VOLUME 2

THE RESTLESS AMERICANS
THE CHALLENGE OF CHANGE IN AMERICAN HISTORY

Edwin C. Rozwenc • **Amherst College**
Edward C. Martin • **Education Development Center**
Martin W. Sandler • **Curriculum Coordinator**

Judy Poe • Art and Design

Xerox College Publishing   Lexington, Massachusetts • Toronto

ISB Number: 0-536-00735-7
Library of Congress
Catalog Card Number: 76-180833

Printed in the United States of America.

In America I have seen the freest and best educated of men in circumstances the happiest to be found in the world; yet it seemed to me that a cloud habitually hung on their brow, and they seemed serious and almost sad even in their pleasures. . . .

It is odd to watch with what feverish ardor the Americans pursue prosperity and how they are ever tormented by the shadowy suspicion that they may not have chosen the shortest route to get it. . . .

Add to this taste for prosperity a social state in which neither law nor custom holds anyone in one place, and that is a great further stimulus to this restlessness of temper. One will then find people continually changing path for fear of missing the shortest cut leading to happiness. . . .

Alexis de Tocqueville,
from *Democracy in America*

This book is designed to meet the needs of the introductory survey course in United States history, but in many ways it is unique. As you will see in the following table of contents, the book is divided into five major topics which focus upon the nature of social, political, and economic change in the history of this nation. While our approach is primarily topical, the five major units of study appear in the order in which they come to the fore in American history. The table of contents also identifies the basic issues raised within each topic and outlines the sources and strategies employed in the text to seek answers to specific questions about the challenge of change in American history.

In order to provide greater classroom flexibility, *The Restless Americans* is available in both a one-volume hardcover edition and a two-volume paperbound edition. Volume 1 of the paperbound edition contains the first three units of study:

America's Revolutionary Heritage
The Dream of Opportunity
Ethnic Identity and Assimilation in American Life

Volume 2 contains:

Ethnic Identity and Assimilation in American Life
Urbanization in America
The United States and Global Politics

Pagination remains the same in all three volumes and each volume has its own individual index.

As you will notice, this book contains many different kinds of material. In addition to extensive readings from primary and secondary sources of historical information, we include photographs, paintings, song lyrics, cartoons, advertisements, comic strips, maps, and various forms of statistical data. All these elements are integral parts of the text. They constitute important records and commentaries which afford depth of insight into our nation's past and help us gather evidence relevant to the questions raised throughout. We have provided introductions to all readings and running commentary linking the various elements to one another and to the dominant themes which recur in American history. Also included are suggested research projects designed to give the student an opportunity to analyze, discover relationships, and apply his understanding of historical study beyond the pages of the text.

The needs and interests of American history students and faculty have changed in recent years. Exploration of enduring issues and consideration of historical developments in terms of their consequences for American society as a whole have assumed their rightful place as focal points for study. The student who uses this book will not approach dates, places, and events out of this context. Instead they become vital tools that must be used in seeking insight into the most penetrating issues of our past and in coming to a better understanding of the problems and opportunities that challenge us today. ∎

iii

3 ETHNIC IDENTITY AND ASSIMILATION IN AMERICAN LIFE

What is an American?

Why, and how, have some racial and ethnic groups been excluded from their full rights as Americans?

What events, policies, and persons have shaped the Indian experience in American history?

How have legislation, political leaders, and black spokesmen outside the political sphere influenced the course of history for black Americans?

Is it possible both to be an American and to maintain a separate cultural identity?

4 URBANIZATION IN AMERICA

How have Americans throughout our history tried to reform their cities?

Should the main object of urban reform be efficiency, the welfare of city residents, or beautification?

Has urban renewal failed?

How are urban governments organized, priorities established, and programs put into action?

Are the problems of modern cities insoluble, or can we remake our urban civilization?

v

5 THE UNITED STATES AND GLOBAL POLITICS

What have been the goals of American foreign policy since World War II?

How have Americans responded to the wars we have fought since 1914?

What aims have American foreign policy-makers pursued in their conduct of foreign affairs?

What is the relationship between public opinion and public policy on foreign affairs?

Can public opinon change the purposes of foreign policy?

THE RESTLESS AMERICANS

What is an American?

Why, and how, have some racial and ethnic groups been excluded from their full rights as Americans?

What events, policies, and persons have shaped the Indian experience in American history?

How have legislation, political leaders, and black spokesmen outside the political sphere influenced the course of history for black Americans?

Is it possible both to be an American and to maintain a separate cultural identity?

ETHNIC IDENTITY
AND ASSIMILATION
IN AMERICAN LIFE

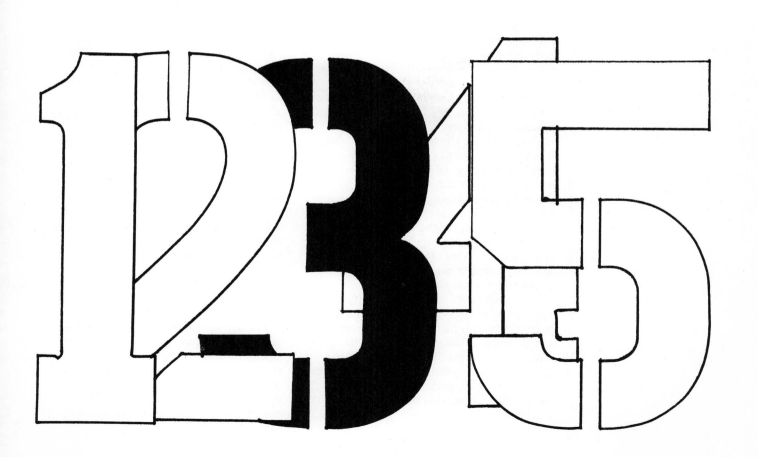

3

ETHNIC IDENTITY AND ASSIMILATION IN AMERICAN LIFE

The history of the United States has in large measure been shaped by the continuous process of absorbing the steady stream of racial and ethnic groups which arrived in the New World. At the time of the Revolution, the American population was largely white, Anglo-Saxon, and Protestant; this group made use of substantial numbers of black Africans as a servile labor force and competed for choice areas of the continental domain with Indian tribes who had arrived in North America long before the first European settlers. For nearly one hundred and fifty years the new nation followed an open door policy regarding immigration which brought over 30 million newcomers to its shores. In the early nineteenth century, most of these migrants came from western or northern Europe—Englishmen, Welshmen, Scotsmen, Irishmen, Frenchmen, Dutchmen, Germans, and Swedes— but, by the end of the century the main tide of migrants was coming from southern and eastern Europe—Italians, Serbians, Greeks, Bulgarians, Hungarians, Czechs, Poles, and Russians. And, whereas the earlier migrants (except for the Irish and some Germans) had been largely Protestant, the later migrants were mainly Catholics, Jews, or communicants of the Greek or Russian Orthodox churches.

The appearance of such a quantity and variety of ethnic groups in so short a period of human history created severe social strains in American society and gave rise to many forms of prejudiced and discriminatory behavior. Yet many Americans —including some historians—have accepted the comfortable belief that America has been a great "melting pot" which has successfully assimilated these diverse immigrants (or at least their descendants) and, in the process, created a new kind of man—the American.

This melting pot idea is closely associated with the democratic aspirations of our society. We like to think that everyone— no matter what his race, nationality, or creed—should have equal rights and opportunities in our society. Hence, if the goal of the society is to provide equal rights and opportunities for all people of whatever racial or religious background, then it seems logical to assume that they should all be assimilated into one unified cultural stock called "American." The term "melting pot," therefore, seemed useful both as a popular metaphor and as a conceptual term to describe the process of assimilation in America.

In recent decades, however, the melting pot idea has been challenged on two grounds: first, because it is an inaccurate description of social reality for minority groups which do not enjoy equal rights and opportunities; second, because, even when relatively free access to rights and opportunities does exist, an ethnic group should not be expected to yield its cultural identity for the sake of absorption into an "American" cultural identity which turns out to be little more than conformity to white, Anglo-Saxon, and Protestant cultural traditions.

The process of assimilation, therefore, is exceedingly complex. It includes certain structural and institutional aspects, such as equal access to the institutional advantages of the society (the right to a job, the right to vote, the right to hold office). But it also contains an important psychological dimension—the right to preserve one's cultural identity. The relationship between these two aspects often creates difficult personal and social problems. Too often, the price of maintaining a separate cultural identity is separation to the point of exclusion and discriminatory treatment. Hence the persisting problem for American society is to find a way of balancing the two aspects of the assimilation process— to ensure full respect for cultural differences and, at the same time, to provide full equality of rights and opportunities.

In this part of our inquiry into the challenge of change in American history, we shall examine the assimilation process as it has affected both the red man and the black man and then move to a consideration of the recent resurgence of ethnicity in American society. This will enable us to test the adequacy of the theories put forth by modern social scientists concerning the process of assimilation in American life. ■

AMERICA AS THE MELTING POT

On the following pages you will find two classic statements of ethnic diversity in America. The first was written by Michel Guillaume Jean de Crèvecoeur, a French-born aristocrat who immigrated to this country in 1765. De Crèvecoeur, in his famous book, *Letters from an American Farmer,* saw the American as a "new breed of man."

The second selection is taken from the final scene of Israel Zangwill's play, *The Melting Pot,* which was first produced at the Capitol Theatre in Washington, D.C., in 1908. The climax of the final scene is an emotional conversation between Vera, the daughter of a Russian who had persecuted Jews, and David, the idealistic Jewish concert violinist.

Source: Michel Guillaume Jean de Crève- coeur, *Letters from an American Farmer* (New York: Fox, Duffield, and Co., 1904), pp. 6–10.

What Then is the American, This New Man?

. . . whence came all these people? they are a mixture of English, Scotch, Irish, French, Dutch, Germans, and Swedes. From this promiscuous breed, that race now called Americans have arisen. The eastern provinces must indeed be excepted, as being the unmixed descendants of Englishmen. I have heard many wish that they had been more intermixed also: for my part, I am no wisher, and think it much better as it has happened. They exhibit a most conspicuous figure in this great and variegated picture; they too enter for a great share in the pleasing perspective displayed in these thirteen provinces. I know it is fashionable to reflect on them, but I respect them for what they have done; for the accuracy and wisdom with which they have settled their territory; for the decency of their manners; for their early love of letters; their ancient college, the first in this hemisphere; for their industry; which to me who am but a farmer, is the criterion of everything. There never was a people, situated as they are, who with so ungrateful a soil have done more in so short a time. Do you think that the monarchical ingredients which are more prevalent in other governments, have purged them from all foul stains? Their histories assert the contrary.

In this great American asylum, the poor of Europe have by some means met together, and in consequence of various causes; to what purpose should they ask one another what countrymen they are? Alas, two thirds of them had no country. Can a wretch who wanders about, who works and starves, whose life is a contin-

211

ual scene of sore affliction or pinching penury; can that man call England or any other kingdom his country? A country that had no bread for him, whose fields procured him no harvest, who met with nothing but the frowns of the rich, the severity of the laws, with jails and punishments; who owned not a single foot of the extensive surface of this planet? No! Urged by a variety of motives, here they came. Every thing has tended to regenerate them; new laws, a new mode of living, a new social system; here they are become men: in Europe they were as so many useless plants, wanting vegetative mould, and refreshing showers; they withered, and were mowed down by want, hunger, and war; but now by the power of transplantation, like all other plants they have taken root and flourished! Formerly they were not numbered in any civil lists of their country, except in those of the poor; here they rank as citizens. By what invisible power has this surprising metamorphosis been performed? By that of the laws and that of their industry. The laws, the indulgent laws, protect them as they arrive, stamping on them the symbol of adoption; they receive ample rewards for their labours; these accumulated rewards procure them lands; those lands confer on them the title of freemen, and to that title every benefit is affixed which men can possibly require. This is the great operation daily performed by our laws. From whence proceed these laws? From our government. Whence the government? It is derived from the original genius and strong desire of the people ratified and confirmed by the crown. This is the great chain which links us all, this is the picture which every province exhibits, Nova Sco-

tia excepted. There the crown has done all; either there were no people who had genius, or it was not much attended to: the consequence is, that the province is very thinly inhabited indeed; the power of the crown in conjunction with the musketos has prevented men from settling there. Yet some parts of it flourished once, and it contained a mild harmless set of people. But for the fault of a few leaders, the whole were banished. The greatest political error the crown ever committed in America, was to cut off men from a country which wanted nothing but men!

What attachment can a poor European emigrant have for a country where he had nothing? The knowledge of the language, the love of a few kindred as poor as himself, were the only cords that tied him: his country is now that which gives him land, bread, protection, and consequence: *Ubi panis ibi patria,* is the motto of all emigrants. What then is the American, this new man? He is either an European, or the descendant of an European, hence that strange mixture of blood, which you will find in no other country. I could point out to you a family whose grandfather was an Englishman, whose wife was Dutch, whose son married a French woman, and whose present four sons have now four wives of different nations. *He* is an American, who, leaving behind him all his ancient prejudices and manners, receives new ones from the new mode of life he has embraced, the new government he obeys, and the new rank he holds. He becomes an American by being received in the broad lap of our great *Alma Mater.* Here individuals of all nations are melted into a new race of men, whose labours and posterity will one day

cause great changes in the world. Americans are the western pilgrims, who are carrying along with them that great mass of arts, sciences, vigour, and industry which began long since in the east; they will finish the great circle. The Americans were once scattered all over Europe; here they are incorporated into one of the finest systems of population which has ever appeared, and which will hereafter become distinct by the power of the different climates they inhabit. The American ought therefore to love this country much better than that wherein either he or his forefathers were born. Here the rewards of his industry follow with equal steps the progress of his labour; his labour is founded on the basis of nature, *self-interest;* can it want a stronger allurement? Wives and children, who before in vain demanded of him a morsel of bread, now, fat and frolicsome, gladly help their father to clear those fields whence exuberant crops are to arise to feed and to clothe them all; without any part being claimed, either by a despotic prince, a rich abbot, or a mighty lord. Here religion demands but little of him; a small voluntary salary to the minister, and gratitude to God; can he refuse these? The American is a new man, who acts upon new principles; he must therefore entertain new ideas, and form new opinions. From involuntary idleness, servile dependence, penury, and useless labour, he has passed to toils of a very different nature, rewarded by ample subsistence. This is an American. . . . ■

Source: Israel Zangwill, *The Melting Pot* (New York: The Macmillan Co., 1909), pp. 193–200.

"There She Lies—the Great Melting Pot"

VERA

[Vehemently, coming still nearer.]

Oh, no! no! I watched the faces—those faces of toil and sorrow, those faces from many lands. They were fired by your vision of their coming brotherhood, lulled by your dream of their land of rest. And I could see that you were right in speaking to the people. In some strange, beautiful way the inner meaning of your music stole into all those simple souls—

DAVID

[Springing up.]

And *my* soul? What of *my* soul? False to its own music, its own mission, its own dream. That is what I mean by failure, Vera. I preached of God's Crucible, this great new continent that could melt up all race-differences and vendettas, that could purge and re-create, and God tried me with his supremest test. He gave me a heritage from the Old World, hate and vengeance and blood, and said, "Cast it all into my Crucible." And I said, "Even thy Crucible cannot melt this hate, cannot drink up this blood." And so I sat crooning over the dead past, gloating over the old blood-stains—I, the apostle of America, the prophet of the God of our children. Oh—how my music mocked me! And you—so fearless, so high above fate—how you must despise me!

VERA

I? Ah no!

DAVID

You must. You do. Your words still sting. Were it seven seas between us, you said, our love must cross them. And I—I who had prated of seven seas—

VERA

Not seas of blood—I spoke selfishly, thoughtlessly. I had not realised that crimson flood. Now I see it day and night. O God!

[She shudders and covers her eyes.]

DAVID

There lies my failure—to have brought it to your eyes, instead of blotting it from my own.

VERA

No man could have blotted it out.

DAVID

Yes—by faith in the Crucible. From the blood of battlefields spring daisies and buttercups. In the divine chemistry the very garbage turns to roses. But in the supreme moment my faith was found wanting. You came to me—and I thrust you away.

VERA

I ought not to have come to you. . . . I ought not to have come to you to-day. We must not meet again.

DAVID

Ah, you cannot forgive me!

VERA

Forgive? It is I that should go down on my knees for my father's sin.

[She is half-sinking to her knees. He stops her by a gesture and a cry.]

DAVID

No! The sins of the fathers shall not be visited on the children.

VERA

My brain follows you, but not my heart. It is heavy with the sense of unpaid debts —debts that can only cry for forgiveness.

DAVID

You owe me nothing—

VERA

But my father, my people, my country. . . .

[She breaks down. Recovers herself.]

My only consolation is, you need nothing.

DAVID

[Dazed.]

I—need—nothing?

VERA

Nothing but your music . . . your dreams.

DAVID

And your love? Do I not need that?

VERA

[Slowly.]

I will kiss you as we Russians kiss at Easter—the three kisses of peace.

[She kisses him three times on the mouth as in ritual solemnity.]

DAVID

[Very calmly.]

Easter was the date of the massacre— see! I am at peace.

VERA

God grant it endure!

[They stand quietly hand in hand.]

Look! How beautiful the sunset is after the storm!

[David turns. The sunset, which has begun to grow beautiful just after Vera's entrance, has now reached its most magnificent moment; below there are narrow lines of saffron and pale gold, but above the whole sky is one glory of burning flame.]

DAVID

[Prophetically exalted by the spectacle.]

It is the fires of God round His Crucible.

[He drops her hand and points downward.]

There she lies, the great Melting-Pot— listen! Can't you hear the roaring and the bubbling? There gapes her mouth

[He points east.]

—the harbour where a thousand mammoth feeders come from the ends of the world to pour in their human freight. Ah, what a stirring and a seething! Celt and Latin, Slav and Teuton, Greek and Syrian, —black and yellow—

VERA

[Softly, nestling to him.]

Jew and Gentile—

DAVID

Yes, East and West, and North and South, the palm and the pine, the pole and the equator, the crescent and the cross— how the great Alchemist melts and fuses them with his purging flame! Here shall they all unite to build the Republic of Man

and the Kingdom of God. Ah, Vera, what is the glory of Rome and Jerusalem where all nations and races come to worship and look back, compared with the glory of America, where all races and nations come to labour and look forward!

[He raises his hands in benediction over the shining city.]

Peace, peace, to all ye unborn millions, fated to fill this giant continent—the God of our *children* give you Peace.

[An instant's solemn pause. The sunset is swiftly fading, and the vast panorama is suffused with a more restful twilight, to which the many-gleaming lights of the town add the tender poetry of the night. Far back, like a lonely, guiding star, twinkles over the darkening water the torch of the Statue of Liberty. From below comes up the softened sound of voices and instruments joining in "My Country, 'tis of Thee." The curtain falls slowly.] ■

THE MELTING POT AS AN IDEOLOGY

Among the most famous statements about assimilation in America are the two you have just read by de Crèvecoeur and Zangwill. These statements, written 127 years apart, encapsulate a central ideological theme in American culture—the melting pot.

1 How does each statement define the process of assimilation in America? Who is involved? How and why does it occur?

2 What emotional tone is established and how is it conveyed to the reader?

3 What are the central values expressed and how do they relate to the process of assimilation?

4 What differences do you find between the two statements? ■

214

THE INDIANS' STRUGGLE FOR SELF-PRESERVATION

Our inquiry in this unit begins with an examination of the first immigrants to the North American continent—the Indians. It is impossible to determine how many Indians were living in North America at the time the first white settlers arrived. Estimates range from one million to one and a half million people. But archeologists are now certain that there were Indians living in the Americas some 20,000 years ago!

From the sixteenth to the beginning of the twentieth century, the Indians with the ever-increasing population of white European immigrants fought a long series of wars not only to determine the ownership of what is now the United States but also to preserve their own identity as a people. Although the military struggle was lost years ago, the Indians' struggle for self-preservation continues today.

Throughout the Indian-white conflict, many government leaders of the United States were deeply perplexed by the issue. The following three statements were made by Thomas Jefferson.

JEFFERSON AND THE INDIANS

Notes on Virginia, 1785

The Indian of North America being more within our reach, I can speak of him somewhat from my own knowledge, but more from the information of others better acquainted with him, and on whose truth and judgment I can rely. From these sources I am able to say, in contradiction to this representation, that he is neither more defective in ardor, nor more impotent with his female, than the white reduced to the same diet and exercise; that he is brave, when an enterprise depends on bravery; education with him making the point of honor consist in the destruction of an enemy by stratagem, and in the preservation of his own person free from injury; or, perhaps, this is nature, while it is education which teaches us to honor force more than finesse; that he will defend himself against a host of enemies, always choosing to be killed, rather than to surrender, though it be to the whites, who he knows will treat him well; that in other situations, also, he meets death with more deliberation, and endures tortures with a firmness unknown almost to religious enthusiasm with us; that he is affectionate to his children, careful of them, and indulgent in the extreme; that his affections comprehend his other connections, weakening, as with us, from circle to circle, as they recede from the centre; that his friendships are strong and faithful to the uttermost extremity; that his sensibility is keen, even the warriors weeping most bitterly on the loss of their children, though in general they endeavor to appear superior to human events; that his vivacity and activity of mind is equal to ours in the same situation; hence his eagerness for hunting, and for

Source: *The Writings of Thomas Jefferson*, ed. Paul L. Ford (New York: G. P. Putnam's Sons, 1894), vol. III, pp. 151–155.

games of chance. The women are submitted to unjust drudgery. This I believe is the case with every barbarous people. With such, force is law. The stronger sex therefore imposes on the weaker. It is civilization alone which replaces women in the enjoyment of their natural equality. That first teaches us to subdue the selfish passions, and to respect those rights in others which we value in ourselves. Were we in equal barbarism, our females would be equal drudges. The man with them is less strong than with us, but their woman stronger than ours; and both for the same obvious reason; because our man and their woman is habituated to labor, and formed by it. With both races the sex which is indulged with ease is the least athletic. An Indian man is small in the hand and wrist, for the same reason for which a sailor is large and strong in the arms and shoulders, and a porter in the legs and thighs. They raise fewer children than we do. The causes of this are to be found, not in a difference of nature, but of circumstance. The women very frequently attending the men in their parties of war and of hunting, child-bearing becomes extremely inconvenient to them. It is said, therefore, that they have learned the practice of procuring abortion by the use of some vegetable; and that it even extends to prevent conception for a considerable time after. During these parties they are exposed to numerous hazards, to excessive exertions, to the greatest extremities of hunger. Even at their homes the nation depends for food, through a certain part of every year, on the gleanings of the forest; that is, they experience a famine once in every year. With all animals, if the female be illy fed, or not fed at all, her young perish; and if both male and female be reduced to like want, generation becomes less active, less productive. To the obstacles, then, of want and hazard, which nature has opposed to the multiplication of wild animals, for the purpose of restraining their numbers within certain bounds, those of labour and of voluntary abortion are added with the Indian. No wonder, then, if they multiply less than we do. Where food is regularly supplied, a single farm will show more of cattle, than a whole country of forests can of buffalos. The same Indian women, when married to white traders, who feed them and their children plentifully and regularly, who exempt them from excessive drudgery, who keep them stationary and unexposed to accident, produce and raise as many children as the white women. Instances are known, under these circumstances, of their rearing a dozen children. An inhuman practice once prevailed in this country, of making slaves of the Indians. It is a fact well known with us, that the Indian women so enslaved produced and raised as numerous families as either the whites or blacks among whom they lived. It has been said that Indians have less hair than the whites, except on the head. But this is a fact of which fair proof can scarcely be had. With them it is disgraceful to be hairy on the body. They say it likens them to hogs. They therefore pluck the hair as fast as it appears. But the traders who marry their women, and prevail on them to discontinue this practice, say, that nature is the same with them as with the whites. Nor, if the fact be true, is the consequence necessary which has been drawn from it. . . . To judge of the truth of this, to form a just estimate of their genius and mental powers, more facts are wanting, and great allowance to be made for those circumstances of their situation which call for a display of particular talents only. This done, we shall probably find that they are formed in mind as well as body, on the same module with the 'Homo sapiens Europæus.' The principles of their society forbidding all compulsion, they are to be led to duty and to enterprise by personal influence and persuasion. Hence eloquence in council, bravery and address in war, become the foundations of all consequence with them. To these acquirements all their faculties are directed. Of their bravery and address in war we have multiplied proofs, because we have been the subjects on which they were exercised. Of their eminence in oratory we have fewer examples, because it is displayed chiefly in their own councils. ■

Source: *The Writings of Thomas Jefferson,* ed. Paul L. Ford (New York: G. P. Putnam's Sons, 1897), vol. VIII, pp. 213–215.

Letter to Benjamin Hawkins, February 18, 1803

Altho' you will receive, thro' the official channel of the War Office, every communication necessary to develop to you our views respecting the Indians, and to direct your conduct, yet, supposing it will be satisfactory to you, and to those with whom you are placed, to understand my personal dispositions and opinions in this particular, I shall avail myself of this private letter to state them generally. I consider the business of hunting as already become insufficient to furnish clothing and subsistence to the Indians. The promotion of agriculture, therefore, and household manufacture, are essential in their preservation, and I am disposed to aid and encourage it liberally. This will enable them to live on much smaller portions of land, and indeed will render their vast forests useless but for the range of cattle; for which purpose, also, as they become better farmers, they will be found useless, and even disadvantageous. While they are learning to do better on less land, our increasing numbers will be calling for more land, and thus a coincidence of interests will be produced between those who have lands to spare, and want other necessaries, and those who have such necessaries to spare, and want lands.

In truth, the ultimate point of rest & happiness for them is to let our settlements and theirs meet and blend together, to intermix, and become one people. Incorporating themselves with us as citizens of the U. S., this is what the natural progress of things will of course bring on, and it will be better to promote than to retard it. Surely it will be better for them to be identified with us, and preserved in the occupation of their lands, than be exposed to the many casualties which may endanger them while a separate people. I have little doubt but that your reflections must have led you to view the various ways in which their history may terminate, and to see that this is the one most for their happiness. And we have already had an application from a settlement of Indians to become citizens of the U. S. It is possible, perhaps probable, that this idea may be so novel as that it might shock the Indians, were it even hinted to them. Of course, you will keep it for your own reflection; but, convinced of its soundness, I feel it consistent with pure morality to lead them towards it, to familiarize them to the idea that it is for their interest to cede lands at times to the U. S., and for us thus to procure gratifications to our citizens, from time to time, by new acquisitions of land. From no quarter is there at present so strong a pressure on this subject as from Georgia for the residue of the fork of Oconee & Ockmulgee; and indeed I believe it will be difficult to resist it. As it has been mentioned that the Creeks had at one time made up their minds to sell this, and were only checked in it by some indiscretions of an individual, I am in hopes you will be able to bring them to it again. I beseech you to use your most earnest endeavors; for it will relieve us here from a great pressure, and yourself from the unreasonable suspicions of the Georgians which you notice, that you are more attached to the interests of the Indians than of the U. S., and throw cold water on their willingness to part with lands. It is so easy to excite suspicion, that none are to be wondered at; but I am in hopes it will be in your power to quash them by effecting the object. ∎

Source: *The Writings of Thomas Jefferson,* ed. Paul L. Ford (New York: G. P. Putnam's Sons, 1897), vol. VIII, pp. 344–345.

Thomas Jefferson's Second Inaugural Address, March 4, 1805

The aboriginal inhabitants of these countries I have regarded with the commiseration their history inspires. Endowed with the faculties and the rights of men, breathing an ardent love of liberty and independence, and occupying a country which left them no desire but to be undisturbed, the stream of overflowing population from other regions directed itself on these shores; without power to divert, or habits to contend against, they have been overwhelmed by the current, or driven before it; now reduced within limits too narrow for the hunter's state, humanity enjoins us to teach them agriculture and the domestic arts; to encourage them to that industry which alone can enable them to maintain their place in existence, and to prepare them in time for that state of society, which to bodily comforts adds the improvement of the mind and morals. We have therefore liberally furnished them with the implements of husbandry and household use; we have placed among them instructors in the arts of first necessity; and they are covered with the ægis of the law against aggressors from among ourselves.

But the endeavors to enlighten them on the fate which awaits their present course of life, to induce them to exercise their reason, follow its dictates, and change their pursuits with the change of circumstances, have powerful obstacles to encounter; they are combated by the habits of their bodies, prejudice of their minds, ignorance, pride, and the influence of interested and crafty individuals among them, who feel themselves something in the present order of

217

things, and fear to become nothing in any other. These persons inculcate a sanctimonious reverence for the customs of their ancestors; that whatsoever they did, must be done through all time; that reason is a false guide, and to advance under its counsel, in their physical, moral, or political condition, is perilous innovation; that their duty is to remain as their Creator made them, ignorance being safety, and knowledge full of danger; in short, my friends, among them is seen the action and counteraction of good sense and bigotry; they, too, have their anti-philosophers, who find an interest in keeping things in their present state, who dread reformation, and exert all their faculties to maintain the ascendency of habit over the duty of improving our reason, and obeying its mandates. ∎

THE AMBIVALENCE OF A POLITICAL LEADER

The attitude of a political leader is of the greatest importance in determining what policy decisions are made. Sometimes we see a leader's attitude as fixed and consistent; often it is ambivalent or ambiguous. In the three statements you have just read, Thomas Jefferson verbalizes his attitude toward the American Indian.

1 What kinds of things is Jefferson describing in each of his statements about the Indians? Does he reflect bias or prejudice?

2 In the three statements, is Jefferson's general attitude toward the Indians consistent? What government policy toward the Indians is advocated or implied by each statement? How would you explain the differences in the statements? What further information would you need to completely explain the differences?

3 What did Jefferson believe would be the final fate of the American Indian? Would you make the same prediction today?

4 In the following selection, President Andrew Jackson states his attitude and policy toward the American Indian. Compare it to the three Jefferson statements. Is Jackson consistent?

JACKSON AND THE INDIANS

Andrew Jackson's Annual Message, 1829
The condition and ulterior destiny of the Indian tribes within the limits of some of our States have become objects of much interest and importance. It has long been the policy of Government to introduce among them the arts of civilization, in the hope of gradually reclaiming them from a wandering life. This policy has, however, been coupled with another wholly incompatible with its success. Professing a desire to civilize and settle them, we have at the same time lost no opportunity to purchase their lands and thrust them farther into the wilderness. By this means they have not only been kept in a wandering state, but been led to look upon us as unjust and indifferent to their fate. Thus, though lavish in its expenditures upon the subject, Government has constantly defeated its own policy, and the Indians in general, receding farther and farther to the west, have retained their savage habits. A portion, however, of the Southern tribes, having mingled much with the whites and made some progress in the arts of civilized life, have lately attempted to erect an independent government within the limits of Georgia and Alabama. These States, claiming to be the only sovereigns within their territories, extended their laws over the Indians, which induced the latter to call upon the United States for protection.

Under these circumstances the question presented was whether the General Government had a right to sustain those people in their pretensions. The Constitution declares that "no new State shall be formed or erected within the jurisdiction of any other State" without the consent of its legislature. If the General Government is

Source: *A Compilation of the Messages and Papers of the Presidents:* 1789–1897, ed. J. D. Richardson (New York: Bureau of National Literature, 1897), vol. II, pp. 456–459.

not permitted to tolerate the erection of a confederate State within the territory of one of the members of this Union against her consent, much less could it allow a foreign and independent government to establish itself there. Georgia became a member of the Confederacy which eventuated in our Federal Union as a sovereign State, always asserting her claim to certain limits, which, having been originally defined in her colonial charter and subsequently recognized in the treaty of peace, she has ever since continued to enjoy, except as they have been circumscribed by her own voluntary transfer of a portion of her territory to the United States in the articles of cession of 1802. Alabama was admitted into the Union on the same footing with the original States, with boundaries which were prescribed by Congress. There is no constitutional, conventional, or legal provision which allows them less power over the Indians within their borders than is possessed by Maine or New York. Would the people of Maine permit the Penobscot tribe to erect an independent government within their State? And unless they did would it not be the duty of the General Government to support them in resisting such a measure? Would the people of New York permit each remnant of the Six Nations within her borders to declare itself an independent people under the protection of the United States? Could the Indians establish a separate republic on each of their reservations in Ohio? And if they were so disposed would it be the duty of this Government to protect them in the attempt? If the principle involved in the obvious answer to these questions be abandoned, it will follow that the objects

of this Government are reversed, and that it has become a part of its duty to aid in destroying the States which it was established to protect.

Actuated by this view of the subject, I informed the Indians inhabiting parts of Georgia and Alabama that their attempt to establish an independent government would not be countenanced by the Executive of the United States, and advised them to emigrate beyond the Mississippi or submit to the laws of those States.

Our conduct toward these people is deeply interesting to our national character. Their present condition, contrasted with what they once were, makes a most powerful appeal to our sympathies. Our ancestors found them the uncontrolled possessors of these vast regions. By persuasion and force they have been made to retire from river to river and from mountain to maintain, until some of the tribes have become extinct and others have left but remnants to preserve for a while their once terrible names. Surrounded by the whites with their arts of civilization, which by destroying the resources of the savage doom him to weakness and decay, the fate of the Mohegan, the Narragansett, and the Delaware is fast overtaking the Choctaw, the Cherokee, and the Creek. That this fate surely awaits them if they remain within the limits of the States does not admit of a doubt. Humanity and national honor demand that every effort should be made to avert so great a calamity. It is too late to inquire whether it was just in the United States to include them and their territory within the bounds of new States, whose limits they could control. That step can not be retraced. A

State can not be dismembered by Congress or restricted in the exercise of her constitutional power. But the people of those States and of every State, actuated by feelings of justice and a regard for our national honor, submit to you the interesting question whether something can not be done, consistently with the rights of the States, to preserve this much-injured race.

As a means of effecting this end I suggest for your consideration the propriety of setting apart an ample district west of the Mississippi, and without the limits of any State or Territory now formed, to be guaranteed to the Indian tribes as long as they shall occupy it, each tribe having a distinct control over the portion designated for its use. There they may be secured in the enjoyment of governments of their own choice, subject to no other control from the United States than such as may be necessary to preserve peace on the frontier and between the several tribes. There the benevolent may endeavor to teach them the arts of civilization, and, by promoting union and harmony among them, to raise up an interesting commonwealth, destined to perpetuate the race and to attest the humanity and justice of this Government.

This emigration should be voluntary, for it would be as cruel as unjust to compel the aborigines to abandon the graves of their fathers and seek a home in a distant land. But they should be distinctly informed that if they remain within the limits of the States they must be subject to their laws. In return for their obedience as individuals they will without doubt be protected in the enjoyment of those possessions which they have improved by their industry. But it seems to me visionary to suppose that in this state of things claims can be allowed on tracts of country on which they have neither dwelt nor made improvements, merely because they have seen them from the mountain or passed them in the chase. . . . ∎

INDIAN LEADERS
IN PROFILE

On the pages which follow you will find three profiles written to identify three great Indian leaders of three different periods in the nineteenth century. These profiles should give you some idea of how these chiefs organized their people and how they perceived the struggle for self-preservation.

Source: Adapted from Alvin M. Josephy, Jr., *The Patriot Chiefs: A Chronicle of American Indian Resistance* (New York: The Viking Press, 1969), pp. 129–174.

Tecumseh

Of all the Indian leaders who resisted American expansion into the West, Tecumseh was clearly the greatest. He was not only a brave warrior and brilliant orator, but he was the one Indian leader who had a vision of combining all of the tribes into something resembling a unified Indian nation with a united racial consciousness. General William Henry Harrison, who had fought Tecumseh's followers in the historic battle of Tippecanoe, later praised Tecumseh as "one of those uncommon geniuses, which spring up occasionally to produce revolutions and overturn the established order of things."

Tecumseh was born in March 1768 in a Shawnee village on the banks of the Mad River in southwestern Ohio. It is said that in Shawnee language and allegory, the name Tecumseh could be interpreted as a "panther lying in wait." The Shawnees, at the time of Tecumseh's birth, were a hunting tribe whose migrations westward had brought them into frequent conflict with white settlers who were advancing into the Ohio Valley. Tecumseh's father was a hunter and warrior who had been continually involved in the bloody warfare that marked the early history of Kentucky and Ohio.

When Tecumseh was still a boy, his father was murdered by a band of white frontiersmen who had crossed into Shawnee territory in violation of a treaty that had temporarily ended one of the frequent Indian wars in the Ohio region. The experience filled Tecumseh with hatred for the white man. He wanted to become a warrior like his father and he hoped that his people would become "like a fire spreading over the hill and valley, consuming the race of dark souls."

When the Americans had won their revolution against the British, the tide of white settlers streaming into the Ohio region became even greater and Tecumseh, still in his teens, joined one of the raiding bands of Shawnees that attacked the settlers' flatboats as they floated down the Ohio River. By the time George Washington became President, Tecumseh was a twenty-one-year-old leader of a Shawnee band that continually harassed the American army forces sent to the West with daring raids and ambushes. When General Anthony Wayne finally defeated a large Indian force at the battle of Fallen Timbers (August 20, 1794), Tecumseh refused to join the other Indian chiefs who parlayed for peace with the victorious white general.

During the ten years of relative peace that followed the battle of Fallen Timbers, Tecumseh married a half-breed woman with whom he quarreled so often that he soon left her. Then he met a sensitive young white girl, the blonde and beautiful Rebecca Galloway, the daughter of a successful pioneer farmer near Chillicothe. A curious, romantic attachment developed between them. Rebecca taught Tecumseh to speak better English and read to him from the Bible, Shakespeare, and works of history. Tecumseh seemed particularly eager to learn about the great leaders of white civilization, and to Rebecca and her father the young Indian appeared to be ready to accept the ways of white civilization. Eventually, when Tecumseh asked Rebecca to marry him, she indicated that she would be willing if he would give up his Indian ways and live with her among white men. Tecumseh took a month to decide, but finally told Rebecca that he could never abandon his people.

Indeed, the plight of his people was giving Tecumseh great anguish. White traders were selling liquor to the Indians and his tribal brothers seemed unable to resist the magic of the white man's alcoholic drink. They traded land and other possessions for whiskey, and within a few years many proud and dignified warriors had become demoralized by constant drunkenness. Tecumseh's younger brother Laulewasika became a drunkard but Tecumseh refused to drink whiskey and preached angrily against it.

During a dreadful epidemic of sickness among the Shawnees in 1805, Laulewasika began to experience the first of many trances which gave him a vision of a new life. He changed his name to Tenskwatawa and became a great Indian prophet who preached the doctrine of abstinence and urged Indians to return to the ways of their fathers. The Prophet's sermons became a source of added strength to Tecumseh who was emerging as the most dynamic Indian leader in the Northwest Territory. Other tribes besides the Shawnees were influenced by the Prophet's teachings and antiwhite feelings began to reach a dangerous peak of intensity in the Northwest Territory in the first decade of the nineteenth century.

America's officials watched the growth of the new spirit of militancy among the Indians with alarm. They were convinced that the British in Canada were giving secret aid to Tecumseh and the Prophet. Their fears were increased when Tecumseh began to appear in village after village and among tribe after tribe appealing for their support with brilliant and impassioned oratory. After covering the northwest region, Tecumseh traveled south to seek the support of the Creeks, Choctaws, and even the Seminoles as far away as Florida.

While Tecumseh was visiting the Southern tribes, the politically ambitious territorial governor of Indiana, William Henry Harrison, began to push an aggressive policy of treaty-making with the Indians to obtain more land cessions. Using considerable gifts of whiskey, Harrison was able to get several chiefs to cede 3,000,000 acres of land. These new cessions infuriated Tecumseh when he learned of them on his return, and he set about immediately to gather a force of a thousand warriors at his brother's headquarters, Prophet Town, to resist any attempt by Americans to settle in the ceded lands.

Governor Harrison was so disturbed by these preparations that he invited Tecumseh and the Prophet to parley with him. On August 11, 1810, a dramatic confrontation took place at the governor's residence in Vincennes. Harrison insisted that Tecumseh had no right to resist the sale of land in Indiana because the Shawnees had never had any settled homeland anyway. Tecumseh stated his position in an eloquent speech. "You endeavor to make distinctions," he said, "you endeavor to prevent the Indians from doing what we, their leaders, wish them to do . . . unite and consider their land common property . . . The only way . . . is for all the red men to unite in claiming a common and equal right in the land, as it was at first, and should be now . . . for it never was divided, but belongs to all. No tribe has a right to sell, even to each other, much less to strangers. . . . Sell a country! Why not sell the air, the clouds, and the great sea, as well as the earth? Did not the Great Spirit make them all for the use of his children?"

The conference revealed that both sides were determined to pursue a collision course. Harrison made clear that he intended to press forward with his policy of treaty-making for more land cessions, and Tecumseh was determined to build more tribal alliances as a means of strengthening the Indians' will to resist. After Tecumseh crossed the Canadian border to induce the tribes there to join his Indian confederation, Harrison and other Western leaders were convinced that the British were giving secret aid to a conspiracy against the Americans. When an Indian band killed some white men in the Illinois country, Harrison demanded that Tecumseh turn over the Indians who had committed the murders to be tried by the territorial courts. Tecumseh refused and soon departed on another long journey in the summer and fall of 1811 to the Southern tribes, seeking to bind them more firmly to his Indian confederation.

Everywhere he went among the Choctaws, Cherokees, Creeks, Osages, and Iowas, Tecumseh sought to arouse a fierce spirit of resistance. "Shall we, without a struggle, give up our homes, our country bequeathed to us by the Great Spirit, the graves of our dead and everything that is dear and sacred to us?" he asked again and again. "I know you will cry with me, Never! Never." Everywhere, the younger warriors shouted their approval of Tecumseh's eloquent words, but the older chiefs held back, unsure of their strength against

the Americans. The Creeks and Seminoles, however, were already full of hatred for the Americans who were pressing into their lands. To them, Tecumseh gave bundles of red-painted sticks, telling them that when he gave the word, they were to throw away one stick each day. When all the sticks were gone, they were to rise up in a simultaneous attack on the whites on every part of the frontier.

But while Tecumseh was among the Southern tribes, Harrison struck first. Convinced that the best defense was an offense, Harrison led an American force of nearly a thousand men up the Wabash River to the Prophet's Town at the mouth of the Tippecanoe. After a sharp engagement on November 7, 1811, in which Harrison's losses were greater than those of the smaller force opposing him, the Indians withdrew from Prophet's Town. Whereupon, Harrison's men marched into the Indian settlement, burning the buildings and destroying stores of food and other materials. On his return, Harrison announced that he had won a great victory, and the legend of the battle of Tippecanoe quickly outgrew any resemblance to reality.

By the time Tecumseh returned, his brother had already sent messengers to all the tribes in the Northwest Territory calling for revenge. When Tecumseh returned to Tippecanoe in March of 1812, he stood, as he said later, "upon the ashes of my own home—and there I summoned the spirits of the braves who had fallen —and as I snuffed up the smell of their blood from the ground, I swore once more eternal hatred—the hatred of the avenger."

The Shawnee chief found important

allies because within a few months the Americans were at war with the British in the War of 1812. "Here is a chance—" Tecumseh declared exultantly at a large council of tribes held at Fort Wayne, Indiana, "yes, a chance such as never will occur again—for us Indians of North America to form ourselves into one great combination and cast our lot with the British in this war. And should they conquer and again get mastery of all North America, our rights to at least a portion of the land of our fathers would be respected by the King." Scornfully, he broke a peace pipe sent to him by the American authorities, and marched off with a large party of Shawnees, Delawares, Kickapoos, and Pottawatomies to join the British.

In the early stages of the war, victory seemed likely as Tecumseh and nearly 3,000 warriors joined the British in the battles which led to the complete surrender of General Hull and the American garrison at Detroit on August 13, 1812. In January 1813, the British and Tecumseh's Indians won a notable victory over a force of nearly a thousand Kentuckians at the Raisin River, but the victory was marred by the wanton butchery of all the Americans, including the wounded, who were captured in the battle. Tecumseh, who was not a bloodthirsty man, was dismayed at the conduct of his tribal followers. Moreover, the news of the grisly massacre aroused the entire American West; and Tecumseh's old foe, General William Henry Harrison, soon assembled a large force of volunteers for a campaign to recapture Detroit.

After several bloody battles on land, and with the help of Commodore Perry's naval victory on Lake Erie, Harrison retook Detroit and crossed the lake into Canada in pursuit of the British and Indian forces. Bitter over what he considered to be the cowardice and duplicity of the British, Tecumseh sought to rally his forces for a major battle with Harrison's forces. On October 5, 1813, a large battle took place at the Thames River between Harrison's force of 3,500 troops and a force of 700 British supported by more than a thousand Indians. Shouting "Remember the River Raisin," a charge by 1,500 mounted Kentuckians disorganized the British forces and in the ensuing battle the British and Indians were cut to pieces.

Even as defeat became a certainty, Tecumseh fought with the desperation of a cornered panther. Americans caught glimpses of him in the battle, running among his men, a bandage tied around a wounded arm, urging them to fight to the last. When the battle was joined at close quarters, Americans hit him again and again and they could see the great chief, blood pouring from his mouth, staggering desperately among his warriors pleading with them to fight on. When darkness halted the battle, the remnants of the Indians slipped away through a swamp, taking with them the body of their dead leader.

Tecumseh's death ended his great dream of an Indian confederation. The Indians of the Northwest were left without a dynamic leader to unite them, and the conclusion of the War of 1812 destroyed any hope of aid from the British. Tecumseh became a legend—and, curiously enough, he became a hero among Americans as well as among the Indians. Five years after the war, the *Indiana Centinel* of Vincennes, Indiana, where the dramatic personal confrontation between Tecumseh and William Henry Harrison had taken place, published a letter praising the once-hated Indian enemy with these words: "Every schoolboy in the Union now knows that Tecumseh was a great man. He was truly great—and his greatness was his own, unassisted by science or the aids of education. As a statesman, a warrior and a patriot, take him all in all, we shall not look upon his like again." ■

Source: Adapted from Alvin M. Josephy, Jr., *The Patriot Chiefs: A Chronicle of American Indian Resistance* (New York: The Viking Press, 1969), pp. 175–205.

Osceola

When Andrew Jackson became President, he was determined to pursue a vigorous policy of removing all Indian tribes to the territory west of the Mississippi River. He did not originate the removal policy; it had already been started by Thomas Jefferson. But Jefferson and his first successors in the White House had made removal treaties in a benign fashion—attempting by negotiation to secure the consent of Indian chiefs to the cession of their tribal lands, and allowing any Indians who so chose the option of remaining on their lands. Under this policy, most of the Indians of the Northwest Territory were removed in the decade or so after the War of 1812. But the Southern Indian tribes in Georgia, Florida, Alabama, and Mississippi were less willing to cede their lands and move to the wild country of the trans-Mississippi West.

Under the Removal Bill passed at Jackson's urging on May 28, 1830, the Southern Indians were offered the privilege of exchanging their tribal lands east of the Mississippi for lands west of the Mississippi and money grants to help them migrate. But they were given no choice; if they did not accept removal treaties, they would be forced to leave anyway.

This policy caused considerable political controversy among the American people, largely because there was great sympathy with the plight of Christianized and civilized tribes like the Cherokees. But all the appeals of the Cherokees and their many white friends failed to change Jackson's inflexible determination to carry out the removal policy. By 1838, the Cherokees had capitulated to military pressure, and

began their long trek westward along the 1,200-mile "trail of tears." By and large, the same was true of the Creeks and Choctaws and other Southern tribes—except for a large faction of the Seminoles. The resistance of an important faction of the Seminoles to the removal policy led to the "Second" Seminole War of 1835–1838.

The "First" Seminole War had been fought in the years immediately after the War of 1812. In 1818, General Andrew Jackson had invaded Florida to destroy Seminole Indian bands who were raiding American settlements north of the Florida line and harboring escaped Negro slaves. Jackson's aggressive invasion of the Seminole "sanctuaries" in Spanish territory also had the effect of increasing Spain's willingness to cede Florida to the United States.

By acquiring Florida, the United States obtained jurisdiction over all the Seminole tribal groups. But in the years following Jackson's ruthless campaign against the Seminole villages, the Seminole will to resist weakened and in 1823 most chiefs agreed to a treaty which designated a restricted area in central Florida as a reservation for the Seminoles.

During these years, a young Creek Indian named Osceola was growing to manhood among the Seminoles. Born to a Creek woman in 1804, Osceola was believed to be the son of a half-breed Scottish-Creek trader named William Powell, and the young Indian boy was known to white men as Billy Powell. Osceola grew up with a Creek band that moved into the area near the Florida border and accepted Tecumseh's "red sticks" when the Southern tribes were being organized for war against the Americans. Oceola was too

young to join the warriors of his village in the War of 1812, but he was among those Creeks who fled Florida when Jackson's Tennessee militia destroyed the Creek forces in the famous battle of Horseshoe Bend, May 14, 1814.

It was during the years that Osceola and his mother lived in Seminole country that he took the Indian name by which he is known to history. Osceola meant "Black Drink Singer," and the name referred to a powerful black drink that was drunk in the rituals of the Southern Indian tribes. The black liquid made from the leaves of the cassina shrub was a strong purgative that also had a pronounced psychological effect—making the drinker feel exhilarated. Warriors often used the drink to cleanse their bodies and to strengthen their will for battle. A practiced black drinker would drink large quantities of the drink and then force himself to throw up the liquid, spouting it six to eight feet in the air. A black drink singer was one who emitted the long drawn-out cries that accompanied the drinking and spouting of the ceremony.

The Seminoles became increasingly troublesome in the eyes of the white settlers in Florida despite the treaty which restricted them to their inland reservation. Many Seminole warriors made hunting forays outside their reservation, and the Seminole villages continued to harbor large numbers of runaway slaves who escaped into the swamps of central Florida. Hence, when Jackson became President, there was growing agitation for removal of the Seminoles to the West.

President Jackson sent an emissary to the Seminole chiefs in 1832 to begin treaty negotiations for removal. With some trickery and bribery, several Seminole chiefs were induced to sign a treaty that provided for a certain number of their people to go west in 1834 and for others to leave the following year. Osceola, however, was among the younger leaders who refused to accept the treaty, denouncing it as a fraud.

In the next few years, Osceola quickly rose to a position of prestige among the Seminoles because of his bold opposition to the American government's policy. When President Jackson sent a new emissary, a Georgia militia general named Wiley Thompson, to get the compliance of the Seminoles, with the threat that he would compel them to go to the West "even in irons, if necessary," Osceola refused to be intimidated. According to a story that has never been fully verified, Osceola is said to have drawn his hunting knife at the treaty table, driving it through the paper on which the treaty was written. Sixteen other chiefs, however, made their marks on the treaty by January 1835.

Osceola and his followers continued to resist. In June 1835, Wiley Thompson made an attempt to put Osceola under arrest, reporting that the recalcitrant chief "came into my office and insulted me by some insolent remarks." Under duress, Osceola agreed to sign the treaty, but he had no intention of obeying its terms. As soon as he was free, he organized a band of followers to capture and execute cooperating chiefs who were preparing their people to emigrate to the West.

General Wiley Thompson was determined to stamp out the terroristic attacks on the government's removal policy. But his small force of federal troops was soon harassed by Seminole war parties who ambushed troops of soldiers who were attempting to find the hiding places of Osceola and his raiding bands. By December 1835, warfare had become widespread throughout Florida; and on December 28, Wiley Thompson and four other Americans were killed in a daring raid that Osceola led against the government headquarters building on the Seminole reservation.

In the summer of 1836, the federal government dispatched a force of a thousand regulars aided by militia units from neighboring states to hunt down Osceola and break the resistance of the Seminoles. After a year of frustration and floundering, the American forces succeeded in isolating the resisting bands of Seminoles and securing the capitulation of their leaders. Osceola fought bitterly and held out as long as he could; but by 1837, a large force of 8,000 American regulars was operating in Florida and causing great suffering among the Seminole people. At one point, in May of 1837, Osceola decided to surrender but then changed his mind when he heard stories of treachery against his people.

The guerrilla war dragged on until 1838. Osceola was ill with malaria, and messengers came to General Hernandez, who commanded a small American force on the eastern side of St. Johns River, with the news that Osceola wished to have a council. Hernandez and an escort of two hundred mounted men went to Osceola's camp where a white flag of truce was flying. Instead of parleying, however, Hernandez' mounted men, on the order of their commander, dashed into the camp, disarmed the Indians, and seized Osceola.

Osceola was imprisoned in Fort Marion near St. Augustine and then, to prevent any attempt at escape, was transported to Fort Moultrie, in Charleston, South Carolina. There the young chief, still in his thirties, slowly wasted away in his final illness. By that time, public sympathy for the stricken chief of the Seminoles was growing. An editorial in the *Charleston Courier* said: "We now owe him the respect which the brave ever feel toward the brave." George Catlin, the famous artist, came to Fort Moultrie to paint his portrait, depicting him wearing his Seminole finery.

On January 30, 1838, Osceola, weakened by malaria and other complicating illnesses, died in the presence of his chiefs, wearing his war dress and his war paint as a final act of defiance. The surgeon-physician at the fort was a Doctor Weedon, who happened to be the brother-in-law of Wiley Thompson whom Osceola had killed at the start of the Seminole War. When death came to Osceola, the doctor cut off the Indian chief's head and took it home as a souvenir. But most Americans have been more generous in their memory of Osceola. They prefer to remember the face and head of the Seminole chief as it was portrayed in Catlin's famous painting. ■

Source: Adapted from Alvin M. Josephy, Jr., *The Patriot Chiefs: A Chronicle of American Indian Resistance* (New York: The Viking Press, 1969), pp. 275–310.

Crazy Horse

The Sioux Indians were a loose federation of tribes who had wandered over vast stretches of the North American continent before finally settling in the plains country along the upper reaches of the Missouri River. During the sixteenth century they were forest Indians, hunting in the woods and raising corn around their villages along the lakes and rivers of the upper Mississippi Valley. They were also constantly at war with neighboring tribes among the Algonquian-speaking Indians. As a result of this warfare, the Sioux were pushed westward, particularly after French and English traders began to furnish the Algonquian tribes with guns and metal weapons.

By the eighteenth century, the Sioux were plains Indians who had learned to use the horse and to hunt the buffalo that roamed in great herds over the grasslands of the Great Plains. Consequently, when the Americans began their removal policy in the nineteenth century, the Sioux did not have to be relocated in the trans-Mississippi West. They were already there.

But white Americans were there too—mostly fur traders working for the powerful American Fur Company which had built trading posts along the Missouri River and across the Rocky Mountains as far west as the Columbia River in Oregon; in the 1830's, rival trading groups joined the scramble for furs. By the 1840's many white settlers were beginning to make the trek through Sioux country on the long trail to Oregon.

Contact with white traders had a demoralizing effect on the Sioux. Rival traders used whiskey to win the Indians' favor and many natives traded whatever they owned—furs, horses, clothing—for liquor and other of the white man's goods. There had always been factionalism among the Sioux, but contact with the white traders seemed to increase the quarreling and fighting among tribal factions.

It was in this time of increasing demoralization and factionalism among the Sioux that Crazy Horse was born in 1842, in an Oglala Sioux village on the eastern side of the Black Hills. His father was a respected Oglala medicine man and his mother was the sister of Spotted Tail, who was to become an important Oglala chief.

As a boy, Crazy Horse was considered somewhat unusual; he was a loner—quiet and aloof—set apart also by his lighter skin and lighter-colored hair. Indeed, in his early years, he was known as Light-Haired Boy. From his father, he acquired a fear and hatred of the white men. The Oglala medicine man often brooded about the demoralizing presence of the white traders and dreamed of a leader who might unite the Sioux and destroy the liquor trade and other corrupting influences.

But another problem, even greater than that of the white traders, began to threaten the future of the Sioux tribes. More and more white settlers were migrating through Sioux country along the Oregon Trail. In 1851, the Superintendent of Indian affairs was sent from Washington to hold a great council with Indians from all parts of the Plains. Ten thousand Indians assembled at Horse Creek near Fort Laramie where they heard the proposal of the emissary from Washington. In return for guarantees for the safety of white migrants who were using the Oregon Trail and for the right to erect forts along the route, the Superintendent of Indian affairs offered to pay specified government annuities to the Sioux over a period of fifty-five years. After much parleying, the chiefs of the various Sioux tribes agreed to the new treaty. They collected their annuities and when the army posts appeared along the Oregon Trail some of the worst excesses of the whiskey trade were stopped.

In 1854, however, this peaceful relationship was shattered when an overzealous Army lieutenant led a punitive raid on a Sioux village after some Indians had apparently stolen and butchered a cow from a party of migrants. Angered by this action, many bands of Sioux put on their war paint and began raiding activities along the Oregon Trail.

This was a crucial period in the life of "Light-Haired Boy." He was already attached to one of the ablest warriors of the village who taught him the skills that a hunter and warrior should know. Before he was twelve, the boy had killed his first buffalo and, at the village ceremony to honor such an exploit, he was renamed "His Horse Looking." When the troubles with the white man began, "His Horse Looking's" father, the medicine man, voiced his hope even more loudly for a great leader who might unite the Sioux.

Soon the time came for "His Horse Looking" to go alone to some wild place in quest of a vision, an important step in the transition of a young Sioux to manhood. After three days and nights of his lonely vigil on a remote hill, and growing hungry and faint from his fast, the young Sioux fell into a half-sleep. According to one account, he dreamed that he saw his horse coming toward him carrying a rider who had a small, smooth stone behind his ear. The horse and rider seemed to be a part of a coming storm, and the rider had a zigzag lightning streak on his cheek and hail-spots dotted his body. All around were his people attempting to reach out to the rider as if to clutch him—and when the storm faded, a hawk flew over the rider's head.

According to the same account, when the young Sioux told his father of his vision, the medicine man believed that this was the sign he had been looking for. If his son trusted the vision, he could become the great leader the Sioux were looking for, and when he rode to battle he would ride through storms of bullets without being touched. So the father bestowed his own name—Crazy Horse—on his son.

In the next ten years, the young Crazy Horse became the daring leader of an Oglala band—participating in constant fights with the Crows and other warlike Indians further west. He became a rival of other young Sioux chiefs for preeminence as a warrior. When renewed warfare broke out between the whites and the Indians after the end of the Civil War brought new waves of white settlers, Crazy Horse was given a leading role in an attack on a large wagon train in the vicinity of Fort Laramie in July of 1865. When a troop of cavalry from the fort rode out to help the wagon train, the large Sioux force of nearly 3,000 warriors overwhelmed both the cavalry and the wagon train.

Three years of bitter warfare followed between cavalry units of the American army and large bands of Sioux Indians. Crazy Horse continually distinguished himself as a daring leader in these hit-and-run battles and, as a result, was designated by his Oglala tribe to be a "shirt-wearer" —with the privilege of wearing the specially decorated buffalo skin which signified that he was a protector of the people. This honor was all the more unusual because Crazy Horse refused to take scalps.

A temporary peace was arranged between the American government and the Sioux in 1868, but Crazy Horse and other younger leaders remained suspicious of the chiefs who had signed the treaty. They distrusted the white men, and for good reason, because their main purpose was to pacify the region as a prelude to building a transcontinental railroad to the northern Pacific region. The treaty promised to respect the large area around the Powder and Bighorn rivers as Indian hunting grounds free from white interference, but in reality it was a way of establishing the Sioux on reservations.

As the railroad men came into the pacified area, the buffalo herds grew smaller and more scattered. Many of the Sioux, including Crazy Horse and his followers, were not satisfied to stay in the reservation areas as virtual dependents of the Indian agencies. When gold was discovered in the Black Hills in the 1870's, white men began pouring into Sioux lands in violation of the treaty of 1868. At the same time, the federal government sent out a new and more formidable body of troops, the 7th Cavalry, commanded by Colonel George Armstrong Custer.

Custer had made a gallant record as a cavalry commander in the Civil War, and he seemed to thirst for more glory to offset the comparatively drab life that was his lot in the army posts of the West. He had already made a reputation as a reckless and unreasonable Indian fighter against the Cheyennes in Kansas and the southern plains; now he was sent to Sioux country at the very moment when matters were reaching a danger point. With scant regard for treaty rights, Custer began leading armed expeditions into Sioux country to gather information and to protect survey parties for the Northern Pacific Raliroad route. By August of 1873, Crazy Horse was already leading raiding parties against Custer's troops in retaliation.

When the gold prospectors rushed into the Black Hills, it was only a question of time before full-scale warfare would begin between the Sioux and the Americans. The Sioux blamed Custer for the failure to keep the gold prospectors out of what was still Indian country. The American commander, already known as "Long Hair" because of his long blond hair, was now called "The Chief of all the Thieves." Hoping to prevent war, the Indian office in Washington sent a commission to negotiate with the Sioux chiefs for the purchase of the Black Hills for $6,000,000. Some chiefs wished to bargain, but Crazy Horse refuse to participate in the council. His war band continually harassed the prospectors and, by the spring of 1876, large forces of American troops were riding into Indian country "to teach the Indians a lesson."

In response, the Oglala Sioux designated Crazy Horse as the supreme war chief of their tribe and called upon other Sioux tribes to join them. Many, but not all, of the other Sioux tribes united with the Oglalas to resist further incursions by American troops. Several Cheyenne tribal groups also joined the Sioux who were determined to fight to the end.

In June of 1876, Colonel Custer, the old enemy of the Sioux, led five companies of cavalry toward the Little Bighorn where 12–15,000 Sioux and Cheyenne were encamped, including as many as 5,000 warriors. Not knowing how many Indians he had before him, but reckless as always, Custer rode his troops into battle, confidently expecting the Indians "to skedaddle." But he found himself encircled by thousands of mounted Indians and other thousands on foot. In a savage battle, on June 25, 1876, Custer's small force of 275 men was wiped out and Custer himself, with his long golden hair, was massacred along with his men. Crazy Horse, his cheeks painted with zigzags of lightning and his body with hailspots, was in the thick of the battle exhorting his warriors to the kill.

The victory over Custer was sweet but temporary. As larger American forces appeared with cavalry and field guns, the Sioux and Cheyenne broke camp and moved south to the Bighorn mountains. From there, Crazy Horse continued to lead raids against the miners and settlers in the Black Hills, but it became clear that the Sioux and Cheyenne lacked the power to drive them out.

By the fall of 1876, large American punitive expeditions began to penetrate the Bighorn mountain country. Soon the tribes were split and isolated by the sustained attacks of the mounted soldiers. When winter came, the Sioux camps were close to starvation, and the army commanders threatened to withhold further supplies of food from the peaceful Sioux who had remained in the reservations if their chiefs did not agree to a new treaty in the name of the whole Sioux nation. The peaceful chiefs capitulated and signed a new agreement which surrendered the Black Hills to the Americans.

Two large Sioux bands still fought on, contemptuously refusing to accept a treaty which was not based on the assent of the majority of the tribes. One was led by Sitting Bull and the other by Crazy Horse. Sitting Bull led his exhausted followers across the border to Canada to spare them from further losses by war and starvation. But Crazy Horse continued to carry on a desperate and hopeless warfare against the relentless campaign of the American cavalry forces. Finally, Crazy Horse and his weakened band were cornered near the fateful Little Bighorn, where they were starving and suffering terribly from the bitter cold of winter.

As winter also impeded the operations of the American cavalry forces, emissaries were sent to Crazy Horse to talk him into surrendering. For months, Crazy Horse remained iron-willed and defiant, but the suffering of his people must have convinced him that renewed warfare in the spring would be impossible. Early in May 1877, Crazy Horse informed General Cook that he would end his resistance if the Americans would give his people an area along the Powder River where they could hunt in peace.

On May 5, 1877, Crazy Horse led his proud band of warriors and their lodges and families to the soldiers' camp near Fort Robinson in the country north of the Platte River. For weeks, Crazy Horse and the army officers held councils without reaching agreement. Rumors developed that Crazy Horse was scheming to return to the warpath. Finally, on September 4, 1877, eight companies of cavalry, and four hundred Sioux led by friendly chiefs, were sent to the encampment of the Oglalas to arrest their chief. Crazy Horse made an attempt to escape by horseback but was overtaken. After a parley, he agreed to return for a further talk with the army commanders.

On the following day, Crazy Horse was taken to Fort Robinson, where he was led to a guardroom. When he realized that he was being imprisoned, he drew a knife from under his blanket and in the commotion that followed, the officer in charge yelled, "kill the son of a bitch." One of the guards lunged at Crazy Horse with his bayonet and thrust it deep into the chief's body. Crazy Horse sagged to the floor saying to the men who were trying to grab hold of him, "Let me go my friends, you have hurt me enough."

As Crazy Horse was laid on the floor in his own blood, his life slowly ebbing away, signal fires sent the news to all the surrounding Sioux camps and by nightfall the father of Crazy Horse was at the side of his dying son. When Crazy Horse saw him and recognized him, he said: "Oh, my father. I am badly hurt. Tell the people it is no use to depend on me anymore now." Shortly afterward, the thirty-five-year-old chief of the Oglala Sioux was dead.

A month later, the Sioux tribes began a new exodus to the new reservations set aside for them on the Missouri River under the watchful eyes of escorts of American cavalry. A few days out on the trek, there was a sudden movement in the long procession. About 2,000 Sioux who had fought with Crazy Horse swung out of line and galloped north towards the Canadian border. The cavalry escorts were too few to leave the procession to stop them. In a matter of days, Crazy Horse's band had joined the camps of Sitting Bull, where their exile could honor the memory of their dead chief as a symbol of continued protest. ■

IMAGES OF THE AMERICAN INDIAN

The paintings on these pages depict the American Indian and his environment in the nineteenth centuury. All are by well-known artists of the period. As you can see, in addition to making a descriptive statement, each artist also imparts his sense of the subject by the particular way in which he arranges and pictures objects and people on canvas. Thus, each painting can be studied with a view to finding out what the artists' conception of the American Indian was.

In this exercise, the first thing you should do is to sort the paintings by artist. Study form, shape, color, perspective, shading, texture, and so forth to help you decide which paintings have enough in common to warrant placing them in a single group. Then, looking at several works by one artist, try to determine his overall view of the Indians.

1 What kinds of Indian activities and life situations are portrayed? What is the relationship between the people, the activities, and the natural setting?

2 What emotional and intellectual response is each artist attempting to achieve? Can you make any assumptions about the painter's feelings, opinions, values, or beliefs? How would you compare the attitudes of the different artists?

3 What other information would you need to confirm that your analysis of the artist's conception is correct? ■

230

OPPOSITE: *The Buffalo Hunt*
Thomas Gilcrease Institute
Tulsa, Oklahoma

ABOVE LEFT: *See-non-ty-a, an Iowa Medicine Man*
National Gallery of Art
Washington, D.C.

ABOVE RIGHT: *The Sun Dance*
Remington Art Museum
Ogdensburg, New York

LEFT: *The Outlier*
Remington Art Museum
Ogdensburg, New York

CENTER: *Attack on the Wagon Train*
Thomas Gilcrease Institute
Tulsa, Oklahoma

RIGHT: *Making Flint Arrowheads — Apache*
National Gallery of Art
Washington, D.C.

233

LEFT: *LaSalle's Party Feasted in the Illinois Village*
National Gallery of Art
Washington, D.C.

Kiowa Indians Gathering Wild Grapes
National Gallery of Art
Washington, D.C.

235

236

LEFT: *The Emigrants*
The Museum of Fine Arts
Houston, Texas
Hogg Brothers Collection

RIGHT: *Salute to the Robe Tribe*
Thomas Gilcrease Institute
Tulsa, Oklahoma

237

INDIAN SPOKESMEN

Previously, we have seen how two early presidents of the United States viewed the fate of the American Indian. Here are three classic statements by Indian leaders expressing their own perceptions of what the future held in store for them and their people. The first was made by Powhatan to John Smith in 1609. The second was voiced by the Sauk-Fox leader Black Hawk in 1832. And the third was spoken by Chief Joseph of the Nez Percé Indians in 1877.

Source: *Lives of Celebrated American Indians* (Boston: Bradbury, Soden, and Co., 1843), pp. 179–180; 310–312.

Powhatan

I have seen two generations of my people die. Not a man of the two generations is alive now but myself. I know the difference between peace and war better than any man in my country. I am now grown old, and must die soon; my authority must descend to my brothers, Opitchapan, Opechancanough and Catatough;— then to my two sisters, and then to my two daughters. I wish them to know as much as I do, and that your love to them may be like mine to you. Why will you take by force what you may have quietly by love? Why will you destroy us who supply you with food? What can you get by war? We can hide our provisions and run into the woods; then you will starve for wronging your friends. Why are you jealous of us? We are unarmed, and willing to give you what you ask, if you come in a friendly manner, and not with swords and guns, as if to make war upon an enemy. I am not so simple as not to know that it is much better to eat good meat, sleep comfortably, live quietly with my wives and children, laugh and be merry with the English, and trade for their copper and hatchets, than to run away from them, and to lie cold in the woods, feed on acorns, roots and such trash, and be so hunted that I can neither eat nor sleep. In these wars, my men must sit up watching, and if a twig break, they all cry out, "Here comes Captain Smith!" So I must end my miserable life. Take away your guns and swords, the cause of all our jealousy, or you may all die in the same manner. ■

Black Hawk

You have taken me prisoner with all my warriors. I am much grieved, for I expected, if I did not defeat you, to hold out much longer, and give you more trouble before I surrendered. I tried hard to bring you into ambush, but your last general understands Indian fighting. The first one was not so wise. When I saw that I could not beat you by Indian fighting, I determined to rush on you, and fight you face to face. I fought hard. But your guns were well aimed. The bullets flew like birds in the air, and whizzed by our ears like the wind through the trees in the winter. My warriors fell around me; it began to look dismal. I saw my evil day at hand. The sun rose dim on us in the morning, and at night it sunk in a dark cloud, and looked like a ball of fire. That was the last sun that shone on Black Hawk. His heart is dead, and no longer beats quick in his bosom. He is now a prisoner to the white men; they will do with him as they wish. But he can stand torture, and is not afraid of death. He is no coward. Black Hawk is an Indian.

He has done nothing for which an Indian ought to be ashamed. He has fought for his countrymen, the squaws and papooses, against white men, who came, year after year, to cheat them and take away their lands. You know the cause of our making war. It is known to all white men. They ought to be ashamed of it. The white men despise the Indians, and drive them from their homes. But the Indians are not deceitful. The white men speak bad of the Indian, and look at him spitefully. But the Indian does not tell lies; Indians do not steal.

An Indian who is as bad as the white men, could not live in our nation; he would be put to death, and eat [sic] up by the wolves. The white men are bad schoolmasters; they carry false looks, and deal in false actions; they smile in the face of the poor Indian to cheat him; they shake them by the hand to gain their confidence, to make them drunk, to deceive them, and ruin our wives. We told them to let us alone; but they followed on and beset our paths, and they coiled themselves among us like the snake. They poisoned us by their touch. We were not safe. We lived in danger. We were becoming like them, hypocrites and liars, adulterers, lazy drones, all talkers, and no workers.

We looked up to the Great Spirit. We went to our great father. We were encouraged. His great council gave us fair words and big promises, but we got no satisfaction. Things were growing worse. There were no deer in the forest. The oppossum and beaver were fled; the springs were drying up, and our squaws and papooses without victuals to keep them from starving; we called a great council and built a large fire. The spirit of our fathers arose and spoke to us to avenge our wrongs or die. . . . We set up the war-whoop, and dug up the tomahawk; our knives were ready, and the heart of Black Hawk swelled high in his bosom when he led his warriors to battle. He is satisfied. He will go to the world of spirits contented. He has done his duty. His father will meet him there, and commend him.

Black Hawk is a true Indian, and disdains to cry like a woman. He feels for his wife, his children and friends. But he does not care for himself. He cares for his nation and the Indians. They will suffer. He laments their fate. The white men do not scalp the head; but they do worse— they poison the heart, it is not pure with them. His countrymen will not be scalped, but they will, in a few years, become like the white men, so that you can't trust them, and there must be, as in the white settlements, nearly as many officers as men, to take care of them and keep them in order.

Farewell, my nation. Black Hawk tried to save you, and avenge your wrongs. He drank the blood of some of the whites. He has been taken prisoner, and his plans are stopped. He can do no more. He is near his end. His sun is setting, and he will rise no more. Farewell to Black Hawk. ∎

Source: Merrill Beal, *I Will Fight No More Forever* (Seattle: University of Washington Press, 1966), p. 372.

Chief Joseph

Tell General Howard I know his heart. What he told me before I have in my heart. I am tired of fighting. Our chiefs are killed. Looking Glass is dead. The old men are all killed. It is the young men who say yes or no. He who led the young men is dead. It is cold and we have no blankets. The little children are freezing to death. My people, some of them, have run away to the hills and have no blankets, no food; no one knows where they are, perhaps freezing to death. I want time to look for my children and see how many of them I can find. Maybe I shall find them among the dead. Hear me, my chiefs, I am tired; my heart is sick and sad. From where the sun now stands, I will fight no more forever. ∎

239

THE ATTEMPT TO DISSOLVE COMMUNAL OWNERSHIP

The two accounts in this section deal with United States government policy toward the Indian in more modern times. By the end of the nineteenth century a growing number of Americans voiced a desire for more humane treatment of the Indians. In 1875 and 1884 the United States Congress passed legislation permitting the Indians to take up homesteads. The acts, however, were almost totally ignored. Then, in 1887, Congress passed the Dawes Act, a measure designed to bring about the dissolution of the reservations through the offer of land to individual Indian owners subject to certain restrictions. In the selection which follows, historian Loring B. Priest describes the nature of the Dawes Act and the effect it had on the way of life of the American Indian.

Source: Loring Benson Priest, *Uncle Sam's Stepchildren: The Reformation of the United States Indian Policy, 1865–1887* (New Brunswick, N.J.: Rutgers University Press, 1942), pp. 218–251.

The Dawes Act—1887

While the portions of the Dawes Act dealing with the problem of Indian citizenship were of the utmost importance, the primary purpose of the measure was to revolutionize the method of Indian land holding. The age-old practice of communal or tribal ownership was to be ended by dividing reservations into plots for distribution to individual Indians. The race would advance more rapidly, reformers held, if each Indian was encouraged by receiving personal title to the land he occupied. As a measure limited to abandoning communal for several ownership would not benefit the whites, however, more than a mere change in the method of land holding was necessary to win the favor of legislators. The Dawes Act was accepted by Congress only after its sponsors had made strange compromises between plans intended to aid the Indian and those meant to annex his land.

Two land holding provisions of the Dawes Act reveal unusually well the way in which Indian and white interests were balanced. Considerations of Indian welfare were uppermost when legislators provided that allotments should not be sold for 25 years. Yet self-interest was just as obviously the motive when Congress insisted that all unallotted land should immediately be opened to white settlement. Although funds from the sale of excess land were to be used for benefit of the Indians, the fact remained that undisputed title to a definite portion of land was to be gained only by surrendering any claim to the rest. Whether such a policy would prove of benefit to whites, to Indians, to both races, or to neither was far from certain.

The significance of the debates regarding land policy can be comprehended much more clearly after a brief summary of the arrangement which was ultimately approved. The process was to begin whenever the President believed that the members of a tribe would benefit from land distribution. An affirmative decision having been reached regarding the advisability of allotment, each head of a family was to receive one-quarter section (160 acres), each single person over eighteen as well as each orphan child was to have one-eighth section (80 acres), and all other single persons under eighteen born prior to an allotment order were to be assigned one-sixteenth section (40 acres). Where insufficient land existed, *pro rata* assignments were to be made in the same proportion; and where reservations were only of use for grazing, the amounts were to be doubled. In no case, however, was full title to an allotment to be granted for twenty-five years. Indians were to be prevented from disposing of their holdings during this time by patents declaring that the land was held in trust by the United States for the exclusive use of the allottee and his heirs. If still further protection proved desirable at the end of the period, government control might be extended indefinitely at presidential discretion. Once the patents had been issued to each Indian, or sooner if felt desirable by the President, unallotted areas were to be sold to white settlers. Sums realized from the disposal of such land were to be deposited in the United States Treasury and the annual interest accumulated by the funds was to be employed for the education and civilization of the tribe. Thus stated, the principles of the Dawes Act seem extremely simple. In reality, the system was pieced together only after extended debate as to what plan would aid whites the most while injuring Indians the least. Land provisions of the Dawes Act were not exclusively a product of sympathy for the Indian.

In stating that many supporters of the Dawes Act were moved by selfish motives, the impression should not be created that self-seeking legislators were from any particular part of the country. Motives were often so mixed even in the case of individual congressmen that no section's attitude can be characterized as either exclusively selfish or unselfish. The desire of frontiersmen to dispossess Indians was naturally strong; but interest in securing land was a powerful factor in winning the support of men from all sections. A conviction that no Indian land should be "a barrier against the swelling tide of American commerce" was universal. Representatives of frontier states were more apt than their colleagues to emphasize the advantage of severalty legislation to whites, but arguments of Easterners explaining the gains to be made by Indians were almost always accompanied by others urging the necessity for commercial expansion. As Easterners had every reason to be more liberal, their emphasis upon the desirability of obtaining more Indian land was especially significant.

The interest of frontiersmen in opening Indian reservations to settlement was shared by both the individual reformers and the organizations of the East. Few Easterners believed that Indians should occupy land they could not use. Even a woman, who held that Indians as "Dece-

dents of Father Abraham" were "within the covenant of mercy," wrote President Grant that if red men felt they had a right to their lands "it was high time they were better inform'd." Undeniable as were the rights possessed by Indians, Senator Dawes believed that the advance of white civilization was as impossible to check as a river. Members of the Indian Rights Association not only agreed, but announced that they would not resist a legitimate advance of civilization if they could. So eager was their Washington representative to open reservations that he declared the purpose of filling the Indian Territory with settlers "ought never to sleep." Similar interest in expansion led the Mohonk conference of 1884 to hail passage of a bill redistributing Sioux land as much because of the opening of a new highway as for any advantage gained by the Indians. Even members of the Board of Indian Commissioners, who were particularly noted for their concern for the Indian, refused to uphold his land claims. Instead, they ably summarized the opinion of a large majority of Americans by writing in their 1879 *Report*:

We may moralize over the natural rights of the Indian as much as we please, but after all they have their limit. His right to the soil is only possessory. He has no title in fee. If he will cultivate it and use it as civilized men use their possessions, it will or should be well with him, but it is evident that no 12,000,000 acres of the public domain, whose hills are full of ores, and whose valleys are waiting for diligent hands to 'dress and keep them,' in obedience to the divine command, can long be

kept simply as a park, in which wild beasts are hunted by wilder men. This Anglo-Saxon race will not allow the car of civilization to stop long at any line of latitude or longitude on our broad domain. If the Indian in his wildness plants himself on the track, he must inevitably be crushed by it.

The white man's passion for possession was too great to protect Indian rights from invasion even by those known for their sympathy with the oppressed.

* * *

The nature of the compromise which enabled passage of the land provisions of the Dawes Act has already been described. No measure could have been successful without provision for the sale of large portions of the reservations. Yet reformers were strong enough to insist that no Indian land should be taken without compensation. As a result, the sale of surplus land was balanced by granting a secure title to the remainder and setting aside all profits to be used for racial advancement. Whether or not such a policy would prove fair to the Indians and whether or not it could be successfully administered remained to be discovered. But as far as most contemporaries were concerned, a plan for remodeling Indian policy had been found which would prove equally advantageous to the members of both races.

The forced sale of surplus land was naturally the most popular administrative provision of the Dawes Act. As early as 1870, Quakers had officially proposed that superfluous Indian land should be sold to secure money for education and the establishment of tribal members upon individual allotments. Since many students of Indian affairs believed advancement would be impossible as long as tribes were permitted to roam over large areas, plans for reducing reservations by the sale of land received wide support and were occasionally adopted for restricted use. Government officials were not enthusiastic about applying the idea generally as they realized the difficulty of securing a satisfactory administration of land sales and tribal funds. Westerners likewise opposed plans for the acquisition of surplus land as long as hope remained that Indians might be completely removed from a reservation instead of being presented with a clear title to any portion of it. But as the impossibility of further removals became apparent, frontiersmen displayed an increasing willingness to grant land to individual Indians in return for admission to areas which were not needed. Enthusiasm for such an arrangement mounted irresistibly when legislators proposed that claims for damages pending against a tribe should be paid from funds obtained from sale of its land! Even though reformers insisted that money derived from land sales should be used exclusively for purposes of civilization, frontiersmen hoped to divert purchase money into the hands of border communities so that the land of the Indians might be secured without expense. This purpose was ultimately defeated; but in the meantime Western support insured success for the proposal to sell surplus land. Action was delayed until 1887 only because details had to be worked out which would facilitate administration and provide adequate compensation for the Indians.

Problems to be decided before the sale of surplus land could be successfully instituted were far more complicated than the apparent simplicity of the process would indicate. Success or failure might well depend upon whether allotments were selected by the Indians or by government administrators. Yet the superiority of neither method was clear. If complete freedom of choice was permitted, unintelligent selections could not be prevented and land necessary for commercial expansion might be absorbed. But if plots were assigned by the government, Indian antagonism would be aroused and opportunity provided for the intrigues of selfish officials. Even though a decision might be avoided on this controversial point, the question remained whether allotments should be compact or scattered throughout a reservation. While Senator Teller of Colorado was so convinced of the need for racial contact that he endeavored to limit severalty assignments to alternate quarter sections, most legislators wished to confine Indian settlements within as restricted an area as possible. Thus all plans for mixing the races were thwarted in spite of Senator Dawes's interest in encouraging contact; and gaps in assignments were not even permitted either for communal use or to supply the future needs of a tribe. Decisions of equal importance also had to be reached concerning the funds obtained from land sales. Congress debated at length whether every cent should be made available for tribal use at presidential discretion. Senator Dawes was willing to allow the executive department to control the entire fund, but fellow senators successfully insisted that only the interest might

be spent without specific congressional authorization. While such problems were only a few of those which arose during discussion of the sale of surplus land, agreement regarding the Dawes Act was even more seriously delayed by the necessity of deciding what protection should be offered Indian allottees.

The portion of the severalty act which made Indian allotments inalienable for twenty-five years was adopted in spite of violent protests against withholding any areas from prospective buyers. Although the speed with which red men had lost their land under early allotment measures emphasized the importance of prohibiting the sale of all land assigned to Indians, a powerful group fought every effort to protect the race. Yet no doubt regarding the validity of such inalienation provisions was possible in the light of Supreme Court decisions. When purchasers endeavored to retain land sold by a Kansas Indian without government consent, the justices refused the claim and discouraged further suits by declaring:

It was considered by Congress to be necessary, in case the reservees should be desirous of relinquishing their occupation of their lands, that some method of disposing of them should be adopted which would be a safeguard against their own improvidence; and the power of Congress to impose a restriction on the right of alienation, in order to accomplish this object, cannot be questioned. Without this power, it is easy to see, there would be no way of preventing the Indians from being wronged in contracts for the sale of their lands, and the history of our country *affords abundant proof that it is at all times difficult, by the most careful legislation, to protect their interests against the superior capacity and adroitness of their more civilized neighbors.*

In cases where Congress failed to forbid sale, the Court subsequently held that Indians might dispose of their title even before a patent had been issued. But the Court made clear that whenever Congress banned alienation of Indian allotments such restrictions were entirely legal.

Although the legality of prohibitions against the sale of Indian land could not be questioned, many Americans refused to admit the justice of providing Indian land holders with special protection. If red men were sufficiently advanced to be granted citizenship, opponents of inalienation insisted that they should be required to take care of themselves. True freedom would be impossible, they pointed out, as long as Indians were prevented from disposing of their allotments. In most cases, this hatred of inalienation was due to hope of obtaining land from Indian owners. Yet some friends of the race also criticized prohibitions against the sale of allotments on the ground that Indian independence should not be jeopardized in any way. Ill-considered insistence that red men must stand upon their own feet was evident, for example, in the remarks of a Baptist reformer who declared:

The land belongs to them or it does not. If it does belong to them, give it to them; but we give it to them as I give anything to my little son. I say, "That is yours, but don't you sell it, my boy.' Well then it is

not his. The Indians are simply playing that it is theirs, while we have everything in our power to do as we please. . . . The time is coming when we should step forth and recognize the rights of these Indians to citizenship and property. If they lose their property, they are doing no more than we have done before them. More than one-half of us are losing ours, but we go to work and get more . . . 'Root hog or die' is a principle; and let us put them in a position to 'root.'

Fortunately such an extreme view of the necessity for independence was exceptional among reformers. Most leaders of the Indian movement were too well informed to disregard the fact that allotment measures must prove ineffective unless provisions were included protecting Indian titles.

Inclusion of an inalienation provision in the Dawes Act did much to counteract portions of the bill which were less favorable to the Indians. Yet some reformers considered the twenty-five-year prohibition inadequate even after a clause had been added allowing an indefinite extension of the period by presidential action. Senator Miller of California believed that Indians would not be ready to forego United States protection in less than fifty years. But even if government control had been made perpetual, officials rarely displayed sufficient interest in protecting Indian land to justify confidence that any prohibition against sale would be of value. In many cases, the United States had been unnecessarily slow in issuing patents. Puyallup Indians were forced to wait thirty years because their land was desired by

the Northern Pacific; while delay in granting inalienable patents to the Crows led their disgruntled agent to expose the folly of inconsistent Washington land administration by writing:

It would be better to maintain the reservations forever (reducing them to reasonable size) than to patent lands to Indians without making them inalienable.

The government is altogether too slow in these matters.

It is too slow in doing what is right, and after going slow for a few years it wakes up and literally 'makes a break' and then is too fast in doing what is wrong (as for instance in patenting lands to Indians in Kansas and other places without making them inalienable).

It is provided by treaty with these Indians—the Crows—that their homesteads shall be inalienable, and there is no reason in this world why with this proviso every patent should have been issued by this date . . . The only reason it has not been done is that the people at Washington dont know anything about this work.

It sometimes seems as if they were incapable of learning or else that they dont care.

Whatever protection was provided at the moment, the safety of the Indians depended upon future legislators and administrators. The very fact that many Americans wished to force severalty upon the Indians regardless of treaty obligations raised the question whether inalienation clauses might not be similarly abrogated if Congress so desired. Yet as long as people feared that Indians would become paupers

243

and vagabonds if freed from government control, special protection was certain to be widely advocated. Even if the effectiveness of inalienation provisions had been indisputable, however, there would still have been reason to question whether the increased protection was worth the price demanded. ■

The Indian New Deal

The administration of Franklin D. Roosevelt is regarded by many historians as a period of vigorous and varied reform. One of the most innovative of these reforms had to do with U.S. policy toward the American Indian. The following was written by John Collier, who was Indian Commissioner of the United States during the New Deal era.

Source: John Collier, *The Indians of the Americas* (New York: W. W. Norton & Co., Inc., 1947), pp. 261–287.

In March, 1933, Franklin D. Roosevelt entered into office as President of the United States. Harold L. Ickes became the new Secretary of the Interior. I was appointed the new Indian Commissioner.

I had been learning a great deal about the American Indian himself, and about other men and women who knew the Indian, for over twelve years; and my staff and I, always with the firm support of Harold L. Ickes and the active and personal interest of the President, formulated a set of principles that have remained dominant. They may be summarized this way:

First, Indian societies must and can be discovered in their continuing existence, or regenerated, or set into being *de novo*— and made use of. This procedure serves equally the purposes of those who believe the ancient Indian ways to be best and those who believe in rapid acculturation to the higher rather than the lower levels of white life.

Second, the Indian societies, whether ancient, regenerated or created anew, must be given status, responsibility and power.

Third, the land, held, used and cherished in the way the particular Indian group desires, is fundamental in any lifesaving program.

Fourth, each and all of the freedoms should be extended to Indians, and in the most convincing and dramatic manner possible. In practice this included repeal of sundry espionage statutes, guarantee of the right to organize, and proclamation and enforcement of cultural liberty, religious liberty and unimpeded relationships of the generations.

Fifth, the grant of freedom must be more, however, than a remission of enslave-

244

ments. Free for what? Organization is necessary to freedom: help toward organizing must be extended by the government. Credit is necessary to freedom: co-operatively managed credit must be supplied. Knowledge is necessary to freedom: education in terms of live local issues and problems must be supplied through activity programs in the schools; technological and business and civic education must be supplied to adults; professional and collegiate training must be opened to the post-adolescent group. Responsibility is necessary to freedom: one responsibility is perpetuation of the natural resources, and conservation must be made mandatory on the tribes, by statute. Capital goods are necessary to freedom, and responsibility must be applied to capital goods: a tribe that handles its revolving credit fund irresponsibly must know that shrunken credit will be its lot tomorrow.

And now, the sixth principle: The experience of responsible democracy is, of all experiences, the most therapeutic, the most disciplinary, the most dynamogenic and the most productive of efficiency. In this one affirmation we, the workers, who knew so well the diversity of the Indian situation and its incalcitrancy toward monistic programs, were prepared to be unreserved, absolute, even at the risk of blunders and of turmoil. We tried to extend to the tribes a self-governing self-determination without any limit beyond the need to advance by stages to the goal. Congress let us go only part way, but the part way, when the administrative will was undeviating, proved to be enough. Often the administrative will was not undeviating, often the administrative resourceful-

ness was not enough, often the Gulliver's threads of the land allotment system and of civil service and the appropriation systems kept the administrator imprisoned. The establishment of living democracy, profound democracy, is a high art; it is the ultimate challenge to the administrator. The Indian Service since 1933 has practiced the art, has met the challenge, in ways varied enough and amid situations diversified enough to enable one to give a verdict which seems genuinely momentous: the democratic way has been proved to be enormously the efficient way, the genius-releasing and the nutritive and life-impelling way, and *the way of order.*

The seventh principle I would call the first and the last: That research and then more research is essential to the program, that in the ethnic field research can be made a tool of action essential to all the other tools, indeed, that it ought to be the master tool. But we had in mind a particular kind of research impelled from central areas of needed action. Since action is by nature not only specialized but also integrative of specialties, and nearly always integrative of more than the specialties, our needed research must be of the integrative sort. Again, since the findings of the research must be carried into effect by the administrator and the layman, and must be criticized by them through their experience, the administrator and the layman must themselves participate creatively in the research, impelled as it is from their own area of need. Through such integrative research, in 1933, the Soil Conservation Service directly originated in the ecological and economic problems of the Navajo Indian tribe. In current years in-

tegrative research (the administrator and layman always participating) has pushed far back our horizons of knowledge and understanding of a whole series of the tribes, and has searched our policies, administration, personnel and operating methods to their foundations. I add, in passing, that such research invariably has operated to deepen our realization of the potentialities of the democratic way, as well as our realization of our own extreme, pathetic shortcomings.

In 1934 the Indian Reorganization bill was laid before Congress, where the hearings on it lasted several months. Some people ridiculed this bill because it contained 52 printed pages. They forgot that it was offered as a successor to the greater part of several thousand pages of Indian law. Until 1934, Indian tribes rarely had been consulted on the legislation introduced for their supposed benefit. In preparing this bill, however, the Indian office first sent to all the tribes questions concerning the Indian problems deemed to be central. Then the bill was furnished them all. Finally, congresses of Indians were held in all the regions, gatherings in which practically every tribe in the United States was represented.

As originally introduced in Congress the bill had six main parts.

1 The Indian societies were to be recognized, and be empowered and helped to undertake political, administrative and economic self-government.

2 Provision was made for an Indian civil service and for the training of Indians in administration, the professions and other vocations.

3 Land allotment was to be stopped, and the revestment of Indians with land was provided for.

4 A system of agricultural and industrial credit was to be established, and the needed funds authorized.

5 Civil and criminal law enforcement, below the level reached by federal court jurisdiction, was to be set up under a system of courts operating with simplified procedures and ultimately responsible to the tribes.

6 The consolidation of fractionalized allotted lands, and the delivery of allotments back into the tribal estate, was provided for under conditions which safeguarded all individual property rights and freedoms.

The first four parts of the Reorganization bill, as listed, became law. The fifth and sixth parts were lost. The fifth part may have been fortunately lost, because the tribes, under the enacted parts of the bill and under court decisions defining the unextinguished, inherent powers of Indian tribes, are coping with law and order more effectively with each passing year. But the loss of the sixth part was a major disaster to the Indians, the Indian Service and the program. Congress has not yet righted that blunder of 1934. The fractionalizing of allotted Indian lands rushes on; the real estate operation of leasing these atomized parcels, collecting, accounting for, and paying out the hundreds of thousands of vanishing incomes becomes increasingly costly, and increasingly a barrier against productive work or thinking in the allotted jurisdictions; millions of their best acres remain unusable to the Indians.

In the meantime, however, the Indian Service and the tribes are struggling to reverse the flood that is eating away the Indians' land-base. This is being done through voluntary exchanges and relinquishments, which require contact with each of the all but innumerable heirs—fifty heirship equities may vest in one Indian, and one allotment may have hundreds of scattered heirs. Despite the difficulties, the wasting flood has been checked and reversed in a few jurisdictions. It is only where this occurs that there can be a beginning of the positive program of using Indian lands through Indian effort. The situation was fully recognized in the report of the House Sub-committee on Indian Investigation, issued in December, 1944. In passing so lightly over this very important subject I wish only to add that in this matter, too, the Indians are wrestling with a problem widely encountered in other lands. One of the heavy drags on the agricultural economy of Asiatic India, for example, is the ever-increasing fractionalization of farm holdings. The formulae that are being successfully used here in the United States (but far too gradually, in the absence of the Congressional authority sought but not obtained) have application in Europe and in Asia.

The Reorganization bill, as finally enacted, contained a requirement that every tribe should accept or reject it in a referendum held by secret ballot. Those who accepted the act could organize under it for local self-government. Through a subsequent referendum they could organize themselves as federal corporations chartered for economic enterprise. Ultimately, about three-fourths of the Indians of the

United States and Alaska came within the act. A related enactment, the Johnson-O'Malley Act, also passed in 1934, provided for the devolution of federal power to states and other political subdivisions, and for the enlistment of private agencies in the Indian task, through a flexible system of contracts and of grants-in-aid.

In the past twelve years the Indian Service, on the basis of this legislation and impelled by the principles enumerated above, has striven to the end that every one of the particular programs—conservation, the cattle program, community organization, schools, the credit program, health, the Indian branch of the Civilian Conservation Corps and the other depression-years programs, the arts and crafts work—that every particular program should serve the primary aims of freeing or regenerating the Indian societies, and infusing them with the spirit of democracy, implementing them with democratic tools, and concentrating their attention upon their basic practical exigencies. Year after year, and cumulatively with the years, we who were doing the work observed sadly our partial failures, here and there our complete failures. Yet we also witnessed a development that has far outweighed the deficiencies.

* * *

From the Indian record we can also draw these conclusions:

First, biological racehood, whether it exists or not, is without practical importance. There accumulate within the around races that are biologically distinguishable, and within and around races that are not biologically distinguishable, those in-group and out-group factors whose aggregate is called "racial." The factors are socially caused and socially transmitted.

Second, in ethnic matters, as in other vital matters, governmental intervention can be baneful or benign. In any field of human relations, when government tries to do the whole job, authoritatively and monopolistically, the result is baneful. The earlier Indian record is replete with evidence of this. But when government makes research an inseparable part of its ethnic operations, eschews monopoly, acts as a catalytic and co-ordinating agent, offers its service through grants-in-aid to local subdivisions, then government can be decisively benign, as the recent Indian record demonstrates. It is of national importance, and necessary to the good role of our Occidental governments in the world, that ethnic groups shall have equality of opportunity, shall be enabled to contribute their ideals and genius to the common task, shall not suffer discriminations, shall be free to breathe deeply the breath of public life. The Bill of Rights and the Constitution within the United States, the Charter of United Nations in the world, must be made good. It follows that governments and the federation of governments should and must concern themselves with ethnic matters, and that the methods should be right and not wrong.

Third, the individual fares best when he is a member of a group faring best. All human beings, in young childhood at least, are members of groups. The group is the tree and they are the fruit it bears. At least up to a certain age-level, the individual reft from his group is hurt or destroyed. The ruin inflicted on Red Indians through the white man's denial of their grouphood,

and his leading them to deny their own grouphood, is only a special case of something that is universal. It may be that contemporary white life is being injured nearly as much by the submergence of its primary social groupings as the denial of Indian grouphood injured Indian life. If the primary social group in white life were regenerated for full functioning, through resourceful and sustained social effort, and were dynamically connected once more with the great society, the hygienic and creative results might be no less startling than those observed in the comeback of Indian societies.

Fourth, in ethnic groups of low prestige the apparent inferiority (acquired or innate) may mask an actual superiority. In most Indian groups the academic lag of children is pronounced, but if these children were given non-language tests that have been standardized on whites, they excel, even to a sensational extent. Their elder brothers excel when they are thrown into critical action, as they have been in the recent world war. In rhythm, so little regarded in our white society, the Indians excel. In public spirit they excel, and in joy of life, and in intensity realized within quietude. They excel in art propensities, and in truthfulness. These superiorities will be masked by an apparent inferiority until their group as a group moves into status and power. Then the mask will fall away. The application of this fact to underprivileged ethnic groups in general is readily apparent.

And last, the Indians and their societies disclose that social heritage is far more perduring than is commonly believed. On how small a life-base, on a diminished and

starved life-base for how many generations, the motivations and expectations of a society, and its world-view and value system and loyalties, can keep themselves alive; how these social possessions, which are of the soul, can endure, like the roots and seeds on the Mojave desert, through long ages, without one social rain; and how they rush, like these roots and seeds, into surprising and wonderful blossom when the social rain does come at last. Perhaps no other ethnic groups have revealed this old, all-important truth so convincingly as the Indians have done. Indeed, this capacity for perdurance is one of the truths on which the hope of our world rests—our world grown so pallid in the last century, through the totalitarian horror. The sunken stream can flow again, the ravaged desert can bloom, the great past is not killed. The Indian experience tells us this. ■

247

THE PROBLEM OF
INDIAN IDENTITY
IN MODERN AMERICA

Source: Vine DeLoria, *Custer Died for Your Sins* (New York: The Macmillan Co., 1969), pp. 10–19; 24–29.

Our inquiry into the American Indian concludes with a statement by a contemporary Indian writer. The selection is by Vine DeLoria and is taken from his book, *Custer Died for Your Sins.* How does he analyze the problem of the American Indian today?

To be an Indian in modern American society is in a very real sense to be unreal and ahistorical. In this book we will discuss the other side—the unrealities that face us as Indian people. It is this unreal feeling that has been welling up inside us and threatens to make this decade the most decisive in history for Indian people. In so many ways, Indian people are re-examining themselves in an effort to redefine a new social structure for their people. Tribes are reordering their priorities to account for the obvious discrepancies between their goals and the goals whites have defined for them.

Indian reactions are sudden and surprising. One day at a conference we were singing "My Country 'Tis of Thee" and we came across the part that goes:

Land where my fathers died
Land of the Pilgrims' pride . . .

Some of us broke out laughing when we realized that our fathers undoubtedly died trying to keep those Pilgrims from stealing our land. In fact, many of our fathers died because the Pilgrims killed them as witches. We didn't feel much kinship with those Pilgrims, regardless of who they did in.

We often hear "give it back to the Indians" when a gadget fails to work. It's a terrible thing for a people to realize that society has set aside all non-working gadgets for their exclusive use.

During my 3 years as Executive Director of the National Congress of American Indians it was a rare day when some white didn't visit my office and proudly proclaim that he or she was of Indian descent.

Cherokee was the most popular tribe of their choice and many people placed the Cherokees anywhere from Maine to Washington State. Mohawk, Sioux, and Chippewa were next in popularity. Occasionally I would be told about some mythical tribe from lower Pennsylvania, Virginia, or Massachusetts which had spawned the white standing before me.

At times I became quite defensive about being a Sioux when these white people had a pedigree that was so much more respectable than mine. But eventually I came to understand their need to identify as partially Indian and did not resent them. I would confirm their wildest stories about their Indian ancestry and would add a few tales of my own hoping that they would be able to accept themselves someday and leave us alone.

Whites claiming Indian blood generally tend to reinforce mythical beliefs about Indians. All but one person I met who claimed Indian blood claimed it on their grandmother's side. I once did a projection backward and discovered that evidently most tribes were entirely female for the first three hundred years of white occupation. No one, it seemed, wanted to claim a male Indian as a forebear.

It doesn't take much insight into racial attitudes to understand the real meaning of the Indian-grandmother complex that plagues certain whites. A male ancestor has too much of the aura of the savage warrior, the unknown primitive, the instinctive animal, to make him a respectable member of the family tree. But a young Indian princess? Ah, there was royalty for the taking. Somehow the white was linked with a noble house of gentility and culture if his grandmother was an Indian princess who ran away with an intrepid pioneer. And royalty has always been an unconscious but all-consuming goal of the European immigrant.

The early colonists, accustomed to life under benevolent despots, projected their understanding of the European political structure onto the Indian tribe in trying to explain its political and social structure. European royal houses were closed to ex-convicts and indentured servants, so the colonists made all Indian maidens princesses, then proceeded to climb a social ladder of their own creation. Within the next generation, if the trend continues, a large portion of the American population will eventually be related to Powhatan.

While a real Indian grandmother is probably the nicest thing that could happen to a child, why is a remote Indian princess grandmother so necessary for many whites? Is it because they are afraid of being classed as foreigners? Do they need some blood tie with the frontier and its dangers in order to experience what it means to be an American? Or is it an attempt to avoid facing the guilt they bear for the treatment of the Indian?

The phenomenon seems to be universal. Only among the Jewish community, which has a long tribal-religious tradition of its own, does the mysterious Indian grandmother, the primeval princess, fail to dominate the family tree. Otherwise, there's not much to be gained by claiming Indian blood or publicly identifying as an Indian. The white believes that there is a great danger the lazy Indian will eventually corrupt God's hard-working people. He is still suspicious that the Indian way of life

is dreadfully wrong. There is, in fact, something *un-American* about Indians for most whites.

I ran across a classic statement of this attitude one day in a history book which was published shortly after the turn of the century. Often have I wondered how many Senators, Congressmen, and clergymen of the day accepted the attitudes of that book as a basic fact of life in America. In no uncertain terms did the book praise God that the Indian had not yet been able to corrupt North America as he had South America:

It was perhaps fortunate for the future of America that the Indians of the North rejected civilization. Had they accepted it the whites and Indians might have inter-married to some extent as they did in Mexico. That would have given us a population made up in a measure of shiftless half-breeds.

I never dared to show this passage to my white friends who had claimed Indian blood, but I often wondered why they were so energetic if they did have some of the bad seed in them.

Those whites who dare not claim Indian blood have an asset of their own. They *understand* Indians.

Understanding Indians is not an esoteric art. All it takes is a trip through Arizona or New Mexico, watching a documentary on TV, having known *one* in the service, or having read a popular book on *them.*

There appears to be some secret osmosis about Indian people by which they can magically and instantaneously communicate complete knowledge about themselves

to these interested whites. Rarely is physical contact required. Anyone and everyone who knows an Indian or who is *interested,* immediately and thoroughly understands them.

You can verify this great truth at your next party. Mention Indians and you will find a person who saw some in a gas station in Utah, or who attended the Gallup ceremonial celebration, or whose Uncle Jim hired one to cut logs in Oregon, or whose church had a missionary come to speak last Sunday on the plight of Indians and the mission of the church.

There is no subject on earth so easily understood as that of the American Indian. Each summer, work camps disgorge teen-agers on various reservations. Within one month's time the youngsters acquire a knowledge of Indians that would astound a college professor.

Easy knowledge about Indians is a historical tradition. After Columbus "discovered" America he brought back news of a great new world which he assumed to be India and, therefore, filled with Indians. Almost at once European folklore devised a complete explanation of the new land and its inhabitants which featured the Fountain of Youth, the Seven Cities of Gold, and other exotic attractions. The absence of elephants apparently did not tip off the explorers that they weren't in India. By the time they realized their mistake, instant knowledge of Indians was a cherished tradition.

Missionaries, after learning some of the religious myths of tribes they encountered, solemnly declared that the inhabitants of the new continent were the Ten Lost Tribes of Israel. Indians thus received a religious-historical identity far greater than they wanted or deserved. But it was an impossible identity. Their failure to measure up to Old Testament standards doomed them to a fall from grace and they were soon relegated to the status of a picturesque species of wildlife.

Like the deer and the antelope, Indians seemed to play rather than get down to the serious business of piling up treasures upon the earth where thieves break through and steal. Scalping, introduced prior to the French and Indian War by the English,[1]

---

[1] Notice, for example the following proclamation:

Given at the Council Chamber in Boston this third day of November 1755 in the twenty-ninth year of the Reign of our Sovereign Lord George the Second by the Grace of God of Great Britain, France, and Ireland, King Defender of the Faith.

By His Honour's command
J. Willard, Secry.
God Save the King

Whereas the tribe of Penobscot Indians have repeatedly in a perfidious manner acted contrary to their solemn submission unto his Majesty long since made and frequently renewed.

I have, therefore, at the desire of the House of Representatives . . . thought fit to issue this Proclamation and to declare the Penobscot Tribe of Indians to be enemies, rebels and traitors to his Majesty. . . . And I do hereby require his Majesty's subjects of the Province to embrace all opportunities of pursuing, captivating, killing and destroy-all and every of the aforesaid Indians.

And whereas the General Court of this Province have voted that a bounty . . . be granted and allowed to be paid out of the Province Treasury . . . the premiums of bounty following viz:

confirmed the suspicion that Indians were wild animals to be hunted and skinned. Bounties were set and an Indian scalp became more valuable than beaver, otter, marten, and other animal pelts.

American blacks had become recognized as a species of human being by amendments to the Constitution shortly after the Civil War. Prior to emancipation they had been counted as three-fifths of a person in determining population for representation in the House of Representatives. Early Civil Rights bills nebulously state that other people shall have the same rights as "white people," indicating there *were* "other people." But Civil Rights bills passed during and after the Civil War systematically excluded Indian people. For a long time an Indian was not presumed capable of initiating an action in a court of law, of owning property, or of giving testimony against whites in court. Nor could an Indian vote or leave his reservation. Indians were America's captive people without any defined rights whatsoever.

Then one day the white man discovered that the Indian tribes still owned some 135 million acres of land. To his horror he learned that much of it was very valuable. Some was good grazing land, some was farm land, some mining land, and some covered with timber.

For every scalp of a male Indian brought in as evidence of their being killed as aforesaid, forty pounds.

For every scalp of such female Indian or male Indian under the age of twelve years that shall be killed and brought in as evidence of their being killed as aforesaid, twenty pounds.

Animals could be herded together on a piece of land, but they could not sell it. Therefore it took no time at all to discover that Indians were really people and should have the right to sell their lands. Land was the means of recognizing the Indian as a human being. It was the method whereby land could be stolen legally and not blatantly.

Once the Indian was thus acknowledged, it was fairly simple to determine what his goals were. If, thinking went, the Indian was just like the white, he must have the same outlook as the white. So the future was planned for the Indian people in public and private life. First in order was allotting them reservations so that they could sell their lands. God's foreordained plan to repopulate the continent fit exactly with the goals of the tribes as they were defined by their white friends.

It is fortunate that we were never slaves. We gave up land instead of life and labor. Because the Negro labored, he was considered a draft animal. Because the Indian occupied large areas of land, he was considered a wild animal. Had we given up anything else, or had anything else to give up, it is certain that we would have been considered some other thing.

Whites have had different attitudes toward the Indians and the blacks since the Republic was founded. Whites have always refused to give non-whites the respect which they have been found to legally possess. Instead there has always been a contemptuous attitude that although the law says one thing, "we all know better."

Thus whites steadfastly refused to allow blacks to enjoy the fruits of full citizenship. They systematically closed schools, churches, stores, restaurants, and public places to blacks or made insulting provisions for them. For one hundred years every program of public and private white America was devoted to the exclusion of the black. It was, perhaps, embarrassing to be rubbing shoulders with one who had not so long before been defined as a field animal.

The Indian suffered the reverse treatment. Law after law was passed requiring him to conform to white institutions. Indian children were kidnapped and forced into boarding schools thousands of miles from their homes to learn the white man's ways. Reservations were turned over to different Christian denominations for governing. Reservations were for a long time church operated. Everything possible was done to ensure that Indians were forced into American life. The wild animal was made into a household pet whether or not he wanted to be one.

Policies for both black and Indian failed completely. Blacks eventually began the Civil Rights movement. In doing so they assured themselves some rights in white society. Indians continued to withdraw from the overtures of white society and tried to maintain their own communities and activities.

Actually both groups had little choice. Blacks, trapped in a world of white symbols, retreated into themselves. And people thought comparable Indian withdrawal unnatural because they expected Indians to behave like whites.

The white world of abstract symbols became a nightmare for Indian people. The words of the treaties, clearly stating that Indians should have "free and undis-turbed" use of their lands under the protection of the federal government, were cast aside by the whites as if they didn't exist. The Sioux once had a treaty plainly stating that it would take the signatures or marks of three-fourths of the adult males to amend it. Yet through force the government obtained only 10 percent of the required signatures and declared the new agreement valid.

Indian solutions to problems which had been defined by the white society were rejected out of hand and obvious solutions discarded when they called for courses of action that were not proper in white society. When Crow Dog assassinated Spotted Tail the matter was solved under traditional Sioux customs. Yet an outraged public, furious because Crow Dog had not been executed, pressured for the Seven Major Crimes Act for the federal government to assume nearly total criminal jurisdiction over the reservations. Thus foreign laws and customs using the basic concepts of justice came to dominate Indian life. If, Indians reasoned, justice is for society's benefit, why isn't our justice accepted? Indians became convinced they were the world's stupidest people.

Words and situations never seemed to fit together. Always, it seemed, the white man chose a course of action that did not work. The white man preached that it was good to help the poor, yet he did nothing to assist the poor in his society. Instead he put constant pressure on the Indian people to hoard their worldly goods, and when they failed to accumulate capital but freely gave to the poor, the white man reacted violently.

The failure of communication created a void into which poured the white do-gooder, the missionary, the promoter, the scholar, and every conceivable type of person who believed he could help. White society failed to understand the situation because this conglomerate of assistance blurred the real issues beyond recognition.

The legend of the Indian was embellished or tarnished according to the need of the intermediaries to gain leverage in their struggle to solve problems that never existed outside of their own minds. The classic example, of course, is the old-time missionary box. People were horrified that Indians continued to dress in their traditional garb. Since whites did not wear buckskin and beads, they equated such dress with savagery. So do-gooders in the East held fantastic clothing drives to supply the Indians with civilized clothes. Soon boxes of discarded evening gowns, tuxedos, tennis shoes, and uniforms flooded the reservations. Indians were made to dress in these remnants so they could be civilized. Then, realizing the ridiculous picture presented by the reservation people, neighboring whites made fun of the Indian people for having the presumption to dress like whites.

But in the East, whites were making great reputations as "Indian experts," as people who devoted their lives to helping the savages. Whenever Indian land was needed, the whites pictured the tribes as wasteful people who refused to develop their natural resources. Because the Indians did not "use" their lands, argued many land promoters, the lands should be taken away and given to people who knew what to do with them.

White society concentrated on the individual Indian to the exclusion of his group, forgetting that any society is merely a composite of individuals. Generalizations by experts universalized "Indianness" to the detriment of unique Indian values. Indians with a common cultural base shared behavior patterns. But they were expected to behave like a similar group of whites and rarely did. Whites, on the other hand, generally came from a multitude of backgrounds and shared only the need for economic subsistence. There was no way, therefore, to combine white values and Indian behavior into a workable program or intelligible subject of discussion.

One of the foremost differences separating white and Indian was simply one of origin. Whites derived predominantly from western Europe. The earliest settlers on the Atlantic seaboard came from England and the low countries. For the most part they shared the common experiences of their peoples and dwelt within the world view which had dominated western Europe for over a millennium.

Conversely Indians had always been in the western hemisphere. Life on this continent and views concerning it were not shaped in a post-Roman atmosphere. The entire outlook of the people was one of simplicity and mystery, not scientific or abstract. The western hemisphere produced wisdom, western Europe produced knowledge.

Perhaps this distinction seems too simple to mention. It is not. Many is the time I have sat in Congressional hearings and heard the chairman of the committee crow about "our" great Anglo-Saxon heritage of law and order. Looking about the hearing room I saw row after row of full-blood Indians with blank expressions on their faces. As far as they were concerned, Sir Walter Raleigh was a brand of pipe tobacco that you got at the trading post.

When we talk about European background, we are talking about feudalism, kings, queens, their divine right to rule their subjects, the Reformation, Christianity, the Magna Charta, and all of the events that went to make up European history.

American Indians do not share that heritage. They do not look wistfully back across the seas to the old country. The Apache were not at Runymede to make King John sign the Magna Charta. The Cherokee did not create English common law. The Pima had no experience with the rise of capitalism and industrialism. The Blackfeet had no monasteries. No tribe has an emotional, historical, or political relationship to events of another continent and age.

Indians have had their own political history which has shaped the outlook of the tribes. There were great confederacies throughout the country before the time of the white invader. The eastern Iroquois formed a strong league because as single tribes they had been weak and powerless against larger tribes. The Deep South was controlled by three confederacies: the Creeks with their town system, the Natchez, and the Powhatan confederation which extended into tidelands Virginia. The Pequots and their cousins the Mohicans controlled the area of Connecticut, Massachusetts, Rhode Island, and Long Island.

True democracy was more prevalent among Indian tribes in pre-Columbian days than it has been since. Despotic power was abhorred by tribes that were loose combinations of hunting parties rather than political entities.

Conforming their absolute freedom to fit rigid European political forms has been very difficult for most tribes, but on the whole they have managed extremely well. Under the Indian Reorganization Act Indian people have generally created a modern version of the old tribal political structure and yet have been able to develop comprehensive reservation programs which compare favorably with governmental structures anywhere. . . . ■

CONTEMPORARY
INDIAN FOLK SONGS

Folk songs are so-called because they are songs of the people. Folk songs are usually spontaneous creations that become part of the heritage and tradition of a group of people. They often express the feelings, beliefs, and ideas of that group toward some person, event, or general situation. The following folk songs express the reactions of contemporary American Indians to their history and problems. Both the lyrics and the music are important to an understanding of the meaning of the songs.

1 What specific ideas, beliefs, and feelings are expressed in each song? What is the general mood of the song?

2 Based on these lyrics, what hypotheses can you make about how contemporary Indians view their history? Their situation today?

Listen to the music of these songs. This can be done by either using the music on these pages and persuading someone who knows guitar to play for the class, or by getting from a library a record of contemporary songs of the American Indian.

3 What is the tone and spirit of the music? How does it reinforce or alter the tone and mood of each song?

4 Does this modify your hypothesis about how Indians view their situation?

5 How would you compare the tone, spirit, and message of these songs with the statements made by Powhatan, Black Hawk, and Chief Joseph? ■

254

Hey, Mr. President

Words and Music by Peter La Farge

Hey, Mr. President, we're going to charge you
   rent
For every treaty broken for every treaty bent.
We are making reservations
That will be just for whites

We will be honest about the white man's
   rights

Hey, Mr. President we're going to charge you
   rent, etc.

We are going to be the tourists,
We'll come to see you dance.
You'll let us know the reason
Why you prance.

Hey, Mr. President, we're going to charge you
   rent, etc.

We're not unpatriotic
We just like to see
Like to see your culture
How intriguing it will be.

Hey, Mr. President, we're going to charge you
   rent, etc.

You get out your medicine men
You get out your squaws
And we will give you justice
Under Indian laws.

Hey, Mr. President, we're going to charge you
   rent, etc.

The Senecas
(As Long as The Grass Shall Grow)

Words and Music by Peter La Farge

The Senecas are an Indian tribe,
Of the Iriquois nation,
Down on the New York Pennsylvania line,
You'll find their reservation,
After the U-S. revolution,
Corn planter was a chief,
He told the tribe these men they could trust
That was his true belief,
He went down to independence hall,
And there a treaty signed,
That promised peace with the USA,
And Indian rights combined,
George Washington gave his signature,
The Government gave its hand,
They said that now and forever more,
This was Indian Land.

As long as the moon shall rise,
As long as the rivers flow,
As long as the sun will shine,
As long as the grass shall grow.

On the Seneca reservation,
There is much sadness now,
Washington's treaty has been broken,
And there is no hope, no how,
Across the Allegheny River,
They're throwing up a dam,
It will flood the Indian Country,
A proud day for Uncle Sam,
It has broke the ancient treaty
With a Politician's grin,
It will drown the Indian's grave yards,
Cornplanter can you swim?
The Earth is Mother to the Senecas,
They're trampling sacred ground,
Change the mint green earth to black mud
    flats,
As honor hobbles down . . .

The Iriquois Indians used to rule,
From Canada way south,
But no one fears the Indians now,
And smiles the liar's mouth,
The Senecas hired an expert,
To figure another site,
But the great good army engineers,
Said that he had no right,
Although he showed them another plan,
And showed them another way,
They laughed in his face and said no deal,
Kinuza dam is here to stay,
Congress turned the Indians down,
Brushed off the Indians' plea,
So the Senecas have renamed the dam,
They call it lake perfidy . . .

Washington, Adams and Kennedy,
Now hear their pledges ring,
The treatys are safe, we'll keep our word,
But what is that gurgaling?
It's the back water from perfidy lake
It's rising all the time,
Over the homes and over the fields,
Over the promises fine,
No boats will sail on lake perfidy,
In winter it will fill,
In summer it will be a swamp,
And all the fish will kill,
But the Government of the USA,
Has corrected George's vow,
The father of our country must be wrong,
What's an Indian, anyhow . . .

Now that the Buffalo's gone

Buffy Sainte-Marie

Can you remember the times
That you held your head high
And told all your friends of your Indian claims
Proud good lady and proud good man.
Your great, great grandfather from Indian
    blood sprang,
And you feel in your heart for these ones.

Oh it's written in books and in songs
That we've been mistreated and wronged
Well, over and over I hear the same words
    from you,
Good lady, from you good man.
Well listen to me—if you care where we stand,
And you feel you're a part of these ones.

When a war between nations is lost
The loser we know pays the cost
But even when Germany fell to your hands
Consider dear lady, consider dear man.
You left them their pride and you left them
    their land
And what have you done to these ones?

Has a change come about Uncle Sam
Or are you still taking our land
A treaty forever George Washington signed
    he did,
Dear lady, he did, dear man
And the treaty's being broken by Kinzua Dam
And what will you do for these ones?

Oh it's all in the past you can say
But it's still going on till today
The government now wants the Iriquois land
That of the Seneca and the Cheyenne
It's here and it's now you must help us,
    dear man
Now that the buffalo's gone.

255

THE BLACK MAN'S STRUGGLE FOR EQUALITY AND IDENTITY

In 1619 the first blacks to come to America from Africa were brought to Jamestown, Virginia. They came as indentured servants bound to serve their masters for a specified period of time before they were to be set free. However, because crops like tobacco and cotton required cheap labor to be profitable, slavery rather than indentured servitude became the lot of the blacks brought from Africa. As early as 1661, the state of Virginia declared that all newly arrived black Africans and any children born to them were to be slaves forever.

Slavery was, of course, one of the prime causes of the Civil War. Yet even though the North proved victorious, the thousands of blacks who were freed as a result of the conflict were not given equal status in American society in the years that followed. It can be said that in the final quarter of the nineteenth century, the institution of slavery was replaced by a new institution designed to maintain racial discrimination—segregation.

In more recent times, the "black revolution" has captured the attention both of America and of the rest of the world. Yet while there is little doubt that blacks have made real strides in the last quarter century, it is equally clear that they are still not fully integrated into American society and that they still do not enjoy the same rights and opportunities possessed by most other citizens.

The materials in this section are designed to help you deal with the problems of identity and assimilation for blacks in America. ■

RACIAL PREJUDICE AS A BASIS FOR SLAVERY AND SEGREGATION

The appearance of an institutionalized pattern of segregation in American society reveals the persistence of racial attitudes even after the abolition of slavery. Many of those who favored abolishing "the peculiar institution" nevertheless retained ambivalent attitudes concerning full equality for the black man. Let us take Abraham Lincoln, for example. On the following pages you will read five statements made by Lincoln between 1858 and 1865.

Source: Political Debates Between Hon. Abraham Lincoln and Hon. Stephen A. Douglas, in *The Celebrated Campaign of 1858* (Columbus: Foller, Foster, and Co., 1860), pp. 232–233.

Lincoln-Douglas Debate—1858

The real issue in this controversy—the one pressing upon every mind—is the sentiment on the part of one class that looks upon the institution of slavery as a wrong and of another class that does not look upon it as a wrong. . . .

That is the real issue. That is the issue that will continue in this country when these poor tongues of Judge Douglas and myself shall be silent. It is the eternal struggle between these two principles—right and wrong—throughout the world. They are the two principles that have stood face to face from the beginning of time and will ever continue to struggle. The one is the common right of humanity and the other the divine right of kings. It is the same principle in whatever shape it develops itself. It is the same spirit that says, "You work and toil and earn bread, and I'll eat it." No matter in what shape it comes, whether from the mouth of a king who seeks to bestride the people of his own nation and live by the fruit of their labor, or from one race of men as an apology for enslaving another race, it is the same tyrannical principle. . . . ■

Source: *Complete Works of Abraham Lincoln*, ed. John Nicolay and John Hay (New York: Century Company, 1894), vol. I, pp. 369–370.

Lincoln-Douglas Debate—1858

I will say, then, that I am not, nor ever have been, in favor of bringing about in any way the social and political equality of the white and black races; that I am not, nor ever have been, in favor of making voters or jurors of negroes, nor of qualifying them to hold office, nor to intermarry with white people; and I will say, in addition to this, that there is a physical difference between the white and black races which I believe will forever forbid the two races living together on terms of social and political equality. And inasmuch as they cannot so live, while they do remain together there must be the position of superior and inferior, and I as much as any other man am in favor of having the superior position assigned to the white race. I say upon this occasion I do not perceive that because the white man is to have the superior position the negro should be denied everything. I do not understand that because I do not want a negro woman for a slave I must necessarily want her for a wife. My understanding is that I can just let her alone. I am now in my fiftieth year, and I certainly never have had a black woman for either a slave or a wife. So it seems to me quite possible for us to get along without making either slaves or wives of negroes. I will add to this that I have never seen, to my knowledge, a man, woman, or child who was in favor of producing a perfect equality, social and political, between negroes and white men. . . . ■

Source: *Collected Works of Abraham Lincoln*, ed. Roy P. Basler (New Brunswick, N.J.: Rutgers University Press, 1953), vol. V, pp. 370–372.

Lincoln To A Deputation of Blacks—1862

You and we are different races. We have between us a broader difference than exists between almost any other two races. Whether it is right or wrong I need not discuss, but this physical difference is a great disadvantage to us both, as I think your race suffer very greatly, many of them by living among us, while ours suffer from your presence. In a word we suffer on each side. If this is admitted, it affords a reason at least why we should be separated. . . .

Your race are suffering, in my judgment, the greatest wrong inflicted on any people. But even when you cease to be slaves, you are yet far removed from being placed on an equality with the white race. You are cut off from many of the advantages which the other race enjoy. The aspiration of men is to enjoy equality with the best when free, but on this broad continent, not a single man of your race is made the equal of a single man of ours. Go where you are treated the best, and the ban is still upon you.

I do not propose to discuss this, but to present it as a fact with which we have to deal. I cannot alter it if I would. It is a fact, about which we all think and feel alike, I and you. We look to our condition, owing to the existence of the two races on this continent. I need not recount to you the effects upon white men, growing out of the institution of Slavery. I believe in its general evil effects on the white race. See our present condition—the country engaged in war!—our white men cutting one another's throats, none knowing how far it will extend; and then consider what we know to be the truth. But for your race among us there could not be war, although many men engaged on either side do not care for you one way or the other. Nevertheless, I repeat, without the institution of Slavery and the colored race as a basis, the war could not have an existence.

It is better for us both, therefore, to be separated. I know that there are free men among you, who even if they could better their condition are not as much inclined to go out of the country as those, who being slaves could obtain their freedom on this condition. I suppose one of the principal difficulties in the way of colonization is that the free colored man cannot see that his comfort would be advanced by it. You may believe you can live in Washington or elsewhere in the United States the remainder of your life [as easily], perhaps more so than you can in any foreign country, and hence you may come to the conclusion that you have nothing to do with the idea of going to a foreign country. This is (I speak in no unkind sense) an extremely selfish view of the case.

But you ought to do something to help those who are not so fortunate as yourselves. There is an unwillingness on the part of our people, harsh as it may be, for you free colored people to remain with us. Now, if you could give a start to white people, you would open a wide door for many to be made free. If we deal with those who are not free at the beginning, and whose intellects are clouded by Slavery, we have very poor materials to start with. If intelligent colored men, such as are before me, would move in this matter, much might be accomplished. It is

Source: **Collected Works of Abraham Lincoln**, ed. Roy P. Basler (New Brunswick, N.J.: Rutgers University Press, 1953), vol. VI, pp. 28–30.

exceedingly important that we have men at the beginning capable of thinking as white men, and not those who have been systematically oppressed.

There is much to encourage you. For the sake of your race you should sacrifice something of your present comfort for the purpose of being as grand in that respect as the white people. It is a cheering thought throughout life that something can be done to ameliorate the condition of those who have been subject to the hard usage of the world. It is difficult to make a man miserable while he feels he is worthy of himself, and claims kindred to the great God who made him. In the American Revolutionary war sacrifices were made by men engaged in it; but they were cheered by the future. Gen. Washington himself endured greater physical hardships than if he had remained a British subject. Yet he was a happy man, because he was engaged in benefiting his race—something for the children of his neighbors, having none of his own.

The colony of Liberia has been in existence a long time. In a certain sense it is a success. The old President of Liberia, Roberts, has just been with me—the first time I ever saw him. He says they have within the bounds of that colony between 300,000 and 400,000 people, or more than in some of our old States, such as Rhode Island, or in some of our newer States, and less than in some of our larger ones. They are not all American colonists, or their descendants. Something less than 12,000 have been sent thither from this country. Many of the original settlers have died, yet, like people elsewhere, their offspring outnumber those deceased.

The question is if the colored people are persuaded to go anywhere, why not there? One reason for an unwillingness to do so is that some of you would rather remain within reach of the country of your nativity. I do not know how much attachment you may have toward our race. It does not strike me that you have the greatest reason to love them. But still you are attached to them at all events.

The place I am thinking about having for a colony is in Central America. It is nearer to us than Liberia—not much more than one-fourth as far as Liberia, and within seven days' run by steamers. Unlike Liberia it is on a great line of travel—it is a highway. The country is a very excellent one for any people, and with great natural resources and advantages, and especially because of the similarity of climate with your native land—thus being suited to your physical condition. ■

The Emancipation Proclamation

January 1, 1863

By the President of the United States of America:

A PROCLAMATION.

Whereas, on the twentysecond day of September, in the year of our Lord one thousand eight hundred and sixty two, a proclamation was issued by the President of the United States, containing, among other things, the following, towit:

"That on the first day of January, in the year of our Lord one thousand eight hundred and sixty-three, all persons held as slaves within any State or designated part of a State, the people whereof shall then be in rebellion against the United States, shall be then, thenceforward, and forever free; and the Executive Government of the United States, including the military and naval authority thereof, will recognize and maintain the freedom of such persons, and will do no act or acts to repress such persons, or any of them, in any efforts they may make for their actual freedom.

"That the Executive will, on the first day of January aforesaid, by proclamation, designate the States and parts of States, if any, in which the people thereof, respectively, shall then be in rebellion against the United States; and the fact that any State, or the people thereof, shall on that day be, in good faith, represented in the Congress of the United States by members chosen thereto at elections wherein a majority of the qualified voters of such State shall have participated, shall, in the absence of strong countervailing testimony, be deemed conclusive evidence that such State, and the people thereof, are not then in rebellion against the United States."

Now, therefore I, Abraham Lincoln, President of the United States, by virtue of the power in me vested as Commander-in-Chief, of the Army and Navy of the United States in time of actual armed rebellion against authority and government of the United States, and as a fit and necessary war measure for suppressing said rebellion, do, on this first day of January, in the year of our Lord one thousand eight hundred and sixty three, and in accordance with my purpose so to do publicly proclaimed for the full period of one hundred days, from the day first above mentioned, order and designate as the States and parts of States wherein the people thereof respectively, are this day in rebellion against the United States, the following, towit:

Arkansas, Texas, Louisiana, (except the Parishes of St. Bernard, Plaquemines, Jefferson, St. Johns, St. Charles, St. James[,] Ascension, Assumption, Terrebonne, Lafourche, St. Mary, St. Martin, and Orleans, including the City of New-Orleans) Mississippi, Alabama, Florida, Georgia, South-Carolina, North-Carolina, and Virginia, (except the fortyeight counties designated as West Virginia, and also the counties of Berkley, Accomac, Northampton, Elizabeth-City, York, Princess Ann, and Norfolk, including the cities of Norfolk & Portsmouth []]; and which excepted parts are for the present, left precisely as if this proclamation were not issued.

And by virtue of the power and for the purpose aforesaid, I do order and declare that all persons held as slaves within said designated States and parts of States are, and henceforward shall be free; and that the Executive government of the United States, including the military and naval authorities thereof, will recognize and maintain the freedom of said persons.

And I hereby enjoin upon the people so declared to be free to abstain from all violence, unless in necessary self-defence; and I recommend to them that, in all cases when allowed, they labor faithfully for reasonable wages.

And I further declare and make known, that such persons of suitable condition, will be received into the armed service of the United States to garrison forts, positions, stations, and other places, and to man vessels of all sorts in said service.

And upon this act, sincerely believed to be an act of justice, warranted by the Constitution, upon military necessity, I invoke the considerate judgment of mankind, and the gracious favor of Almighty God.

In witness whereof, I have hereunto set my hand and caused the seal of the United States to be affixed.

Done at the City of Washington, this first day of January, in the
[L.S.] year of our Lord one thousand eight hundred and sixty three, and of the Independence of the United States of America the eighty-seventh.

By the President: Abraham Lincoln
William H. Seward,
Secretary of State. ∎

Roger Malloch, Magnum

Source: *Collected Works of Abraham Lincoln*, ed. Roy P. Basler (New Brunswick, N.J.: Rutgers University Press, 1953), vol. VIII, pp. 254–255.

Lincoln on the 13th Amendment—1865

February 1, 1865

The President said he supposed the passage through Congress of the Constitutional amendment for the abolishment of Slavery throughout the United States, was the occasion to which he was indebted for the honor of this call. [Applause.] The occasion was one of congratulation to the country and to the whole world. But there is a task yet before us—to go forward and consummate by the votes of the States that which Congress so nobly began yesterday. [Applause and cries—"They will do it," &c.] He had the honor to inform those present that Illinois had already to-day done the work. [Applause.] Maryland was about half through; but he felt proud that Illinois was a little ahead. He thought this measure was a very fitting if not an indispensable adjunct to the winding up of the great difficulty. He wished the reunion of all the States perfected and so effected as to remove all causes of disturbance in the future; and to attain this end it was necessary that the original disturbing cause should, if possible, be rooted out. He thought all would bear him witness that he had never shrunk from doing all that he could to eradicate Slavery by issuing an emancipation proclamation. [Applause.] But that proclamation falls far short of what the amendment will be when fully consummated. A question might be raised whether the proclamation was legally valid. It might be added that it only aided those who came into our lines and that it was inoperative as to those who did not give themselves up, or that it would have no effect upon the children of the slaves born hereafter. In fact it would be urged that it did not meet the evil. But this amendment is a King's cure for all the evils. [Applause.] It winds the whole thing up. He would repeat that it was the fitting if not indispensable adjunct to the consummation of the great game we are playing. He could not but congratulate all present, himself, the country and the whole world upon this great moral victory. ■

LINCOLN'S AMBIVALENCE TOWARD BLACK AMERICANS

Earlier in this unit you examined Thomas Jefferson's attitude toward the Indians. In the statements you have just read, Abraham Lincoln expressed his attitude on slavery and black Americans.

1 What kinds of statements does Lincoln make about slavery and the American black in each item? Do his words reflect bias or prejudice?

2 In the five statements, is Lincoln's general attitude toward slavery and the black Americans consistent? What government policy toward the black is stated or implied by each statement? How are these similar to or different from each other? How would you explain the differences in the statements? What further information would you need to explain the differences more completely?

3 What do you think Lincoln believed would be the final fate of the American black? Would you make the same prediction? ■

THE HISTORIC ROOTS OF RACISM IN AMERICA

Winthrop Jordan in his book *White Over Black* argues that the white American's relationship to the black has been determined by a basic dilemma in the thinking of white Americans. Do you think that the dilemma described by Jordan applies or does not apply to Lincoln's attitude toward slavery and the American black? Does his argument apply to Jefferson's attitude toward the American Indian?

Source: Winthrop D. Jordan, *White Over Black* (Chapel Hill, N.C.: University of North Carolina Press, 1968), pp. 573–574, 581–582.

I shall need, too, the favor of that Being in whose hands we are, who led our forefathers, as Israel of old, from their native land, and planted them in a country flowing with all the necessaries and comforts of life; who has covered our infancy with his providence, and our riper years with his wisdom and power; and to whose goodness I ask you to join with me in supplications, that he will so enlighten the minds of your servants, guide their councils, and prosper their measures, that whatsoever they do, shall result in your good, and shall secure to you the peace, friendship, and approbation of all nations.

These words concluded the second inaugural address of President Thomas Jefferson in 1805. Coming from him, from the Enlightenment, from rationalism and natural philosophy, from Virginia, they effuse a special illumination. It was exactly two and a half centuries since Englishmen had first confronted Negroes face to face. Richard Hakluyt was then in his cradle and the idea of America not yet fully alive in England. Now, what had once been the private plantations of the English nation was transformed into an independent state seeking not only the "peace" but the "approbation" of all the nations. The transformation had been accompanied by similarly impressive alterations in the character of society and thought. The people had become what so many sixteenth-century Englishmen feared they might become—the governors. As Jefferson said, magistrates were "servants" of the people. God no longer governed—much less judged—his people immediately; indeed "that Being" was now to be

given "supplications" so that his "goodness" might endorse a people's continuance in peace and prosperity.

It would seriously mistake the meaning of Jefferson's words to see them as entirely a bland acclamation of the new society in America or as merely another stanza to God-on-our-side. They were these and more. His explicit identification of Americans with the covenanted people of Israel suggests that all Americans were very much in touch with what has been called too narrowly the old New England firm of Moses and Aaron. The American people had been led out "from their native land," though here there was a crucial difference, for Americans had once been truly "native" to England in a way that Israel had never been in Egypt. They had been planted in a land "flowing" with "comforts," a land of plenty, a land surely of milk and honey. In their earliest years, as the process of maturation was so persuasively described, they had "providence"; later they had "wisdom and power." As they grew they dispossessed the tribes of the land and allotted it in various portions to themselves. They killed and enslaved those people not of their own house, both the dispossessed tribes and the black sons of the cursed Canaanites whom their very ancient intellectual forefathers had driven out and killed when they achieved *their* deliverance from bondage.

All of which suggests that the most profound continuities ran through the centuries of change. Particularly, there were the tightly harnessed energies of a restless, trafficking, migrating people emerging from dearth and darkness into plenty and enlightenment. These were a people of the Word, adventuring into a New World; they sought to retain their integrity—their identity—as a peculiar people; they clamped hard prohibitions on themselves as they scented the dangers of freedom.

Which in turn rings of the twin themes which coursed through Elizabethan England—freedom and control. The same themes were changed upon in America; they may be summarized and at the same time most clearly illuminated by looking at a single, undramatic development in the heart of Jeffersonian America.

In 1806 Virginia restricted the right of masters to manumit their slaves. On its face not a remarkable measure, in fact it was the key step in the key state and more than any event marked the reversal of the tide which had set in strongly at the Revolution. It was the step onto the slippery slope which led to Appomattox and beyond.

There had been some sentiment in Virginia favoring restriction of manumission ever since passage of the law permitting private manumissions by will or deed in 1782. However, the appearance of widespread and insistent demand for restriction may be dated precisely at September 1800. The next year in the Virginia Senate, an amendment was offered to a consolidated slave bill requiring anyone freeing a slave to post $1,000 bond as security that the freedman would leave the state within two months; the amendment failed, seven votes to eleven. Public pressure mounted inexorably during the next few years, especially as it became apparent that the Assembly's resolutions on colonization were not going to bring results. In 1805,

the year of the last such resolution before 1816, a vigorous debate took place in the House of Delegates on a bill prohibiting private manumission; the bill was narrowly defeated, 81 to 72. At next year's session the House considered a similar bill which was finally defeated by only two votes. Undaunted, the proponents of restriction switched tactics by utilizing the popularity of Negro removal. Into a separate bill for the regulation of slaves the Senate quietly inserted an amendment providing that any Negro freed in Virginia had to depart the state within one year or face reenslavement. The delegates, many of them now reconciled by the absence of direct restriction on the property rights of slaveowners, approved the provision 94 to 65.

Although some newly manumitted Negroes actually did leave Virginia in the following years, this provision was in fact a drastic restriction on manumission and was intended as such by members of the General Assembly. At the time of passage, Ohio already prohibited the entry of Negroes, and within a year the other three key states, Kentucky, Maryland, and Delaware, predictably forbade Negroes from entering to take up permanent residence. Furthermore, the Virginia act of 1806 effectively prevented benevolent masters from providing manumitted slaves with the one endowment they most needed—land. As it turned out, the act did help cut appreciably the rate of increase of the free Negro population, and the opponents of emancipation remained satisfied with the measure's effectiveness as long as slavery lasted.

The pattern of voting in the House to

some extent mirrored sectional differences, for of course the more heavily Negro tidewater and piedmont counties aligned generally in favor of restriction; but so many delegates voted against what might be presumed to be the interests of their locality that it is clear that differences in personality played fully as important a role in determining individual votes—as one would expect to begin with.

No record of debate on the provision has survived, if in fact there was any. Fortunately, however, the spirited debates on the two directly restrictionist bills of 1805 and 1806 were partially reported in the Richmond newspapers. Brief as they are, these reports reveal with unusual clarity the attitudes which led the Virginia legislature to repudiate Virginia's most tangible expression of dedication to the principle of liberty for all men.

Within every white American who stood confronted by the Negro, there had arisen a perpetual duel between his higher and lower natures. His cultural conscience—his Christianity, his humanitarianism, his ideology of liberty and equality—demanded that he regard and treat the Negro as his brother and his countryman, as his equal. At the same moment, however, many of his most profound urges, especially his yearning to maintain the identity of his folk, his passion for domination, his sheer avarice, and his sexual desire, impelled him toward conceiving and treating the Negro as inferior to himself, as an American leper. At closer view, though, the duel appears more complex than a conflict between the best and worst in the white man's nature, for in a variety of ways the white man translated his "worst" into his "best." Raw sexual aggression became retention of purity, and brutal domination became faithful maintenance of civilized restraints. These translations, so necessary to the white man's peace of mind, were achieved at devastating cost to another people set permanently apart because they looked different from the white man generation after generation. But the enormous toll of human wreckage was by no means paid exclusively by the Negro, for the subtle translations of basic urges in the white man necessitated his treating the Negro in a fashion which lacerated his own conscience, that very quality in his being which necessitated those translations. So the peace of mind the white man sought by denying his profound inexorable drives toward creation and destruction (a denial accomplished by correlated affirmations of virtue in himself and depravity in the Negro) was denied the white man; he sought his own peace at the cost of others and accordingly found none. In fearfully hoping to escape the animal within himself the white man debased the Negro, surely, but at the same time he debased himself.

Conceivably there was and is a way out from the vicious cycle of degradation, an opening of better hope demanding an unprecedented and perhaps impossible measure of courage, honesty, and sheer nerve. If the white man turned to stare at the animal within him, if he once admitted unashamedly that the beast was there, he might see that the old foe was a friend as well, that his best and his worst derived from the same deep well of energy. If he once fully acknowledged the powerful forces which drove his being,

the necessity of imputing them to others would drastically diminish. If he came to recognize what had happened and was still happening with himself and the Negro in America, if he faced the unpalatable realities of the tragedy unflinchingly, if he were willing to call the beast no more the Negro's than his own, then conceivably he might set foot on a better road. Common charity and his special faith demanded that he make the attempt. But there was little in his historical experience to indicate that he would succeed. ∎

LEGALIZING SEGREGATION

By the end of the nineteenth century, segregation of blacks from whites was not only a way of life throughout most of America—it was sanctioned by the highest court in the land as well. This was evidenced by the historic *Plessy* v. *Ferguson* decision handed down by the Supreme Court in 1896.

In 1890 the legislature of the state of Louisiana passed a law requiring all railway companies carrying passengers within the state to provide equal but separate accommodations for the white and black races. The legislature stated that "no person or persons shall be admitted to occupy seats in coaches other than the ones assigned to them on account of the race they belong to."

Plessy, who was a light-skinned mulatto, took a seat in a car reserved for whites. When he refused to leave the car he was arrested. Legal proceedings were started against him and his case was eventually appealed to the Supreme Court. Here is a portion of that court's decision in this important case.

Source: *Plessy v. Ferguson*, 163 U.S. 537 (1896).

This case turns upon the constitutionality of an act of the General Assembly of the State of Louisiana, passed in 1890, providing for separate railway carriages for the white and colored races.

The first section of the statute enacts "that all railway companies carrying passengers in their coaches in this State, shall provide equal but separate accommodations for the white and colored races, by providing two or more passenger coaches for each passenger train, or by dividing the passenger coaches by a partition so as to secure separate accommodations: *Provided,* That this section shall not be construed to apply to street railroads. No person or persons, shall be admitted to occupy seats in coaches, other than the ones assigned to them, on account of the race they belong to." . . .

The information filed in the criminal District Court charged in substance that Plessy, being a passenger between two stations within the State of Louisiana, was assigned by officers of the company to the coach used for the race to which he belonged, but he insisted upon going into a coach used by the race to which he did not belong. Neither in the information nor plea was his particular race or color averred.

The petition for the writ of prohibition averred that petitioner was seven eighths Caucasian and one eighth African blood, that the mixture of colored blood was not discernible in him, and that he was entitled to every right, privilege and immunity secured to citizens of the United States of the white race; and that, upon such theory, he took possession of a vacant seat in a coach where passengers of the white race

were accommodated, and was ordered by the conductor to vacate said coach and take a seat in another assigned to persons of the colored race, and having refused to comply with such demand he was forcibly ejected with the aid of a police officer, and imprisoned in the parish jail to answer a charge of having violated the above act.

The constitutionality of this act is attacked upon the ground that it conflicts both with the Thirteenth Amendment of the Constitution, abolishing slavery, and the Fourteenth Amendment, which prohibits certain restrictive legislation on the part of the States.

1 That it does not conflict with the Thirteenth Amendment, which abolished slavery and involuntary servitude, except as a punishment for crime, is too clear for argument. . . .

2 By the Fourteenth Amendment, all persons born or naturalized in the United States, and subject to the jurisdiction thereof, are made citizens of the United States and of the State wherein they reside; and the States are forbidden from making or enforcing any law which shall abridge the privileges or immunities of citizens of the United States, or shall deprive any person of life, liberty or property without due process of law, or deny to any person within their jurisdiction the equal protection of the laws. . . .

The object of the amendment was undoubtedly to enforce the absolute equality of the two races before the law, but in the nature of things it could not have been intended to abolish distinctions based upon color, or to enforce social, as distinguished from political equality, or a commingling of the two races upon terms

unsatisfactory to either. Laws permitting, and even requiring, their separation in places where they are liable to be brought into contact do not necessarily imply the inferiority of either race to the other, and have been generally, if not universally, recognized as within the competency of the state legislatures in the exercise of their police power. The most common instance of this is connected with the establishment of separate schools for white and colored children, which has been held to be a valid exercise of the legislative power even by courts of States where the political rights of the colored race have been longest and most earnestly enforced. . . .

While we think the enforced separation of the races, as applied to the internal commerce of the State, neither abridges the privileges or immunities of the colored man, deprives him of his property without due process of law, nor denies him the equal protection of the laws, within the meaning of the Fourteenth Amendment, we are not prepared to say that the conductor, in assigning passengers to the coaches according to their race, does not act at his peril, or that the provision of the second section of the act, that denies to the passenger compensation in damages for a refusal to receive him into the coach in which he properly belongs, is a valid exercise of the legislative power. Indeed, we understand it to be conceded by the State's attorney, that such part of the act as exempts from liability the railway company and its officers is unconstitutional. The power to assign to a particular coach obviously implies the power to determine to which race the passenger belongs, as well as the power to determine who, under the laws of the particular State, is to be deemed a white, and who a colored person. This question, though indicated in the brief of the plaintiff in error, does not properly arise upon the unconstitutionality of the act, so far as it requires the railway to provide separate accommodations, and the conductor to assign passengers according to their race.

It is claimed by the plaintiff in error that, in any mixed community, the reputation of belonging to the dominant race, in this instance the white race, is *property,* in the same sense that a right of action, or of inheritance, is property. Conceding this to be so, for the purposes of this case, we are unable to see how this statute deprives him of, or in any way affects his right to, such property. If he be a white man and assigned to a colored coach, he may have his action for damages against the company for being deprived of his so called property. Upon the other hand, if he be a colored man and be so assigned, he has been deprived of no property, since he is not lawfully entitled to the reputation of being a white man.

In this connection, it is also suggested by the learned counsel for the plaintiff in error that the same argument that will justify the state legislature in requiring railways to provide separate accommodations for the two races will also authorize them to require separate cars to be provided for people whose hair is of a certain color, or who are aliens, or who belong to certain nationalities, or to enact laws requiring colored people to walk upon one side of the street, and white people upon the other, or requiring white

men's houses to be painted white, and colored men's black, or their vehicles or business signs to be of different colors, upon the theory that one side of the street is as good as the other, or that a house or vehicle of one color is as good as one of another color. The reply to all this is that every exercise of the police power must be reasonable, and extend only to such laws as are enacted in good faith for the promotion of the public good, and not for the annoyance or oppression of a particular class. . . .

So far, then, as a conflict with the Fourteenth Amendment is concerned, the case reduces itself to the question whether the statute of Louisiana is a reasonable regulation, and with respect to this there must necessarily be a large discretion on the part of the legislature. In determining the question of reasonableness it is at liberty to act with reference to the established usages, customs and traditions of the people, and with a view to the promotion of their comfort, and the preservation of the public peace and good order. Gauged by this standard, we cannot say that a law which authorizes or even requires the separation of the two races in public conveyances is unreasonable, or more obnoxious to the Fourteenth Amendment than the acts of Congress requiring separate schools for colored children in the District of Columbia, the constitutionality of which does not seem to have been questioned, or the corresponding acts of state legislatures.

We consider the underlying fallacy of the plaintiff's argument to consist in the assumption that the enforced separation of the two races stamps the colored race

with a badge of inferiority. If this be so, it is not by reason of anything found in the act, but solely because the colored race chooses to put that construction upon it. The argument necessarily assumes that if, as has been more than once the case, and is not unlikely to be so again, the colored race should become the dominant power in the state legislature, and should enact a law in precisely similar terms, it would thereby relegate the white race to an inferior position. We imagine that the white race, at least, would not acquiesce in this assumption. The argument also assumes that social prejudices may be overcome by legislation, and that equal rights cannot be secured to the negro except by an enforced commingling of the two races. We cannot accept this proposition. If the two races are to meet upon terms of social equality, it must be the result of natural affinities, a mutual appreciation of each other's merits and a voluntary consent of individuals. . . . ■

BLACK RESPONSES TO SEGREGATION

The *Plessy* v. *Ferguson* decision established the legal basis for segregation in the last years of the nineteenth century. One of the most important black figures at that time was Booker T. Washington, a man who had risen from a life of slavery to become a leading black educator in America. Washington did not challenge the principle of social segregation. But his position did not go unchallenged. One of the most important black leaders to take issue with him was W. E. B. DuBois, a sociologist and one of the founders of the National Association for the Advancement of Colored People.

Source: Booker T. Washington, *Up From Slavery* (New York: Doubleday and Co., 1903).

Washington: Atlanta Exposition Address—1895

A ship lost at sea for many days suddenly sighted a friendly vessel. From the mast of the unfortunate vessel was sent the signal: "Water, water, we die of thirst." The answer from the friendly vessel at once came back, "Cast down your bucket where you are." A second time the signal, "Water, water, send us water," ran up from the distressed vessel and was answered, "Cast down your bucket where you are," and a third and fourth signal for water was answered, "Cast down your bucket where you are." The captain of the distressed vessel, at last heeding the injunction, cast down his bucket and it came up full of fresh, sparkling water from the mouth of the Amazon River.

To those of my race who depend on bettering their condition in a foreign land, or who underestimate the importance of cultivating friendly relations with the southern white man who is their next door neighbor, I would say, cast down your bucket where you are. Cast it down in making friends, in every manly way, of the people of all races by whom you are surrounded. Cast it down in agriculture, in mechanics, in commerce, in domestic service, and in the professions. And in this connection it is well to bear in mind that, whatever other sins the South may be called upon to bear, when it comes to business pure and simple it is in the South that the Negro is given a man's chance in the commercial world; and in nothing is this Exposition more eloquent than in emphasizing this chance. Our greatest danger is that in the great leap from slavery to freedom, we may overlook the fact that the masses of us are to live by the production of our hands, and fail to keep in mind that we shall prosper in proportion as we learn to dignify and glorify common labor and put brains and skill into the common occupations of life; shall prosper in proportion as we learn to draw the line between the superficial and the substantial, the ornamental gewgaws of life and the useful. No race can prosper till it learns that there is as much dignity in tilling a field as in writing a poem. It is at the bottom of life we must begin and not at the top. Nor should we permit our grievances to overshadow our opportunities. . . .

To those of the white race who look to the incoming of those of foreign birth and strange tongue and habits for the prosperity of the South, were I permitted, I would repeat what I say to my own race, "Cast down your bucket where you are." Cast it down among the eight millions of Negroes whose habits you know, whose fidelity and love you have tested in days when to have proved treacherous meant the ruin of your firesides. Cast down your bucket among those people who have, without strikes and labor wars, tilled your fields, cleared your forests, builded your railroads and cities, and brought forth treasures from the bowels of the earth and helped make possible this magnificent representation of the progress of the South. Casting down your bucket among my people, helping and encouraging as you are doing on these grounds, and with education of head, hand, and heart, you will find that they will buy your surplus land, make blossom the waste places in your fields, and run your factories. While doing this you can be sure in the future, as you have been in the past, that you and your families will be surrounded by the most patient, faithful, law-abiding, and unresentful people that the world has seen.

As we have proved our loyalty to you in the past, in nursing your children, watching by the sickbeds of your mothers and fathers, and often following them with tear-dimmed eyes to their graves, so in the future, in our humble way, we shall stand by you with a devotion that no foreigner can approach, ready to lay down our lives, if need be, in defense of yours; interlacing our industrial, commercial, civil, and religious life with yours in a way that shall make the interests of both races one. In all things that are purely social we can be as separate as the fingers, yet one as the hand in all things essential to mutual progress.

Gentlemen of the Exposition: As we present to you our humble effort at an exhibition of our progress, you must not expect overmuch; starting thirty years ago with ownership here and there in a few quilts and pumpkins and chickens (gathered from miscellaneous sources), remember, the path that has led us from these to the invention and production of agricultural implements, buggies, steam engines, newspapers, books, statuary, carvings, paintings, the management of drug stores and banks, has not been trodden without contact with thorns and thistles. While we take pride in what we exhibit as a result of our independent efforts, we do not for a moment forget that our part in this exhibition would fall far short of your expectations but for the constant help

that has come to our educational life, not only from the southern states, but especially from northern philanthropists who have made their gifts a constant stream of blessing and encouragement.

The wisest among my race understand that the agitation of questions of social equality is the extremest folly, and that progress in the enjoyment of all the privileges that will come to us must be the result of severe and constant struggle, rather than of artificial forcing. No race that has anything to contribute to the markets of the world is long in any degree ostracized. It is important and right that all privileges of the law be ours, but it is vastly more important that we be prepared for the exercises of these privileges. The opportunity to earn a dollar in a factory just now is worth infinitely more than the opportunity to spend a dollar in an opera house. ∎

Source: W. E. B. DuBois, *Souls of Black Folk* (Chicago: A. C. McClurg and Co., 1904), pp. 3–6; 50–53.

"Atlanta Compromise" Challenged

The Negro is a sort of seventh son, born with a veil, and gifted with second-sight in this American world,—a world which yields him no true self-consciousness, but only lets him see himself through the revelation of the other world. It is a peculiar sensation, this double-consciousness, this sense of always looking at one's self through the eyes of others, of measuring one's soul by the tape of a world that looks on in amused contempt and pity. One ever feels his twoness,—an American, a Negro; two souls, two thoughts, two unreconciled strivings; two warring ideals in one dark body, whose dogged strength alone keeps it from being torn asunder.

The history of the American Negro is the history of this strife,—this longing to attain self-conscious manhood, to merge his double self into a better and truer self. In this merging he wishes neither of the older selves to be lost. He would not Africanize America, for America has too much to teach the world and Africa. He would not bleach his Negro soul in a flood of white Americanism, for he knows that Negro blood has a message for the world. He simply wishes to make it possible for a man to be both a Negro and an American, without being cursed and spit upon by his fellows, without having the doors of Opportunity closed roughly in his face.

* * *

Easily the most striking thing in the history of the American Negro since 1876 is the ascendancy of Mr. Booker T. Washington. It began at the time when war memories and ideals were rapidly passing; a day of astonishing commercial development was dawning; a sense of doubt and

267

hesitation overtook the freedmen's sons,—then it was that his leading began. Mr. Washington came, with a single definite programme, at the psychological moment when the nation was a little ashamed of having bestowed so much sentiment on Negroes, and was concentrating its energies on Dollars. His programme of industrial education, conciliation of the South, and submission and silence as to civil and political rights, was not wholly original; the Free Negroes from 1830 up to war-time had striven to build industrial schools, and the American Missionary Association had from the first taught various trades; and Price and others had sought a way of honorable alliance with the best of the Southerners. But Mr. Washington first indissolubly linked these things; he put enthusiasm, unlimited energy, and perfect faith into this programme, and changed it from a by-path into a veritable Way of Life. And the tale of the methods by which he did this is a fascinating study of human life.

It startled the nation to hear a Negro advocating such a programme after many decades of bitter complaint; it startled and won the applause of the South, it interested and won the admiration of the North; and after a confused murmur of protest, it silenced if it did not convert the Negroes themselves.

To gain the sympathy and cooperation of the various elements comprising the white South was Mr. Washington's first task; and this, at the time Tuskegee was founded, seemed, for a black man, well-nigh impossible. And yet ten years later it was done in the word spoken at Atlanta: "In all things purely social we can be as

separate as the five fingers, and yet one as the hand in all things essential to mutual progress." This "Atlanta Compromise" is by all odds the most notable thing in Mr. Washington's career. The South interpreted it in different ways; the radicals received it as a complete surrender of the demand for civil and political equality; the conservatives, as a generously conceived working basis for mutual understanding. So both approved it, and to-day its author is certainly the most distinguished Southerner since Jefferson Davis, and the one with the largest personal following.

Next to this achievement comes Mr. Washington's work in gaining place and consideration in the North. Others less shrewd and tactful had formerly essayed to sit on these two stools and had fallen between them; but as Mr. Washington knew the heart of the South from birth and training, so by singular insight he intuitively grasped the spirit of the age which was dominating the North. And so thoroughly did he learn the speech and thought of triumphant commercialism, and the ideals of material prosperity, that the picture of a lone black boy poring over a French grammar amid the weeds and dirt of a neglected home soon seemed to him the acme of absurdities. One wonders what Socrates and St. Francis of Assisi would say to this.

And yet this very singleness of vision and thorough oneness with his age is a mark of the successful man. It is as though Nature must needs make men narrow in order to give them force. So Mr. Washington's cult has gained unquestioning followers, his work has wonderfully pros-

pered, his friends are legion, and his enemies are confounded. To-day he stands as the one recognized spokesman of his ten million fellows, and one of the most notable figures in a nation of seventy millions. One hesitates, therefore, to criticize a life which, beginning with so little, has done so much. And yet the time is come when one may speak in all sincerity and utter courtesy of the mistakes and shortcomings of Mr. Washington's career, as well as of his triumphs, without being thought captious or envious, and without forgetting that it is easier to do ill than well in the world.

The criticism that has hitherto met Mr. Washington has not always been of this broad character. In the South especially has he had to walk warily to avoid the harshest judgments,—and naturally so, for he is dealing with the one subject of deepest sensitiveness to that section. Twice—once when at the Chicago celebration of the Spanish-American War he alluded to the color-prejudice that is "eating away the vitals of the South," and once when he dined with President Roosevelt—has the resulting Southern criticism been violent enough to threaten seriously his popularity. In the North the feeling has several times forced itself into words, that Mr. Washington's counsels of submission overlooked certain elements of true manhood, and that his educational programme was unnecessarily narrow. Usually, however, such criticism has not found open expression, although, too, the spiritual sons of the Abolitionists have not been prepared to acknowledge that the schools founded before Tuskegee, by men of broad ideals and self-sacrificing spirit, were wholly failures or worthy of ridicule. While, then, criticism has not failed to follow Mr. Washington, yet the prevailing public opinion of the land has been but too willing to deliver the solution of a wearisome problem into his hands, and say, "If that is all you and your race ask, take it."

Among his own people, however, Mr. Washington has encountered the strongest and most lasting opposition, amounting at times to bitterness, and even to-day continuing strong and insistent even though largely silenced in outward expression by the public opinion of the nation. Some of this opposition is, of course, mere envy; the disappointment of displaced demagogues and the spite of narrow minds. But aside from this, there is among educated and thoughtful colored men in all parts of the land a feeling of deep regret, sorrow, and apprehension at the wide currency and ascendancy which some of Mr. Washington's theories have gained. These same men admire his sincerity of purpose, and are willing to forgive much to honest endeavor which is doing something worth the doing. They cooperate with Mr. Washington as far as they conscientiously can; and, indeed, it is no ordinary tribute to this man's tact and power that, steering as he must between so many diverse interests and opinions, he so largely retains the respect of all.

But the hushing of the criticism of honest opponents is a dangerous thing. It leads some of the best of the critics to unfortunate silence and paralysis of effort, and others to burst into speech so passionately and intemperately as to lose listeners. Honest and earnest criticism from those whose interests are most nearly touched,—

criticism of writers by readers, of government by those governed, of leaders by those led,—this is the soul of democracy and the safeguard of modern society. If the best of the American Negroes receive by outer pressure a leader whom they had not recognized before, manifestly there is here a certain palpable gain. Yet there is also irreparable loss,—a loss of that peculiarly valuable education which a group receives when by search and criticism it finds and commissions its own leaders. The way in which this is done is at once the most elementary and the nicest problem of social growth. History is but the record of such group-leadership; and yet how infinitely changeful is its type and character! And of all types and kinds, what can be more instructive than the leadership of a group within a group?—that curious double movement where real progress may be negative and actual advance be relative retrogression. All this is the social student's inspiration and despair.

Now in the past the American Negro has had instructive experience in the choosing of group leaders, founding thus a peculiar dynasty which in the light of present conditions is worthwhile studying. When sticks and stones and beasts form the sole environment of a people, their attitude is largely one of determined opposition to and conquest of natural forces. But when to earth and brute is added an environment of men and ideas, then the attitude of the imprisoned group may take three main forms,—a feeling of revolt and revenge; an attempt to adjust all thought and action to the will of the greater group; or, finally, a determined effort at self-realization and self-development despite environing

opinion. The influence of all of these attitudes at various times can be traced in the history of the American Negro, and in the evolution of his successive leaders.

Before 1750, while the fire of African freedom still burned in the veins of the slaves, there was in all leadership or attempted leadership but the one motive of revolt and revenge,—typified in the terrible Maroons, the Danish blacks, and Cato of Stono, and veiling all the Americas in fear of insurrection. The liberalizing tendencies of the latter half of the eighteenth century brought, along with kindlier relations between black and white, thoughts of ultimate adjustment and assimilation. Such aspiration was especially voiced in the earnest songs of Phyllis, in the martyrdom of Attucks, the fighting of Salem and Poor, the intellectual accomplishments of Banneker and Derham, and the political demands of the Cuffes.

Stern financial and social stress after the war cooled much of the previous humanitarian ardor. The disappointment and impatience of the Negroes at the persistence of slavery and serfdom voiced itself in two movements. The slaves in the South, aroused undoubtedly by vague rumors of the Haytian revolt, made three fierce attempts at insurrection,—in 1800 under Gabriel in Virginia, in 1822 under Vesey in Carolina, and in 1831 again in Virginia under the terrible Nat Turner. In the Free States, on the other hand, a new and curious attempt at self-development was made. In Philadelphia and New York color-prescription led to a withdrawal of Negro communicants from white churches and the formation of a peculiar socio-religious institution among the Negroes known as the African Church,—an organization still living and controlling in its various branches over a million of men.

Walker's wild appeal against the trend of the times showed how the world was changing after the coming of the cotton-gin. By 1830 slavery seemed hopelessly fastened on the South, and the slaves thoroughly cowed into submission. The free Negroes of the North, inspired by the mulatto immigrants from the West Indies, began to change the basis of their demands; they recognized the slavery of slaves, but insisted that they themselves were freemen, and sought assimilation and amalgamation with the nation on the same terms with other men. Thus, Forten and Purvis of Philadelphia, Shad of Wilmington, DuBois of New Haven, Barbadoes of Boston, and others, strove singly and together as men, they said, not as slaves; as "people of color," not as "Negroes." The trend of the times, however, refused them recognition save in individual and exceptional cases, considered them as one with all the despised blacks, and they soon found themselves striving to keep even the rights they formerly had of voting and working and moving as freemen. Schemes of migration and colonization arose among them; but these they refused to entertain, and they eventually turned to the Abolition movement as a final refuge.

Here, led by Remond, Nell, Wells-Brown, and Douglass, a new period of self-assertion and self-development dawned. To be sure, ultimate freedom and assimilation was the ideal before the leaders, but the assertion of the manhood rights of the Negro by himself was the main reliance, and John Brown's raid was the extreme of

270

its logic. After the war and emancipation, the great form of Frederick Douglass, the greatest of American Negro leaders, still led the host. Self-assertion, especially in political lines, was the main programme, and behind Douglass came Elliot, Bruce, and Langston, and the Reconstruction politicians, and, less conspicuous but of greater social significance Alexander Crummell and Bishop Daniel Payne.

Then came the Revolution of 1876, the suppression of the Negro votes, the changing and shifting of ideals, and the seeking of new lights in the great night. Douglass, in his old age, still bravely stood for the ideals of his early manhood,—ultimate assimilation *through* self-assertion, and on no other terms. For a time Price arose as a new leader, destined, it seemed, not to give up, but to re-state the old ideals in a form less repugnant to the white South. But he passed away in his prime. Then came the new leader. Nearly all the former ones had become leaders by the silent suffrage of their fellows, had sought to lead their own people alone, and were usually, save Douglass, little known outside their race. But Booker T. Washington arose as essentially the leader not of one race but of two, —a compromiser between the South, the North, and the Negro. Naturally the Negroes resented, at first bitterly, signs of compromise which surrendered their civil and political rights, even though this was to be exchanged for larger chances of economic development. The rich and dominating North, however, was not only weary of the race problem, but was investing largely in Southern enterprises, and welcomed any method of peaceful cooperation. Thus, by national opinion, the Negroes

began to recognize Mr. Washington's leadership; and the voice of criticism was hushed.

Mr. Washington represents in Negro thought the old attitude of adjustment and submission; but adjustment at such a peculiar time as to make his programme unique. This is an age of unusual economic development, and Mr. Washington's programme naturally takes an economic cast, becoming a gospel of Work and Money to such an extent as apparently almost completely to overshadow the higher aims of life. Moreover, this is an age when the more advanced races are coming in closer contact with the less developed races, and the race-feeling is therefore intensified; and Mr. Washington's programme practically accepts the alleged inferiority of the Negro races. Again, in our own land, the reaction from the sentiment of war time has given impetus to race-prejudice against Negroes, and Mr. Washington withdraws many of the high demands of Negroes as men and American citizens. In other periods of intensified prejudice all the Negro's tendency to self-assertion has been called forth; at this period a policy of submission is advocated. In the history of nearly all other races and peoples the doctrine preached at such crises has been that manly self-respect is worth more than lands and houses, and that a people who voluntarily surrender such respect, or cease striving for it, are not worth civilizing.

In answer to this, it has been claimed that the Negro can survive only through submission. Mr. Washington distinctly asks that black people give up, at least for the present, three things —

First, political power,

Second, insistence on civil rights,

Third, higher education of Negro youth —

and concentrate all their energies on industrial education, the accumulation of wealth, and the conciliation of the South. This policy has been courageously and insistently advocated for over fifteen years, and has been triumphant for perhaps ten years. As a result of this tender of the palm-branch, what has been the return? In these years there have occurred:

1 The disfranchisement of the Negro.

2 The legal creation of a distinct status of civil inferiority for the Negro.

3 The steady withdrawal of aid from institutions for the higher training of the Negro.

These movements are not, to be sure, direct results of Mr. Washington's teachings; but his propaganda has, without a shadow of doubt, helped their speedier accomplishment. The question then comes: Is it possible, and probable, that nine millions of men can make effective progress in economic lines if they are deprived of political rights, made a servile caste, and allowed only the most meagre chance for developing their exceptional men? If history and reason give any distinct answer to these questions, it is an emphatic *No*. And Mr. Washington thus faces the triple paradox of his career:

1 He is striving nobly to make Negro artisans business men and property-owners; but it is utterly impossible, under modern competitive methods, for workingmen and property-owners to defend their rights and exist without the right of suffrage.

2 He insists on thrift and self-respect, but at the same time counsels a silent submission to civic inferiority such as is bound to sap the manhood of any race in the long run.

3 He advocates common-school and industrial training, and depreciates institutions of higher learning; but neither the Negro common-schools, nor Tuskegee itself, could remain open a day were it not for teachers trained in Negro colleges, or trained by their graduates.

This triple paradox in Mr. Washington's position is the object of criticism by two classes of colored Americans. One class is spiritually descended from Toussaint the Savior, through Gabriel, Vesey, and Turner, and they represent the attitude of revolt and revenge; they hate the white South blindly and distrust the white race generally, and so far as they agree on definite action, think that the Negro's only hope lies in emigration beyond the borders of the United States. And yet, by the irony of fate, nothing has more effectually made this programme seem hopeless than the recent course of the United States toward weaker and darker peoples in the West Indies, Hawaii, and the Philippines, —for where in the world may we go and be safe from lying and brute force?

The other class of Negroes who cannot agree with Mr. Washington has hitherto said little aloud. They deprecate the sight of scattered counsels, of internal disagreement; and especially they dislike making their just criticism of a useful and earnest man an excuse for a general discharge of venom from small-minded opponents. Nevertheless, the questions involved are so fundamental and serious

that it is difficult to see how men like the Grimkes, Kelly Miller, J. W. E. Bowen, and other representatives of this group, can much longer be silent. Such men feel in conscience bound to ask of this nation three things:

1 The right to vote.

2 Civic equality.

3 The education of youth according to ability. ∎

GONE
WITH THE
WIND

From its beginnings the motion picture was destined to become one of the most important media of mass entertainment. Even after the advent of television, movies continued to hold their own either by cornering considerable time on T.V. or by moving into areas which T.V. could not or would not enter. As part of the mass media, movies both reflect and shape popular opinion about events. For example, many young Americans in the 1940's and 1950's got their image of war from the countless films which portrayed World War II. Films can also convey images of groups of people. For example, the World War II movies routinely treated the Japanese as a vicious and treacherous people.

The movies have also given us a variety of images of black Americans. On the next pages are stills and advertisements from some famous movies of the past which

1 What image of the black does each movie project? On the basis of these portrayals, can any general interpretation of American society be made? ·

2 What change over time do you notice in the portrayals?

3 How would you compare these historic film images of blacks with those you have seen in films recently?

4 Another group often portrayed in the movies is the American Indian. How does the film image of the black man compare with that of the red man in the nineteenth-century paintings presented earlier in this unit? ■

CAROLINA

Photos on these pages and following pages from
Culver Pictures

**FIFTY ROADS
TO TOWN**

274

**THE
LITTLEST REBEL**

**THE
DEFIANT ONES**

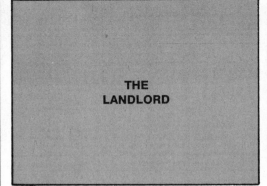

THE LANDLORD

276

COTTON COMES TO HARLEM

THE LEGAL BASIS
OF SEGREGATION
OVERTHROWN

There is no question but that the most important of all modern decisions regarding the rights of blacks in America was made in 1954 by the Supreme Court in its *Brown* v. *Board of Education* ruling. It was this decision that overturned the "separate but equal" doctrine established in the *Plessy* v. *Ferguson* case.

Source: *Brown* v. *Board of Education*, 347 U.S. 483 (1954).

Mr. Chief Justice Warren delivered the opinion of the Court.

These cases come to us from the States of Kansas, South Carolina, Virginia, and Delaware. They are premised on different facts and different local conditions, but a common legal question justifies their consideration together in this consolidated opinion.

In each of the cases, minors of the Negro race, through their legal representatives, seek the aid of the courts in obtaining admission to the public schools of their community on a nonsegregated basis. In each instance, they had been denied admission to schools attended by white children under laws requiring or permitting segregation according to race. This segregation was alleged to deprive the plaintiffs of the equal protection of the laws under the Fourteenth Amendment. In each of the cases other than the Delaware case, a three-judge federal district court denied relief to the plaintiffs on the so-called "separate but equal" doctrine announced by this Court in *Plessy* v. *Ferguson*. Under that doctrine, equality of treatment is accorded when the races are provided substantially equal facilities, even though these facilities be separate. In the Delaware case, the Supreme Court of Delaware adhered to that doctrine, but ordered that the plaintiffs be admitted to the white schools because of their superiority to the Negro schools.

The plaintiffs contend that segregated public schools are not "equal" and cannot be made "equal," and that hence they are deprived of the equal protection of the laws. Because of the obvious importance

of the question presented, the Court took jurisdiction. Argument was heard in the 1952 Term, and reargument was heard this Term on certain questions propounded by the Court.

Reargument was largely devoted to the circumstances surrounding the adoption of the Fourteenth Amendment in 1868. It covered exhaustively consideration of the Amendment in Congress, ratification by the states, then existing practices in racial segregation, and the views of proponents and opponents of the Amendment. This discussion and our own investigation convince us that, although these sources cast some light, it is not enough to resolve the problem with which we are faced. At best, they are inconclusive. The most avid proponents of the post-War Amendments undoubtedly intended them to remove all legal distinctions among "all persons born or naturalized in the United States." Their opponents, just as certainly, were antagonistic to both the letter and the spirit of the Amendments and wished them to have the most limited effect. What others in Congress and the state legislatures had in mind cannot be determined with any degree of certainty.

An additional reason for the inconclusive nature of the Amendment's history, with respect to segregated schools, is the status of public education at that time. In the South, the movement toward free common schools, supported by general taxation, had not yet taken hold. Education of white children was largely in the hands of private groups. Education of Negroes was almost non-existent, and practically all of the race were illiterate. In fact, any education of Negroes was forbidden by law in some states. Today, in contrast, many Negroes have achieved outstanding success in the arts and sciences as well as in the business and professional world. It is true that public school education at the time of the Amendment had advanced further in the North, but the effect of the Amendment on Northern States was generally ignored in the congressional debates. Even in the North, the conditions of public education did not approximate those existing today. The curriculum was usually rudimentary; ungraded schools were common in rural areas; the school term was but three months a year in many states; and compulsory school attendance was virtually unknown. As a consequence, it is not surprising that there should be so little in the history of the Fourteenth Amendment relating to its intended effect on public education.

In the first cases in this Court construing the Fourteenth Amendment, decided shortly after its adoption, the Court interpreted it as proscribing all state-imposed discriminations against the Negro race. The doctrine of "separate but equal" did not make its appearance in this Court until 1896 in the case of *Plessy* v. *Ferguson* involving not education but transportation. American courts have since labored with the doctrine for over half a century. In this Court, there have been six cases involving the "separate but equal" doctrine in the field of public education. In *Cumming* v. *County Board of Education* and *Gong Lum* v. *Rice* the validity of the doctrine itself was not challenged. In more recent cases, all on the graduate school level, inequality was found in that specific benefits enjoyed by white students were denied to Negro students of the same educational qualifications. In none of these cases was it necessary to re-examine the doctrine to grant relief to the Negro plaintiff. And in *Sweatt* v. *Painter* the Court expressly reserved decision on the question whether *Plessy* v. *Ferguson* should be held inapplicable to public education.

In the instant cases, that question is directly presented. Here, unlike *Sweatt* v. *Painter*, there are findings below that the Negro and white schools involved have been equalized, or are being equalized, with respect to buildings, curricula, qualifications and salaries of teachers, and other "tangible" factors. Our decision, therefore, cannot turn on merely a comparison of these tangible factors in the Negro and white schools involved in each of the cases. We must look instead to the effect of segregation itself on public education.

In approaching this problem, we cannot turn the clock back to 1868 when the Amendment was adopted, or even to 1896 when *Plessy* v. *Ferguson* was written. We must consider public education in the light of its full development and its present place in American life throughout the Nation. Only in this way can it be determined if segregation in public schools deprives these plaintiffs of the equal protection of the laws.

Today, education is perhaps the most important function of state and local governments. Compulsory school attendance laws and the great expenditures for education both demonstrate our recognition of the importance of education to our democratic society. It is required in the performance of our most basic public responsibilities, even service in the armed forces. It is the very foundation of good citizenship. Today it is a principal instrument in awakening the child to cultural values, in preparing him for later professional training, and in helping him to adjust normally to his environment. In these days, it is doubtful that any child may reasonably be expected to succeed in life if he is denied the opportunity of an education. Such an opportunity, where the state has undertaken to provide it, is a right which must be made available to all on equal terms.

We come then to the question presented: Does segregation of children in public schools solely on the basis of race, even though the physical facilities and other "tangible" factors may be equal, deprive the children of the minority group of equal educational opportunities? We believe that it does.

In *Sweatt* v. *Painter* in finding that a segregated law school for Negroes could not provide them equal educational opportunities, this Court relied in large part on "those qualities which are incapable of objective measurement but which make for greatness in a law school." In *McLaurin* v. *Oklahoma State Regents* the Court, in requiring that a Negro admitted to a white graduate school be treated like all other students, again resorted to intangible considerations: ". . . his ability to study, to engage in discussions and exchange views with other students, and, in general, to learn his profession." Such considerations apply with added force to children in grade and high schools. To separate them from others of similar age and qualifications solely because of their race generates a feeling of inferiority as to their status in the community that may affect their hearts and minds in a way unlikely ever to be undone. The effect of this separation on their educational opportunities was well stated by a finding in the Kansas case by a court which nevertheless felt compelled to rule against the Negro plaintiffs:

"Segregation of white and colored children in public schools has a detrimental effect upon the colored children. The impact is greater when it has the sanction of the law; for the policy of separating the races is usually interpreted as denoting the inferiority of the negro group. A sense of inferiority affects the motivation of a child to learn. Segregation with the sanction of law, therefore, has a tendency to [retard] the educational and mental development of negro children and to deprive them of some of the benefits they would receive in a racial[ly] integrated school system."

Whatever may have been the extent of psychological knowledge at the time of *Plessy* v. *Ferguson,* this finding is amply supported by modern authority. Any language in *Plessy* v. *Ferguson* contrary to this finding is rejected.

We conclude that in the field of public education the doctrine of "separate but equal" has no place. Separate educational facilities are inherently unequal. Therefore, we hold that the plaintiffs and others similarly situated for whom the actions have been brought are, by reason of the segregation complained of, deprived of the equal protection of the laws guaranteed by the Fourteenth Amendment. This disposition makes unnecessary any discussion whether such segregation also violates the Due Process Clause of the Fourteenth Amendment.

Because these are class actions, because of the wide applicability of this decision, and because of the great variety of local conditions, the formulation of decrees in these cases presents problems of considerable complexity. On reargument, the consideration of appropriate relief was necessarily subordinated to the primary question—the constitutionality of segregation in public education. We have now announced that such segregation is a denial of the equal protection of the laws. In order that we may have the full assistance of the parties in formulating decrees, the cases will be restored to the docket, and the parties are requested to present further argument on Questions 4 and 5 previously propounded by the Court for the reargument this Term. The Attorney General of the United States is again invited to participate. The Attorneys General of the states requiring or permitting segregation in public education will also be permitted to appear as *amici curiae* upon request to do so by September 15, 1954, and submission of briefs by October 1, 1954. ∎

THE SUPREME COURT AS A DECISION-MAKER

The Supreme Court decision you have read was a critical one in the black's struggle for equal rights. It is also an excellent example of how the Supreme Court sometimes functions as a political decision-maker. In reaching a decision, justices make use of the facts of the case, precedent, and logical reasoning to justify their conclusions.

1 How are the facts in the case used to support the final decision? How are other legal cases used? What other kinds of information do the justices rely on?

2 Trace the logical reasoning in the argument. How does this reasoning move the argument to the decision reached? ∎

Wall of Respect, Chicago, detail
Mike Mauney, Black Star

BLACK SELF-EXPRESSION IN WALL ART

In recent years blacks have used many different methods to emphasize their needs and highlight their accomplishments. One of the most dramatic of these is the use of wall art. Walls on buildings in several American cities are now adorned with vivid self-expression by blacks. Examples of this art form appear on the next seven pages.

1 What particular techniques do the wall artists use to dramatize their work?

2 What emotions do the paintings appeal to?

3 What black self-image does each painting project?

281

Wall of Respect, Chicago, and details
Mike Mauney, Black Star

284

A Wall in Boston's South End, and detail
Talbot Lovering, photographer, Boston

From "Paint the Promenade" festival of the Denver Art Museum

Photo at left by Don Rutledge, Black Star

Photo at right courtesy of the Denver Art Museum

287

INTEGRATION:
Choices for Black Americans

Since 1954 integration has been one of the most widely discussed—and emotionally charged—issues in America. In recent years the desirability of assimilation itself has been seriously questioned by some blacks. Separatist and black nationalist movements have flourished and black radicals have brought their own interpretations to the complex problems connected with integration.

On the following pages you will encounter three statements by black leaders who have addressed themselves to the issue of assimilation. The first is the classic "I Have A Dream" speech delivered by Martin Luther King, Jr., at the Lincoln Memorial during the civil rights march on Washington in 1963.

288

Source: Martin Luther King, Jr., in *Speeches by the Leaders: The March on Washington for Jobs and Freedom* (New York: NAACP, 1963).

Martin Luther King, Jr.

And as we walk we must make the pledge that we shall always march ahead. We cannot turn back. There are those who are asking the devotees of civil rights: "When will you be satisfied?" We can never be satisfied as long as our bodies, heavy with the fatigue of travel, cannot gain lodging in the motels of the highways and the hotels of the cities. We cannot be satisfied as long as the Negro's basic mobility is from a smaller ghetto to a larger one. We can never be satisfied as long as our children are stripped of their selfhood and robbed of their dignity by signs stating: "For Whites Only." We cannot be satisfied as long as the Negro in Mississippi cannot vote and the Negro in New York believes he has nothing for which to vote. No, no, we are not satisfied and we will not be satisfied until justice rolls down like the waters and righteousness like a mighty stream.

I am not unmindful that some of you have come here out of great trials and tribulations, some of you have come fresh from narrow jail cells, some of you have come from areas where your quest for freedom left you battered by the storms of persecution and staggered by the winds of police brutality. You have been the veterans of creative suffering. Continue to work with the faith that unearned suffering is redemptive.

Go back to Mississippi, go back to Alabama, go back to South Carolina, go back to Georgia, go back to Louisiana, go back to the slums and ghettos of our northern cities, knowing that somehow this situation can and will be changed. Let us not wallow in the valley of despair.

I say to you today, my friends, even though we face the difficulties of today and tomorrow, I still have a dream. It is a dream deeply rooted in the American dream. I have a dream that one day this nation will rise up and live out the true meaning of its creed: "We hold these truths to be self-evident that all men are created equal."

I have a dream that one day on the red hills of Georgia the sons of former slaves and the sons of former slaveowners will be able to sit down together at the table of brotherhood.

I have a dream that one day even the State of Mississippi, a state sweltering with the heat of injustice, sweltering with the heat of oppression, will be transformed into an oasis of freedom and justice. I have a dream that my four little children will one day live in a nation where they will not be judged by the color of their skin but by the content of their character. I have a dream today.

I have a dream that one day down in Alabama with its vicious racists, with its Governor having his lips dripping with the words of interposition and nullification—one day right there in Alabama, little black boys and black girls will be able to join hands with little white boys and white girls as sisters and brothers.

I have a dream today.

I have a dream that one day every valley shall be exalted, every hill and mountain shall be made low, the rough places will be made plain and the crooked places will be made straight, and the glory of the Lord shall be revealed, and all flesh shall see it together.

This is our hope. This is the faith that

I go back to the South with. With this faith we will be able to hew out of the mountain of despair a stone of hope. With this faith we will be able to transform the jangling discords of our nation into a beautiful symphony of brotherhood. With this faith we will be able to work together, to pray together, to struggle together, to go to jail together, to stand up for freedom together, knowing that we will be free one day.

This will be the day when all of God's children will be able to sing with new meaning:

> My country 'tis of thee,
> Sweet land of liberty,
> Of thee I sing:
> Land where my fathers died,
> Land of the pilgrims' pride,
> From every mountain-side
> Let Freedom ring.

Five score years ago, a great American, in whose symbolic shadow we stand today, signed the Emancipation Proclamation. This momentous decree came as the great beacon light of hope for millions of Negro slaves who had been seared in the flames of withering injustice. It came as the joyous daybreak to end the long night of their captivity.

But one hundred years later the Negro still is not free. One hundred years later, the life of the Negro is still badly crippled by the manacles of segregation and the chains of discrimination. One hundred years later, the Negro lives on a lonely island of poverty in the midst of a vast ocean of material prosperity. One hundred years later, the Negro is still languished in the corners of American society and finds himself an exile in his own land. So we have come here today to dramatize the shameful condition.

In a sense we've come to our Nation's Capital to cash a check. When the architects of our republic wrote the magnificent words of the Constitution and the Declaration of Independence, they were signing a promissory note to which every American was to fall heir. This note was a promise that all men, yes, black men as well as white men, should be guaranteed the unalienable rights of life, liberty and the pursuit of happiness.

It is obvious today that America has defaulted on this promissory note insofar as her citizens of color are concerned. Instead of honoring this sacred obligation, America has given the Negro people a bad check, a check which has come back marked "Insufficient Funds." But we refuse to believe the bank of justice is bankrupt. We refuse to believe that there are insufficient funds in the great vaults of opportunity of this nation. So we have come to cash this check, a check that will give us upon demand, the riches of freedom and the security of justice. We have also come to this hallowed spot to remind America of the fierce urgency of now.

This is no time to engage in the luxury of cooling off or to take the tranquilizing drug of gradualism. Now is the time to make real the promises of democracy. Now is the time to rise from the dark and desolate valley of segregation to the sunlit path of racial justice. Now is the time to lift our nation from the quicksands of racial injustice to the solid rock of brotherhood. Now is the time to make justice a reality for all of God's children.

It would be fatal for the nation to overlook the urgency of the moment. This sweltering summer of the Negro's legitimate discontent will not pass until there is an invigorating autumn of freedom and equality. Nineteen sixty-three is not an end but a beginning. Those who hoped that the Negro needed to blow off steam and will now be content will have a rude awakening if the nation returns to business as usual. There will be neither rest nor tranquility in America until the Negro is guaranteed his citizenship rights. The whirlwinds of revolt will continue to shake the foundations of our nation until the bright day of justice emerges.

But there is something I must say to my people who stand on the warm threshold which leads them to the palace of justice. In the process of gaining our rightful place we must not be guilty of wrongful deeds. Let us not seek to satisfy our thirst for freedom by drinking from the cup of bitterness and hatred. We must forever conduct our struggle on the high plane of dignity and discipline. We must not allow our creative protest to degenerate into physical violence. Again and again we must rise to the majestic heights of meeting physical force with soul force.

The marvelous new militancy which has engulfed the Negro community must not lead us to a distrust of all white people, for many of our white brothers, as evidenced by their presence here today, have come to realize that their destiny is tied up with our destiny. They have come to realize that their freedom is inextricably bound to our freedom. We cannot walk alone.

And if America is to be a great nation,

this must become true. So, let freedom ring from the prodigious hill tops of New Hampshire. Let freedom ring from the mighty mountains of New York. Let freedom ring from the heightening Alleghenies of Pennsylvania. Let freedom ring from the snowcapped Rockies of Colorado. Let freedom ring from the curvaceous slopes of California. But not only that, let freedom ring from Stone Mountain of Georgia.

Let freedom ring from Lookout Mountain of Tennessee.

Let freedom ring from every hill and molehill of Mississippi. From every mountainside, let freedom ring. And when we allow freedom to ring, when we let it ring from every village, from every hamlet, from every state and every city, we will be able to speed up that day when all of God's children, black men and white men, Jews and Gentiles, Protestants and Catholics, will be able to join hands and sing in the words of the old Negro spiritual: "Free at last! free at last! thank God almighty, we are free at last!" ■

Malcolm X

By the 1960's the Black Muslim movement had become a potent force in the black ghettos of America and was even gaining recognition abroad. The chief spokesman for this nationalistic group was Malcolm X, a man who had surmounted poverty, drugs, and imprisonment to become one of the most powerful black voices ever heard in the country. The statements which follow were made by Malcolm in 1962, a year before he broke with the Muslims and three years before he was murdered while giving a speech.

Source: Malcolm X, "Separation or Integration: A Debate," *Dialogue Magazine,* May 1962, pp. 14–18.

I might point out that it makes America look ridiculous to stand up in world conferences and refer to herself as the leader of the free world. Here is a country, Uncle Sam, standing up and pointing a finger at the Portuguese, and at the French, and at other colonizers, and there are 20 million black people in this country who are still confined to second-class citizenship, 20 million black people in this country who are still segregated and Jim-Crowed, as my friend, Dr. Farmer has already pointed out. And despite the fact that 20 million black people here yet don't have freedom, justice and equality, Adlai Stevenson has the nerve enough to stand up in the United Nations and point the finger at South Africa, and at Portugal and at some of these other countries. All we say is that South Africa preaches what it practices and practices what it preaches; America preaches one thing and practices another. And we don't want to integrate with hypocrites who preach one thing and practice another.

The good point in all of this is that there is an awakening going on among whites in America today, and this awakening is manifested in this way: two years ago you didn't know that there were black people in this country who didn't want to integrate with you; two years ago the white public had been brainwashed into thinking that every black man in this country wanted to force his way into your community, force his way into your schools, or force his way into your factories; two years ago you thought that all you would have to do is give us a little token integration and the race problem would be solved. Why? Because the people in the black community who didn't want integration were never given a voice, were never given a platform, were never given an opportunity to shout out the fact that integration would never solve the problem. And it has only been during the past year that the white public has begun to realize that the problem will never be solved unless a solution is devised acceptable to the black masses, as well as the black bourgeoisie—the upper class or middle class Negro. And when the whites began to realize that these integration-minded Negroes were in the minority, rather than in the majority, then they began to offer an open forum and give those who want separation an opportunity to speak their mind too.

We who are black in the black belt, or black community, or black neighborhood can easily see that our people who settle for integration are usually the middle-class so-called Negroes, who are in the minority. Why? Because they have confidence in the white man; they have absolute confidence that you will change. They believe that they can change you; they believe that there is still hope in the American dream. But what to them is an American dream to us is an American nightmare, and we don't think that it is possible for the American white man in sincerity to take the action necessary to correct the unjust conditions that 20 million black people here are made to suffer morning, noon, and night. And because we don't have any hope or confidence or faith in the American white man's ability to bring about a change in the injustices that exist, instead of asking or seeking to integrate into the American society we

want to face the facts of the problem the way they are, and separate ourselves. And in separating ourselves this doesn't mean that we are anti-white or anti-American, or anti-anything. We feel, that if integration all these years hasn't solved the problem yet, then we want to try something new, something different and something that is in accord with the conditions as they actually exist.

The honorable Elijah Muhammad teaches us that there are over 725 million Moslems or Muslims on this earth. I use both words interchangeably. I use the word Moslem for those who can't undergo the change, and I use the word Muslim for those who can. He teaches us that the world of Islam stretches from the China Seas to the shores of West Africa and that the 20 million black people in this country are the lost-found members of the nation of Islam. He teaches us that before we were kidnaped by your grandfathers and brought to this country and put in chains, our religion was Islam, our culture was Islam. We came from the Muslim world, we were kidnaped and brought here out of the Muslim world. And after being brought here we were stripped of our language, stripped of our ability to speak our mother tongue, and it's a crime today to have to admit that there are 20 million black people in this country who not only can't speak their mother tongue, but don't even know they ever had one. This points up the crime of how thoroughly and completely the black man in America has been robbed by the white man of his culture, of his identity, of his soul, of his self. And because he has been robbed of his self, he is trying to accept your

self. Because he doesn't know who he is, now he wants to be who you are. Because he doesn't know what belongs to him, he is trying to lay claim to what belongs to you. You have brain-washed him and made him a monster. He is black on the outside, but you have made him white on the inside. Now he has a white heart and a white brain, and he's breathing down your throat and down your neck because he thinks he's a white man the same as you are. He thinks that he should have your house, that he should have your factory, he thinks that he should even have your school, and most of them even think that they should have your woman, and most of them are after your woman.

The honorable Elijah Muhammad teaches us that the black people in America, the so-called Negroes, are the people who are referred to in the Bible as the lost sheep, who are to be returned to their own in the last days. He says that we are also referred to in the Bible, symbolically, as the lost tribe. He teaches us in our religion, that we are those people whom the Bible refers to who would be lost until the end of time. Lost in a house that is not theirs, lost in a land that is not theirs, lost in a country that is not theirs, and who will be found in the last days by the Messiah who will awaken them and enlighten them, and teach them that which they had been stripped of, and then this would give them the desire to come together among their own kind and go back among their own kind.

And this, basically, is why we who are followers of the honorable Elijah Muhammad don't accept integration: we feel that we are living at the end of time, by

Declan Haun, Black Star

292

this, we feel that we are living at the end of the world. Not the end of the earth, but the end of the world. He teaches us that there are many worlds. The planet is an earth, and there is only one earth, but there are many worlds on this earth, the Eastern World and the Western World. There is a dark world and a white world. There is the world of Christianity, and the world of Islam. All of these are worlds and he teaches us that when the book speaks of the end of time, it doesn't mean the end of the earth, but it means the end of time for certain segments of people, or a certain world that is on this earth. Today, we who are here in America who have awakened to the knowledge of ourselves; we believe that there is no God but Allah, and we believe that the religion of Islam is Allah's religion, and we believe that it is Allah's intention to spread his religion throughout the entire earth. We believe that the earth will become all Muslim, all Islam, and because we are in a Christian country we believe that this Christian country will have to accept Allah as God, accept the religion of Islam as God's religion, or otherwise God will come in and wipe it out. And we don't want to be wiped out with the American white man, we don't want to integrate with him, we want to separate from him.

The method by which the honorable Elijah Muhammad is straightening out our problem is not teaching us to force ourselves into your society, or force ourselves even into your political, economic or any phase of your society, but he teaches us that the best way to solve this problem is for complete separation. He says that since the black man here in America is

actually the property that was stolen from the East by the American white man, since you have awakened today and realized that this is what we are, we should be separated from you, and your government should ship us back from where we came from, not at our expense, because we didn't pay to come here. We were brought here in chains. So the honorable Elijah Muhammad and the Muslims who follow him, we want to go back to our own people. We want to be returned to our own people.

But in teaching this among our people and the masses of black people in this country, we discover that the American government is the foremost agency in opposing any move by any large number of black people to leave here and go back among our own kind. The honorable Elijah Muhammad's words and work is harassed daily by the F.B.I. and every other government agency which use various tactics to make the so-called Negroes in every community think that we are all about to be rounded up, and they will be rounded up too if they will listen to Mr. Muhammad; but what the American government has failed to realize, the best way to open up a black man's head today and make him listen to another black man is to speak against that black man. But when you begin to pat a black man on the back, no black man in his right mind will trust that black man any longer. And it is because of this hostility on the part of the government toward our leaving here that the honorable Elijah Muhammad says then, if the American white man or the American government doesn't want us to leave, and the government has proven its inability to bring about integration or

give us freedom, justice and equality on a
basis, equally mixed up with white people,
then what are we going to do? If the government doesn't want us to go back among
our own people, or to our own people,
and at the same time the government has
proven its inability to give us justice, the
honorable Elijah Muhammad says if
you don't want us to go and we can't stay
here and live in peace together, then the
best solution is separation. And this is
what he means when he says that some of
the territory here should be set aside,
and let our people go off to ourselves and
try and solve our own problem.

   Some of you may say, Well, why should
you give us part of this country? The honorable Elijah Muhammad says that for
400 years we contributed our slave labor
to make the country what it is. If you were
to take the individual salary or allowances of each person in this audience it
would amount to nothing individually, but
when you take it collectively all in one
pot you have a heavy load. Just the weekly
wage. And if you realize that from anybody who could collect all of the wages
from the persons in this audience right
here for one month, why they would be so
wealthy they couldn't walk. And if you
see that, then you can imagine the result of
millions of black people working for nothing for 310 years. And that is the contribution that we made to America. Not
Jackie Robinson, not Marian Anderson, not
George Washington Carver, that's not
our contribution; our contribution to
American society is 310 years of free slave
labor for which we have not been paid
one dime. We who are Muslims, followers
of the honorable Elijah Muhammad, don't

Charles Moore, Black Star

293

think that an integrated cup of coffee is
sufficient payment for 310 years of slave
labor. ■

Source: Kenneth Clark, "Letter of Resignation from Board of Directors of Antioch College in Black Studies, Myths and Realities" (A. Philip Randolph Educational Fund, September 1969), pp. 32–34.

Kenneth Clark

In the 1960's and 1970's, the demand for black studies programs, Afro-American institutes, and the like grew in great volume on the nation's campuses. Not all black leaders were in agreement with these demands. In the letter below, psychologist Kenneth B. Clark explains why he resigned from the Board of Directors of Antioch College when that institution decided to support an all-black Afro-American Studies Institute.

The problem of Antioch's support of the Afro-American Institute and the controversy with the HEW as to whether Antioch's support of this racially organized and exclusionary facility on its campus did or did not violate Title VI of the Civil Rights Act is to me a serious matter involving racial justice and dignity, and the role of the college and university in helping to free the human mind and body of primitive passions. As you know from my previous letters to you and to President Dixon and from our series of discussions, I have been, not only disturbed, but vigorously opposed to the college's decision to participate in any form of racial exclusion.

I opposed this for the same reasons that we fought together in the school segregation cases which led to the Brown decision. I continue to believe, as I know you do, that racial prejudice, discrimination and segregation are damaging to the human personality without regard to the racial rationalizations or excuses offered in support of such practices.

There is absolutely no evidence to support the contention that the inherent damage to human beings of primitive exclusion on the basis of race is any less damaging when demanded or enforced by the previous victims than when imposed by the dominant group. There is absolutely no valid basis by which educational institutions can or should make any distinctions on the basis of race or color. Some argue that blacks and whites must be separated because they represent different cultures and that cultures, like oil and water, cannot mix. Segregationists have argued so for generations against integrated transportation, drinking fountains, integrated schools, and intermarriage—maintaining that mixture would lead to mongrelization of the races. Such racial distinctions are arbitrary, dangerously ignorant, and cruel. They are destructive and inimical to all of the goals of serious education. In this regard I am in complete agreement with the editorial in the New York Times of Wednesday, May 7, 1969, which said among other things that HEW did "a serious disservice to the cause of racial integration by authorizing Antioch College to operate an all-Negro black studies institute." I am not, however, particularly surprised that practical and political men would find such justification consistent with their political needs to seek to accept a patently racist arrangement by subterfuge.

To exclude someone of one race—or to admit that it would be appropriate to do so—on the grounds that his background or experience is irrelevant, that they render him unable to achieve is precisely what white segregationists have been doing to blacks for centuries. Yet this seems to be the burden of rationalization at Antioch for a black separatist policy. Yet, it is whites who need a black studies program most of all.

The white liberal for his part who concedes black separatism so hastily and benevolently must look to his own reasons, not the least of them perhaps an exquisite relief. To encourage or endorse a separate black program not academically equivalent to the college curriculum generally, indeed to endorse any such program, is to reinforce the Negro's inability to compete with whites for the real power of the real world. It is no excuse to justify the deed by citing the demand.

The history of the Civil Rights movement, the pattern of evasion since the Brown decision 15 years ago prepared me for this HEW type of logic and evasion of the fundamental moral and legal implications of this problem. What I am *not* prepared to accept is continued association with an educational institution which is an accessory, if not an instigator of this type of game-playing with the lives of human beings and with the life and stability of the society. I am personally not prepared to continue an association with Antioch College in which as a member of the Board of Directors I am, and must be considered educationally responsible for and a participant in what is to me, a shoddy evasion of the moral and educational responsibility which a college must assume or frankly admit that it is indistinguishable from the political areas of our society.

I believe that above all under times of tension, stress, and pressures to conform to the shouting demands of the populace, colleges must have the courage to stand firmly for the rule of reason and for those principles and values considered indispensable to serious education. I do not believe that Antioch, in acceding to the demands for a separate facility for its Negro students, has showed this type of courage. I do not believe that Antioch, in permitting some of the more hostile Negro students to coerce and intimidate other Negroes and whites by quashing vocal dissent, has showed the courage necessary

to maintain that type of academic climate which permits man that freedom of inquiry, freedom of thought, and freedom of dissent which are essential to the life of the intellect.

Colleges and universities must be the custodians of the rational and intellectual approach to the study and eventual solution of difficult and complex human problems. To succumb to any form of dogmatism, to institutionalize the irrational is to fail in fulfilling this important obligation. I am convinced that Antioch has not only violated this sacred obligation by its approach to the Afro-American Studies Institute, and by permitting the existence of and financially supporting the racially exclusionary Unity house on its campus, Antioch has also tarnished its own glorious traditions of stubborn resistance to the fashionable. It was this history which made me profoundly proud to be identified with Antioch College.

In permitting a group of students to inflict their dogmatism and ideology on other students and on the total college community; and in being silent while some students intimidate, threaten, and in some cases physically assault the Negro students who disagree with them, the Administration at Antioch has not only defaulted in its responsibilities, but, I believe has made a mockery of its concern for the protection and development of human dignity without regard to cost. ■

A SPECTRUM OF POLITICAL OPINIONS

We have already encountered a spectrum of opinion on political issues. It is also possible to find a spectrum running from radical to reactionary on a fundamental social issue such as integration. Classify the three black leaders whose statements you have just read in terms of their positions on assimilation into American society. Use the following criteria to determine where each man should be located:

1 Beliefs about the nature of the relationship between blacks and whites in America.

2 Beliefs about the relationship of blacks to American society in general.

3 Beliefs about what constitutes proper political action. ■

THE MULTIPLYING PROBLEMS OF ASSIMILATION

The black revolution of the 1960's was accompanied by, and indeed gave rise to, a remarkable resurgence of ethnic feeling among a variety of groups in America. The following newspaper articles which appeared in the spring of 1971 testify to this resurgence and to the heightened consciousness of power relationships that underlie it.

Source: Kay Longcope, "The Identity Crisis of 'Harvard's Chicanos'," *Boston Sunday Globe,* May 2, 1971.

The Identity Crisis of "Harvard's Chicanos"

"My parents pushed me very hard in an Anglo (Caucasian) direction. I rejected every Chicano value. For 29 years I have lived a life of total pretension. It has led to horrible complications in myself. I am just now learning who I am."

The young man in levis and blue and gray striped sport shirt could have been black, Oriental, or American Indian. His words are equally applicable to them. His name, however, is Ben Moya and he is a Mexican-American (Chicano) from the Southwest.

Moya, a Teaching Fellow at the Harvard Law School, in September became the University's first and only Chicano faculty member. He also has the dubious distinction of being the country's only Mexican-American serving full time on a law school faculty, though there are 60 Mexican-American lawyers in the United States.

In the minority community from which he comes, he is an exception in other ways. Statistically, he is one of only 6.4 percent of the nation's 5 to 6 million Mexican-Americans who have received even a high school education: he is among 1.6 percent who finished college.

Because "my parents pushed me very hard" toward white society's success standards—getting a good education so he could get a good job—Moya graduated first in his class at the University of New Mexico in Albuquerque, where he was raised.

He also has attended Princeton University and now, in conjunction with his Teaching Fellow duties, is working toward completion of a Master of Legal Letters.

Anglo Values

"I have worked very hard to adopt all Anglo values to 'get ahead' and that has created a huge gulf between me and my family and between me and my race," he confessed. But the worst has been "the horrible complications and conflicts in myself."

These conflicts, which constitute an agonizing identity crisis, forge a common bond between Moya and his . . . Chicano students, most of whom are on scholarship at Harvard.

Moya's conflicts "are applicable to all of us here," said Jaime Cervantes, 23, of Laverne, Calif. And Ben added: "None of us would be here if we hadn't tried to be Anglo."

The trickier part, as they have learned in a society that prizes whiteness and downplays the value of other cultures, is to revert to their heritage without a sense of shame because "we're different."

"It's a constant dilemma because, from the moment we enter school, we're taught we're going to fail if we don't reject our own culture," said Cervantes.

Henry Gutierrez of East Los Angeles, which has the largest Mexican population outside of Mexico, angrily added: "We're made to become agents of repression . . . destroying our own people by the Anglicized ideas we carry around with us."

How does one become un-Anglicized?

Ben Moya recalls the exact date so quickly that you know the hurt two years ago still throbs.

"March 25, 1969," after not being selected editor of the University of New Mexico's law journal.

"Traditionally," Moya explained, "the

person first in his class or the one who writes the best published article is named editor. I was both, but I wasn't picked."

Not Mature

"They told me that since I wasn't married, I wasn't mature enough to handle the law journal. When someone uses an excuse like that, you have to sit back and think."

Similar wounds were exposed to a visitor as Moya and several of his students chatted in his office at the Harvard Law school's main library building.

Jorge Rangel of Alice, Texas, a 1970 University of Houston political science graduate, told of being elected president of the high school student body, but of being barred from social activities outside of school.

Henry Gutierrez, the only one here with a full beard, said he was "introduced to America" late one night as he watched Los Angeles police beat up an acquaintance who "was so drugged he couldn't walk out of the restaurant by himself."

Roy Cazares of National City, Calif., an 11th grade dropout who subsequently made Dean's List at San Diego State College, felt "the bottom drop out" in witnessing court proceedings in which a friend was sentenced to five days in jail for changing a car's transmission in the street. An Anglo man, in a case just previous, was merely fined $60 for being drunk and kicking out windows in a police car.

In assessing the meaning of these and various instances of discrimination, the light gradually dawns that regardless of how Anglo the Chicanos try to become, acceptance based solely on themselves as persons is always beyond their grasp.

Discrimination

"It doesn't matter that you go to Harvard Law School and leave with good credentials if the majority viewpoint is still 'you're just a Chicano'," said Cervantes.

The discrimination factor against Chicanos and other Hispanos—the nation's second largest minority group—is borne out in a national survey recently conducted by the US Census Bureau. Census data (1970) on the Spanish-speaking will not be available for several more months, but survey figures show that Spanish-surnamed persons have an average family income of $5600, only 70 percent of the national average, and an unemployment rate almost twice that of the nation, along with poorer education, more illiteracy and fewer white collar jobs.

The Census Bureau estimates there are 9.5 million Hispanos in the US (though Spanish leaders put the figure at 10 or 12 million), of whom 55 percent are Mexican-American, 15.8 percent are Puerto Rican, 6.1 percent are Cuban, 6 percent come from other Central and South American countries, and 17.1 percent are simply listed as "other Spanish."

An estimated 4.3 percent of the Mexican-Americans live in the five Southwestern states of California, Arizona, New Mexico, Colorado, and Texas. There also are sizeable Chicano populations in the Midwestern states of Illinois, Ohio, Michigan, and Wisconsin.

Is the discrimination factor less at Harvard or in the East?

"We're used very much as window dressing so Harvard can say, 'look, we have Chicanos'," Moya said.

"It's a colonial experience," added Cervantes. "They're just beginning to recognize Puerto Ricans in Massachusetts, so how can we expect them to recognize Chicanos?"

(Just last week, however, two Chicano undergraduates representing the United Mexican American Students of Boston and four members of Harvard's admissions staff hammered out a first step toward development of a comprehensive Chicano recruitment program.)

(The admissions staff agreed to conduct training sessions to prepare undergraduates for summer and fall recruiting. It also indicated openness to hiring a person "sensitive to the cultural distinctiveness of the Chicano experience should a vacancy develop on the admissions staff.")

("The very fact that they ever met is an encouraging first step," said Moya.)

Easterners' vast ignorance of Mexican-Americans was vividly pointed up in two related incidents.

Several months ago, a Mexican-American student at the University of New Mexico queried Harvard's Division of Medical Sciences about financial assistance in pursuing a PhD degree there. He received this answer:

"As you probably know, the course of study leading to a PhD degree is a long one, averaging four or five years. Financial support for this long period is not easy to obtain, *especially for foreign students.* It might be well for you to apply to a foundation in *your own country,* a US government agency, or the Institute of International Education." (Emphasis added.)

More recently, Cervantes visited officials at Boston's regional HEW office to explain who Mexican-Americans are and where

298 Charles Harbutt, Magnum

they live. His host seemed to be paying attention, but as Cervantes was leaving, he said:

"I'm sure that with your Harvard education, you'll be very successful when you go back to Mexico."

"When men of that importance can negate 10 to 12 million people—most of whom are American citizens—that's serious," declared Cervantes. "There's just no concept here that Mexicans are Americans."

"Tossed Salad"

Another problem they are facing, along with other Hispanos, is "attempts to push us into black molds" since Easterners primarily are used to dealing with the black community, which has an entirely different cultural orientation to that of the Spanish-speaking.

"This country recognizes minority possibility of a multi-culture and the knowledge that it is not a melting pot but a tossed salad," said Cervantes.

"This country recognizes minority groups as they become more vociferous, but we don't like the concept of 'squeeky wheels getting the most grease'." We don't want to melt. We don't want to yell.

"We do want to help correct the notion that everything not Anglo is dirty."

To effect such change, not only for Chicanos but in concert with the nation's other struggling minorities, the Mexican-Americans at Harvard plan to return to homes in Texas, New Mexico, Arizona and California to put law expertise to work in "changing systems that have never worked for us."

The most repressive systems needing change, they feel, are judicial and educational systems. Their feeling is certainly shared by most other minority group members in Boston and elsewhere who have met stone walls in attempts to better police-community relations and make school boards more responsive to language and other cultural needs. In the educational realm, Puerto Ricans and Chinese in Boston are specific cases in point.

Among Mexican-Americans in the Southwest—the nation's second largest minority—charges of police brutality run rampant. They were most explosively underscored last summer and fall in East Los Angeles, when Chicano Moratoriums against the Indochina War erupted into violent confrontations with police. Several Mexican-Americans were killed, including Reuben Salazar, the *Los Angeles Times*' respected columnist.

"There is a hiatus for the police to do anything they want," said Moya. "Injunctive relief against them is very rare."

He added: "There has always been a problem between the Chicano community and the criminal justice system, from the police to courts of appeals. The more sophisticated Chicanos become in attempts to involve themselves in mainstream society—getting elected to school boards, city councils, etc.—the more sophisticated repressive systems become."

"We're willing to compete with Anglos in any walk of life," the students made clear, "but not with shackles put on us at the beginning. We want equal treatment under law."

Learning to obtain that equal treatment for themselves and for other members of their race is why they have become transplanted Easterners . . . and Harvard's Chicanos. ■

Source: Kevin Lahart, "The Anger of the Ethnics: Was the Melting Pot a Myth; the American Dream Not Worth It?" *The Boston Globe*, July 11, 1971.

The Anger of the Ethnics

Picture Joe Colombo. Chubby, smiling, television lights illuminating his countenance for the clicking cameras, rays of brightness flashing back from between strands of hair on his balding pate. Speaking: "I say there is a conspiracy against all Italian-Americans. I feel that Mr. Nixon is behind it . . . Mitchell, I believe, has a vendetta against Italian-Americans."

(Colombo was shot in the head on Nov. 28 and has since been in critical condition in a New York City hospital. The shooting, following which his would-be assassin was shot and killed, took place during a daytime rally following the same theme.)

More than 1400 people turned up in March for the $125-a-plate fete for Colombo—Joseph Colombo Sr.—a man convicted of perjury, indicted for income-tax evasion and for gambling violations, a man described by law-enforcement officials as a Cosa Nostra family chieftain; a man who describes himself as honest and hardworking, persecuted because of his ethnic background.

They cheered him.

Two months earlier, the Ford Foundation announced grants totaling a shade under one million dollars for research and action programs "related to the problems of America's white working-class population." Then, covering the foundation's flank, its press release on the grant said: "The foundation stressed at the same time that it was continuing its work to widen opportunities for black and other racial minorities."

Thus the Ford Foundation climbed on the coaster wagon that may well become a bandwagon headed toward giving substance to the slogan "power to the people."

The people in this case being those popularly described as the angry "ethnics."

50 Million People

While both the Ford grants and the Colombo celebration can be viewed with cynicism—on the one hand a cover for the mob; on the other a sellout to the racist proletariat—a more benign and probably more correct view is that they are intimately related and that their root source is the immense dissatisfaction, disaffection and anger felt by those who are called "ethnics."

There are now, according to government and social agencies, at least 50 million persons in the US in families with incomes between $5000 and $11,000 a year and within three generations of their European roots. Spokesmen for those agencies say that unless that mass of people is understood—and remedies found for their real grievances—the polarization that now exists will pull the country beyond the breaking point.

Part of the polarization can be attributed to racism.

It is more than racism. An image of Eastern European groups as racist was reinforced in the early 1960s when a national opinion research center survey showed Polish-Americans as the most bigoted of several ethnic groups. But when the Poles are contrasted with white Anglo-Saxon Protestants, even in the major cities, according to a National Urban League-sponsored Harris poll, it is the WASPS who are the more racist.

Beyond racism, the causes of the polarization revolve around economic and cultural issues.

"The last thing anyone did for the workingman," says Barbara Mikulski, who helped organize Baltimore's Southeast Community Organization, "was the GI Bill of Rights after World War II. Federal, state and local programs are not helping the working class guy. He gets no subsidies, no tax loopholes. Yet he is the one who is paying for the programs."

All Don't Make It

Other threads are woven into the fabric of dissatisfaction. Msgr. Geno Baroni came out of the coalfields of Western Pennsylvania, where his father was a miner. In 1963, the Catholic priest helped coordinate the civil rights march on Washington. Now he heads the United States Catholic Conference's Center for Urban Ethnic Affairs, in Washington.

The myths of the Melting Pot and the American Dream, he says, are no longer functional. "What we were taught was that everyone is going to make it, everyone is going to be the same. What has happened is that everyone has not made it, and a lot of people have lost a sense of their own heritage, a sense of their own culture," as they have submerged those things in their attempts to become "American."

The theme is expanded a bit by Ralph Perrotta, executive associate for ethnic affairs for the National Urban Coalition in Washington. He explains, "You're brought up feeling that you're not quite American and develop feelings of self-hatred. One of my earliest recollections is my mother referring to the Irish families on the block as the 'Americans.' "

How completely the myth of the melting

pot was accepted—and how it was pushed on immigrants—is shown by the Ford English School, set up by the Ford Motor Co. in 1914 to Americanize its immigrant workers. A statement by the company preserved in the archives of the Henry Ford Museum says:

". . . We prefer that classes be mixed as to race and country, for our great aim is to impress these men that they are, or should be, Americans and that their former racial, national and linguistic differences are to be forgotten."

The same document described a ceremony marking the graduation of a class from the school: "Not long ago this school graduated over 500 men. Commencement exercises were held in the largest hall in the city. On the stage was represented an immigrant ship. In front of it was a huge melting pot. Down the gangplank came the members of the class dressed in their national garbs and carrying luggage such as they carried when they landed in this country. Down they poured into the Ford melting pot and disappeared. Then the teachers began to stir the contents of the pot with long ladles. Presently the pot began to boil over and out came the men dressed in their best American clothes and waving American flags."

"But the melting pot theory just didn't work," says the Rev. Paul Asciolla of Chicago, assistant editor of the Italian newspaper *Fra Noi*. "You can't," says the priest, "kill your grandfather."

"Who Am I"

And if you think you have, says Dr. Andrew Greeley, a priest who heads the Center for the Study of Ethnic Pluralism at the University of Chicago, you may have to resurrect him to find out who you are. "I have Irish kids coming to me now who want to do their dissertations on their own ethnic groups. They say they don't know who they are and want to find out," he says.

While those who have made it to graduate school want to discover their history, many of their aunts and uncles and cousins remain close to their ethnic roots and within the economic margins of what is facilely described as Middle America, the white lower middle class, the silent majority.

The estimates on the size of the group range up to 70 million. The majority traces its origins to eastern and southern Europe—Poles, Lithuanians, Czechs, Slovaks, Ukrainians, Italians. Of the total, between 20 and 30 million are white Anglo-Saxon Protestants and those descended from earlier immigrant groups: the Irish, Germans, Scandinavians and other northern Europeans.

It is this mass, tied together by little more than the tenuous thread of economic position, that began to give off discernible rumblings of discontent in the late 1960s as a number of factors became operative.

For starters, they began to lose—or barely break even—economically. Irving Levine, director of the National Project on Ethnic America, sponsored by the American Jewish Committee, points to US Labor Department figures and concludes that the American worker has suffered a decline in real income of 3 percent between 1965 and 1970.

The years saw more than an economic squeeze. According to Harvard sociologist Nathan Glazer, "What made the ethnic thing important was the post-1963 black revolution. People became more aware of ethnic distinctions. The black power movement brought a rise in black consciousness, black pride, and made black demands more visible."

At the same time that he was beginning to feel the economic pinch, the white worker was perceiving that blacks and their problems were getting more attention. Added to that, says policy scientist James Barry of the State University of New York at Buffalo, was the rise in antiwar feeling—a feeling shared by great numbers of workers—among segments of the youth culture and spin-off attacks on being an American.

Unbearable Idea

"And since the working-class white 'ethnic' wasn't quite sure of his own 'Americanism'," Barry says, "the attack scared the hell out of him. He perceived the attack as coming from upper-middle-class WASPS, kids who were saying that the achievement of the American dream wasn't worth it. That was just unbearable."

The white working class, then, which had formed a crucial bloc in the New Deal coalition, began to feel cut out of the action. Its neighborhoods were increasingly threatened. It found itself locked into the decaying cities, as blockbusters used it—and blacks—as pawns in a game of "Let's you and him fight."

The media projected a provoking image of students as freaks who called policemen (working-class in their origins and lifestyles) pigs, burned the American flag and supported the Viet Cong.

White "ethnics" felt deserted by their civic and religious leaders. The media, the intellectual elite and even their own sons and daughters—in some instances—seemed to be against them. The government was doing nothing for them since they were, after all, white Americans and thereby affluent. They found themselves the victims of labeling: Middle Americans, Silent Majority, Hardhats, Racists, "ethnics"—stereotypes that dealt with the mass but missed the complexity within the mass.

One thing that began shaping the view of many academics, community organizers and agency people was George Wallace's 1968 presidential campaign. James Wright, a community organizer in Gary, Ind., says, "Wallace came around and the people went for him." Not, he says, because they are racist but because they felt helpless, because they felt "they couldn't do a thing." Wright, a Mexican-American—his non-Hispanic name stems from the day five generations ago "when some dude from Virginia wandered through the town in Mexico my people come from"—says of the people in the Calumet Community Congress, which he helped organize: "These people are the salt of the earth. Given a democratic vehicle, they're going to go in the right direction. You've got to accept the workingman as many-dimensioned."

Levine, picking up the theme, calls for a wideangle view of the "ethnics." "Once you've dramatized people as racists, you throw them on the junk pile. It's not enough. You have to see their real grievances."

In the mid-'60s, push came to shove and then shove came to punch. A variety of factors conspired to submerge the roots of lower middle-class unrest. "Too many people were seeing group conflict—a phenomenon as old as America and as American as cherry pie—purely in terms of racism," Levine says. In addition, he continues, there were not, and are still not, enough facts about the lower middle class. And since assimilation was presumed to have taken place, "None of the mainstream thinkers was adequately talking about the lower middle class." In addition:

• Blacks developed a tactic that Tom Wolfe calls "Mau-Mauing the flak-catchers"—an ingenious and highly visible method of terrorizing bureaucrats.

• The Federal government declared war on poverty and aimed to build the "Great Society."

• The soaring national economy induced euphoria (from 1966 through 1969, the unemployment rate never went above 4 percent).

Glazer, co-author with Daniel Patrick Moynihan of "Beyond the Melting Pot," traces the lack of interest in ethnicity back to the mid-'50s, when everyone had pretty much dismissed group conflict and saw cooperation developing along the lines of religious groupings.

It didn't. So Glazer and Moynihan's book, first published in 1963, was reissued last year with a new 100-page introduction that put group conflict back into ethnic terms.

Polarizing

Who first went beyond racism in looking at and dealing with the problems of the marginal folks in Middle America?

"Irv Levine," say Greeley and others.

Why did Levine get into it? "In late 1967," he says, "we saw the country polarizing and thought there was no chance of decent movement toward depolarization unless we could discover a workable strategy to do that. In addition, ethnicity was becoming increasingly important and we felt we would like to see where it moved and help explain the phenomenon."

Out there—between the Hudson River and the Sierra Nevada mountains, out there in Middle America—the people were growing restive over unclearly defined grievances. In New York, where half the nation's Jewish population lives, a series of events was bringing great clarity to the question of polarization. Some segments of the black population were singling out the Jews as the ultimate white racists.

Allies Needed

What was perceived by many as black anti-Semitism was developing, and, as one Jewish agency staffer put it, "We needed new allies."

It was much more than anti-Semitism, according to Levine. "I'm a lower-middle-class kid from Brownsville. I grew up on the streets. In 1966 I came back to New York after spending six years in the Shaker Heights of the world working as a civil rightsnik, and moved into Flatbush.

"I had almost forgotten my own roots. On visits home during the six years I was away I would hear things from the brothers and dismiss them as exaggeration. My own motivations were more pro-black than pro-my own family. I came back and began to have great sympathy for the members of my own family who were being destroyed.

"I began to see the emergence of Jewish reaction to the black school movement. What was happening was not just fear of integration. I was shocked at the rather meaningless life-style, a troubled life-style among the people. I got the feeling that the only viable institution in the neighborhood was the beauty parlor.

"There were so few options for lower-middle-class whites. Education was the only way up, but there was tremendous black dissatisfaction with the schools and white resistance to change. What was happening was that the white kids and black kids were being trapped in no-win schools.

"And I said to myself, 'If Jews, who are the most liberal of New Yorkers, are reacting this way, then something other than racism is at work here.' "

If it was not racism, what was it?

"Legitimate group self-interest in conflict," responds Levine.

Another event of the late '60s that Levine reads as an out-cropping of legitimate self-interest is the 1967 school-board election of Wayne Township, N.J. The vice president of the Board of Education, Newton Miller, issued a statement urging the defeat of two Jewish board candidates on the ground that "most Jewish people are liberals, especially when it comes to spending money for education . . ." and ". . . we could lose what is left of Christ in our Christmas celebrations in our schools . . ."

"People," says Levine, "said that the Wayne scandal and the New York City teachers' strike in the autumn of 1968 were heavy with anti-Semitism. But it was more than that. It was a struggle of legitimate group self-interest; the interest of non-Jews

302

to maintain their own traditions and of Jews asserting their prerogatives and their tradition of what they believed to be the best education. We said right away that both struggles were legitimate. Not everyone agreed."

Conferences Held

Levine developed, and the American Jewish Committee sponsored, a series of conferences that have brought together various ethnic and neighborhood leaders, academics, union people, church groups and government agencies. Their aim is to "Turn on mainstream leadership" to the problems and possibilities of cooperation. A National Consultation on Ethnic America at Fordham University in June, 1968, has been followed with local and regional conferences in Philadelphia, Newark, Chicago, Kansas City, St. Louis, Detroit, New Haven and Buffalo.

Close on the heels of the American Jewish Committee came the Catholic Church. If there are 50 million in the country who might be considered "ethnics," 40 million are Roman Catholics. "When you look at the major cities," says Msgr. Baroni, "and see who's left that's white, you see the working class, not the bankers, not the professionals, but the working class, and the blacks in a city like Detroit, two out of three persons are either black or Polish."

In November, 1969, the American Catholic Bishops approved plans submitted by the US Catholic Conference's Urban Task Force. According to Baroni, work was proposed in three areas—with blacks, with the Spanish-speaking and with whites. "The whites," he says, "were left to work with the white groups."

Baroni and his staff are working with community organization in several cities with large "ethnic" populations, attempting to define and deal with problems of the working-class population—problems which Msgr. Baroni says have been "ignored since the end of World War II."

Both the AJC program and Msgr. Baroni's efforts were funded by Ford Foundation grants. Additional Ford money went to the Center for the Study of Ethnic Pluralism headed by Greeley, the University of Michigan and the Research Foundation of the City University of New York.

Why did the foundation put up the money?

Greeley sees two reasons. "What's sauce for the blacks," he says, "is sauce for everyone else. Secondly, the world of the foundation, the world of government, has awakened to the existence of places like the northwest side of Chicago."

Problems Real

That interpretation is not quite shared by the Ford Foundation's Basil Whiting. "We were concerned about the polarization and conflict in the cities of the northeast and saw a need to try to reduce that. In addition," he says, "there are problems relating to this segment of the population, which, while they are by no means as severe as those faced by the blacks and poor, are real. Finally, we wanted to explore the possibility of joint or parallel action and cooperation between blacks and whites in getting services they both need."

The foundation, Whiting says, "didn't look at this in terms of ethnicity. We're not emphasizing ethnicity. What we talk about here in the program is not 'ethnics' but the working class."

There is, nevertheless, heavy emphasis on ethnicity in the programs of those who received grants. According to Levine, "The ethnicity factor" must be taken into account. "You can't say that (the problem) is either ethnicity or class . . . and it's been that way in group struggles in American history . . . class and ethnicity must be taken together."

Greeley thinks that the extended family relationships and sense of identity found in "ethnic" neighborhood communities may well be a solution to much of what's ailing America. He is also zeroing in on ethnicity with the hope that he can explode "the myth that the white 'ethnic' is a blue-collar worker."

Out of all this, what a high proportion of those involved are looking for is wide-ranging acceptance of ethnic diversity, pride in heritage and a development of broad-based coalitions based on converging self-interest.

"The blacks began to say you've got to know who you are," Msgr. Baroni says, "and turned a negative image into a positive one."

Ethnics, he says, must do the same thing. "There's enough stress in a fast-changing society. A person needs his sources of strength. If they reject their culture and heritage, they have nothing to stand on." ∎

RACE, ETHNICITY, AND THE MASS MEDIA

Mass media often try to shape our opinions or sell something to us—whether it be an idea or a product. They also reflect public opinion. Whatever their aim, the media always incorporate some point of view in the material they present to the public. In the advertisements and comic strips on these pages race and ethnicity are featured.

1 What purpose does race or ethnicity serve in each advertisement?

2 What position toward racial and ethnic assimilation does each advertisement take?

3 Compare the treatment of race and ethnicity in the ads with their treatment in the comic strips.

4 How do these approaches compare with how race and ethnicity are treated on television? ■

We don't talk about opportunities. We create them.

Billy Joe Hooper is the boss. His income is better than good because he successfully runs a Texaco service station.

What's more, he owns his own home, a new car, and his three children are assured a college education. And now he's become a Texaco wholesaler with two trucks to make deliveries.

Things weren't always so good for Billy Joe; back in 1959 he was working in a lesser job. At night, to earn extra money, he worked as an attendant in a Texaco service station.

Impressed by his hard work and determination, we arranged financing so he could go into business for himself.

Today, Billy Joe Hooper is just one of 1,700 minority group retailers who operate their own Texaco stations. We have a special program to train minority group members who are interested in doing this. We call it Operation Opportunity.

Call it what you will, it proves a point. We at Texaco don't just talk about opportunities. We create them. If you know someone who may be interested, please write to us:

Manager, Training
Sales—United States,
Texaco Inc., 135 East 42nd Street,
New York, N.Y. 10017.

We're working to keep your trust. TEXACO

Courtesy of Texaco Inc.

Engineering Teamw all-American style

These three young peopl Bethlehem's reinforcing department in Seattle.

Charles James, at right trainee to assistant chief years. He is responsible struction in his office. B Indian Reservation near part-time as a commerci nance his education at bo and college. After gradu eral jobs before joining trainee detailer.

Now it is Charles Jame trainees to learn the rope

Marvin Williams, at lef trainees. He was an iron but a back injury made it to seek less strenuous em terest in the trainee prog his enrollment in a night knowledge of drafting sk

When asked how she like Hoyer, a detailer trainee, I work with are terrific. T had is from a few cust believe I was a Bethlehe telephoned to ask some construction job. They c firm that I was a Bethlehe

These three employees o grounds serve to remind is nothing in modern tech the place of dedicated p close harmony.

At Bethlehem Steel we be portunity for all. We emp people without regard to gion, sex, age or national o

BETHLEHEM S

Courtesy of Bethlehem Steel

began as a simple
shot of two blind
ren. One of those
e visions that a
and a camera
times capture.
became a message
Bea Lavery pencilled
a copy line.
d it became an
ertisement when a
p of professional
unicators recognized
t was an idea which
d be shared.
hat is advertising?
entially, it's free
ch that somebody
for.
a force that
rts free choice in
marketplace of ideas,
es and products.
d the way we look
free choice is the
amental purpose of
ocracy.

Carson/Roberts/Inc.,
ox 48458 A,
geles, Calif. 90048

THE BLIND ARE ALSO COLOR BLIND

CARSON/ROBERTS/INC/

Welcome aboard our magnificent 747

306

You don't have to be Jewish

to love Levy's
real Jewish Rye

Henry S. Levy & Sons, Inc. © 1967

LUTHER

WHAT'S WRONG WITH OREO?

FLU?

NO, SHE HEARD ABOUT THE FLU EPIDEMIC AND HER FRIEND LILY CAME DOWN WITH IT...

...BUT SHE DIDN'T! NOW SHE DOESN'T BELIEVE IN THE...

THE CAPTAIN AND THE KIDS   By R. Dirks

307

ASSIMILATION IN AMERICA: Melting Pot or Boiling Pot?

During the 1960's and 1970's, intellectuals felt obliged to undertake a reexamination of the whole complex question of assimilation in American life. In this final section we shall look at three statements made by serious students of the assimilation process. The first is by a well known historian of immigration, Oscar Handlin.

Source: Oscar Handlin, *The Newcomers: Negroes and Puerto Ricans in a Changing Metropolis* (Cambridge, Mass.: Harvard University Press, 1959), pp. 118–119.

The Assimilation Process Continues

In historical perspective, the Negroes and the Puerto Ricans in the New York Metropolitan Region do not present the radically new problem they seem to pose in the columns of the daily newspaper. Rather, their adjustment, difficult as it is, is but the most recent of a long series. The hardships such people have created and suffered have been concomitants of the necessity for accommodating in the city a large, unskilled, and poorly paid labor force needed for urban growth. These newest arrivals have thus but assumed the role formerly played by European immigrants.

In the past, New York benefited greatly from the presence of such laborers; but the city and the immigrants paid the cost in debilitating social disorders. Recovery from those disorders came from the capacity to expand and from the freedom with which the newcomers and their children could rise to the opportunities created by the expansion.

The Negroes and the Puerto Ricans have followed the general outline of the experience of earlier immigrants. These latest arrivals diverged from that earlier experience because color prejudice and the social and economic conditions they encountered impeded their freedom of movement, both in space and in social and economic status. That divergence in experience need not be more than temporary, however.

The available evidence sustains the following more concrete conclusions.

1 A pool of potential emigrants will persist in both Puerto Rico and in the South, but it will be drawn upon only to the extent that opportunities for unskilled labor in New York exist. Both groups will, in any case, however, increase in numbers through internal growth.

2 The genuine problems of social disorder in which Negroes and Puerto Ricans are involved can best be solved through the development of communal institutions, under responsible leadership that will give order and purpose to their lives.

3 The reduction of prejudice and the expansion of opportunities are essential to such development.

4 Such development will not come primarily through the general dispersal of these people in the whole population. Although some individuals, given the freedom to do so, will prefer to scatter in many different districts, the great majority of Negroes and Puerto Ricans, like the other ethnic groups, will continue to live in cohesive settlements. They will be accommodated through the evolution, in the suburbs and in the central city, of numerous neighborhoods at various income levels to which clusters of them will be voluntarily drawn by common interests and tastes.

5 The Negroes and Puerto Ricans are likely to continue, as they have in the past, to depend more on governmental services for education and welfare than did earlier immigrants.

Ultimately the future will be shaped by the men and women who will live through it. But the experience of the past offers a solid foundation for the belief that the newest immigrants to a great cosmopolitan city will come to play as useful a role in it as any of their predecessors. They themselves need only show the will and energy, and their neighbors the tolerance, to make it possible. ■

Source: Milton M. Gordon, *Assimilation In American Life* (New York: Oxford University Press, 1964), pp. 60–83.

Sociologist Milton Gordon is particularly noted for his studies of ethnic subcultures and the assimilation process in American life. In the selection below, Professor Gordon analyzes the nature of assimilation itself.

The Assimilation Variables

What happens "when peoples meet," as the phrase goes? Such meetings in the modern world are likely to take place under a variety of circumstances: colonial conquest, military occupation, redrawing of national boundaries to include diverse ethnic groups, large-scale trade and missionary activity, technical assistance to underdeveloped countries, displacement of an aboriginal population, and voluntary immigration which increases the ethnic diversity of the host country. In the American continental experience, the last two types have been the decisive ones. The displacement and attempted incorporation of the American Indian on the white conqueror's terms, and the massive immigration into this land of over 41 million people, largely from Europe but also from the other Americas and to a smaller extent from the Orient, from the days of the thinly populated and, even then, ethnically varied seaboard republic to the continent-spanning nation of the present, constitute the setting for the "meeting of peoples" in the American context.

Sociologists and cultural anthropologists have described the processes and results of ethnic "meetings" under such terms as "assimilation" and "acculturation." Sometimes these terms have been used to mean the same thing; in other usages their meanings, rather than being identical, have overlapped. (Sociologists are more likely to use "assimilation"; anthropologists have favored "acculturation" and have given it a narrower but generally consistent meaning.) With regard to the term "assimilation," particularly, there is a certain amount of confusion, and there is, further, a compelling need for a rigorous and systematic analysis of the concept of assimilation which would "break it down" into all the possible relevant factors or variables which could conceivably be included under its rubric.

* * *

Let us first of all, imagine a hypothetical situation in which a host country, to which we shall give the fictitious name of "Sylvania," is made up of a population all members of which are of the same race, religion, and previous national extraction. Cultural behavior is relatively uniform except for social class divisions. Similarly, the groups and institutions, i.e., the "social structure," of Sylvanian society are divided and differentiated only on a social class basis. Into this country, through immigration, comes a group of people who differ in previous national background and in religion and who thus have different cultural patterns from those of the host society. We shall call them the Mundovians. Let us further imagine that within the span of another generation, this population group of Mundovian national origin (now composed largely of the second generation, born in Sylvania) has taken on completely the cultural patterns of the Sylvanians, has thrown off any sense of peoplehood based on Mundovian nationality, has changed its religion to that of the Sylvanians, has eschewed the formation of any communal organizations made up principally or exclusively of Mundovians, has entered and been hospitably accepted into the social cliques, clubs, and institutions of the Sylvanians at various class levels, has intermarried freely and frequently with the Sylvanians, encounters no prejudice or discrimination (one reason being that they are no longer distinguishable culturally or structurally from the rest of the Sylvanian population), and raises no value conflict issues in Sylvanian public life. Such a situation would represent the ultimate form of assimilation—complete assimilation to the culture and society of the host country. Note that we are making no judgment here of either the sociological desirability, feasibility, or moral rightness of such a goal. We are simply setting it up as a convenient abstraction—an "ideal type"—ideal not in the value sense of being most desirable but in the sense of representing the various elements of the concept and their interrelationships in "pure," or unqualified, fashion (the methodological device of the "ideal type" was developed and named by the German sociologist, Max Weber).

Looking at this example, we may discern that seven major variables are involved in the process discussed—in other words, seven basic subprocesses have taken place in the assimilation of the Mundovians to Sylvanian society. These may be listed in the following manner. We may say that the Mundovians have
1 changed their cultural patterns (including religious belief and observance) to those of the Sylvanians;
2 taken on large-scale primary group relationships with the Sylvanians, i.e., have entered fully into the societal network of groups and institutions, or societal structure, of the Sylvanians;
3 have intermarried and interbred fully with the Sylvanians;

Table 1

THE ASSIMILATION VARIABLES

Subprocess or Condition	Type or Stage of Assimilation	Special Term
Change of cultural patterns to those of host society	Cultural or behavioral assimilation	Acculturation
Large-scale entrance into cliques, clubs, and institutions of host society, on primary group level	Structural assimilation	None
Large-scale intermarriage	Marital assimilation	Amalgamation
Development of sense of peoplehood based exclusively on host society	Identificational assimilation	None
Absence of prejudice	Attitude receptional assimilation	None
Absence of discrimination	Behavior receptional assimilation	None
Absence of value and power conflict	Civic assimilation	None

4 have developed a Sylvanian, in place of a Mundovian, sense of peoplehood, or ethnicity;

5 have reached a point where they encounter no discriminatory behavior;

6 have reached a point where they encounter no prejudiced attitudes;

7 do not raise by their demands concerning the nature of Sylvanian public or civic life any issues involving value and power conflict with the original Sylvanians (for example, the issue of birth control).

Each of these steps or subprocesses may be thought of as constituting a particular stage or aspect of the assimilation process. Thus we may, in shorthand fashion, consider them as types of assimilation and characterize them accordingly. We may, then, speak, for instance, of "structural assimilation" to refer to the entrance of Mundovians into primary group relationships with the Sylvanians, or "identificational assimilation" to describe the taking on of a sense of Sylvanian peoplehood. For some of the particular assimilation subprocesses there are existing special terms, already reviewed. For instance, cultural or behavioral assimilation is what has already been defined as "acculturation." The full list of assimilation subprocesses or variables with their general names, and special names, if any, is given in Table 1.

Not only is the assimilation process mainly a matter of degree, but, obviously, each of the stages or subprocesses distinguished above may take place in varying degrees.

In the example just used there has been assimilation in all respects to the society and culture which had exclusively occupied the nation up to the time of the immigrants' arrival. In other instances there may be other subsocieties and subcultures already on the scene when the new group arrives but one of these subsocieties and its way of life is dominant by virtue of original settlement, the preemption of power, or overwhelming predominance in numbers. In both cases we need a term to stand for the dominant subsociety which provides the standard to which other groups adjust or measure their relative degree of adjustment. We have tentatively used the term "host society"; however, a more neutral designation would be desirable. A. B. Hollingshead, in describing the class structure of New Haven, has used the term "core group" to refer to the Old Yankee families of colonial, largely Anglo-Saxon ancestry who have traditionally dominated the power and status system of the community, and who provide the "master cultural mould" for the class system of the other groups in the city. Joshua Fishman has referred to the "core society" and the "core culture" in American life, this core being "made up essentially of white Protestant, middle-class clay, to which all other particles are attracted." If there is anything in American life which can be described as an over-all American culture which serves as a reference point for immigrants and their children, it can best be described, it seems to us, as the middle-class cultural patterns of, largely, white Protestant, Anglo-Saxon origins, leaving aside for the moment the question of minor reciprocal influences on this culture exercised by the cultures of later entry into the United States, and ignoring also, for this purpose, the distinction between the upper-middle class and the lower-middle class cultural worlds.

There is a point on which I particularly do not wish to be misunderstood. I am not for one moment implying that the contribution of the non-Anglo-Saxon stock to the nature of American civilization has been minimal or slight. Quite the contrary. The qualitative record of achievement in industry, business, the professions, and the arts by Americans whose ancestors came from countries and traditions which are not British, or in many cases not even closely similar to British, is an overwhelmingly favorable one, and with reference to many individuals, a thoroughly brilliant one. Taken together with the substantial quantitative impact of these non-Anglo-Saxon groups on American industrial and agricultural development and on the demographic dimensions of the society, this record reveals an America in mid-twentieth century whose greatness rests on the contributions of many races, religions, and national backgrounds. My point, however, is that, with some exceptions, as the immigrants and their children have become Americans, their contributions, as laborers, farmers, doctors, lawyers, scientists, artists, etc., have been made *by way* of cultural patterns that have taken their major impress from the mould of the overwhelmingly English character of the dominant Anglo-Saxon culture or subculture in America, whose dominion dates from colonial times and whose *cultural* domination in the United States has never been seriously threatened. One must make a distinction between influencing the cultural patterns themselves and contributing to the progress and development of the society. It is in the latter area that the influence of the immigrants and their children in the United States has been decisive.

Accordingly, I shall follow Fishman's usage in referring to middle-class white Protestant Americans as constituting the "core society," or in my terms, the "core subsociety," and the cultural patterns of this group as the "core culture" or "core subculture." I shall use Hollingshead's term "core group" to refer to the white Protestant element at any social class level.

Let us now, for a moment, return to our fictitious land of Sylvania and imagine an immigration of Mundovians with a decidedly different outcome. In this case the Sylvanians accept many new behavior patterns and values from the Mundovians, just as the Mundovians change many of their ways in conformance with Sylvanian customs, this interchange taking place with appropriate modifications and compromises, and in this process a new cultural system evolves which is neither exclusively Sylvanian nor Mundovian but a mixture of both. This is a cultural blend, the result of the "melting pot," which has melted down the cultures of the two groups in the same societal container, as it were, and formed a new cultural product with standard consistency. This process has, of course, also involved thorough social mixing in primary as well as secondary groups and a large-scale process of intermarriage. The melting pot has melted the two groups into one, societally and culturally.

Whether such a process as just described is feasible or likely of occurrence is beside the point here. It, too, is an "ideal type," an abstraction against which we can measure the realities of what actually happens. Our point is that the seven variables of the assimilation process which we have isolated can be measured against the "melting pot" goal as well as against the "adaptation to the core society and culture" goal. That is, assuming the "melting pot" goal, we can then inquire how much acculturation of both groups has taken place to form such a blended culture, how much social structural mixture has taken place, and so on. We now have a model of assimilation with seven variables which can be used to analyze the assimilation process with reference to either of two variant goal-systems: 1) "adaptation to the core society and culture," and 2) the "melting pot." Theoretically, it would be possible to apply the analysis model of variables with reference to carrying out the goal-system of "cultural pluralism" as well. However, this would be rather premature at this point since the concept of cultural pluralism is itself so meagerly understood. . . .

Let us now apply this model of assimilation analysis in tentative fashion to selected "minority" ethnic groups on the American scene. The applied paradigm presented in Table 2 allows us to record and summarize a great deal of information compactly and comparatively. We shall deal here, for illustrative purposes, with four groups: Negroes, Jews, Catholics (excluding Negro and Spanish-speaking Catholics), and Puerto Ricans. The basic goal-referent will be "adaptation to core society and culture." The entries in the table cells may be regarded, at this point, as hypotheses. . . .

One of the tasks of sociological theory is not only to identify the factors or variables present in any given social process or situation, but also to hypothesize how these variables may be related to each other. Let us look at the seven assimilation variables from this point of view. We note that in Table 2, of the four ethnic groups listed, only one, the Puerto Ricans, are designated as being substantially unassimilated culturally. The Puerto Ricans are the United States' newest immigrant group of major size. If we now examine the entries for the Negro, one of America's oldest minorities, we find that assimilation has not taken place in most of the other variables, but with allowance for social class factors, *has* taken place culturally. These two facts in juxtaposition should give us a clue to the relation of the cultural assimilation variable to all the others. This relationship may be stated as follows: 1) *cultural assimilation, or acculturation, is likely to be the first of the types of assimilation to occur when a minority group arrives on the scene; and 2) cultural assimilation, or acculturation, of the minority group may take place even when none of the other types of assimilation occurs simultaneously or later, and this condition of "acculturation only" may continue indefinitely.*

If we examine the history of immigration into the United States, both of these propositions are seen to be borne out. After the birth of the republic, as each succeeding wave of immigration, first from Northern and Western Europe, later from Southern and Eastern Europe and the Orient, has spread over America, the first process that has occurred has been the taking on of the English language and American behav-

312

ior patterns, even while the creation of the immigrant colonies sealed off their members from extensive primary contacts with "core society" Americans and even when prejudice and discrimination against the minority have been at a high point. While this process is only partially completed in the immigrant generation itself, with the second and succeeding generations, exposed to the American public school system and speaking English as their native tongue, the impact of the American acculturation process has been overwhelming; the rest becomes a matter of social class mobility and the kind of acculturation that such mobility demands. On the other hand, the success of the acculturation process has by no means guaranteed entry of each minority into the primary groups and institutions—that is, the subsociety—of the white Protestant group. With the exception of white Protestant immigrant stock from Northern and Western Europe—I am thinking here particularly of the Scandinavians, Dutch, and Germans—by and large such structural mixture on the primary level has not taken place. Nor has such acculturation success eliminated prejudice and discrimination or in many cases led to large-scale intermarriage with the core society.

The only qualifications of my generalizations about the rapidity and success of the acculturation process that the American experience suggests are these: 1) If a minority group is spatially isolated and segregated (whether voluntarily or not) in a rural area, as is the case with the American Indians still on reservations, even the acculturation process will be very slow; and 2) Unusually marked discrimination,

Table 2

PARADIGM OF ASSIMILATION

Applied to Selected Groups in the United States—
Basic Goal Referent: Adaptation to Core Society and Culture

Group	Type of Assimilation						
	Cultural	Structural	Marital	Identificational	Attitude Receptional	Behavior Receptional	Civic
Negroes	Variation by class	No	No	No	No	No	Yes
Jews	Substantially Yes	No	Substantially No	No	No	Partly	Mostly
Catholics (excluding Negro and Spanish-speaking)	Substantially Yes	Partly (variation by area)	Partly	No	Partly	Mostly	Partly
Puerto Ricans	Mostly No	No	No	No	No	No	Partly

313

such as that which has been faced by the American Negro, if it succeeds in keeping vast numbers of the minority group deprived of educational and occupational opportunities and thus predestined to remain in a lower-class setting, may indefinitely retard the acculturation process for the group. Even in the case of the American Negro, however, from the long view or perspective of American history, this effect of discrimination will be seen to have been a delaying action only; the quantitatively significant emergence of the middle-class Negro is already well on its way.

Before we leave specific examination of the acculturation variable and its relationships, it would be well to distinguish between two types of cultural patterns and traits which may characterize any ethnic group. Some, like its religious beliefs and practices, its ethical values, its musical tastes, folk recreational patterns, literature, historical language, and sense of a common past, are essential and vital ingredients of the group's cultural heritage, and derive exactly from that heritage. We shall refer to these as *intrinsic* cultural traits or patterns. Others, such as dress, manner, patterns of emotional expression, and minor oddities in pronouncing and inflecting English, tend to be products of the historical vicissitudes of a group's adjustment to its local environment, including the present one (and also reflect social class experiences and values), and are in a real sense, external to the core of the group's ethnic cultural heritage. These may conveniently be referred to as *extrinsic* cultural traits or patterns. To illustrate, the Catholicism or Judaism of the immigrant from Southern or Eastern Europe repre-

sents a difference in *intrinsic culture* from the American core society and its Protestant religious affiliation. However, the greater volatility of emotional expression of the Southern and Eastern European peasant or villager in comparison with the characteristically greater reserve of the upper-middle class American of the core society constitutes a difference in *extrinsic culture*. To take another example, the variant speech pattern, or argot, of the lower-class Negro of recent southern background, which is so widespread both in the South and in northern cities, is a product of external circumstances and is not something vital to Negro culture. It is thus an *extrinsic* cultural trait. Were this argot, which constitutes such a powerful handicap to social mobility and adjustment to the core culture, to disappear, nothing significant for Negro self-regard as a group or the Negro's sense of ethnic history and identity would be violated. While this distinction between intrinsic and extrinsic culture is a tentative one, and cannot be uniformly applied to all cultural traits, it is still a useful one and may help cast further light on the acculturation process, particularly in its relationship to prejudice and discrimination.

As we examine the array of assimilation variables again, several other relationships suggest themselves. One is the indissoluble connection, in the time order indicated, between structural assimilation and marital assimilation. That is, entrance of the minority group into the social cliques, clubs, and institutions of the core society at the primary group level inevitably will lead to a substantial amount of intermarriage. If children of different ethnic backgrounds belong to the same play-group,

later the same adolescent cliques, and at college the same fraternities and sororities; if the parents belong to the same country club and invite each other to their homes for dinner; it is completely unrealistic not to expect these children, now grown, to love and to marry each other, blithely oblivious to previous ethnic extraction. Communal leaders of religious and nationality groups that desire to maintain their ethnic identity are aware of this connection, which is one reason for the proliferation of youth groups, adult clubs, and communal institutions which tend to confine their members in their primary relationships safely within the ethnic fold.

If marital assimilation, an inevitable by-product of structural assimilation, takes place fully, the minority group loses its ethnic identity in the larger host or core society, and identificational assimilation takes place. Prejudice and discrimination are no longer a problem, since eventually the descendants of the original minority group become indistinguishable, and since primary group relationships tend to build up an "in-group" feeling which encloses all the members of the group. If assimilation has been complete in all intrinsic as well as extrinsic cultural traits, then no value conflicts on civic issues are likely to arise between the now dispersed descendants of the ethnic minority and members of the core society. Thus the remaining types of assimilation have all taken place like a row of tenpins bowled over in rapid succession by a well placed strike. We may state the emergent generalization, then, as follows: *Once structural assimilation has occurred, either simultaneously with or subsequent to acculturation, all of the other types of assimilation will naturally follow.* It need hardly be pointed out that while acculturation, as we have emphasized above, does not necessarily lead to structural assimilation, structural assimilation inevitably produces acculturation. Structural assimilation, then, rather than acculturation, is seen to be the keystone of the arch of assimilation. The price of such assimilation, however, is the disappearance of the ethnic group as a separate entity and the evaporation of its distinctive values.

There are a number of other crucial hypotheses and questions which can be phrased by the manipulation of these variables. One of the most important, of course, is whether "attitude receptional" and "behavior receptional" assimilation—that is, elimination of prejudice and discrimination—may take place when acculturation, *but not structural assimilation,* occurs. This can be shown to be one of the key questions in the application of our analytical model to "cultural pluralism." . . . Another interesting question is whether prejudice and discrimination are more closely related to differences between the core group and the ethnic minority in intrinsic culture traits or extrinsic culture traits. I would hypothesize that, at least in our era, differences in extrinsic culture are more crucial in the development of prejudice than those of an intrinsic nature. Differences in religious belief, *per se,* are not the occasion for bitter acrimony in twentieth-century America, particularly when these differences occur in middle-class Americans of native birth whose external appearance, speech patterns, and manner are notably uniform. On the other hand, the gap in extrinsic cultural traits between the zoot-suited side-burned slum juvenile and the conservatively clothed and behaving middle-class American distinctly gives the signal for mutual suspicion and hostility. This is not to say that differences in intrinsic values among ethnic groups in America, particularly as these differences spill over into demands on the shaping of American public life, may not result in power conflict. But one must make a distinction between irrational ethnic prejudice, in what might be called the old-fashioned sense, and the conflict of groups in the civic arena over issues based on opposing value-premises, sincerely held in each case.

We shall forgo additional manipulation of the variables in the analytical model at this point since the preceding discussion should have clarified its potential use. We now have an analytical scheme—a set of conceptual categories—which allows us to appreciate the true complexity of the assimilation process, to note the varying directions it may take, and to discern the probable relationships of some of its parts. This set of analytical tools should serve us well as we consider the theories of assimilation and minority group life which have arisen historically in America. ■

316

Many observers regard the Japanese Americans as a classic example of a racial minority that has "made it" in America in relatively recent times. In the following selection, sociologist Harry H. L. Kitano explains the nature of the assimilation of Japanese Americans and why this process has been possible.

Source: Harry H. L. Kitano, *Japanese Americans: The Evolution of a Subculture* (Englewood Cliffs, N.J.: Prentice-Hall, 1969), pp. 143–147.

American Assimilation and the Japanese Subculture

Sixty years has produced a marked change in the attitudes of both the Caucasian majority and the Japanese minority in the United States. Marital preference remains ingroup, but the groups themselves are less rigid in their attitudes, and intermarriage brings little opprobrium. The results of the postwar occupation of Japan and the large numbers of Japanese warbrides are obvious. As a Caucasian airlines pilot once remarked to this writer, speaking of his Japanese bride, "No one pays much attention to us since there was that movie (*Sayonara*) with Marlon Brando." Perhaps this generalization sounds somewhat too "Hollywoodish," but there is little doubt that the general direction of assimilation, generation by generation, will include biological as well as social integration. An important but often overlooked integration variable also includes the desirability of the Japanese female from American eyes, although such an attraction may be somewhat overexaggerated. Another important point concerning race and acceptance for the Japanese was the factor of differential perception and differential acceptance from the majority group. Although it may have seemed to the Japanese that most everybody in the United States was always against them (especially during certain periods), this was not so. There were regional differences; there were social class differences and there were always a number of influential "Japanophiles"—those who "loved" Japan and the Japanese. Therefore, he was not subjected to the well-nigh universal degree of constant hostility that has been the lot of other ethnic groups.

Cultural Pluralism

This leads to a pertinent question: What has been the most significant factor in the Japanese acculturative process? The answer seems to be the pluralistic development of a congruent Japanese culture within the framework of the larger American society. If we may be permitted a somewhat elaborate metaphor, this development may be envisioned as two trees, sprung from different seeds but flourishing in the same soil, in identical climatic conditions, the younger of them springing up by the side of the older, so that although the two trunks, rooted in similar values and aspirations, nourished by similar factors of education and industry, are separate, their branches intermingle, and eventually, it may be difficult to distinguish the leaves of one from the leaves of the other. The organic and gradual nature of this metaphor is particularly appropriate to cultural pluralism, yet it must be emphasized that this mode of acculturation seems only to work when two cultures spring from relatively similar seeds. The exotic plant of some cultures seems not to flourish in American soil. For some groups it seems apparent that cultural pluralism hinders acculturation and assimilation simply because the discrepancies between the cultures seem to lead to increased divergence and intergroup tensions. In such cases, assimilation seems to require the dissolution of one of the cultures, and its substitution by more "American" patterns of behavior. Such a process inevitably requires more time, more conflict, raises critical questions of value, and creates more difficulties for the individuals and cultures caught in the process. Further, as we have

San Francisco Convention and Visitors Bureau

mentioned in our opening chapter, there may be a functional order so that the smoothest method of adaptation follows an acculturation, integration, and assimilation sequence.

A comparison of cultural pluralism with other modes of acculturation immediately involves one in the subtleties of possible modes of selective cultural pluralism. For instance, a purely cultural-pluralistic development might imply, say, the retention of the native language as well as its customs and values. Yet the Japanese have quickly and almost completely discarded the Japanese language, and artificial attempts to preserve it (e.g., Japanese language school) have largely failed. In other dimensions, too, certain unwieldy Japanese customs were almost immediately supplanted by more efficient American ones. The potential inherent in cultural

pluralism for retaining some elements of a distinctive way of life and discarding others is one of its most attractive elements. It is a cliché to say of America that it is a great melting pot, meaning, presumably, that the disparate elements that comprise it are eventually commingled in an amorphous brew labeled "the norm," and that this is desirable. Yet, surely, the distinctive contribution of Oriental, of Mexican, of African, and many other cultures, could greatly improve the savour of the bland American brew. The cultural-pluralistic development of the Japanese-American group so far provides another example of how the native and American may coexist.

Structural Pluralism

The problem of structural pluralism is a related issue. Followed to an ultimate

extreme, it might describe a society with a vast number of independent groups maintained through restrictions on friendship, dating, and marriage. There is an obvious danger to the proliferation of such structures—the restriction of friendship and marriage to persons within one's own network could very well foster a strong "we" and "they" feeling, leading to less communication, more misunderstanding, more prejudiced attitudes and higher levels of discrimination.

The development of pluralistic structures for the Japanese was originally based more on necessity than choice—there was little opportunity for Japanese to enter into the social structure of the larger community. Currently, however, the matter of choice appears to be of a more voluntary nature—most Japanese can enter into the social structures of the larger society, although there is always the element of greater risk and possible rejection for those choosing this path. The continued existence of the ethnic structures, however, limits the opportunity for "risk-taking," and many Japanese who might otherwise have ventured into the larger society choose the easy way out through participation in the ethnic structures (even though these groups are as "American" as any). The comment of "being more comfortable and at ease with one's own kind" covers many situations. However, many Japanese still need the ethnic structures and the justification for the cradle-to-grave services (e.g., a Japanese doctor will be on hand at delivery; a Japanese priest will perform over the burial; and in between, one can live a life of friends, dating, and marriage primarily with other Japanese) provided by the ethnic community is important; however, the structures may be playing a negative role when their strength pulls back some who might venture into the larger society. This writer feels that social interaction based primarily on interest and achievement is healthier than one based on ethnicity.

Judged by most standards, the coexistence between the Japanese and American cultures has been successful. Education, productivity, and "Americanism" have been high, and crime, delinquency, and other forms of social deviance have been low. And if we remember that this has been accomplished by a nonwhite group, the progress appears even more remarkable.

Interestingly enough, the adaptation of the Japanese to the United States is similar to that of many European groups. . . . A typical pattern of interaction between groups starts with contact, followed by competition, then by accommodation. Accommodation is usually accompanied by segregated ethnic islands, which eventually leads to the final stage of assimilation. When an observer takes a long-range historical view of the interaction between two cultures, the process as described by Park appears to have high validity. It must be added, however, that this model can function best when there are equal opportunities (e.g., especially in education and employment) and where there is a willingness on the part of both cultures to accommodate to each other.

The unusual part of the Japanese adaptation is that it is being accomplished by a "nonwhite" group and a population heretofore considered to be "unassimilable." In fact, the adaptation has been of such a quality that it has been termed a "model American minority."

But we must also be reminded that the judgment of Japanese Americans as the "model American minority" is made from a strictly majority point of view. Japanese Americans are good because they conform —they don't "make waves"—they work hard and are quiet and docile. As in a colonial situation, there tends to be one set of prescriptions for those in power and another for the subject people. But, ideally, members of the ethnic community should share in any evaluation of the efficacy of their adjustment. For if the goals of the American society include freeing an individual for self-expression and creativity, and if social maturity includes originality, participation, and the opportunity for individuals to function at their highest levels, then certain questions may be asked about the Japanese. It may be a disservice to some of them to continue calling them "good" and reinforcing their present adaptation. The kind of goodness that led them to accept the wartime evacuation can, in the long run, be a drawback as well as a strength. Perhaps this is one group where emphasis on the self—the development of individual self and the satisfaction of ego needs—can be more highly emphasized.

However, it would be tragic if some of the strengths of the Japanese culture were to be forgotten. The ability to look beyond self and to act in relation to others is an admirable quality, and the ethnic identity, whether in terms of a nation and manifested as pride, or in terms of a community, helped the Japanese achieve a degree of cohesion and group loyalty that appears important for a meaningful life. Without an abstraction that leads beyond self, life may regress to self-indulgence and to self-gratification so that the accumulation of wealth and power—often associated with "success"—may only be an empty victory. Hopefully, the next generation of Japanese Americans will integrate the best of the Japanese and the American cultures so that their lives will reflect the richness of both. But, at the risk of being unduly pessimistic, the probability that they may draw from the more negative elements of both of the cultures is also a realistic prospect.

We have described a group that has been effective in social organization, effective in socialization, effective in controlling deviant behavior, and effective in "becoming successful" in American terms. When we look back on the past prejudice and discrimination faced by the Japanese, we find that even their most optimistic dreams have been surpassed. Such a story may give us some optimism for the future of race relations in the American society.

1 How does each author define the assimilation process? What kinds of evidence and criteria does each use? Are their premises similar or different?

2 What values show in each acccunt?

3 Do any of the accounts agree with the melting pot theory put forth by de Crèvecoeur and Zangwill at the beginning of this unit?

4 How would you explain your own opinion about assimilation in American life? ■

PREPARING
A CASE STUDY
ON ASSIMILATION

In this unit we have sought to analyze the assimilation process as it has affected the American Indian and the American black. We have also raised certain broader questions regarding ethnicity and ethnic tensions in American society. To further your understanding of the problems involved, select any other racial or ethnic group resident in the United States and prepare a case study on that group's response to the assimilation process. You may wish to use some of the criteria established by Oscar Handlin, Milton Gordon, and Harry H. L. Kitano, but you can also make use of some other set of variables. However, your case study should include:

1 The definition of assimilation you have adopted for the purposes of your research.

2 Historic perceptions of the group both by insiders and outsiders.

3 The political, social, and economic relationship of the group to the larger society.

4 Present perceptions of cultural assimilation by leaders of the group.

The following bibliography should help you begin your study.

Gordon, Milton. *Assimilation in American Life.* New York: Oxford University Press, 1964. A basic sociological treatise on the acceptance of various ethnic and racial groups into American society.

Glazer, Nathan, and Moynihan, Daniel. *Beyond the Melting Pot.* Cambridge: MIT Press, 1970. A new edition of the classic study of minorities in New York City.

Handlin, Oscar. *The Newcomers: Negroes and Puerto Ricans in a Changing Metropolis.* Cambridge: Harvard University Press, 1959. Handlin's theory of assimilation as applied to newcomers to American cities. ■

How have Americans throughout our history tried to
reform their cities?

Should the main object of urban reform be efficiency,
the welfare of city residents, or beautification?

Has urban renewal failed?

How are urban governments organized, priorities
established, and programs put into action?

Are the problems of modern cities insoluble, or can we
remake our urban civilization?

URBANIZATION IN AMERICA

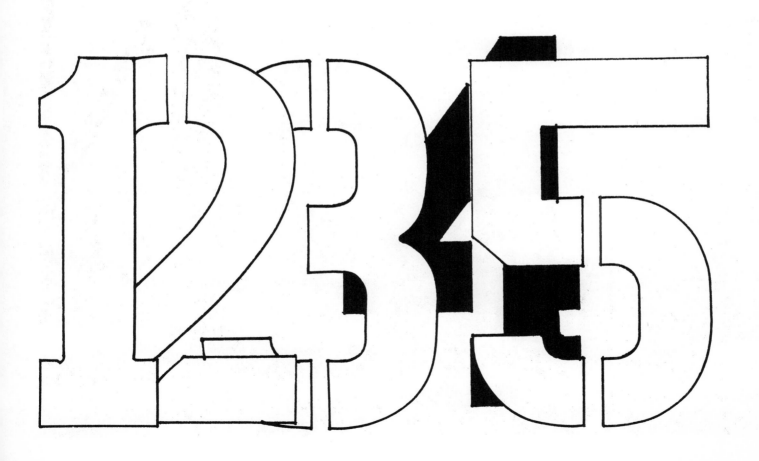

IMAGES OF THE CITY IN AMERICAN ART

paintings were done by the same artist. Study form, shape, color, perspective, shading, texture, and content in making this determination. Then, by means of a comparative approach, answer the following questions.

1 What kinds of people, in what kinds of activities and situations, are portrayed? What kinds of natural and man-made objects are shown? What is the relationship between the natural and the man-made?

2 What emotional and intellectual response to the city is the artist attempting to evoke? Can you make any assumptions about the artist's values or about his feelings toward the city? How would you compare the attitudes of the artists?

3 What other information would you need to confirm that this was in fact the artist's conception? ∎

The paintings on these pages depict the city as it was seen by American artists at the turn of the twentieth century. Several are by painters who belonged to the so-called Ashcan school of art. This designation is an indication that these artists were looking at themes new to American art. The subject matter of their paintings focused on aspects of the growing city, and by the particular people and scenes they chose to portray they were in fact expressing their own thoughts and feelings about the urban complexes rising around them. In this exercise, you are asked to study these paintings to find out what the artists' conceptions of the American city were and how they translated them to canvas.

The first thing you should do is to sort the paintings by artist. Ask yourself which

Blue Morning
National Gallery of Art
Washington, D.C.

Backyards, Greenwich Village
Collection Whitney Museum of American Art

324

Madison Square, New York
Collection of Mrs. Charles Prendergast

Herald Square
Museum of Fine Arts, Boston

Steaming Streets
Santa Barbara Museum of Art

Pigeons
Museum of Fine Arts, Boston

326

Park Street, Boston
Museum of Fine Arts, Boston

The Lone Tenement
National Gallery of Art
Washington, D.C.

328

The Mall, Central Park
Courtesy of the Art Institute of Chicago

Fifth Avenue Critics
Library of Congress

Late Afternoon, Public Garden
Museum of Fine Arts, Boston

330

THE RISE OF THE CENTRAL CITY

The rapid growth of cities after the Civil War brought about profound alterations in American society as more and more Americans left the slower rhythms of life in the rural countryside to crowd into cities where the opportunities for economic success and for new excitements of every kind seemed almost unlimited. In 1860, only one sixth of the American population lived in cities of 8,000 or more. By 1900, more than 25,000,000 Americans, or one third of the entire population, were living in cities—most of them in the larger cities that were being created by the accelerating pace of the Industrial Revolution. In 1960, more than 110,000,000 Americans, three fifths of the total population, lived in urban areas of over 50,000.

Within a hundred years, then, America was transformed from a society of rural towns and villages into a highly urbanized society in which nearly half the population lived in the great population clusters that had collected around the larger metropolitan centers of the eastern seaboard, the Middle West, the Southwest, and California. But the growth of cities in the first decades of this transformation was quite different from the urban sprawl that has occurred in more recent decades. In the period before 1910, most of the population movement was flowing into the central city. The most viable part of the city was its central core, where factories, office buildings, warehouses, banks, libraries, schools, and theaters were located. Laborers, office clerks, bankers, and professional men and women—nearly everyone—lived close to their places of employment and recreation.

Since 1910, the electric trolley car, the commuter train, and especially the automobile have made it possible for people to live in residences farther away from their places of work. Cities began to spread out and suburban rings around them began to grow faster than the central core. Indeed, little by little, the central city became a place of great skyscrapers, office buildings, and apartments owned and inhabited by the rich and the powerful which was surrounded by blighted areas inhabited by the poor and the powerless.

In both periods of urban growth, the problems of organizing and governing the city have been enormous. Much of the history of twentieth-century America has been shaped by the effort to deal with these problems, and the future of this country will depend, to a large degree, upon our ability to turn these huge megalopolitan clusters into attractive and livable places for people of all social backgrounds.

In the first stage of our inquiry into the problems of the city we will look at the politics of urbanization at the turn of the twentieth century, when the central cities seemed strong and viable. At this time, municipal power was in the hands of political bosses who had organized powerful political machines to take advantage of the opportunities for extortion and graft offered by the need for the rapid development of a whole host of municipal services such as water and sewer lines, gas and electric services, paved streets, and rapid transit systems. At the same time, municipal reformers saw the possibility of developing new techniques for the efficient organization of municipal services

and new methods of urban planning that would make cities beautiful and attractive places where human beings could live. The battle between bosses and reformers at the beginning of the twentieth century, therefore, sets the stage for an informed dialogue about the quality of life in our cities that has continued down to today. ■

THE ELECTIVE SYSTEM; OR, MASTER AND SLAVE.

"GROSS IRREGULARITY NOT 'FRAUDULENT.'"

BOSS SWEED. "To make this *book straight* is the hardest job I ever had. What made WATSON go sleigh-riding?"

TWEEDLEDEE AND SWEEDLEDUM.

(*A New Christmas Pantomime at the Tammany Hall.*)

CLOWN (*to PANTALOON*). "Let's Blind them with *this*, and then take *some more*."

PERCEPTIONS OF
BOSS POLITICS

On the following pages are several different images of the "political boss" who played such a prominent role in American urban life in the fifty-year period following the Civil War. One such image can be found in the collection of political cartoons by Thomas Nast; the second is taken from a magazine article by Lincoln Steffens, the famous muckraker; the third is a selection from the writings of Jane Addams, the pioneer social worker; and the fourth is a collection of anecdotes by several political bosses.

Who the hell are the truant officers to say that a boy ought to be sent to reform school? Frank Hague was a problem child. Suppose those guys had sent him to an institution? He'd have learned how to be really bad and he might have come out Frank Hague, the public enemy, instead of Frank Hague, the first citizen of his city and the leading citizen of New Jersey.

NO VICE, NO CRIME,
NO RACKETEERING.

I made the city. Nobody cared a damn about it until I came along.

Frank Hague
Jersey City, New Jersey

Mr. Crump won't 'low no easy riders here, Mr. Crump won't 'low no easy riders here. We don't care what Mr. Crump don't 'low, We goin' to barrelhouse anyhow, Mr. Crump can go catch hisself some air!

Memphis should be conducted as a great business corporation in which there are 200,000 stockholders, and not as a place to be exploited by politicians.

We all expect to work for the interest of the city. If we do, we will get good results under the new form of government. I've only this to say: Everyone must work; there must be no grafting and no drunkenness.

Ed Crump
Memphis, Tennessee

If there's a fire in Ninth, Tenth or Eleventh Avenue, for example, any hour of the day or night, I'm usually there with some of my election district captains as soon as the fire engines. If a family is burned out, I don't ask whether they are Republicans or Democrats, and I don't refer them to the Charity Organization Society, . . .
If there's a family in my district in want I know it before the Charitable Societies do, and me and my men are first on the ground. I have a special corps to look up such cases. The consequence is that the poor look up to George W. Plunkitt as a father, come to him in trouble — and don't forget him on election day.

Puttin' on style don't pay in politics. The people won't stand for it. If you've got an achin' for style, sit down on it till you have made your pile and landed a Supreme Court Justiceship with a fourteen-year term at $17,500 a year, or some job of that kind.

The civil service law is the biggest fraud of the age. It is the curse of the nation. There can't be no real patriotism while it lasts. How are you goin' to interest our young men in their country if you have no offices to give them when they work for their party?

George Plunkitt
New York

Brown Brothers

1 How are these portrayals of the boss alike or different? How would you account for the differences in perception?

2 How does each source describe the boss? What kind of details are given of his personal characteristics? Of his methods of operation? Of the goals to which he aspired? Of the sources of his popularity and power? Of the uses to which he put power?

3 On which of these factors does each source concentrate? Which factors are ignored?

4 Based on all four sources, what would you hypothesize were the principal characteristics of an American city "boss"? ■

334

Source: Lincoln Steffens, *The Shame of the Cities* (New York: S. S. McClure Co., 1904), pp. 69–96.

"Boodlers" in St. Louis:
A Case Study

In other cities mere exposure has been sufficient to overthrow a corrupt régime. In St. Louis the conviction of the boodlers leaves the felons in control, the system intact, and the people—spectators. It is these people who are interesting—these people, and the system they have made possible.

The convicted boodlers have described the system to me. There was no politics in it—only business. The city of St. Louis is normally Republican. Founded on the home-rule principle, the corporation is a distinct political entity, with no county to confuse it. The State of Missouri, however, is normally Democratic, and the legislature has taken political possession of the city by giving to the Governor the appointment of the Police and Election Boards. With a defective election law, the Democratic boss in the city became its absolute ruler.

This boss is Edward R. Butler, better known as "Colonel Ed," or "Colonel Butler," or just "Boss." He is an Irishman by birth, a master horseshoer by trade, a good fellow—by nature, at first, then by profession. Along in the seventies, when he still wore the apron of his trade, and bossed his tough ward, he secured the agency for a certain patent horseshoe which the city railways liked and bought. Useful also as a politician, they gave him a blanket contract to keep all their mules and horses shod. Butler's farrieries glowed all about the town, and his political influence spread with his business; for everywhere big Ed Butler went there went a smile also, and encouragement for your

weakness, no matter what it was. Like "Doc" Ames, of Minneapolis—like the "good fellow" everywhere—Butler won men by helping them to wreck themselves. A priest, the Rev. James Coffey, once denounced Butler from the pulpit as a corrupter of youth; at another time a mother knelt in the aisle of a church, and during service audibly called upon Heaven for a visitation of affliction upon Butler for having ruined her son. These and similar incidents increased his power by advertising it. He grew bolder. He has been known to walk out of a voting-place and call across a cordon of police to a group of men at the curb, "Are there any more repeaters out here that want to vote again?"

They will tell you in St. Louis that Butler never did have much real power, that his boldness and the clamor against him made him seem great. Public protest is part of the power of every boss. So far, however, as I can gather, Butler was the leader of his organization, but only so long as he was a partisan politician; as he became a "boodler" pure and simple, he grew careless about his machine, and did his boodle business with the aid of the worst element of both parties. At any rate, the boodlers, and others as well, say that in later years he had about equal power with both parties, and he certainly was the ruler of St. Louis during the Republican administration of Ziegenhein, which was the worst in the history of the city. His method was to dictate enough of the candidates on both tickets to enable him, by selecting the worst from each, to elect the sort of men he required in his business. In other words, while honest

Democrats and Republicans were "loyal to party" (a point of great pride with the idiots) and "voted straight," the Democratic boss and his Republican lieutenants decided what part of each ticket should be elected; then they sent around Butler's "Indians" (repeaters) by the van load to scratch ballots and "repeat" their votes, till the worst had made sure of the government by the worst, and Butler was in a position to do business.

His business was boodling, which is a more refined and a more dangerous form of corruption than the police blackmail of Minneapolis. It involves, not thieves, gamblers, and common women, but influential citizens, capitalists, and great corporations. For the stock-in-trade of the boodler is the rights, privileges, franchises, and real property of the city, and his source of corruption is the top, not the bottom, of society. Butler, thrown early in his career into contact with corporation managers, proved so useful to them that they introduced him to other financiers, and the scandal of his services attracted to him in due course all men who wanted things the city had to give. The boodlers told me that, according to the tradition of their combine, there "always was boodling in St. Louis."

Butler organized and systematized and developed it into a regular financial institution, and made it an integral part of the business community. He had for clients, regular or occasional, bankers and promoters; and the statements of boodlers, not yet on record, allege that every transportation and public convenience company that touches St. Louis had dealings with Butler's combine. And my best information is that these interests were not victims. Blackmail came in time, but in the beginning they originated the schemes of loot and started Butler on his career. Some interests paid him a regular salary, others a fee, and again he was a partner in the enterprise, with a special "rake-off" for his influence. "Fee" and "present" are his terms, and he has spoken openly of taking and giving them. I verily believe he regarded his charges as legitimate (he is the Croker type); but he knew that some people thought his services wrong. He once said that, when he had received his fee for a piece of legislation, he "went home and prayed that the measure might pass," and, he added facetiously, that "usually his prayers were answered."

His prayers were "usually answered" by the Municipal Assembly. This legislative body is divided into two houses—the upper, called the Council, consisting of thirteen members, elected at large; the lower, called the House of Delegates, with twenty-eight members, elected by wards; and each member of these bodies is paid twenty-five dollars a month salary by the city. With the mayor, this Assembly has practically complete control of all public property and valuable rights. Though Butler sometimes could rent or own the mayor, he preferred to be independent of him, so he formed in each part of the legislature a two-thirds majority—in the Council nine, in the House nineteen—which could pass bills over a veto. These were the "combines." They were regularly organized, and did their business under parliamentary rules. Each "combine" elected its chairman, who was elected chairman also of the legal bodies, where he appointed the committees, naming to each a majority of combine members.

In the early history of the combines, Butler's control was complete, because it was political. He picked the men who were to be legislators; they did as he bade them do, and the boodling was noiseless, safe, and moderate in price. Only wrongful acts were charged for, and a right once sold was good; for Butler kept his word. The definition of an honest man as one who will stay bought fitted him. But it takes a very strong man to control himself and others when the money lust grows big, and it certainly grew big in St. Louis. Butler used to watch the downtown districts. He knew everybody, and when a railroad wanted a switch, or a financial house a franchise, Butler learned of it early. Sometimes he discovered the need and suggested it. Naming the regular price, say $10,000, he would tell the "boys" what was coming, and that there would be $1,000 to divide. He kept the rest, and the city got nothing. The bill was introduced and held up till Butler gave the word that the money was in hand; then it passed. As the business grew, however, not only illegitimate, but legitimate permissions were charged for, and at gradually increasing rates. Citizens who asked leave to make excavations in streets for any purpose, neighborhoods that had to have street lamps—all had to pay, and they did pay. In later years there was no other way. Business men who complained felt a certain pressure brought to bear on them from most unexpected quarters downtown.

A business man told me that a railroad which had a branch near his factory suggested that he go to the Municipal Legislature and get permission to have a switch run into his yard. He liked the idea, but when he found it would cost him eight or ten thousand dollars, he gave it up. Then the railroad became slow about handling his freight. He understood, and, being a fighter, he ferried the goods across the river to another road. That brought him the switch; and when he asked about it, the railroad man said:

"Oh, we got it done. You see, we pay a regular salary to some of those fellows, and they did it for us for nothing."

"Then why in the deuce did you send me to them?" asked the manufacturer.

"Well, you see," was the answer, "we like to keep in with them, and when we can throw them a little outside business we do."

In other words, a great railway corporation, not content with paying bribe salaries to these boodle aldermen, was ready, further to oblige them, to help coerce a manufacturer and a customer to go also and be blackmailed by the boodlers. "How can you buck a game like that?" this man asked me.

Very few tried to. Blackmail was all in the ordinary course of business, and the habit of submission became fixed—a habit of mind. The city itself was kept in darkness for weeks, pending the payment of $175,000 in bribes on the lighting contract, and complaining citizens went for light where Mayor Ziegenhein told them to go—to the moon.

Boodling was safe, and boodling was fat. Butler became rich and greedy, and neglectful of politics. Outside capital came in, and finding Butler bought, went over

his head to the boodle combines. These creatures learned thus the value of franchises, and that Butler had been giving them an unduly small share of the boodle.

Then began a struggle, enormous in its vile melodrama, for control of corruption—Butler to squeeze the municipal legislators and save his profits, they to wring from him their "fair share." Combines were formed within the old combines to make him pay more; and although he still was the legislative agent of the inner ring, he had to keep in his secret pay men who would argue for low rates, while the combine members, suspicious of one another, appointed their own legislative agent to meet Butler. Not sure even then, the cliques appointed "trailers" to follow their agent, watch him enter Butler's house, and then follow him to the place where the money was to be distributed. Charles A. Gutke and John K. Murrell represented Butler in the House of Delegates, Charles Kratz and Fred G. Uthoff in the Council. The other members suspected that these men got "something big on the side," so Butler had to hire a third to betray the combine to him. In the House, Robertson was the man. When Gutke had notified the chairman that a deal was on, and a meeting was called, the chairman would say:

"Gentlemen, the business before us to-night is [say] the Suburban Railway Bill. How much shall we ask for it?"

Gutke would move that "the price be $40,000." Some member of the outer ring would move $100,000 as fair boodle. The debate often waxed hot, and you hear of the drawing of revolvers. In this case (of the Suburban Railway) Robertson rose

and moved a compromise of $75,000, urging moderation, lest they get nothing, and his price was carried. Then they would lobby over the appointment of the agent. They did not want Gutke, or anyone Butler owned, so they chose some other; and having adjourned, the outer ring would send a "trailer" to watch the agent, and sometimes a second "trailer" to watch the first.

They began to work up business on their own account, and, all decency gone, they sold out sometimes to both sides of a fight. The Central Traction deal in 1898 was an instance of this. Robert M. Snyder, a capitalist and promoter, of New York and Kansas City, came into St. Louis with a traction proposition inimical to the city railway interests. These felt secure. Through Butler they were paying seven members of the Council $5,000 a year each, but as a precaution John Scullin, Butler's associate, and one of the ablest capitalists of St. Louis, paid Councilman Uthoff a special retainer of $25,000 to watch the salaried boodlers. When Snyder found Butler and the combines against him, he set about buying the members individually, and, opening wine at his headquarters, began bidding for votes. This was the first break from Butler in a big deal, and caused great agitation among the boodlers. They did not go right over to Snyder; they saw Butler, and with Snyder's valuation of the franchise before them, made the boss go up to $175,000. Then the Council combine called a meeting in Gast's Garden to see if they could not agree on a price. Butler sent Uthoff there with instructions to cause a disagreement, or fix a price so high that

Snyder would refuse to pay it. Uthoff obeyed, and, suggesting $25,000, persuaded some members to hold out for it, till the meeting broke up in a row. Then it was each man for himself, and all hurried to see Butler, and to see Snyder too. In the scramble various prices were paid. Four councilmen got from Snyder $10,000 each, one got $15,000, another $17,500, and one $50,000; twenty-five members of the House of Delegates got $3,000 each from him. In all, Snyder paid $250,000 for the franchise, and since Butler and his backers paid only $175,000 to beat it, the franchise was passed. Snyder turned around and sold it to his old opponents for $1,250,000. It was worth twice as much.

The man who received $50,000 from Snyder was the same Uthoff who had taken $25,000 from John Scullin, and his story as he has told it since on the stand is the most comical incident of the exposure. He says Snyder, with his "overcoat full of money," came out to his house to see him. They sat together on a sofa, and when Snyder was gone Uthoff found beside him a parcel containing $50,000. This he returned to the promoter, with the statement that he could not accept it, since he had already taken $25,000 from the other side; but he intimated that he could take $100,000. This Snyder promised, so Uthoff voted for the franchise.

The next day Butler called at Uthoff's house. Uthoff spoke first.

"I want to return this," he said, handing Butler the package of $25,000.

"That's what I came after," said Butler.

When Uthoff told this in the trial of Snyder, Snyder's counsel asked why he returned this $25,000.

"Because it wasn't mine," exclaimed Uthoff, flushing with anger. "I hadn't earned it."

But he believed he had earned the $100,000, and he besought Snyder for that sum, or, anyway, the $50,000. Snyder made him drink, and gave him just $5,000, taking by way of receipt a signed statement that the reports of bribery in connection with the Central Traction deal were utterly false; that "I [Uthoff] know you [Snyder] to be as far above offering a bribe as I am of taking one."

Irregular as all this was, however, the legislators kept up a pretense of partisanship and decency. In the debates arranged for in the combine caucus, a member or two were told off to make partisan speeches. Sometimes they were instructed to attack the combine, and one or two of the rascals used to take delight in arraigning their friends on the floor of the House, charging them with the exact facts.

But for the serious work no one knew his party. Butler had with him Republicans and Democrats, and there were Republicans and Democrats among those against him. He could trust none not in his special pay. He was the chief boodle broker and the legislature's best client; his political influence began to depend upon his boodling instead of the reverse.

He is a millionaire two or three times over now, but it is related that to someone who advised him to quit in time he replied that it wasn't a matter of money alone with him; he liked the business, and would rather make fifty dollars out of a switch than $500 in stocks. He enjoyed buying franchises cheap and selling them dear. In the lighting deal of 1899 Butler

received $150,000, and paid out only $85,000—$47,500 to the House, $37,500 to the Council—and the haggling with the House combine caused those weeks of total darkness in the city. He had Gutke tell this combine that he could divide only $20,000 among them. They voted the measure, but, suspecting Butler of "holding out on them," moved to reconsider.

The citizens were furious, and a crowd went with ropes to the City Hall the night the motion to reconsider came up; but the combine was determined. Butler was there in person. He was more frightened than the delegates, and the sweat rolled down his face as he bargained with them. With the whole crowd looking on, and reporters so near that a delegate told me he expected to see the conversation in the papers the next morning, Butler threatened and pleaded, but finally promised to divide $47,500. That was an occasion for a burst of eloquence. The orators, indicating the citizens with ropes, declared that since it was plain the people wanted light, they would vote them light. And no doubt the people thought they had won, for it was not known till much later that the votes were bought by Butler, and that the citizens only hastened a corrupt bargain.

The next big boodle measure that Butler missed was the Suburban Traction, the same that led long after to disaster. This is the story Turner and Stock have been telling over and over in the boodle trials. Turner and his friends in the St. Louis Suburban Railway Company sought a franchise, for which they were willing to pay large bribes. Turner spoke about it to Butler, who said it would cost $145,000.

This seemed too much, and Turner asked Stock to lobby the measure through. Stock managed it, but it cost him $144,000—$135,000 for the combine, $9,000 extra for Meysenburg—and then, before the money was paid over and the company in possession of its privilege, an injunction put a stop to all proceedings. The money was in safe-deposit vaults—$75,000 for the House combine in one, $60,000 for the Council combine in the other—and when the legislature adjourned, a long fight for the money ensued. Butler chuckled over the bungling. He is said to have drawn from it the lesson that "when you want a franchise, don't go to a novice for it; pay an expert, and he'll deliver the goods."

But the combine drew their own conclusions from it, and their moral was, that though boodling was a business by itself, it was a good business, and so easy that anybody could learn it by study. And study it they did. Two of them told me repeatedly that they traveled about the country looking up the business, and that a fellowship had grown up among boodling aldermen of the leading cities in the United States. Committees from Chicago would come to St. Louis to find out what "new games" the St. Louis boodlers had, and they gave the St. Louisans hints as to how they "did the business" in Chicago. So the Chicago and St. Louis boodlers used to visit Cleveland and Pittsburgh and all the other cities, or, if the distance was too great, they got their ideas by those mysterious channels which run all through the "World of Graft." The meeting place in St. Louis was Decker's stable, and ideas unfolded there were developed into plans which, the boodlers say to-day, are only in abeyance. In Decker's stable the idea was born to sell the Union Market; and though the deal did not go through, the boodlers, when they saw it failing, made the market men pay $10,000 for killing it. This scheme is laid aside for the future. Another that failed was to sell the court-house, and this was well under way when it was discovered that the ground on which this public building stands was given to the city on condition that it was to be used for a court-house and nothing else.

But the grandest idea of all came from Philadelphia. In that city the gas-works were sold out to a private concern, and the water-works were to be sold next. The St. Louis fellows have been trying ever since to find a purchaser for their water-works. The plant is worth at least $40,-000,000. But the boodlers thought they could let it go at $15,000,000, and get $1,-000,000 or so themselves for the bargain. "The scheme was to do it and skip," said one of the boodlers who told me about it, "and if you could mix it all up with some filtering scheme it could be done; only some of us thought we could make more than $1,000,000 out of it—a fortune apiece. It will be done some day."

Such, then, is the boodling system as we see it in St. Louis. Everything the city owned was for sale by the officers elected by the people. The purchasers might be willing or unwilling takers; they might be citizens or outsiders; it was all one to the city government. So long as the members of the combines got the proceeds they would sell out the town. Would? They did and they will. If a city treasurer runs away with $50,000 there is a great halloo about it. In St. Louis the regularly

"WHAT ARE YOU GOING TO DO ABOUT IT," IF "OLD HONESTY" LETS HIM LOOSE AGAIN?

organized thieves who rule have sold $50,000,000 worth of franchises and other valuable municipal assets. This is the estimate made for me by a banker, who said that the boodlers got not one-tenth of the value of the things they sold, but were content because they got it all themselves. . . . ■

338

Source: Jane Addams, *Democracy and Social Ethics* (Cambridge, Mass.: Belknap Press, 1964), pp. 222–226; 229–230; 242–245; 265–269.

What Reformers Must Do

It is difficult both to interpret sympathetically the motives and ideals of those who have acquired rules of conduct in experience widely different from our own, and also to take enough care in guarding the gains already made, and in valuing highly enough the imperfect good so painfully acquired and, at the best, so mixed with evil. This wide difference in daily experience exhibits itself in two distinct attitudes toward politics. The well-to-do men of the community think of politics as something off by itself; they may conscientiously recognize political duty as part of good citizenship, but political effort is not the expression of their moral or social life. As a result of this detachment, "reform movements," started by business men and the better element, are almost wholly occupied in the correction of political machinery and with a concern for the better method of administration, rather than with the ultimate purpose of securing the welfare of the people. They fix their attention so exclusively on methods that they fail to consider the final aims of city government. This accounts for the growing tendency to put more and more responsibility upon executive officers and appointed commissions at the expense of curtailing the power of the direct representatives of the voters. Reform movements tend to become negative and to lose their educational value for the mass of the people. The reformers take the role of the opposition. They give themselves largely to criticisms of the present state of affairs, to writing and talking of what the future must be and of certain results which should be obtained. In trying to better matters, however, they have in mind only political achievements which they detach in a curious way from the rest of life, and they speak and write of the purification of politics as of a thing set apart from daily life.

On the other hand, the real leaders of the people are part of the entire life of the community which they control, and so far as they are representative at all, are giving a social expression to democracy. They are often politically corrupt, but in spite of this they are proceeding upon a sounder theory. Although they would be totally unable to give it abstract expression, they are really acting upon a formulation made by a shrewd English observer; namely, that, "after the enfranchisement of the masses, social ideals enter into political programmes, and they enter not as something which at best can be indirectly promoted by government, but as something which it is the chief business of government to advance directly."

Men living near to the masses of voters, and knowing them intimately, recognize this and act upon it; they minister directly to life and to social needs. They realize that the people as a whole are clamoring for social results, and they hold their power because they respond to that demand. They are corrupt and often do their work badly; but they at least avoid the mistake of a certain type of business men who are frightened by democracy, and have lost their faith in the people. The two standards are similar to those seen at a popular exhibition of pictures where the cultivated people care most for the technique of a given painting, the moving mass for a subject that shall be domestic and human.

This difference may be illustrated by the writer's experience in a certain ward of Chicago, during three campaigns, when efforts were made to dislodge an alderman who had represented the ward for many years. In this ward there are gathered together fifty thousand people, representing a score of nationalities; the newly emigrated Latin, Teuton, Celt, Greek, and Slav who live there have little in common save the basic experiences which come to men in all countries and under all conditions. In order to make fifty thousand people, so heterogeneous in nationality, religion, and customs, agree upon any demand, it must be founded upon universal experiences which are perforce individual and not social.

An instinctive recognition of this on the part of the alderman makes it possible to understand the individualistic basis of his political success, but it remains extremely difficult to ascertain the reasons for the extreme leniency of judgment concerning the political corruption of which he is constantly guilty.

*   *   *

The successful candidate, then, must be a good man according to the morality of his constituents. He must not attempt to hold up too high a standard, nor must he attempt to reform or change their standards. His safety lies in doing on a large scale the good deeds which his constituents are able to do only on a small scale. If he believes what they believe and does what they are all cherishing a secret ambition to do, he will dazzle them by his success and win their confidence. There is a certain wisdom in this course.

339

There is a common sense in the mass of men which cannot be neglected with impunity, just as there is sure to be an eccentricity in the differing and reforming individual which it is perhaps well to challenge.

* * *

We are constantly underestimating the amount of sentiment among simple people. The songs which are most popular among them are those of a reminiscent old age, in which the ripened soul calmly recounts and regrets the sins of his youth, songs in which the wayward daughter is forgiven by her loving parents, in which the lovers are magnanimous and faithful through all vicissitudes. The tendency is to condone and forgive, and not hold too rigidly to a standard. In the theatres it is the magnanimous man, the kindly reckless villain who is always applauded. So shrewd an observer as Samuel Johnson once remarked that it was surprising to find how much more kindness than justice society contained.

On the same basis the alderman manages several saloons, one down town within easy access of the city hall, where he can catch the more important of his friends. Here again he has seized upon an old tradition and primitive custom, the good fellowship which has long been best expressed when men drink together. The saloons offer a common meeting ground, with stimulus enough to free the wits and tongues of the men who meet there.

He distributes each Christmas many tons of turkeys not only to voters, but to families who are represented by no vote. By a judicious management some families get three or four turkeys apiece; but what

of that, the alderman has none of the nagging rules of the charitable societies, nor does he declare that because a man wants two turkeys for Christmas, he is a scoundrel who shall never be allowed to eat turkey again. As he does not distribute his Christmas favors from any hardly acquired philanthropic motive, there is no disposition to apply the carefully evolved rules of the charitable societies to his beneficiaries. Of course, there are those who suspect that the benevolence rests upon self-seeking motives, and feel themselves quite freed from any sense of gratitude; others go further and glory in the fact that they can thus "soak the alderman." An example of this is the young man who fills his pockets with a handful of cigars, giving a sly wink at the others. But this freedom from any sense of obligation is often the first step downward to the position where he is willing to sell his vote to both parties, and then scratch his ticket as he pleases. The writer recalls a conversation with a man in which he complained quite openly, and with no sense of shame, that his vote had "sold for only two dollars this year," and that he was "awfully disappointed." The writer happened to know that his income during the nine months previous had been but twenty-eight dollars, and that he was in debt thirty-two dollars, and she could well imagine the eagerness with which he had counted upon this source of revenue. After some years the selling of votes becomes a commonplace, and but little attempt is made upon the part of the buyer or seller to conceal the fact, if the transaction runs smoothly.

* * *

A reformer who really knew the people and their great human needs, who believed that it was the business of government to serve them, and who further recognized the educative power of a sense of responsibility, would possess a clue by which he might analyze the situation. He would find out what needs, which the alderman supplies, are legitimate ones which the city itself could undertake, in counter-distinction to those which pander to the lower instincts of the constituency. A mother who eats her Christmas turkey in a reverent spirit of thankfulness to the alderman who gave it to her, might be gradually brought to a genuine sense of appreciation and gratitude to the city which supplies her little children with a Kindergarten, or, to the Board of Health which properly placarded a case of scarlet-fever next door and spared her sleepless nights and wearing anxiety, as well as the money paid with such difficulty to the doctor and the druggist. The man who in his emotional gratitude almost kneels before his political friend who gets his boy out of jail, might be made to see the kindness and good sense of the city authorities who provided the boy with a playground and reading room, where he might spend his hours of idleness and restlessness, and through which his temptations to petty crime might be averted. A man who is grateful to the alderman who sees that his gambling and racing are not interfered with, might learn to feel loyal and responsible to the city which supplied him with a gymnasium and swimming tank where manly and well-conducted sports are possible. The voter who is eager to serve the alderman at all times,

340

because the tenure of his job is dependent upon aldermanic favor, might find great relief and pleasure in working for the city in which his place was secured by a well-administered civil service law.

After all, what the corrupt alderman demands from his followers and largely depends upon is a sense of loyalty, a standing-by the man who is good to you, who understands you, and who gets you out of trouble. All the social life of the voter from the time he was a little boy and played "craps" with his "own push," and not with some other "push," has been founded on this sense of loyalty and of standing in with his friends. Now that he is a man, he likes the sense of being inside a political organization, of being trusted with political gossip, of belonging to a set of fellows who understand things, and whose interests are being cared for by a strong friend in the city council itself. All this is perfectly legitimate, and all in the line of the development of a strong civic loyalty, if it were merely socialized and enlarged. Such a voter has already proceeded in the forward direction in so far as he has lost the sense of isolation, and has abandoned the conviction that city government does not touch his individual affairs. Even Mill claims that the social feelings of man, his desire to be at unity with his fellow-creatures, are the natural basis for morality, and he defines a man of high moral culture as one who thinks of himself, not as an isolated individual, but as a part in a social organism.

Upon this foundation it ought not to be difficult to build a structure of civic virtue. It is only necessary to make it clear to the voter that his individual needs are common needs, that is, public needs, and that they can only be legitimately supplied for him when they are supplied for all. If we believe that the individual struggle for life may widen into a struggle for the lives of all, surely the demand of an individual for decency and comfort, for a chance to work and obtain the fulness of life may be widened until it gradually embraces all the members of the community, and rises into a sense of the common weal. ∎

SENATOR TWEED IN A NEW ROLE.

URBAN SLUMS

By the turn of the century, an increasing number of journalists and social observers were beginning to comment on such growing urban problems as overcrowding, unsanitary conditions, and the plight of the immigrant and the poor. One of the most important writers and social observers of this period was Jacob Riis. His book *How The Other Half Lives* is a powerful commentary on city conditions at the beginning of the twentieth century. In the selection which follows, Riis describes slum conditions in New York City.

Source: Jacob Riis, *The Battle with the Slum* (New York: The Macmillan Company, 1902), pp. 16–25.

"Dens of Death"

The sketches of the Fourth Ward and Wooster Street barracks are reproduced in an old report of the Association for Improving the Condition of the Poor. They rightly made out, those early missionaries, that the improvement must begin with the people's homes, or not at all, and allowed no indifference on the part of the public to turn them from their path. It is worth the while of Chicago and the other Western cities that are growing with such joyful metropolitan ambitions, to notice that their slums look to-day very much as New York's did then. In fifty years how will it be? "The offspring of municipal neglect" the Assembly Committee of 1857 called our "tenement-house" system. "Forgetfulness of the poor" was the way a citizens' council put it. It comes to the same thing. Whether seen from the point of view of the citizen, the philanthropist, or the Christian, the slum is the poorest investment a city can make, and once made it is not easily unmade. In a Mississippi river town, when pleading for the turning over to the people's use of some vacant land on the river-shore that would make a fine breathing space, I was told that by and by they would consider it. Just now it was too valuable for factory purposes. When the city had grown opulent, in say twenty-five years, they would be willing to hand it over. Fatal delusion! Men do not grow that kind of sense as they grow rich. The land will be always "too valuable." When we in New York were scandalized at last into making a park of the Mulberry Bend, it cost us a million and a half, and it had made the slum a fixture, not to be dis-lodged. No! the way to fight the slum is to head it off. It is like fighting a fire. Chasing it up is hard and doubtful work; the chances are that you will not overtake it till the house is burned down.

There were those who thought when the Civil War was over, that a big fire would not be the worst thing that could happen to New York; and, if it could have burned sense into men's minds as it burned up the evidence of their lack of it, they would have been right. But forty per cent—the rent some of the barracks brought—is a powerful damper on sense and conscience, even with the cholera at the door. However, the fear of it gave us the Citizens' Council of Hygiene, and New York heard the truth for once.

"Not only," it ran, "does filth, overcrowding, lack of privacy and domesticity, lack of ventilation and lighting, and absence of supervision and of sanitary regulation still characterize the greater number of the tenements; but they are built to a greater height in stories; there are more rear houses built back to back with other buildings, correspondingly situated on parallel streets; the courts and alleys are more greedily encroached upon and narrowed into unventilated, unlighted, damp, and well-like holes between the many-storied front and rear tenements; and more fever-breeding wynds and *culs-de-sac* are created as the demand for the humble homes of the laboring poor increases." The Council, which was composed of sixteen of New York's most distinguished physicians, declared that by ordinary sanitary management the city's death-rate should be reduced thirty per cent. Its judgment has been more than

343

Photograph by Jacob A. Riis
The Jacob A. Riis Collection
Museum of the City of New York

borne out. In the thirty-five years that have passed since, it has in fact been reduced over fifty per cent.

Men and women were found living in cellars deep down under the ground. One or two of those holes are left still in Park Street near the Five Points Mission, but they have not been used as living-rooms for a generation. In cellars near the river the tide rose and fell, compelling the tenants "to keep the children in bed till ebb-tide." The plumber had come upon the field, but his coming brought no relief. His was not a case of conscience. "Untrapped soil pipes opened into every floor and poisoned the tenants."

Where the "dens of death" were in Baxter Street, big barracks crowded out the old shanties. More came every day. I remember the story of those shown in the picture. They had been built only a little while when complaint came to the Board of Health of smells in the houses. A sanitary inspector was sent to find the cause. He followed the smell down in the cellar and, digging there, discovered that the waste pipe was a blind. It had simply been run three feet into the ground and was not connected with the sewer.

The houses were built to sell. That they killed the tenants was no concern of the builder's. His name, by the way, was Buddensiek. A dozen years after, when it happened that a row of tenements he was building fell down ahead of time, before they were finished and sold, and killed the workmen, he was arrested and sent to Sing Sing for ten years, for manslaughter.

That time he had forgotten to put lime in the mortar. It was just sand. When the houses fell in the sight of men, the law was at last able to make him responsible. It failed in the matter of the soil pipe. It does sometimes to this very day. Knocking a man in the head with an axe, or sticking a knife into him, goes against the grain. Slowly poisoning a hundred so that the pockets of one be made to bulge may not even banish a man from respectable society. We are a queer lot in some things. However, that is hardly quite fair to society. It is a fact that that part of it which would deserve the respect of its fellow-citizens has got rid of its tenement-house property in recent years. It speculates in railway shares now.

Twenty cases of typhoid fever from a single house in one year was the record that had gone unconsidered. Bedrooms in tenements were dark closets, utterly without ventilation. There couldn't be any. The houses were built like huge square boxes, covering nearly the whole of the lot. Some light came in at the ends, but the middle was always black. Forty thousand windows, cut by order of the Health Board that first year, gave us a daylight view of the slum: "damp and rotten and dark, walls and banisters sticky with constant moisture." Think of living babies in such hell-holes; and make a note of it, you in the young cities who can still head off the slum where we have to wrestle with it for our sins. Put a brand upon the murderer who would smother babies in dark holes and bedrooms. He is nothing else. Forbid the putting of a house five stories high, or six, on a twenty-five foot lot, unless at least thirty-five per cent of the lot be reserved for sunlight and air. Forbid it absolutely, if you can. It is the devil's job, and you will have to pay his dues in the end, depend on it.

And while you are about it make a note of a fact we let go unheeded too long to our harm, and haven't grasped fully yet. The legislative committee of 1857 said it: "to prevent drunkenness provide every man with a clean and comfortable home." Call it paternalism, crankery, any other hard name you can think of, all the same it goes down underneath the foundation of things. I have known drunkards to wreck homes a plenty in my time; but I have known homes, too, that made drunkards by the shortest cut. I know a dozen now—yes, ten dozen—from which, if I had to live there, I should certainly escape to the saloon with its brightness and cheer as often and as long as I could to brood there perhaps over the fate which sowed desolation in one man's path that another might reap wealth and luxury. That last might not be my way, but it is a human way, and it breeds hatred which is not good mortar for us to build with. It does not bind. Let us remember that and just be sensible about things, or we shall not get anywhere.

By which I do not mean that we are not getting anywhere; for we are. Look at Gotham Court, described in the health reports of the sixties as a "packing-box tenement" of the hopeless back-to-back type, which meant that there was no ventilation and could be none. The stenches from the "horribly foul cellars" with their "infernal system of sewerage" must needs poison the tenants all the way up to the fifth story. I knew the court well, knew the gang that made its headquarters with the rats in the cellar, terrorizing the

helpless tenants; knew the well-worn rut of the dead-wagon and the ambulance to the gate, for the tenants died there like flies in all seasons, and a tenth of its population was always in the hospital. I knew the story of how it had been built by a Quaker with good intentions, but without good sense, for the purpose of rescuing people from the awful cellar-holes they burrowed in around there,—this within fifty-one years of the death of George Washington, who lived just across the street on the crest of Cherry Hill when he was President,—and how in a score of years from the time it was built it had come to earn the official description, "a nuisance which, from its very magnitude, is assumed to be unremovable and ir-remediable." That was at that time. But I have lived to see it taken in hand three times, once by the landlord under com-pulsion of the Board of Health, once by Christian men bent upon proving what could be done on their plan with the worst tenement house. And a good deal was accomplished. The mortality was brought below the general death-rate of the city, and the condition of the living was made by comparison tolerable. Only the best was bad in that spot, on account of the good Quaker's poor sense, and the third time the court was taken in hand it was by the authorities, who destroyed it, as they should have done a generation before. Oh, yes, we are getting there; but that sort of thing takes time. ■

345

Photograph by Jacob A. Riis
The Jacob A. Riis Collection
Museum of the City of New York

Source: W. E. B. DuBois, *The Philadelphia Negro, A Social Study* (Philadelphia: McClurg, 1899), pp. 287; 292–297.

Blacks in Philadelphia Slums

After the Civil War, slowly at first, an increasing number of blacks moved to northern cities. In the selection which follows, the distinguished black sociologist W. E. B. DuBois describes the condition of the urban black in the nineteenth century and states why he thinks blacks, from the beginning of the rise of the central city, have had such an unusually difficult time.

Houses and Rent.—The inquiry of 1848 returned quite full statistics of rents paid by the Negroes. In the whole city at that date 4019 Negro families paid $199,665.46 in rent, or an average of $49.68 per family each year. Ten years earlier the average was $44 per family. Nothing better indicates the growth of the Negro population in numbers and power when we compare with this the figures for 1896 for one ward; in that year the Negroes of the Seventh Ward paid $25,699.50 each month in rent, or $308,034 a year, an average of $126.19 per annum for each family. This ward may have a somewhat higher proportion of renters than most other wards. At the lowest estimate, however, the Negroes of Philadelphia pay at least $1,-250,000 in rent each year.

* * *

The accommodations furnished for the rent paid must now be considered. The number of rooms occupied is the simplest measurement, but is not very satisfactory in this case owing to the lodging system which makes it difficult to say how many rooms a family really occupies. A very large number of families of two and three rent a single bedroom and these must be regarded as one-room tenants, and yet this renting of a room often includes a limited use of a common kitchen; on the other hand this sub-renting family cannot in justice be counted as belonging to the renting family. The figures are:

829 families live in 1 room,   or 35.2 percent.
    including families lodging,
104 families live in 2 rooms . . or 4.4   "
371 families live in 3 rooms . . or 15.7   "

170 families live in 4 rooms ⎱ . or 12.7 percent.
127 families live in 5 rooms ⎰
754 families live in 6 rooms . . or 32.0 percent.
    or more

The number of families occupying one room is here exaggerated as before shown by the lodging system; on the other hand the number occupying six rooms and more is also somewhat exaggerated by the fact that not all sub-rented rooms have been subtracted, although this has been done as far as possible.

Of the 2441 families only 334 had access to bathrooms and water-closets, or 13.7 percent. Even these 334 families have poor accommodations in most instances. Many share the use of one bath-room with one or more other families. The bath-tubs usually are not supplied with hot water and very often have no water-connection at all. This condition is largely owing to the fact that the Seventh Ward belongs to the older part of Philadelphia, built when vaults in the yards were used exclusively and bathrooms could not be given space in the small houses. This was not so unhealthful before the houses were thick and when there were large back yards. To-day, however, the back yards have been filled by tenement houses and the bad sanitary results are shown in the death rate of the ward.

Even the remaining yards are disappearing. Of the 1751 families making returns, 932 had a private yard 12 × 12 feet, or larger; 312 had a private yard smaller than 12 × 12 feet; 507 had either no yard at all or a yard and outhouse in common with the other denizens of the tenement or alley.

Of the latter only sixteen families had water-closets. So that over 20 per cent and possibly 30 per cent of the Negro families of this ward lack some of the very elementary accommodations necessary to health and decency. And this too in spite of the fact that they are paying comparatively high rents. Here too there comes another consideration, and that is the lack of public urinals and water-closets in this ward and, in fact, throughout Philadelphia. The result is that the closets of tenements are used by the public. A couple of diagrams will illustrate this; the houses of older Philadelphia were built like this:

When, however, certain districts like the Seventh Ward became crowded and given over to tenants, the thirst for money-getting led landlords in large numbers of cases to build up their back yards like this:

This is the origin of numbers of the blind alleys and dark holes which make some parts of the Fifth, Seventh and Eighth Wards notorious. The closets in such cases are sometimes divided into compartments for different tenants, but in many cases not even this is done; and in all cases the alley closet becomes a public resort for pedestrians and loafers. The back tenements thus formed rent usually for from $7 to $9 a month, and sometimes for more. They consist of three rooms one above the other, small, poorly lighted and poorly ventilated. The inhabitants of the alley are at the mercy of its worst tenants; here policy shops abound, prostitutes ply their trade, and criminals hide. Most of these houses have to get their water at a hydrant in the alley, and must store their fuel in the house. These tenement

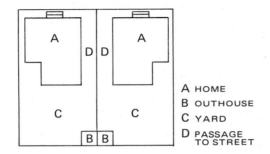

A HOME
B OUTHOUSE
C YARD
D PASSAGE TO STREET

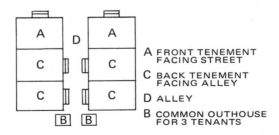

A FRONT TENEMENT FACING STREET
C BACK TENEMENT FACING ALLEY
D ALLEY
B COMMON OUTHOUSE FOR 3 TENANTS

abominations of Philadelphia are perhaps better than the vast tenement houses of New York, but they are bad enough, and cry for reform in housing.

The fairly comfortable working class live in houses of 3-6 rooms, with water in the house, but seldom with a bath. A three room house on a small street rents from $10 up; on Lombard street a 5-8 room house can be rented for from $18 to $30 according to location. The great mass of comfortably situated working people live in houses of 6-10 rooms, and sub-rent a part or take lodgers. A 5-7 room house on South Eighteenth street can be had for $20; on Florida street for $18; such houses have usually a parlor, dining room and kitchen on the first floor and two to four bedrooms, of which one or two are apt to be rented to a waiter or coachman for $4 a month, or to a married couple at $6-10 a month. The more elaborate houses are on Lombard street and its cross streets.

The rents paid by the Negroes are without doubt far above their means and often from one-fourth to three-fourths of the total income of a family goes in rent. This leads to much non-payment of rent both intentional and unintentional, to frequent shifting of homes, and above all to stinting the families in many necessities of life in order to live in respectable dwellings. Many a Negro family eats less than it ought for the sake of living in a decent house.

Some of this waste of money in rent is sheer ignorance and carelessness. The Negroes have an inherited distrust of banks and companies, and have long neglected to take part in Building and Loan Associations. Others are simply careless in the spending of their money and lack the shrewdness and business sense of differently trained peoples. Ignorance and carelessness however will not explain all or even the greater part of the problem of rent among Negroes. There are three causes of even greater importance: these are the limited localities where Negroes may rent, the peculiar connection of dwelling and occupation among Negroes and the social organization of the Negro. The undeniable fact that most Philadelphia white people prefer not to live near Negroes limits the Negro very seriously in his choice of a home and especially in the choice of a cheap home. Moreover, real estate agents knowing the limited supply usually raise the rent a dollar or two for Negro tenants, if they do not refuse them altogether. Again, the occupations which the Negro follows, and which at present he is compelled to follow, are of a sort that makes it necessary for him to live near the best portions of the city; the mass of Negroes are in the economic world purveyors to the rich—working in private houses, in hotels, large stores, etc. In order to keep this work they must live near by; the laundress cannot bring her Spruce street family's clothes from the Thirtieth Ward, nor can the waiter at the Continental Hotel lodge in Germantown. With the mass of white workmen this same necessity of living near work, does not hinder them from getting cheap dwellings; the factory is surrounded by cheap cottages, the foundry by long rows of houses, and even the white clerk and shop girl can, on account of their hours of labor, afford to live further out in the suburbs than the black porter who opens the store.

Thus it is clear that the nature of the Negro's work compels him to crowd into the centre of the city much more than is the case with the mass of white working people. At the same time this necessity is apt in some cases to be overestimated, and a few hours of sleep or convenience serve to persuade a good many families to endure poverty in the Seventh Ward when they might be comfortable in the Twenty-fourth Ward. Nevertheless much of the Negro problem in this city finds adequate explanation when we reflect that here is a people receiving a little lower wages than usual for less desirable work, and compelled, in order to do that work, to live in a little less pleasant quarters than most people, and pay for them somewhat higher rents.

The final reason of the concentration of Negroes in certain localities is a social one and one peculiarly strong: the life of the Negroes of the city has for years centred in the Seventh Ward; here are the old churches, St. Thomas, Bethel, Central, Shiloh and Wesley; here are the halls of the secret societies; here are the homesteads of old families. To a race socially ostracised it means far more to move to remote parts of a city, than to those who will in any part of the city easily form congenial acquaintances and new ties. The Negro who ventures away from the mass of his people and their organized life, finds himself alone, shunned and taunted, stared at and made uncomfortable; he can make few new friends, for his neighbors however well-disposed would shrink to add a Negro to their list of acquaintances. Thus he remains far from friends and the concentred social life

of the church, and feels in all its bitterness what it means to be a social outcast. Consequently emigration from the ward has gone in groups and centred itself about some church, and individual initiative is thus checked. At the same time color prejudice makes it difficult for groups to find suitable places to move to—one Negro family would be tolerated where six would be objected to; thus we have here a very decisive hindrance to emigration to the suburbs.

It is not surprising that this situation leads to considerable crowding in the homes, *i. e.*, to the endeavor to get as many people into the space hired as possible. It is this crowding that gives the casual observer many false notions as to the size of Negro families, since he often forgets that every other house has its sub-renters and lodgers. It is however difficult to measure this crowding on account of this very lodging system which makes it very often uncertain as to just the number of rooms a given group of people occupy. In the following table therefore it is likely that the number of rooms given is somewhat greater than is really the case and that consequently there is more crowding than is indicated. This error however could not be wholly eliminated under the circumstances; a study of the table shows that in the Seventh Ward there are 9302 rooms occupied by 2401 families, an average of 3.8 rooms to a family, and 1.04 individuals to a room. A division by rooms will better show where the crowding comes in.

Families occupying five rooms and less: 1648, total rooms per family, 2.17; total individuals per room, 1.53.

HOMES ACCORDING TO ROOMS AND PERSONS LIVING IN THEM

Rooms	One	Two	Three	Four	Five	Six	Seven	Eight	Nine	Ten	Eleven	Twelve	Thirteen	Fourteen	Fifteen	Sixteen	Seventeen and over	Unknown	Homes, Total	Total Rooms
One	47	572	154	58	25	6	5	—	1	2	—	—	—	—	—	—	—	—	870	870
Two	5	38	33	19	6	1	2	—	1	—	—	—	—	—	—	—	—	—	105	210
Three	13	54	69	87	60	36	25	17	8	2	1	1	1	—	—	1	—	—	375	1125
Four	6	24	35	42	19	19	7	7	5	4	—	3	—	—	—	—	—	—	171	684
Five	—	11	20	21	21	17	14	8	7	5	3	—	—	—	—	—	—	—	127	635
Six	1	5	14	46	38	47	40	24	20	9	10	5	2	—	1	1	—	—	263	1578
Seven	—	2	10	26	19	23	13	12	14	7	7	5	3	1	2	—	4	—	148	1036
Eight	4	9	7	17	17	19	12	15	11	8	6	9	2	3	—	1	3	—	143	1144
Nine	—	1	10	13	8	14	10	8	12	7	5	2	1	2	1	1	—	—	95	855
Ten	—	2	5	6	2	4	5	4	—	5	2	3	3	1	1	1	4	—	48	480
Eleven	—	1	—	1	5	3	4	2	3	2	—	—	1	—	2	4	—	—	28	308
Twelve and over .	—	1	1	1	1	—	2	1	4	4	2	1	2	1	—	—	7	—	28	377
Unknown	—	—	2	4	1	1	—	—	—	—	—	—	—	—	—	—	—	32	40	—
Total	76	720	360	341	222	190	139	98	86	55	36	29	15	8	7	9	18	32	2441	9302

Families occupying three rooms and less: 1350, total rooms per family, 1.63; total individuals per room, 1.85.

The worst cases of crowding are as follows:

Two cases of 10 persons in 1 room.
One case of   9   ··   ·· 1   ··
Five cases of 7   ··   ·· 1   ··
Six cases of   6   ··   ·· 1   ··
Twenty-five cases of 5 persons in 1 room.
One case of 9 persons in 2 rooms.
One case of 16   ··   ·· 3   ··
One case of 13   ··   ·· 3   ··
One case of 11   ··   ·· 3   ··

As said before, this is probably some-thing under the real truth, although per-haps not greatly so. The figures show considerable overcrowding, but not nearly as much as is often the case in other cities. This is largely due to the character of Philadelphia houses, which are small and low, and will not admit many inmates. Five persons in one room of an ordinary tenement would be almost suffocating. The large number of one-room tenements with two persons should be noted. These 572 families are for the most part young or childless couples, sub-renting a bed-room and working in the city. ■

URBAN REFORMERS OF THE PROGRESSIVE ERA

Source: *The American Monthly Review of Reviews*, vol. XVI, no. 1 (July 1897), pp. 33–37.

The period from the end of the nineteenth century to World War I has long been termed the Progressive Era. It coincided with the period of the cities' greatest growth, and not surprisingly, the reforms sought or achieved often represented specific responses to the ever-growing social and political problems of the American city.

Many of these reforms were initiated at the local level by progressive-minded mayors. Two of the most important of these were Seth Low of Brooklyn, New York, and Samuel "Golden Rule" Jones of Toledo, Ohio. The following selections are profiles of these two men written by contemporaries.

Mayor Seth Low

Seth Low, LL.D., President of Columbia University in the City of New York, was forty-seven years old on the 18th of last January. He looks ten years younger. Of medium height, square-shouldered, deep-chested, strongly built, his bearing is erect, his carriage vigorous and easy. There is a suggestion of gray in his thick dark-brown hair, but his fresh complexion, his clear, bright glance, his frank and genial expression and a certain air of quiet but eager energy offset the effect of years and wide experience and sustained toil. None of his portraits that I have seen do him justice, and I do not quite understand why, for his face in repose seems to me one that ought to awaken an artist's keenest interest. Curiously enough, there is more suggestion of the strongest elements of his character in a superb portrait bust of his father by the lamented Olin Warner, recently shown at the Century Club, than in any of his own portraits. And though the careers of the two men differ widely enough, one who has known them both at all well can see the distinct force of heredity in the son's determined deliberation, sound and clear judgment, capacity for large views and patient pursuit of them and in his ingrained benevolence of spirit.

President Low must be called a New York man, since his dream is now realized of an imperial city embracing all the communities within a dozen miles of the harbor. He was educated at a New York college; he was for a number of years the head of a great New York trading house and has long been an active member of the Chamber of Commerce of New York. But he was born in Brooklyn, and his family has the familiar history of English origin, early settlement in Massachusetts and final establishment in New York. His grandfather, for whom he was named, was one of the Harvard-bred merchants, and previous to his removal to New York was in business in Salem. His father, Abiel Abbott Low, followed the Salem bent, went out to China, and returned to found the great tea and silk house of A. A. Low & Brother, to which Seth Low went on graduating from Columbia in 1870. Here it will be seen are all the elements of the vocation of an enlightened merchant, with the inheritance of traditions, power, wealth, opportunity—all to be broken in upon by the imperative call of a greater career appealing to a mind responding to its broader inspiration.

My acquaintance with Seth Low dates from the saddle rides we used to take in the lovely country below what is now Prospect Park—a region then of winding lanes and frequent woods, and rough sand roads skirting the bay and the ocean. He was a lad in the Polytechnic Institute, and what I recall chiefly is that he rode a spirited pony with unusual prudence in avoiding risks and great coolness and promptness in dealing with them when they came—a habit he has never abandoned. The Polytechnic had not at that time a collegiate course, and young Low went, at seventeen, to Columbia. In the spring of 1870 President Barnard said, in a letter a friend has recently unearthed: "I have just been having a long talk with young Low of the senior class, the first scholar in college, and the most manly young man we have had here for many years." On leaving college he went, as has been noted, to his father's business house.

Here he entered as a clerk and traversed the regular grades until he was admitted to the firm in 1875, and four years later, on the retirement of the seniors, succeeded with his brothers to the business, which was finally liquidated in 1888.

Meanwhile he became greatly interested in certain phases of public life. Brooklyn has always been peculiarly a city of churches and charities. In the latter Mr. Low took an active part. It was largely due to him that there was introduced the organization now so generally adopted in other cities, by which the forces and resources available were developed and saved from waste and misapplication. He joined the Republican association of his ward and took energetically to the sort of political work which in those days more readily than now could be done by young men of brains and character within the strict lines of party.

In 1880, in the campaign of Garfield and Arthur, there was organized in Brooklyn "The Young Republican Club," and Mr. Low was chosen as its president. It was purely a campaign club, and a very effectual one, with a large membership and lots of energy, under shrewd guidance. Naturally its conspicuous success brought its president prominently into public view. At the close of the triumphant campaign Mr. Low retired from the presidency and the club was reorganized. Its basis was entirely changed, and though Mr. Low no longer led it, it was to have a decisive influence on his future. Its work was now to include specifically the improvement of the city government, though it was not confined to that. For the first time, so far as I am aware, the principle was definitely adopted that

the object should be pursued without regard to national or state politics. In practice this meant that partisan nominations should not necessarily be binding on the club in municipal elections. The next year brought an occasion for the application of the principle, and it was applied with decision, courage, vigor and complete success. The politics of Brooklyn have always been peculiar, as its situation has been. It was in 1881 a city of great population and wide area and of limited resources. Of corporate wealth it had little; its personal property, like that of most other cities, evaded taxation; its real estate was very largely devoted to dwellings only, and its business was widely scattered, so that there was no business quarter in which taxable values accumulated. With these attributes of a great overgrown village, its population had certain qualities that made efficient city government difficult to attain. Most of the men of Brooklyn, from the laborer or truckman to the president of the New York Chamber of Commerce, did their work or carried on their business across the East River. The place had neither the concentrated public spirit of a small town nor the pride and energy in public matters that a great city awakens in its capable men in emergencies. Its "better class" was divided by limited interests and prejudices, while the mass of voters were in great part led, on both sides, by politicians of little distinction and some of them of extreme unscrupulousness. There were exceptions, and bright ones, but they were decidedly exceptions.

Brooklyn had felt the wave of extravagance and corruption that swept over the land in the wake of the civil war—the in-

evitable effect of the enormous inflation of the currency, the treatment as money of a debt incurred for purposes of destruction. At the time that the Tweed ring, with its unholy alliance with Tammany Republicans, seized on New York, a ring of like composition and with like purposes seized upon Brooklyn. The plunder was not so great, because there was not the wealth, but the burden imposed on the city was relatively even greater. The resources of many a decade were mortgaged in a few years, and all beneficent and even most of the necessary functions of city administration were hampered for a generation.

The revolt against Tweed in New York and the overthrow of the Democratic power in the state and, still more valuable, the overthrow of the corrupt combination within the Democratic party was accompanied by a like movement in Brooklyn, which with varying success had continued to the time when the Young Republican Club had run up the flag of independence in city politics. One of its most fruitful victories, largely due to Mr. Schroeder—a representative of the best type of German-American citizenship, who had been elected first to the mayoralty and afterward to the state Senate—was the passage of a charter for Brooklyn by which the mayor was given the sole power of appointment of the heads of departments and the power of their removal at discretion within thirty days of the beginning of his term of office. The charter was to go into effect on the 1st of January, 1882. The reformers in Brooklyn saw the immense importance of securing a mayor who would worthily use these unprecedented powers.

In the autumn of 1881 the Republicans

nominated for mayor Mr. B. F. Tracy, since Secretary of the Navy in the Harrison administration. He was at that time the strongest party leader the Republicans had known, a man of rectitude of character and great ability, but distinctly a partisan. On a partisan division he was sure to be beaten. Mr. Ripley Ropes, a conservative Republican, independent in city matters, was supported by the Young Republican Club.

It was plain that a union must be made or the defeat of the Democratic candidate, who was supported by if not identified with the ring, would be impossible. Mr. Low was chairman of a delegation appointed to secure the withdrawal of both Messrs. Tracy and Ropes. To his surprise and, it is needless to say, without his aid, his own nomination became the condition of this withdrawal and the solution of the complicated problem. He finally consented, and was elected by a decided though not great majority.

This is not the place to review in detail Mr. Low's administration as mayor. I shall seek only to indicate the principles by which he was guided and the way in which his personal character impressed his administration. He was a very young man in an entirely novel position. He was thirty-two years old, wholly without experience in public affairs and with only limited familiarity with men who had been engaged in them for good or ill. He was the first mayor of a great American city to take upon himself the unrestricted choice of practically the entire executive force of the government. He was the candidate of a minority party and had been elected only by the aid of voters opposed in national politics to himself. His direct responsibility was great, and he felt indirect responsibility for the permanence of the system he represented as well as for its immediate success.

Responsibility has no terrors for Mr. Low. He is quite ready to meet it if he has the power fairly to discharge it. His first act as mayor proved this. He asked of every man whom he appointed to office a promise to resign if requested by the mayor. It was a very bold thing to do. It was without authority in law. Probably had the question been raised it would have been decided to be contrary to law. The power to appoint under certain definite conditions does not embrace and probably excludes the power to impose quite other conditions upon the appointee. However this may be, it is plain that this act concentrated in the mayor a responsibility that a weak man would have shunned. It was a striking demonstration of Mr. Low's devotion to the principle of city government which the charter incompletely embodied, and of the unflinching resolution with which he assumed what he decided to be his duty in its full measure.

The two characteristics of Mr. Low's administration, I think, were, first, the standard he established and maintained; second, his intimate reliance on public opinion.

I should hardly say that his work showed extraordinary administrative ability. The men to whom he gave in charge the various departments of the city affairs were none of them of conspicuous strength and did not leave behind them, nor did their chief, any great work of improvement or any comprehensive or novel system of administration. In these respects the later administration of Mayor Schieren, for example, was distinctly superior. But the mayoralty of Mr. Low made that of Mr. Schieren possible. It did so chiefly by setting up plainly before the people a general and continuous example of honest, open, unselfish administration. Especially all concerned worked together. Every one, in and out of office, was made to feel that there was absolutely only one aim to be pursued —the common good, and nothing would be undertaken or considered save in broad daylight. Mr. Low established what was known as his cabinet. He had regular meetings with the heads of all the departments, in which the general affairs of each were discussed, and he gave constant hearings, within reasonable limits, on all questions in which any considerable interest was involved. No man could claim that he possessed any secret influence with the mayor or that he could secure favor for any measure or policy that could not publicly be explained and justified. Mr. Low was decidedly the mayor. He shirked the determination of no question that it fell to him to determine. But equally he shirked no fair inquiry as to his reasons and permitted no one concerned to be less frank or less distinctly responsible than he was. There was no power behind the mayor's chair, and the occupant of the chair was always the independent but responsible agent of the city in the management of the common business.

In no branch of his work did this high standard of public action show more clearly than in the administration of the civil service, and in this it showed with especial distinctness because he intrusted

Source: *The Outlook,* vol. 62, no. 1 (March 6, 1899), pp. 17–20.

it to a board who were more radical in their views than he at first was, and after thrashing out the matter, as his custom was, he followed the course they proposed. The result in practice was the substantial abolition of patronage. For the first time in the history of Brooklyn and more completely than in any other great city, public places, great and small, ceased to be rewards or incentives for party service or personal support, and became trusts, precisely as places are and must be in private business. It is not easy to put too high a value on this then unprecedented change. Its greatest value lay, not in the single unrelated fact that the city got good service. That might have come from a partisan mayor of exceptional strength and sagacity. It lay in the establishment of a system, in the painstaking, intelligent application of a general principle with a view to its permanent maintenance. It was a part of the setting up of a standard which might be departed from, but which could never again be ignored. ■

Mayor "Golden Rule" Jones

Is the Mayor's chair to be the *terminus a quo* of the popular leaders? We all know what once happened to a Mayor of Buffalo and what is now happening to a Mayor of Detroit. Are such experiences likely to become frequent? There is some reason why they should be. The city is the *crux* of American politics; the man who boldly solves it is entitled to the highest confidence of his fellow-citizens. In truth, the questions now right at the front in municipal politics are the questions around which National issues will soon be made up, and the leaders of municipal reform will be the natural leaders of National reform.

Young Mayor Harrison, of Chicago, has suddenly sprung into National fame through his resolute and successful resistance to the schemes of a voracious corporation; the people were willing to forgive a loose police administration because of his fidelity to a great trust; and they were wise. The saloons and the gambling-houses are public enemies, but their influence is far less deadly in a democracy than that of the great organization of corporate wealth which is ready to spend money by the millions in the bribery of legislatures and city councils and judges and newspapers, in order that it may fasten its grip on the people and suck their blood by slow tribute through generations. It is sometimes supposed that, while the saloon question is a moral question, the question of the success of such an attempt as that which was made by the street-car companies in Chicago and the gas combine in Philadelphia is only a financial question; and that moral questions ought to outrank financial questions. But this is a grievous

misconception. There are no moral questions more vital than those which are raised in our cities by the bold, and generally successful, attempts to rob the people through the acquisition of public utilities.

All this is pertinent to the interesting history of Mayor Jones, of Toledo, who has become pretty well known throughout the country during his two years' incumbency just concluded, and whose remarkable success in the recent election has made more talk, not only among the politicians, but also among the common people, than any recent political event.

Samuel M. Jones was born in Wales in 1846, and his parents came to America when he was only three years old. Poverty and severe toil were the portion of his childhood. At the age of eighteen he found himself in Titusville, Pa., in search of work, and with fifteen cents in his pocket; his quest was soon rewarded by an opportunity to work among the oil-producers, and from that time to this he has kept in close connection with this important industry. In the rough life of the oil-fields he won his vigorous frame, his practical sense, and his intimate acquaintance with the conditions of the working people. With small opportunities of education, he so well employed his leisure that we find him now possessed of considerable knowledge of literature, a keen relish for the best that has been said in prose and verse, and a good, clear English style, often lit up with a felicitous phrase or a telling quotation. He is a well-made man physically, about five feet ten, muscular, with a large blue eye, a genial face, and a manner of great frankness and directness.

353

Clearly he was too brainy a man to be long working by the day; he soon rose to positions of responsibility, and became an employer himself. In 1893 he invented an important improvement in the apparatus of the oil-wells, and, finding no manufacturer willing to produce his device, he set up his own shop in Toledo. "This brought me," he says in an interview, "in contact with ordinary labor conditions for the first time in my life. As a rule, labor in the oil-fields had enjoyed large wages compared to similar classes outside. I found men working in Toledo for a fraction of a dollar a day. I began to wonder how it was possible for men to live on such a small sum of money, as citizens of a free Republic. I studied social conditions, and these led me to feel very keenly the degradation of my fellow-men, and I at once declared that the so-called 'going wages' should not govern our business. I said the rule that every man is entitled to such a share of the products of his toil as will enable him to live decently, and in such a way that he and his children may be fitted to be citizens of a free Republic, should be the rule governing the wages of our establishment."

"Without waiting for any," Mr. Jones set up the principle of a "minimum wage" in his shop; no man should work for him for less than a specified wage. After a year or so he became convinced that one remedy for the prevailing unemployment was the shortening of the labor day, and the adoption of the eight-hour day in his shop was accompanied, not by a reduction, but by an increase in the daily wage. At the same time he changed the hours of labor in the oil-fields under his control from twelve to eight, employing three shifts instead of two for the twenty-four hours. For the wider introduction of this reform in the oil-fields he has labored enthusiastically, but with little success; there are few wells besides his own in which the men do not work twelve hours.

Mr. Jones recognizes the fact that his patent enables him to disregard the competitive rate of wages in his factory; he does not take great credit to himself for maintaining a standard higher than would be possible in unprotected industries; he simply declines to appropriate the whole of this advantage, and divides it with his men. Every year, in addition to the wage, a labor dividend of five per cent upon the amount earned by each man is distributed, and every man who has worked six months or more in the establishment is given a week's vacation with full pay at some time during the year.

In addition to these efforts to improve their material conditions, Mayor Jones has sought to put himself into the most brotherly relations with his men and their families. Let me quote again from that interview:

I soon discovered that the men were lacking in something else besides wages. The men were conscious of social inferiority, and I could not understand how a man who had done no wrong could or should feel inferior to any other man simply because he worked with his hands. Without any organized plan for the purpose or without hardly knowing myself what I was doing, I determined that no such feeling should exist. To break down the feeling of social inequality, we began to "get to-gether"—that is, we had little excursions down the bay. We invited our workmen and their families, and also some other people who live in big houses and who do not work with their hands. We sought to mix them, to let them understand that we are all people—just people, you know.

As business prospered, Mr. Jones built for himself a fine house in one of the beautiful residence districts; but when the house-warming came, the party was made up of his workmen and their wives and sweethearts.

Mayor Jones has been a wide reader of literature relating to social questions; he has made the acquaintance of many of the leaders of social reform; he has invited many of them to Toledo to give free lectures for the education of the people. But his social theories all rest on the Sermon on the Mount. The one thing that he believes with all his heart and soul and mind and strength is that the teachings of Jesus Christ are practicable. Early in the history of his industrial enterprise in Toledo he came, as he says, to feel the need of a rule to govern the place. "So we had the following printed on a piece of tin and nailed to the wall. It's there to-day: 'The rule governing this factory: *Therefore whatsoever ye would that men should do to you, do ye even so to them.*' We told the boys that this was a double-acting rule, which, to be carried out, required that they should do their work as they would want us to do it if they were working the office and we were in the other end of the shop. After nearly four years of a test, I am pleased to say that the Golden Rule works. It is perfectly practicable and is worthy of a trial. It is nearly nineteen hundred years since Jesus gave it to the world, and the least his professed followers can do is to try it."

Adjoining the Golden Rule factory was a vacant lot 150 feet square, with several fine old trees; Mr. Jones bought it, and has made a pretty park of it—Golden Rule Park—with chairs and settees and swings and a May-pole for the children, and a speakers' and music stand. Here, every Sunday afternoon in the mild weather, there is music, and speaking by some one competent to teach, usually on some phase of the social question. "Golden Rule Hall" has also been fitted up in the second story of the factory, where similar meetings are held in the cold weather.

By all these manifestations of his spirit and purpose Mr. Jones became pretty well known, especially to the working classes of Toledo; and when, at the Republican Convention held two years ago for the nomination of municipal officers, a deadlock occurred in the attempt to select a candidate for office, some daring individual ventured to suggest as a compromise candidate the name of Samuel M. Jones. The nomination went through like a whirlwind; and Mr. Jones was elected by a handsome majority, though the corporations and the saloons both stoutly opposed him.

His two years' incumbency has wrought many changes in his following. Not a few who shouted for him in his first campaign denounced him in the second; and a great many of those who feared him then are now his enthusiastic supporters. This is due, no doubt, to a considerable change in the attitude of the Mayor himself.

During the two years he has been advancing pretty rapidly in the direction of Socialism. He is not an advocate of any sudden or radical changes in the industrial order, but his attempts to grapple with the question of employment and his experience with the corporate ownership of public utilities have convinced him that the existing economic system must be greatly modified. He insists, for one thing, that the right to work is a natural and sacred right; and that the State must never ask any man to eat the bread of a pauper until it has given him a chance to earn his own bread. The failure of employment, as he has constantly confronted it during his term of office, he believes to be a chronic condition for which public provision must be made. And this opinion modifies, to a considerable extent, his ideas about municipal administration. It leads him to feel that drunkenness is the effect, more than the cause, of poverty; and to have less faith than once he had in the suppression of drunkenness by law. His enforcement of the law against the saloons has been much less rigid than was expected of him, and those to whom this seems the principal thing have lost faith in him. Mayor Jones claims, however, that there has been less drunkenness during the last year than formerly; that the administration of the police force has been of such a nature that vice and crime have been prevented; and that prevention is better than punishment.

His last message indicated the extent to which he wishes to go in the direction of Socialism. Omitting a few items of local interest, the following is a summary of its recommendations:

The establishment of a city plant for the manufacture of fuel gas.

The control and operation by the city of the electric lighting plant.

The establishment of civil service in all departments of the municipality.

The enactment by the Legislature of laws that will give the city such a measure of Home Rule as will enable it to "bring out the best that is in its own people."

No grant or extension of franchises to private enterprise without the approval of the people.

The abandonment of the contract system on all public work, such as paving, sewers, etc.

The compilation and publication of the city directory by the municipality itself.

The establishment of kindergartens as part of the public-school system.

The sprinkling of the streets by the city itself.

A larger appropriation for public parks.

An appropriation for music in the parks.

The establishment of playgrounds for the children.

The establishment of free public baths.

The veto power to be abolished, and the referendum to the people substituted in its place. ■

Source: *Harper's Weekly*, vol. 137 (June 1918), pp. 106–113.

City Manager Henry M. Waite

The politics of reform during the Progressive Era went beyond the search for reform-minded mayors. Most significant was the inauguration of the city-manager plan, best exemplified by that established in Dayton, Ohio. The magazine article which follows describes the nature of this new idea of municipal government and explains the role of Dayton's city manager, Henry M. Waite.

There is nothing spectacular, or possibly even interesting, about the personality of Mr. Henry M. Waite, the much-talked-about "City Manager" of Dayton, Ohio. This new idea in municipal government found little favor at first with the newspaper men. Mr. Waite's long tabulations of statistics, showing the people precisely how their money had been spent, and what they had obtained for it, furnished few opportunities for headlines. The every-day squabblings of political factions, the picturesque romances involved in the distribution of patronage, the Homeric conflicts of party leaders, the alternating emotions inspired by "wide-open" and "closed towns," the extravagant descriptions of waste and corruption—these details, however humiliating and sordid their implications may have been, at least made American municipal politics exciting and entertaining. Compared to this lurid atmosphere, the present régime of efficiency in Dayton hangs over the community almost like a pall. The City Hall itself symbolizes the new and quiet spirit. Ordinarily this building in American cities is a headquarters of animation and "human interest." It is the place where politicians and their retainers gather to discuss and determine questions of state and too frequently its disheveled appearance suggests the personal motives and the waste and extravagance that dominate municipal policies. The Dayton City Hall, an inconspicuous building of unspeakable architecture, astonishes by its neatness. The floors are carefully swept; the clerks and other employees are industriously bending over their work; no local statesmen, with upturned cigars and hats perched on the back of their heads, are gathered in mysterious corners discussing momentous issues in whispers and now and then buttonholing more important gentlemen who pass in and out of the executive offices. The whole situation suggests that here we have a large number of prosaic rooms in which several hundred people are engaged in performing certain daily tasks, quite as part of an industrial or corporate organization.

One of these offices bears the sign "City Manager." The door is always open, and Mr. Waite is always completely within view. Quite commonly he is talking to one of the stockholders in his unique corporation—one of the men or women, or even children who make up the citizenship of Dayton. If it is summer-time he may be sitting in his shirt-sleeves; always he is dressed in an easy-fitting business suit, never assuming the frock coat and the white necktie that usually distinguish urban statesmanship in this country. He is a trim-looking, smoothly shaven, somewhat stocky gentleman of forty-seven; his steady poise, his quietly resting body, the gray eyes that calmly gaze at his callers through eye-glasses indicate not only assurance, but extreme self-command. He does not greet his callers with effervescence; neither does he treat them with disdain. While talking with them he does not glance at the ceiling and nervously finger his mail; neither does he encourage protracted interviews. There is a feeling that Mr. Waite has all the time necessary for the details of the business in hand; yet it is equally apparent that he has no time for ordinary small talk or extraneous matters. He listens attentively, asks questions quickly, smiles pleasantly at the right moment, and develops a perceptible eagerness if he happens to touch upon the general merits of the Dayton plan. The fact is that Mr. Waite behaves admirably in character; he is precisely what he has always been—a man with the technical training of an engineer, experienced in problems of public works, accustomed to dealing with figures and facts, and having none of the talents that make the great American politician. It is plain why the reporters, in the first days of his incumbency, found him so little to their liking. The one quality that he lacked was the gift of publicity. Mr. Waite solved this problem in a way that sheds the utmost light upon his methods. He placed at the disposal of the reporters the entire official correspondence of Dayton; duplicates of every letter, as they are written, are placed in a basket, to which the newspapers have free and constant access. They even see the mail which, in most cities, would be regarded as extremely confidential; in case publication of the facts would work a business injury, a hint from the manager keeps them out of the press. In this way Mr. Waite has developed publicity of a novel kind. The government of Dayton has no secrets from its constituents, for at any moment any citizen can learn precisely how his public servants are spending his money. They can get the names of everybody with whom the city is doing business and the terms upon which they are doing it, and they can learn every night the city's financial situation to the last penny. The manager's open door and open reception-room, his open books and open correspondence emphasize the basic principles

of publicity upon which the new system is based.

Yet this city of Dayton, and the sixty others which have adopted the same municipal organization, are perhaps working out the final experiment in the much-vexed problem of American municipal government. It seems probable that, after trying endless "plans," we shall reorganize all American cities in accordance with the Dayton idea. The first fact concerning the manager plan immediately argues in its favor. It does not represent the idealistic conception of some closet philosopher; like the British constitution itself, the Dayton plan represents the working of immutable and insistent forces. A group of visionary men did not develop this scheme from their inner consciousness; external circumstances forced the city to adopt it. Until April, 1913, the city of Dayton had followed the historic course of all American municipalities, and the inefficiency and corruption of its administration represented the commonplace American standard. It possessed two great parties and several smaller ones constantly struggling for supremacy—that is, for the spoils; it had the usual easy-going electorate; and, like most American cities, it had its periodical eruptions of virtue and "reform administrations," followed by the usual relapse into civic indifference. Like the "decent element" of New York, Chicago, and San Francisco, Dayton's citizens were "too busy" to keep a constant watch upon their public servants. Occasionally the "business men" lamented the growth of "socialism" among the city's increasing foreign population; women's clubs and civic associations became anxious over the

progress of the Red Light district, and in all other details Dayton simply played true to the American type. Indeed, Dayton reached a depth of municipal inefficiency almost unexampled even in the United States. "Government by deficit" was the description frequently applied to it. "What Dayton needs is not a manager, but a receiver," was Mr. Waite's first remark after glancing through the books. That Dayton should have no budget, that local politicians instead of experts should be filling the offices, that each department should be a separate entity in itself, that taxes should be high, that the public health should be neglected—all this we should have expected, for that is the American plan; what rendered Dayton almost unique was that it floated bond issues to pay current expenses, such as the salaries of school-teachers, policemen, and the like.

All this time, however, the city of Dayton presented precisely that contrast which has astounded so many foreign commentators on the United States. That was the difference between its municipal organization and the organization of private business. Alongside this absurd city government great business enterprises had developed in recent years. These industries had acquired a world-wide reputation for the skill with which they were organized and the energy and success with which they were conducted, and experts from America and Europe frequently came to Dayton to study the last word in modern business organization. These factories did more than turn out a huge annual product and enrich their owners. They were really great industrial communities, and their proprietors had acquired a great reputation for the interest which they displayed in the human side of their enterprises; they had private training establishments for their employees, pension systems, night schools, hospitals, playgrounds, and the like. They regarded it as part of their duty not only to make their employees successful breadwinners but successful citizens, and they even established facilities for teaching their foreign workingmen English and training them in American history and the meaning of American institutions. Thus here, existing side by side, Dayton had these two glaring phenomena: a dirty, unkempt City Hall, full of tobacco-chewing loafers, a high death rate, a high infant-mortality rate, a Red Light district, an insufficient water-supply, streets full of uncollected ashes and rubbish, unsanitary jails, frenzied municipal finance; on the other side great industrial establishments whose watchword was efficiency, whose success and whose attractiveness to industry had increased the population of Dayton from 61,000 to 116,000 in twenty years.

It seems strange, does it not, that these two contrasting facts should not have conveyed their own lesson? For years the enlightened people of Dayton had fussed over the ever-present problem, "How can we improve our city government?" They sent experts abroad to study the matter in all its phases, hoping to find elsewhere a scheme that would fit local conditions. They ran the whole gamut of single-chamber plans, borough plans, commission plans, initiative, referendum, recall, and what not. Yet all this time the answer to their queries apparently lay at their very feet. Dayton's great industries had clearly

evolved a system of government that produced the most satisfactory results. The business of administering Dayton—building roads, sewers, water works, collecting garbage and ashes, managing schools, police and fire departments—was just as much a business as that of making cash-registers, automobiles, and other manufactured products. Why not take the system that had proved so successful in business and use it for the city government? Already certain far-seeing citizens had caught a glimmering of this truth; it took a great natural calamity, however, to make it as clear as daylight. In March, 1913, came that great convulsion that will always figure in Dayton history as the "high water." The melting snows of winter rushed down into the Miami Valley, overwhelmed Dayton, flooded her banks, factories, and schools and forced the citizens to take to rowboats, high buildings, and the roofs of floating houses. This was the greatest crisis in the city's history, and it called for quick action. Dayton's officials stood around and wrung their hands helplessly, not having the slightest idea how to meet the situation. Since their lives had been spent in winning elections, making speeches, cultivating popularity among voters, and distributing political jobs, their helplessness in face of such a crisis is not surprising. The managers and sub-managers of Dayton's factories immediately assumed control, and in a few hours they had completely organized the business of rescuing citizens, providing them with food and shelter and clothing. By the time the water went down a new Dayton had been planned to take the place of the old. Not only had the people been

saved from destruction; they had had an unparalleled example of efficiency in government.

In this great crisis, however, their regularly elected officials had failed them; their privately conducted enterprises had performed the duties with which certain mayors, corporation counsels, comptrollers, and aldermen had been intrusted by the electorate. The activities of the corporation presidents, superintendents, department heads, and the like had been "extra-constitutional," and their only justification had been their success. For a year or two Dayton, as already said, had been seeking a new form of government. If it were really seeking a plan that would produce efficiency, apparently it was not necessary to look far. The hand of Providence itself had pointed the way. Why not adopt the system that had worked so well in this great natural crisis? Why not take over the administration ideas that had given Dayton precisely the organization which had displaced its feudal charter when real administration was needed? It seemed not improbable that the same business organization that produced cash-registers, automobiles, agricultural implements, turbines, railway cars, and sewing-machines, could also sweep the streets, construct highways, remove garbage, build water-supply, maintain parks, manage the police and fire departments; in fine, perform the numerous activities which we have usually regarded as the exclusive province of politicians. Already a few inconspicuous communities elsewhere had experimented with this idea, and Dayton's new Bureau of Municipal Research had given some attention to the plan.

The Third Section Edition

FLOOD EDITION   # The N C R Weekly   **FLOOD EDITION**

Volume III   DAYTON, OHIO, SATURDAY, APRIL 12, 1913   Number 13

Dayton Suffers From Most Destructive Flood in Its History

Third Street, Looking Toward Business Section of City

A Portion of Flooded District Near N. C. R. Factory

West on First Street. Office Buildings in the Distance

The Miami River valley in which Dayton is located, under ordinary conditions one of the most beautiful and peaceful valleys in this country, was suddenly transformed on Tuesday, March 25, into a channel of death and destruction. This was the culmination of a series of unusually severe wind and rain storms which had been in progress for several days throughout the north central section of the United States. As a result of these cyclones and floods a large portion of the country has been devastated from Nebraska on the west to Pennsylvania on the east.

Storm Began Easter Sunday

The storm proper did not reach Dayton until Easter Sunday, March 23, when it rained at intervals during the afternoon and night. On Monday the waters seemed to fall from the clouds in torrents, and by Monday evening, the twenty-fourth, the Miami River, which flows through Dayton, was higher than it had been at any time this year. It continued to rise rapidly and by five o'clock in the evening much of the lowlands surrounding the city and a few of the lowest streets began to fill with water. The rain continued to fall all through the night, and early Tuesday morning the blowing of steam whistles and the ringing of fire alarms and church bells gave warning to those in the lower sections to seek safety from the currents which were rapidly growing in volume and fury. Many heeded the warning and reached the higher points. Others apparently did not appreciate the gravity of the situation and hesitated to leave.

Rapid Rise of Waters

The waters after once breaking over the banks and levees rose with such alarming rapidity that only those who acted promptly were able to escape. There was no time for a second thought.

Hundreds had left their homes in the morning for their daily work only to be caught in the floods on the way and compelled to seek refuge in residences, office buildings and shops in the business districts. Thus they were imprisoned and separated from their families and with no knowledge as to the fate of those whom they had left at home a few minutes before.

The cellars were filled and the first floors of the houses in the residential districts were covered early Tuesday morning. This forced the people to the second floors, attics and roofs of their houses in order to escape with their lives. By nine o'clock in the morning the streets of the greater portion of the city were filled with floating rubbish, lumber, horses and houses. The telephones and telegraph lines were put out of service. Railroad trains could neither enter nor leave the city. There was no method of communication with the outside world or with the different sections of the city.

Terrible Plight of Refugees

The rains continued to fall during all of Tuesday and Tuesday night, and the waters as a consequence continued to rise. The air, growing cold and chilly, was filled with snow flurries. The skies were brightly illuminated at different points by fires which had broken out in both the business and residence sections of the city.

These were the conditions which faced thousands of people who were left marooned on the second floors, attics and roofs of the houses on Tuesday evening. Added to the discomforts of being without food, water, heat, light and dry clothing, the worry and distress which accompanied the separation of families, and the danger of being carried away by the flood, was the apparent necessity of fighting the flames should they continue to spread. On Wednesday, the twenty-sixth, the waters began to recede and by Thursday evening or Friday morning practically all persons in the flooded district had been brought to dry land and their physical wants provided for.

Millions of Dollars Worth of Property Destroyed

This is considered one of the greatest disasters in the history of this country. It is impossible to estimate the loss and damage to property, but it will run into the hundreds of millions of dollars. In this city the merchandise on the first floors of the stores in the principal business sections of the city is completely ruined. The large plate glass windows and the expensive store fixtures are broken and destroyed.

Several business blocks have been destroyed by fire. Numerous houses have been completely wiped out of existence, while hundreds of others are so badly damaged that their repair is almost impossible. Along with the loss of the houses themselves is the furniture and personal property which is usually found in them, including many articles which cannot possibly be replaced by money alone. Horses, carriages and automobiles are also numbered among the property which was swept away by the waters.

Members of Foreign Department Safe

A number of the members of the Foreign Department were in the submerged district and lost their household effects and valuable personal property. They were fortunate, however, in escaping with their lives and all were able to resume their usual duties on Monday, April 7.

The loss of life was not as great as at first estimated. Approximately one hundred bodies have so far been recovered. Others will, no doubt, be found as the waters recede, but it is not likely that the number will exceed two hundred. This is remarkably low considering the nature and extent of the flood and speaks volumes for those who risked their lives in the work of rescue and for the devotion of the doctors, nurses and others who assisted in caring for the refugees.

Dayton's experiences with the flood gave the example and created the public sentiment that made possible the change. The secret of business success, as illustrated in Dayton's corporations, was concentration of authority and responsibility. The stockholders elected a board of directors who had general supervision over affairs. This board did not attempt to control the detail of the business; in most instances it selected a president, or vice-president, gave him complete authority, and demanded results. This manager appointed the heads of departments, giving them authority in turn and in turn exacting results. Thus those twin forces of efficiency, authority and responsibility, became the predominant factors in the whole system. Why not introduce them as the governing powers in the city administration? Fundamentally that is the idea that lies at the basis of the "City Manager" plan. The stockholders—the citizens—elect a board of directors, the five commissioners. These gentlemen have a free hand to engage a manager, to purchase him in the open American market, and to pay him such a salary as the circumstances may warrant. This manager has complete authority to run the business of the city, and, since he has this authority, he can be held completely responsible for its success. He selects the heads of his departments, and is not obliged to select them from the city of Dayton. The relation of these heads to the city manager is identically that of the department heads of a great corporation to the chief executive; the relation of the manager to the city commission is the same as that of the executive to the directorate; and the relation of the commission to the voters is the same as that of the directorate to the stockholders.

Naturally this proposal aroused much antagonism. The socialists opposed it for good socialistic reasons; since it was based upon the organization of successful private business, its origin was clearly "capitalistic." The politicians ridiculed the idea, and their opposition was similarly logical. Why should they submit to "government by non-residents," when "there are plenty of men right here in Dayton who know how to run our town?" Yet there were other opponents, less logical though they may have been more honest and sincere. These respectable conservatives damned the suggestion as "un-American." It seemed inconceivable that an American city could exist and that municipal liberties could be preserved without the usual division of the city into wards, without a frock-coated mayor, a local legislature, an elected comptroller, sealers of weights and measures, coroners, and all the lengthy list who made voting a Dayton ballot, as some one remarked, "like voting a bed-quilt." Still many of these functionaries descend from the days of Magna Charta, and their position seemed as sacred as habeas corpus and trial by jury. But Dayton's electorate is an intelligent and progressive one, and, for the most part, has outlived the age of superstition. And it had just had a persuasive illustration of efficiency and inefficiency. So Dayton turned its back upon the past, and, by a large majority, accepted the City Manager plan.

Let us not forget that ultimate responsibility to the voters resides, not in the manager, but in a commission of five men.

There are no aldermen, no councilmen, no Board of Estimate, none of the useless lumber that usually makes city administration so cumbersome and intricate. But the duties of the commission are not entirely ornamental. One of them, the one who gets the most votes, has the title of Mayor; he presides over the weekly meetings, represents the city on ceremonial occasions, and gets $1,800 a year salary, whereas the other commissioners get $1,200. This commission is the local legislature, in the same sense that the directorate is the legislature of the corporation. It meets weekly and passes such ordinances as its wisdom prescribes, and its approval is needed to perform the greatest function of government—the adoption of a budget. Its most important direct responsibility, however, is the selection of the manager, and, after performing this duty, its main occupation is keeping a close eye upon this important employee, and assuring itself that he measures up to the job. It engages this gentleman for no specific term, for it can "fire" him summarily if convinced that he is not properly doing his work. Clearly, therefore, the position of commissioner is one of great dignity and responsibility, and the first commission elected was almost ideally representative, its members comprising a labor leader in the printing trade, an office manager for a large industrial corporation, a manufacturer, a brick contractor, and a merchant.

The new charter did not prescribe that these gentlemen should select their manager outside of Dayton; it gave them free scope to seek him anywhere. Business prudence indicated that a non-resident might prove most satisfactory at that particular moment, for Dayton resembled a bankrupt business house that badly needed a "new deal." When reorganization demands the elimination of the unfit and the selection of the fit, a private business ordinarily selects its reorganizer outside of its own ranks. A stranger, since he has no accumulated loyalties and is uninfluenced by personal associations and long-standing friendships, is clearly best fitted to "hire and fire." Dayton's new commission offered this job first to General Goethals, suggesting the salary, hitherto unparalleled in American cities, of $25,000 a year. But General Goethals had duties elsewhere, and it was necessary to get some one not quite so well known. The procedure was precisely that of a large corporation looking for an executive head. Several possible candidates were summoned to Dayton, and their personal and professional qualities were carefully examined. Of them all Mr. Henry M. Waite made the most favorable impression. Mr. Waite was not eagerly soliciting the job; he had just declined a place that offered him $16,000 a year; he was therefore an independent agent, and was not obliged to accept the novel opportunity except on his own terms. He was forty-four years old, had been educated at the Massachusetts Institute of Technology, had started his professional career as a transit-man on the Big Four Railroad, and had worked his way up, serving as division engineer, bridge engineer, road-master, superintendent on different lines, finally becoming chief engineer and vice-president of the Clinchfield Coal Corporation. His only contact with a municipality had been as chief engineer of public works in Cincinnati, under the administration of Henry T. Hunt. Amid the howls of protesting politicians the Dayton commission offered Mr. Waite $12,500 a year. To those who shouted that no man with any public spirit would accept such a "monstrous" salary Mr. Waite's retort was eloquent and direct. He was not accepting the job out of any sense of public spirit. Naturally he had that pride in his work which should inspire any properly constituted professional craftsman, and he was not blind to the opportunities for social service which it presented. Primarily, however, he had something to sell to Dayton—his efficiency as an executive, and Dayton, if it really wished his services, must somewhere approximate their market value. This being a City Manager was as much a job as that of being a lawyer, a doctor, or a railroad president; he was not undertaking the work from any passion for public life, or as a stepping-stone to a Governorship, a Senatorship, or possibly the Presidency. Any time Dayton thinks that a cheaper man can do the work better, Mr. Waite is ready to quit the City Hall.

And Mr. Waite selected his subordinates on the same basis. As an evidence of lack of prejudice, he asked representative Dayton organizations to furnish him names of the most competent men who were available to head each of his departments, but he neglected to ask the advice of that order of society who would have been most prolific in suggestions—the machine politicians. As head of the Department of Finance he made an obvious but somewhat unusual appointment— Mr. Hugh E. Wall, a distinguished certified public accountant. Mr. J. E. Barlow, a man with a high reputation as an engineer, became head of the Department of Public Service —another instance of "government by non-residents." Dr. D. F. Garland, a man who, as pastor of a Lutheran church, had displayed that quality known as "social consciousness," was made superintendent of the Department of Public Welfare. Mr. H. P. James, who had served as a member of Dayton's fire department for fourteen years, became Director of Public Safety, an office which included the supervision of the fire and police departments. The net result of these and other appointments was that elimination of political control for which so many American cities have struggled but which few have realized. In selecting minor employees, all political considerations have likewise been disregarded, complete dependence being placed on a Civil Service Commission. Mr. Waite has now had five years in which to test this new municipal system. What, then, have been the results?

In view of the fact that we have in Dayton, almost for the first time in the nation's history, a municipal organization that is spending money purely on business principles, it would be surprising if there should not be definite evidences of improvement. The facts brought forward are not spectacular or dramatic; the details of municipal housekeeping comprise columns of figures, contrasting the price of hose now with the prices paid under the old system, tangible evidences of economy in the purchase of typewriter ribbons, paper clips, and even more substantial items such as the reduction of the debt.

The Waite régime has not been a cheese-paring one. It has not hesitated to pay market prices for city employees, and there has been a slight increase in the tax rate. However, there has been an even greater decrease in other things. One of these is the death rate. Before the Waite régime this stood at 15.7; since, it has dropped to 13. Another detail is the decreased infant-mortality rate—perhaps the severest test of enlightened civic administration; this has dropped from 124 per thousand in 1913 to 87 in 1916. Yet the average Daytonian needs no elaborate statistics to prove that he is living in a changed municipal environment. He sees the signs on every hand. His streets are now painstakingly repaired and cleanly swept, whereas six years ago they were filled with filth and rubbish. Under the old political control the Daytonian had difficulty in drawing water from the tap for his morning bath; the pressure was low and the supply so uncertain that water famines were not infrequent. Now water is as plentiful as heaven intended that it should be; new pumps, new pipe-lines, new meters, new turbines have produced a practically reconstructed water system; and, while these facilities have been so completely modernized, the cost to the citizen has appreciably gone down. Dayton now collects its garbage, whereas formerly it was permitted to gather unheeded in unsalubrious heaps; a modern reduction plant, built by Mr. Waite, not only protects the city's sanitation, but brings a large revenue from the sale of grease and tankage. The city now has its own asphalt plant—an experiment in municipal ownership that has produced excellent results; it has adopted an elaborate plan of conservancy which, unless the nation's greatest engineers are wrong, will prevent future floods; it has planned and begun building a new comprehensive sewer system based upon the requirements, so far as they can be foreseen, of 1950; it has acquired large properties which have been set aside for parks; it has built a municipal greenhouse, constructed several new bridges, planted thousands of trees, and lighted the streets as they had never been lighted before. Dayton's police force, although it has not succeeded in solving the eternal vice question, has abolished graft, closed the Red Light district, and made the city outwardly decent and safe.

And the City Manager is a leading American exponent of that new conception of city government—that it exists not only to safeguard life and property, but to promote social betterment, and to make existence more comfortable, enjoyable, and edifying for the everyday man, woman, and child. Perhaps we shall find Dayton's greatest contribution to municipal administration, not in her water plant, her sewerage system, and accounting methods, but in that branch of her civic life known as the Department of Public Welfare. Dayton, like all American cities, especially those which have had a rapid industrial development, has its poor quarters, its thousands of underfed children, its idle working classes, its army of vagrants and social delinquents, and its babies dying for lack of fresh air and decent surroundings. What is the City Manager doing about this elementary problem? The new Department of Public Welfare is Dayton's public acknowledgment that its responsibility extends to these classes. And here again

Dayton's business enterprises have pointed the way. Its great manufacturers have long been famous for those attempts to benefit its employees which are comprehended under the name of "welfare work"; in their organizations baths, lunch-rooms, gardens, playgrounds, clubs, rest-rooms, lectures, schools, and kindergartens have figured almost as conspicuously as the finished product. Since these men were reorganizing the city on the plans which had been developed in private industry, "welfare work" necessarily became a part of the system. Doctor Garland, who has charge of this department, is responsible for the public health, recreation, parks, correctional and reformatory institutions, outdoor relief, legal aid, municipal lodging-house, and public nursing, while he is also expected constantly to study the causes that produce poverty, delinquency, disease, and crime. Besides reducing the death rate, he has revised the milk standard and lowered by 80 per cent, its bacterial content; he has cleaned the public markets, the bakeries and candy-factories, and improved the sanitation of the food-supply. His department examines nearly two hundred thousand school-children every year, vaccinating the unvaccinated and providing free clinics where most ailments can be treated. Its energies in "cleaning up" the city extend to cutting weeds on vacant lots, and conducting campaigns against those citizens who scatter broadcast papers and rubbish. Doctor Garland has much simplified the municipal lodging-house problem by demanding of its prospective guests half a day's work and a bath—stipulations that have cut the patronage down 75 per cent. A city employ-

ment agency furnishes saleswomen to department stores, seamstresses to households, and "hands" to the local factories. A city legal-aid service furnishes legal advice to hundreds of citizens, most of them representing those poor and ignorant classes that so easily become the victims of legal technicalities. This department has driven all loan sharks out of town and made life exceedingly uncomfortable for fraudulent instalment houses.

Most cities are built for adults; the city plans, with their streets, their alleys, their ornate parks, and their speedways, clearly signify that only grown-ups are expected to inhabit them. Dayton has suddenly awakened to the fact that children form an important part of its population, and it is recasting its physical organization with that as a starting-point. Streets and alleys are all right for mature pedestrians and draymen, but nature never intended that children should live in them and derive from them their education. In 1915 Mr. Waite's Department of Welfare established eighteen playgrounds, and each public school added a similar annex to its equipment. Now marble-shooting, jackstones, kite-flying, baseball, and swimming are regular municipal activities. Wherever Mr. Waite finds a vacant lot he immediately attempts to convert it into a baseball diamond. He has placed the full force of the city government behind the amateur baseball league; he is himself one of the most pertinacious "fans" at these contests and has personally established a prize cup. Play festivals are more important functions than the "inaugurations" that are still the great days in most American municipalities. On such occasions one may witness the folk games and folk dances of dozens of countries. There are municipal water carnivals, with rowboat, canoe, swimming races, and firework displays. Dayton lights the river-front for night bathing, and conducts a municipal dance-hall, where Mr. and Mrs. Waite may sometimes be detected two-stepping with the proletariat. And the city gives entertainments of a more intellectual kind. Its municipal concerts, where the Metropolitan Opera stars and the works of the greatest composers may be heard, have demonstrated the power of music as an educative force in a democracy.

And this spirit of benevolence extends to those who, despite great progress in recent years, are still too much neglected in this country—the wayward and criminal classes. The Dayton workhouse, like most urban institutions of the kind, presented that galaxy of habitual offenders which has long been the despair of prison-reformers. A statistical study disclosed that many Daytonians had spent the larger part of their lives within its walls, serving sentences of thirty and sixty days. Can society do anything to transform these derelicts into normal human beings? Perhaps not; Dayton, however, is trying, though it is too early to draw conclusions concerning its success. One thing it can say: these men and women are making some return to society for the dislocations which they have caused. Doctor Garland has abolished the contract-labor plan. The women do all the sewing and mending for the institution; they remodel cast-off clothing into children's dresses, which are distributed through the Associated Charities to needy families. Besides doing all the routine

work of the workhouse the men labor on the levees, in the river channels and vegetable gardens. A new parole system has been established; prisoners are distributed in the local shops and factories; while sometimes the women are placed out in such private houses as will receive them. Their weekly wages are paid to the Superintendent of Correction, who pays the prisoner's debts, and uses the rest for the support of his wife and children. Less than 10 per cent. of those granted these privileges have violated them.

The old-style politician, who still exists in Dayton, momentarily looking for opportunities to retake his old trenches, has a characteristic and somewhat vulgar name for this system. He calls it "government by bugs." He has that same hostility recently voiced by Mayor Hylan of New York for "experts" of all kinds—especially those from out of town. He reluctantly admits that "that feller Waite is the best of the bunch," and that he does give "good enough government," but he has all the animosity of De Tocqueville himself toward a system in which the legislative and executive powers reside in the same body. He dislikes an order in which the average citizen calls on the Manager for enlightenment instead of coming around to visit the ward boss in the back room of a saloon.

"Can't the politicians come back?" I asked Mr. Waite. "Is your scheme boss-proof?"

"Not at all," he replied, quickly. "They can corrupt the city under this system even more completely than under any other. That in itself is an argument in its favor. All power here lies with a commission of five men who are elected by popular suffrage. If the people elect five politicians these five politicians can dismiss the City Manager and choose one with whom they can plunder and betray the city in every conceivable way. That is just as it should be. We cannot give a man complete power to run a city well without also giving him complete power to do all manner of evil. But the great advantage of the Dayton system is that we know precisely who is to blame. It fixes responsibility in one place instead of scattering it among a dozen different agencies. If Dayton becomes a corrupt and inefficiently managed town, it will only be because the citizens prefer to have it so." ■

363

PERCEPTIONS OF
REFORM POLITICS

The preceding pages all convey an image of the urban reformer at the turn of the century. Most of these portraits come from magazines and newspapers of the day. Two are profiles of reform mayors and another is a profile of a city manager. Also included is a collection of anecdotes by reform mayors.

1 Are the images of the urban reformer projected by these different sources pretty much the same? How would you account for the similarities and differences?

2 Based on these sources, what hypotheses can you make about the dominant characteristics of the American "urban reformer" around the turn of the century?

3 How would you compare the "urban reformer" to the city "boss"? In what ways are the two types most unlike one another? Do they have any characteristics in common? Which characteristics do you think would be most appropriate in a big-city politician of the 1970's? ■

EVERY MAN IS ENTITLED TO SUCH A SHARE IN THE PRODUCTS OF HIS TOIL AS WILL ENABLE HIM TO LIVE DECENTLY, AND IN SUCH A WAY THAT HE AND HIS CHILDREN MAY BE FITTED TO BE CITIZENS OF A FREE REPUBLIC.

DRIVE PROSTITUTES OUT OF TOLEDO! TO WHERE? I SUGGEST THAT INSTEAD WE CALL UPON OUR MINISTERS TO TAKE THESE ERRANT SISTERS INTO THEIR HOMES, GET THEM JOBS AND REHABILITATE THEM.

LET US TAKE CLUBS AWAY FROM POLICEMEN AN SUBSTITUTE LIGHT CANES; DISMISS DRUNKS WITH A LECTURE ON TEMPERANCE AND THIEVES WITH ONE ON THE EVILS OF STEALING; SENTENCE A MAN CAUGHT ILLEGALLY CARRYING A GUN TO SMASHING IT IN PUBLIC WITH A SLEDGE; LECTURE ONE ACCUSED OF ASSAULT ON THE USELESSNESS OF FORCE AND THE POWER OF LOVE.

Sam Jones
MAYOR OF TOLEDO

IT WAS LIKE SEEING A CAPTAIN OF INDUSTRY ON
THE STAGE: HE RECEIVED HIS CALLERS ONE BY
ONE, SWIFTLY, WITHOUT HASTE; HE LISTENED, ALL
ATTENTION, TILL HE UNDERSTOOD; THEN HE
WOULD SMILE OR LAUGH, GIVE A DECISION,
AND — 'NEXT!' NO ASKING FOR TIME TO 'THINK
IT OVER' OR TO 'CONSULT HIS COLLEAGUES;
NO TALK OF 'COMMISSIONS TO INVESTIGATE',
NO 'COME AGAIN NEXT WEEK.' IT WAS
NO OR YES, GENIAL, JOLLY, BUT FINAL:

IT'S FUN, RUNNING THE BUSINESS OF THE CITY
OF CLEVELAND; IT'S THE BIGGEST, MOST
COMPLICATED, MOST DIFFICULT, AND MOST
SATISFYING BUSINESS IN CLEVELAND. A
STREET RAILWAY IS CHILD'S PLAY, COMPARED
WITH IT; A COAL MINE IS A SNAP; A BANK?—
BAH. THERE'S SOMETHING THAT BLINDS YOU
FELLOWS, AND I KNOW WHAT IT IS. IT'S WHAT
FOOLED ME SO LONG WHEN I WAS RUNNING
FOR PUBLIC OFFICE 'ORATIONS. AND I'LL TELL
YOU SOMETHING YOU WANT TO KNOW: HOW TO
BEAT ME .

IF I COULD TAKE AWAY FROM YOU THE THINGS
YOU HAVE, THE FRANCHISES, THE PRIVILEGES

THAT MAKE YOU ENEMIES OF YOUR CITY,
YOU WOULD SEE WHAT I SEE AND RUN
FOR MY JOB YOURSELVES, AND YOU'D
BEAT ME FOR MAYOR AND MANAGE
THE CITY OF CLEVELAND BETTER
THAN I DO.

IT IS PRIVILEGE THAT CAUSES EVIL IN THE
WORLD, NOT WICKEDNESS; AND NOT MEN.

Tom Johnson
MAYOR OF CLEVELAND

IN MY 'POTATO PATCH PLAN', VACANT LOTS
WERE DONATED TO NEEDY FAMILIES FOR
VEGETABLE GROWING. INVOLVED WERE
MORE THAN A THOUSAND DETROIT FAMILIES.

BUT I DO SAY EMPHATICALLY. BETTER TAKE
THE UTILITIES OUT OF PRIVATE HANDS THAN
ALLOW THEM TO STAND AS THE GREATEST
CORRUPTORS OF PUBLIC MORALS THAT
EVER BLACKENED THE PAGES OF HISTORY.

Hazen Pingree
MAYOR OF DETROIT

I AM NOT A REPUBLICAN
MAYOR, AS YOU SAY I AM.
I AM MAYOR OF THE
WHOLE PEOPLE OF
BROOKLYN.

Seth Low
MAYOR OF BROOKLYN

IT IS TIME TO COME OUT
IN THE OPEN AND HAVE
A SQUARE STAND-UP
FIGHT AGAINST THE
REPUBLICAN BOSS, THE
DEMOCRATIC BOSS, AND
THE TROLLEY AND RAIL-
ROAD CORPORATIONS
WHICH CONTROL THEM
BOTH.

Mark Fagan
MAYOR OF JERSEY CITY

PROGRESSIVE URBAN REFORMERS: A Reassessment

Source: Samuel Hays, "The Politics of Reform in Municipal Government in the Progressive Era," *Pacific Northwest Quarterly*, vol. 55, no. 4 (October 1964), pp. 102–117.

The magazine profiles of urban reformers that you have just read reflect the hopeful optimism of writers living in the Progressive Era. The next selection is taken from the researches of an historian who has recently reassessed the politics of municipal reform in the Progressive Era. It is taken from an article written by Samuel Hays, a social historian who has written extensively about America during this period.

Although reformers used the ideology of popular government, they in no sense meant that all segments of society should be involved equally in municipal decision-making. They meant that their concept of the city's welfare would be best achieved if the business community controlled city government. As one businessman told a labor audience, the businessman's slate represented labor "better than you do yourself."

The composition of the municipal reform movement in Pittsburgh demonstrates its upper-class and professional as well as its business sources. Here the two principal reform organizations were the Civic Club and the Voters' League. The 745 members of these two organizations came primarily from the upper class. Sixty-five per cent appeared in upper-class directories which contained the names of only 2 per cent of the city's families. Furthermore, many who were not listed in these directories lived in upper-class areas. These reformers, it should be stressed, comprised not an old but a new upper class. Few came from earlier industrial and mercantile families. Most of them had risen to social position from wealth created after 1870 in the iron, steel, electrical equipment, and other industries and they lived in the newer rather than the older fashionable areas.

Almost half (48 per cent) of the reformers were professional men: doctors, lawyers, ministers, directors of libraries and museums, engineers, architects, private and public school teachers, and college professors. Some of these belonged to the upper class as well, especially the lawyers, ministers, and private school teachers. But

for the most part their interest in reform stemmed from the inherent dynamics of their professions rather than from their class connections. They came from the more advanced segments of their organizations, from those in the forefront of the acquisition and application of knowledge. They were not the older professional men, seeking to preserve the past against change; they were in the vanguard of professional life, actively seeking to apply expertise more widely to public affairs.

Pittsburgh reformers included a large segment of businessmen; 52 per cent were bankers and corporation officials or their wives. Among them were the presidents of fourteen large banks and officials of Westinghouse, Pittsburgh Plate Glass, U.S. Steel and its component parts (such as Carnegie Steel, American Bridge, and National Tube), Jones and Laughlin, lesser steel companies (such as Crucible, Pittsburgh, Superior, Lockhart, and H. K. Porter), the H. J. Heinz Company, and the Pittsburgh Coal Company, as well as officials of the Pennsylvania Railroad and the Pittsburgh and Lake Erie. These men were not small businessmen; they directed the most powerful banking and industrial organizations of the city. They represented not the old business community, but industries which had developed and grown primarily within the past fifty years and which had come to dominate the city's economic life.

These business, professional, and upper-class groups who dominated municipal reform movements were all involved in the rationalization and systematization of modern life; they wished a form of government which would be more consistent with the objectives inherent in those developments. The most important single feature of their perspective was the rapid expansion of the geographical scope of affairs which they wished to influence and manipulate, a scope which was no longer limited and narrow, no longer within the confines of pedestrian communities, but was now broad and city-wide, covering the whole range of activities of the metropolitan area.

The migration of the upper class from central to outlying areas created a geographical distance between its residential communities and its economic institutions. To protect the latter required involvement both in local ward affairs and in the larger city government as well. Moreover, upper-class cultural institutions, such as museums, libraries, and symphony orchestras, required an active interest in the larger municipal context from which these institutions drew much of their clientele.

Professional groups, broadening the scope of affairs which they sought to study, measure, or manipulate, also sought to influence the public health, the educational system, or the physical arrangements of the entire city. Their concerns were limitless, not bounded by geography, but as expansive as the professional imagination. Finally, the new industrial community greatly broadened its perspective in governmental affairs because of its new recognition of the way in which factors throughout the city affected business growth. The increasing size and scope of industry, the greater stake in more varied and geographically dispersed facets of city life, the effect of floods on many business concerns, the need to promote

traffic flows to and from work for both blue-collar and managerial employees—all contributed to this larger interest. The geographically larger private perspectives of upper-class, professional, and business groups gave rise to a geographically larger public perspective.

These reformers were dissatisfied with existing systems of municipal government. They did not oppose corruption per se—although there was plenty of that. They objected to the structure of government which enabled local and particularistic interests to dominate. Prior to the reforms of the Progressive Era, city government consisted primarily of confederations of local wards, each of which was represented on the city's legislative body. Each ward frequently had its own elementary schools and ward-elected school boards which administered them.

These particularistic interests were the focus of a decentralized political life. City councilmen were local leaders. They spoke for their local areas, the economic interests of their inhabitants, their residential concerns, their educational, recreational, and religious interests—i.e., for those aspects of community life which mattered most to those they represented. They rolled logs in the city council to provide streets, sewers, and other public works for their local areas. They defended the community's cultural practices, its distinctive languages or national customs, its liberal attitude toward liquor, and its saloons and dance halls which served as centers of community life. One observer described this process of representation in Seattle:

The residents of the hill-tops and the suburbs may not fully appreciate the faithfulness of certain downtown ward councilmen to the interests of their constituents. . . . The people of a state would rise in arms against a senator or representative in Congress who deliberately misrepresented their wishes and imperiled their interests, though he might plead a higher regard for national good. Yet people in other parts of the city seem to forget that under the old system the ward elected councilmen with the idea of procuring service of special benefit to that ward.

In short, pre-reform officials spoke for their constituencies, inevitably their own wards which had elected them, rather than for other sections or groups of the city.

The ward system of government especially gave representation in city affairs to lower- and middle-class groups. Most elected ward officials were from these groups, and they, in turn, constituted the major opposition to reforms in municipal government. In Pittsburgh, for example, immediately prior to the changes in both the city council and the school board in 1911 in which city-wide representation replaced ward representation, only 24 per cent of the 387 members of those bodies represented the same managerial, professional, and banker occupations which dominated the membership of the Civic Club and the Voters' League. The great majority (67 per cent) were small businessmen—grocers, saloonkeepers, livery-stable proprietors, owners of small hotels, druggists—white-collar workers such as clerks and bookkeepers, and skilled and unskilled workmen.

This decentralized system of urban growth and the institutions which arose from it reformers now opposed. Social, professional, and economic life had developed not only in the local wards in a small community context, but also on a larger scale had become highly integrated and organized, giving rise to a superstructure of social organization which lay far above that of ward life and which was sharply divorced from it in both personal contacts and perspective.

By the late 19th century, those involved in these larger institutions found that the decentralized system of political life limited their larger objectives. The movement for reform in municipal government, therefore, constituted an attempt by upper-class, advanced professional, and large business groups to take formal political power from the previously dominant lower- and middle-class elements so that they might advance their own conceptions of desirable public policy. These two groups came from entirely different urban worlds, and the political system fashioned by one was no longer acceptable to the other.

Lower- and middle-class groups not only dominated the pre-reform governments, but vigorously opposed reform. It is significant that none of the occupational groups among them, for example, small businessmen or white-collar workers, skilled or unskilled artisans, had important representation in reform organizations thus far examined. The case studies of city-manager government undertaken in the 1930's under the direction of Leonard White detailed in city after city the particular opposition of labor. In their analysis

of Jackson, Michigan, the authors of these studies wrote:

The Square Deal, *oldest Labor paper in the state, has been consistently against manager government, perhaps largely because labor has felt that with a decentralized government elected on a ward basis it was more likely to have some voice and to receive its share of privileges.*

In Janesville, Wisconsin, the small shopkeepers and workingmen on the west and south sides, heavily Catholic and often Irish, opposed the commission plan in 1911 and in 1912 and the city-manager plan when adopted in 1923. "In Dallas there is hardly a trace of class consciousness in the Marxian sense," one investigator declared, "yet in city elections the division has been to a great extent along class lines." The commission and city-manager elections were no exceptions. To these authors it seemed a logical reaction, rather than an embarrassing fact that had to be swept away, that workingmen should have opposed municipal reform.

In Des Moines working-class representatives, who in previous years might have been council members, were conspicuously absent from the "businessman's slate." Workingmen acceptable to reformers could not be found. A workingman's slate of candidates, therefore, appeared to challenge the reform slate. Organized labor, and especially the mineworkers, took the lead; one of their number, Wesley Ash, a deputy sheriff and union member, made "an astonishing run" in the primary, coming in second among a field of more than twenty candidates. In fact, the strength

of anticommission candidates in the primary so alarmed reformers that they frantically sought to appease labor.

The day before the final election they modified their platform to pledge both an eight-hour day and an "American standard of wages." They attempted to persuade the voters that their slate consisted of men who represented labor because they had "begun at the bottom of the ladder and made a good climb toward success by their own unaided efforts." But their tactics failed. In the election on March 30, 1908, voters swept into office the entire "opposition" slate. The business and professional community had succeeded in changing the form of government, but not in securing its control. A cartoon in the leading reform newspaper illustrated their disappointment; John Q. Public sat dejectedly and muttered, "Aw, What's the Use?"

The most visible opposition to reform and the most readily available target of reform attack was the so-called "machine," for through the "machine" many different ward communities as well as lower- and middle-income groups joined effectively to influence the central city government. Their private occupational and social life did not naturally involve these groups in larger city-wide activities in the same way as the upper class was involved; hence they lacked access to privately organized economic and social power on which they could construct political power. The "machine" filled this organizational gap.

Yet it should never be forgotten that the social and economic institutions in the wards themselves provided the "machine's" sustaining support and gave it larger significance. When reformers attacked the "machine" as the most visible institutional element of the ward system, they attacked the entire ward form of political organization and the political power of lower- and middle-income groups which lay behind it.

Reformers often gave the impression that they opposed merely the corrupt politician and his "machine." But in a more fundamental way they looked upon the deficiencies of pre-reform political leaders in terms not of their personal shortcomings, but of the limitations inherent in their occupational, institutional, and class positions. In 1911 the Voters' League of Pittsburgh wrote in its pamphlet analyzing the qualifications of candidates that "a man's occupation ought to give a strong indication of his qualifications for membership on a school board." Certain occupations inherently disqualified a man from serving:

Employment as ordinary laborer and in the lowest class of mill work would naturally lead to the conclusion that such men did not have sufficient education or business training to act as school directors. . . . Objection might also be made to small shopkeepers, clerks, workmen at many trades, who by lack of educational advantages and business training, could not, no matter how honest, be expected to administer properly the affairs of an educational system, requiring special knowledge, and where millions are spent each year.

These, of course, were precisely the groups which did dominate Pittsburgh government prior to reform. The League deplored the fact that school boards contained only a small number of "men prominent throughout the city in business life . . . in professional occupations . . . holding positions as managers, secretaries, auditors, superintendents and foremen" and exhorted these classes to participate more actively as candidates for office.

Reformers, therefore, wished not simply to replace bad men with good; they proposed to change the occupational and class origins of decision-makers. Toward this end they sought innovations in the formal machinery of government which would concentrate political power by sharply centralizing the processes of decision-making rather than distribute it through more popular participation in public affairs. According to the liberal view of the Progressive Era, the major political innovations of reform involved the equalization of political power through the primary, the direct election of public officials, and the initiative, referendum, and recall. These measures played a large role in the political ideology of the time and were frequently incorporated into new municipal charters. But they provided at best only an occasional and often incidental process of decision-making. Far more important in continuous, sustained, day-to-day processes of government were those innovations which centralized decision-making in the hands of fewer and fewer people.

The systematization of municipal government took place on both the executive and the legislative levels. The strong-mayor and city-manager types became the most widely used examples of the former. In the first decade of the 20th century, the commission plan had considerable appeal, but its distribution of administrative responsibility among five people gave rise to a demand for a form with more centralized executive power; consequently, the city-manager or the commission-manager variant often replaced it.

A far more pervasive and significant change, however, lay in the centralization of the system of representation, the shift from ward to city-wide election of councils and school boards. Governing bodies so selected, reformers argued, would give less attention to local and particularistic matters and more to affairs of city-wide scope. This shift, an invariable feature of both commission and city-manager plans, was often adopted by itself. In Pittsburgh, for example, the new charter of 1911 provided as the major innovation that a council of twenty-seven, each member elected from a separate ward, be replaced by a council of nine, each elected by the city as a whole.

Cities displayed wide variations in this innovation. Some regrouped wards into larger units but kept the principle of areas of representation smaller than the entire city. Some combined a majority of councilmen elected by wards with additional ones elected at large. All such innovations, however, constituted steps toward the centralization of the system of representation.

Liberal historians have not appreciated the extent to which municipal reform in the Progressive Era involved a debate over the system of representation. The ward form of representation was universally condemned on the grounds that it gave too much influence to the separate units and not enough attention to the larger problems of the city. Harry A. Toulmin, whose book, *The City Manager,* was published by the National Municipal League, stated the case:

The spirit of sectionalism had dominated the political life of every city. Ward pitted against ward, alderman against alderman, and legislation only effected by "log-rolling" extravagant measures into operation, mulcting the city, but gratifying the greed of constituents, has too long stung the conscience of decent citizenship. This constant treaty-making of factionalism has been no less than a curse. The city manager plan proposes the commendable thing of abolishing wards. The plan is not unique in this for it has been common to many forms of commission government. . . .

Such a system should be supplanted, the argument usually went, with city-wide representation in which elected officials could consider the city "as a unit." "The new officers are elected," wrote Toulmin, "each to represent all the people. Their duties are so defined that they must administer the corporate business in its entirety, not as a hodge-podge of associated localities."

Behind the debate over the method of representation, however, lay a debate over who should be represented, over whose views of public policy should prevail. Many reform leaders often explicitly, if not implicitly, expressed fear that lower-

and middle-income groups had too much influence in decision-making. One Galveston leader, for example, complained about the movement for initiative, referendum, and recall:

We have in our city a very large number of negroes employed on the docks; we also have a very large number of unskilled white laborers; this city also has more barrooms, according to its population, than any other city in Texas. Under these circumstances it would be extremely difficult to maintain a satisfactory city government where all ordinances must be submitted back to the voters of the city for their ratification and approval.

At the National Municipal League convention of 1907, Rear Admiral F. E. Chadwick (USN Ret.), a leader in the Newport, Rhode Island, movement for municipal reform, spoke to this question even more directly:

Our present system has excluded in large degree the representation of those who have the city's well-being most at heart. It has brought, in municipalities . . . a government established by the least educated, the least interested class of citizens.
It stands to reason that a man paying $5,000 taxes in a town is more interested in the well-being and development of his town than the man who pays no taxes. . . . It equally stands to reason that the man of the $5,000 tax should be assured a representation in the committee which lays the tax and spends the money which he contributes. . . . Shall we be truly democratic and give the property owner a fair

show or shall we develop a tyranny of ignorance which shall crush him.

Municipal reformers thus debated frequently the question of who should be represented as well as the question of what method of representation should be employed.

That these two questions were intimately connected was revealed in other reform proposals for representation, proposals which were rarely taken seriously. One suggestion was that a class system of representation be substituted for ward representation. For example, in 1908 one of the prominent candidates for commissioner in Des Moines proposed that the city council be composed of representatives of five classes: educational and ministerial organizations, manufacturers and jobbers, public utility corporations, retail merchants including liquor men, and the Des Moines Trades and Labor Assembly. Such a system would have greatly reduced the influence in the council of both middle- and lower-class groups. The proposal revealed the basic problem confronting business and professional leaders: how to reduce the influence in government of the majority of voters among middle- and lower-income groups. ■

371

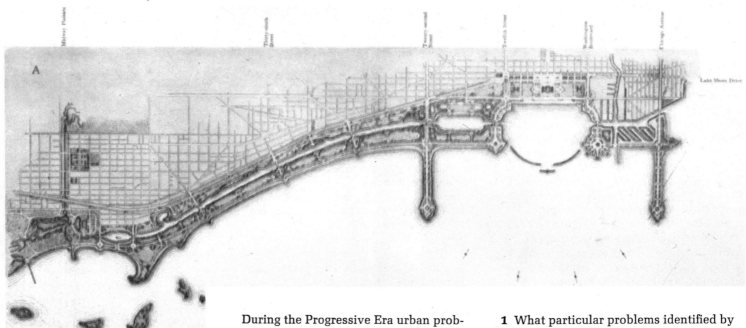

372

Lakeshore from Chicago Avenue on the north to Jackson Park on the south.   From Plan for Chicago, © 1909, The Commercial Club

During the Progressive Era urban problems began to be seen as something more than a political failure involving corruption and inefficiency. Urban architects, housing reformers, and conservationists started to think of ways in which they might physically shape the city so as to make of it a place in which people, space, and nature together would form a whole that was a work of art. The city would become, as Frederick Howe, the Progressive urban reformer suggested, "the hope of democracy." Following are diagrams, sketches, and photographs which portray such plans.

1 What particular problems identified by Progressive reformers was each plan seeking to alleviate?

2 How does the conception of urban life underlying each plan take account of technology, the "natural" environment, and the social needs of people?

3 What potentialities of city living is each plan seeking to develop?

4 Judging from the photographs portraying the plan as it was realized, do you think the planner's hopes for his conception were fulfilled? What evidence supports your conclusion? What other kinds of evidence would be helpful in estimating the effect of the plan? ■

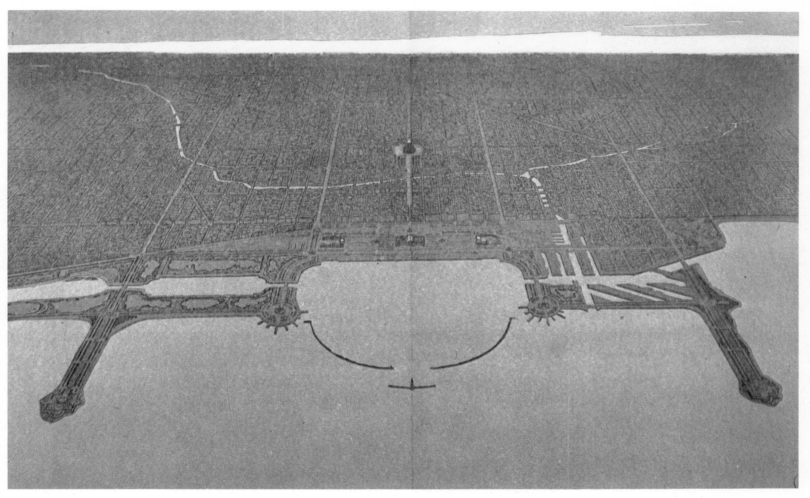

373

Chicago looking west, showing proposed Civic Center, The Grand Axis, Grant Park and the harbor. Painted by Jules Guerin   From Plan for Chicago, © 1909, The Commercial Club

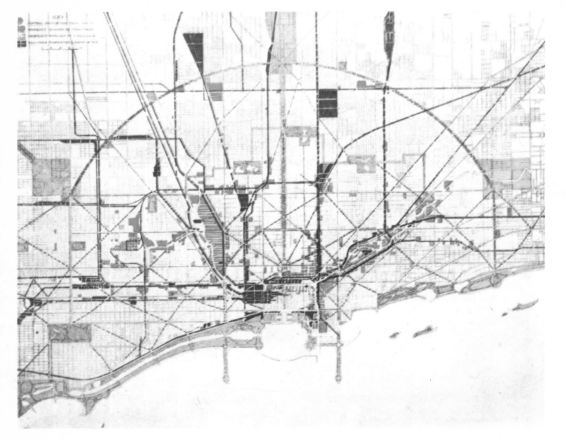

Diagram of general scheme of street circulation and parks in relation to areas covered by industries. From Plan for Chicago, © 1909, The Commercial Club

Proposed plan for Michigan Avenue painted by Jules Guerin, © 1909, The Commercial Club

Proposed plan for waterways, painted by Jules Guerin, © 1909, The Commercial Club

376

ABOVE LEFT:
The Senate Park Commission Plan, 1901, for Washington   From a rendering by Jules Guerin

LEFT:
The Senate Park Commission Plan of 1901 for the west front of the Capitol.

LOWER RIGHT:
The Senate Park Commission Plan for Washington, 1901, showing proposed treatment of the Washington Monument grounds and the Mall

THE CITY BEAUTIFUL

The following selection will help you reflect further on the significance of urban planning during the Progressive Era. It is taken from a book written by Roy Lubove, a leading authority on urban history.

Source: Roy Lubove, *The Urban Community: Housing and Planning in the Progressive Era* (Englewood Cliffs, N.J.: Prentice-Hall, Inc., 1967), pp. 1–10.

During the late nineteenth and early twentieth centuries, the American city entered a new phase of its history. The long-term demographic revolution, which concentrated a majority of the population in urban areas, was completed by 1920. Americans of the progressive era were thus the first to confront the reality of urban dominance. Many reform efforts of the period—labor legislation, Americanization, prohibition, housing, public health, and good government—were related to problems of city life. More generally, urbanization was synonymous with industrialization and its challenge to traditional institutions. The fact that the progressive era witnessed the definitive transition from a rural to an urban civilization has important implications for the historiography of the period. Potentially, urbanization might serve as a fruitful conceptual framework for interpreting political, economic, and social change.

A substantial body of historical literature on progressivism deals with political events, particularly on the national level. Business developments, including the rise of the corporation, have received considerable attention. In recent years, a number of historians have examined social reform ideologies, welfare organization, and related social issues such as immigration and prohibition. Necessarily, the city often provides the setting for these studies, but a more systematic analysis of the relationship between urbanization and institutional change is needed.

Any such analysis will require that historians devote greater attention to the shaping of the urban physical environment. The city, after all, is basically an artifact,

a physical container within which complex human interactions occur; social organization and relationships are greatly influenced by land-use and housing patterns. Prior to the late nineteenth century, urban land and housing were viewed as commodities, subject to the laws of supply and demand. As in the broader economic system, competitive market disciplines presumably guaranteed order and progress. By the late nineteenth century, however, Americans had become less confident that market disciplines would suffice. Planners, housing reformers, and others launched a search for norms of public intervention. They aspired to enlarge the scope of public decision-making. These efforts to institute public controls over land-use and to improve the quality of the housing environment are central to a historiography which adopts urbanization as a conceptual tool. Conservation, housing codes, zoning, city planning, park development, the City Beautiful movement, and the Garden City idea differed in origin, but shared a common objective—an enhanced role for the architect, planner, and welfare expert at the expense of the business interests which had traditionally determined urban land-use policy. The remainder of this essay will be devoted to these movements.

Conservation experts made profound, if indirect, contributions to urban planning. They introduced the concept of scientific, efficient resource utilization. Urban land could be interpreted as one such resource; and urban social reformers frequently adopted the rhetoric of conservation to justify their efforts to improve living and working conditions. They spoke in terms of the need to "conserve" human resources often wasted or exploited in a complex industrial society. Conservation leaders such as John Wesley Powell, Elwood Mead, and Benton MacKaye moved beyond resource policy into the realm of social and community theory. Linking up with the "country life" and "back-to-the-land" movements, these men sought to coordinate new land use and rural community organization principles. Critical of American pioneer tradition which acquiesced in rapid, speculative disposition of the national domain, conservation leaders proposed a policy of administered land use combined with group settlement and the introduction of cooperative institutions.

The settlement of the Plains and Rocky Mountain Region after the Civil War had dramatized the need for radical changes in the national land system. The familiar rectilinear survey and the principle of Homestead dispersed settlement proved increasingly inappropriate as the frontier reached the 100th meridian, where rainfall averaged less than twenty inches a year. John Wesley Powell, geologist in charge of the United States Geographical and Geological Survey of the Rocky Mountain Region, was among the first to formulate an alternative policy. He emphasized that scientific land classification was imperative in a region containing a limited amount of arable land, dependent upon irrigation. These same circumstances demanded a more flexible formula than the rectangular, 160-acre Homestead allotment. Powell suggested that farms of 80 acres and ranches of 2,560 acres were better suited to the region. To insure equitable and efficient water-use, he proposed the establishment of irrigation and pasturage districts. Each would be controlled by nine or more individuals who would be guaranteed access and title to water. These districts might form the nucleus of rural communities; if settlers grouped their homes "to the greatest possible extent," they would benefit more than in the case of the dispersed homestead from the "local social organizations of civilization."

Powell's emphasis upon the advantages of cooperative institutions and group settlement and his interest in the social implications of contrasting land-use systems represented a major contribution to the American planning tradition. He anticipated subsequent programs of scientific land-use, rural cooperation, and rural community planning. The basic principle of administered land-use, coordinated with social objectives, was as applicable to an urban setting as to a rural setting.

Landscape architects served to some degree as the urban counterpart of Powell and his successors in the conservation field. They exerted a major influence in establishing new criteria for urban form and social welfare. Post-Civil War landscape architects such as Frederick Law Olmsted, H. W. S. Cleveland, and Charles Eliot were genuine radicals who espoused the ideal of an urban-rural continuum, or continuous city-park-garden. In their haste to conquer the wilderness, Americans had come to view the city as a man-made environment which subdued nature, if it did not obliterate it. Landscape architects, heirs to the romantic Gothic revival and the "picturesque" estate planning of Andrew Jackson Downing, evolved a new conception of urban form the long-range significance of which cannot be exaggerated. Their ideal was the community which "would combine the advantages of both town and country" and would "so alternate open spaces with areas occupied by dwellings that it would practically occupy one vast garden."

This community norm resulted in a number of distinctive planning objectives. A naturalized urban environment or urban-rural continuum implied, first of all, a democratization of the country estate and suburb, with their attributes of spaciousness and beauty. Landscape architects sought to bring the country into the city, providing environmental amenities hitherto reserved for those who possessed mobility and wealth. In large measure, this achievement depended upon the development of a comprehensive park-boulevard system which would include not only large rural reservations, but also small neighborhood parks or squares.

Comprehensive park development necessitated long-range, systematic planning. If a city failed to reserve land for future park use according to a definite plan, it would become increasingly difficult to acquire suitable sites at reasonable prices. The ideal of a comprehensive park system directed the attention of landscape architects beyond city limits. They were among the first to emphasize the functional interdependence of city and regional hinterland and to urge the establishment of regional planning agencies. The Boston Metropolitan Park Commission pioneered in American regional planning. As early as the 1890's it voiced the need for cooperative effort among park, water, and sewerage authorities.

In seeking a satisfactory relationship between man, space, and nature in the urban community, landscape architects not only popularized the notion of public planning, but undermined the tyranny of the gridiron subdivision. They stressed, first, the desirability of a differentiated street system. Inspired by the great boulevards of Europe, particularly those of Haussmann's Paris, they advocated their use in American cities to expedite travel, to link the units of the city-regional park system, and to serve as a kind of linear park. Basically, the standardized gridiron plan was incompatible with the urban-rural continuum principle. Often the gridiron was a form of pseudo-planning. It brilliantly served the purposes of rapid, speculative subdivision and transfer, but sacrificed existing advantages of site and topography. Landscape architects maintained that the principles of picturesque planning were as valid for the ordinary residential subdivision as for the great rural park or country estate.

The romantic suburb became the most extreme, exotic example of the naturalistic residential subdivision. Llewellyn Park (New Jersey), the first, was begun in the ante-bellum period. The romantic suburb was subsequently popularized by Olmsted and Vaux's Riverside (Illinois), where a picturesque informality contrasted sharply with the "constantly repeated right angles, straight lines, and flat surfaces which characterize our large modern town." In its spaciousness, elimination of the corridor street, and integration of human and natural environment, the romantic suburb suggested an entirely new approach to residential design.

The urban-rural continuum principle contributed to one of the great social achievements of the so-called Gilded Age. Between the 1860's and 1890's many American cities established the foundations for their modern park system. New York and Philadelphia had begun in the 1850's with Central Park and Fairmount Park, respectively. Park commissions were later established in Brooklyn, Boston, Detroit, Chicago, Indianapolis, Kansas City, Milwaukee, Minneapolis, St. Paul, and other cities. The significance of these commissions transcended that of the parks they created. They were among the first municipal planning agencies, and marked a major step in the expansion of municipal welfare functions.

In their crusade for parks and open space, landscape architects did not respond solely to esthetic imperatives. They interpreted parks as a means to the creation of an urban environment compatible with health and social stability. Parks and boulevards acted as buffers against the spread of fires. They provided a salubrious relief from the "artificial" stimuli of urban life, and in tenement districts they offered amenities "which the rich win by travel or by living in luxurious country seats." Extensive, embellished open spaces filled a void in the existence of the urban masses, setting in motion the "purest and most ennobling of external influences." They provided alternatives to "unwholesome, vicious, and destructive methods of seeking recreation." Though they may have exaggerated the social advantages of parks, landscape architects pioneered in efforts to coordinate environmental and social planning in the urban community.

In certain respects, landscape architects and housing reformers pursued similar ends. Both sought to achieve social objectives through environmental melioration. Both favored a greater measure of public decision-making at the expense of private interests. They viewed the tenement park, or playground as an oasis in a concrete jungle, offering sunlight, fresh air, and opportunities to satisfy gregarious instincts in a socially permissible fashion. The park thus served as an instrument of social control.

For housing reformers, however, open space was supplementary to the main objective—enactment of legislation which imposed minimum structural and sanitary standards. In pursuit of restrictive legislation, the housing movement developed close ties with public health officials. Enforcement of housing codes was frequently assigned to health departments. Public health experts were, for obvious reasons, equally concerned with problems of overcrowding, impure water, and faulty sewerage. The accomplishments of housing reformers after 1900 were attributable, in good measure, to their association with the broader public health movement. Confirmation of the germ theory of disease had opened a new era in public health; the claims of housing reformers that substandard housing generated disease were established on a scientific, rather than empirical, basis. The struggle against tuberculosis, rampant in overcrowded, low-income neighborhoods, cemented the alliance between the health and housing movements. Finally, as strongly as any group, health officials endorsed the principle of public environmental control, and in the process greatly enlarged the scope of municipal welfare functions.

Housing and health reformers looked upon restrictive legislation as the key to housing betterment. They also hoped that widespread investment in semi-philanthropic "model" tenements would increase the supply of good, low-cost housing. The Octavia Hill method of housing management represented a third approach. Originating in England, the Octavia Hill method implied resident supervision, high maintenance standards, and some control over the tenants' personal lives. Both the model housing and Octavia Hill schemes were designed, in effect, to withdraw low-income housing from the speculative market. Public service, rather than maximum profit, constituted the rationale for investment. Restrictive legislation, on the other hand, did not substitute for speculative development. It insured, presumably, that housing standards did not drop below statutory minimums. Otherwise, competitive market mechanisms were free to operate.

The Octavia Hill method, of course, did not produce houses. Model tenement schemes never attracted enough investors to seriously challenge the speculative builder. Surplus capital in an expanding economy found more profitable outlets. For all practical purposes, housing remained the province of the petty entrepreneur, tempered by community standards embodied in restrictive legislation. Despite European precedents, few proposals for direct or indirect government subsidy appeared before World War I. Beginning around 1917 a number of architects and housing economists—Edith Elmer Wood,

Robert D. Kohn, Frederick L. Ackerman, and Charles H. Whitaker—launched a drive to discredit the "negative" approach to housing in favor of "constructive" European-type legislation. They looked enviously to England, Germany, and Belgium, where public housing, tax exemption, and low-interest loans to cooperatives, limited-dividend companies, or building and loan associations were used to increase the supply of low-cost housing.

Constructive housing legislation in this country was consistently opposed by Lawrence Veiller, the leading apostle of restrictive codes, founder of the National Housing Association, and author of the influential New York State Tenement House Law of 1901. Most city and state housing codes after 1901 were based upon the New York law or the model laws prepared by Veiller and published by the Russell Sage Foundation. Veiller condemned constructive legislation as socialistic and self defeating in the long run. A limited program of government financial assistance would not supply the need; a massive program would drive out private enterprise entirely and place an enormous burden upon taxpayers.

Under Veiller's leadership the housing movement progressed in organization and effectiveness. Yet restrictive legislation possessed severe limitations. At best it could prevent the worst housing, but could not insure a sufficient supply of good housing at costs or rentals appropriate to the lowest income groups. The same objections raised against government subsidy could apply to restrictive legislation. High standards, rigidly enforced, might discourage private enterprise by cutting profit

margins. Restrictive legislation, finally, did not provide adequate guidance for improvements in residential site-planning and design.

In view of the objections to constructive housing legislation in America, the only alternative way to improve housing standards while reducing costs was through progress in construction and design. Few American architects, however, applied their talents to problems of low-cost housing. I. N. Phelps Stokes of New York represented a notable exception. Stokes diverged from the mainstream of American housing reform in stressing design innovation rather than restrictive legislation. The latter, Stokes complained, not only raised costs but also discouraged experimentation and architectural creativity. Stokes linked his proposals for design innovation with an ingenious plan for urban renewal. He proposed to the New York State Tenement House Commission of 1901 that the municipality acquire and raze tenement blocks. The two perimeter strips, about 40 feet wide and running lengthwise along each block, would then be sold to limited-dividend companies, who would build tenements two rooms in depth. The central portion of the blocks would be used for parks and courts.

Nothing came of Stokes' proposals, which implied an expansion of the building unit from the single lot to the block. Working with limited capital and one or a few lots at a time, the builder had no opportunity, let alone desire, to experiment with new designs or groupings of mass and space. Decentralized and technologically primitive, the building industry could not benefit from the economies of scale.

It was confronted by a challenge of mass production for which it was unequipped by modern standards of technology and management.

Implicit in the movements discussed was the belief that men could consciously control the physical and social environment of their communities. Competitive market disciplines, the "invisible hand," had not sufficed as a source of order and progress. Landscape architects and conservation leaders sought not only an enlargement of public administrative and welfare functions, but also major reconstructions in community form. The same was true of the City Beautiful movement, which flourished from approximately 1893 to 1910.

The City Beautiful, although important in the evolution of the comprehensive city planning idea in America, has frequently been described as a catastrophe. It allegedly stimulated a neo-classicism which stifled functionalist expression in architecture. An exaggerated emphasis upon municipal ornamentation and embellishment presumably diverted attention from utilitarian concerns in the formative years of American city planning. Despite its limitations, which included a failure to deal with the urban housing problem, the City Beautiful did make several useful contributions to American urban life. It helped incorporate the park movement of the nineteenth century into twentieth-century city planning. Landscape architects such as Charles M. Robinson and George E. Kessler were conspicuous among the leaders of the City Beautiful. Few of their plans lacked provision for extensive park

boulevard development. Through their work, in part, the urban-rural continuum principle entered the mainstream of twentieth-century planning. The almost universal interest in park improvement suggests, furthermore, that the City Beautiful was not entirely devoid of utilitarian or social significance. Similarly, though City Beautiful contributions to housing betterment were minimal, the movement encouraged municipal regulation of eyesores or nuisances: bill-board displays, poles, noise, and overhead wires. In the Brunner-Carrère plan for Grand Rapids, Michigan (1909), one even finds early proposals for comprehensive zoning.

Probably the most distinctive legacy of the City Beautiful was the ideal it embodied of the city as a deliberate work of art. It aspired to universalize the beauty and planned unity which Americans had perceived in the Chicago World's Fair of 1893. The dream city which had risen along Chicago's lake front struck with the force of revelation: "The fair! The fair! Never had the name such significance before. Fairest of all the world's present sights it is. A city of palaces set in spaces of emerald, reflected in shining lengths of water which stretch in undulating lines under flat arches of marble bridges, and along banks planted with consummate skill." The Fair's vital lesson was the supreme "need of design and plan for whole cities," now that "everyone saw plainly that though a pond be beautiful, a grassy lawn or bank beautiful, a building beautiful, all of these elements wrought into a harmonious design attain another and greater beauty, and that the beauty of the whole is superior to that of each of the several parts

of the composition exploited separately."
The ephemeral White City stimulated a
mood of dissatisfaction with the "awful
monotony of ugliness" which reigned in
the real cities where people lived and
worked. This mood the City Beautiful
translated into a quest for communities
planned as works of art.

The ideal of the city as a work of art
invigorated the tradition of civic design
which extended back to colonial Williams-
burg, Annapolis, and, not least, L'Enfant's
Washington. It was necessary, however,
to divest this tradition of its aristocratic
connotations. Prophets of the City Beautiful thus assured Americans that the proposed civic centers, grand boulevards, and
sculptural and artistic embellishments were
truly democratic in contrast to the "work of
art in its secluded gallery." Such amenities
expressed the pride of a democratic people
in their communities and, like public
parks, insured equal access to advantages
once reserved for the affluent. The City
Beautiful elevated public standards of taste
and inspired a civic loyalty which transcended ethnic and class fragmentation.

The City Beautiful led to the preparation
of plans for numerous American communities. These schemes usually ignored housing and other social problems, but the City
Beautiful nonetheless performed a valuable
service in introducing new environmental
ideals. It popularized the notion that the
city was more than an economic machine
and that planning was necessary to prevent
further visual deterioration. The City
Beautiful aspired, through planning, to
reconcile industrialization with the great
Renaissance-Baroque and indigenous traditions of urban beautification. ■

383

URBAN RENEWAL

Housing Projects

The high hopes of urban planners for a "city beautiful" were never fully realized. The rapid development of automobile transportation intensified the processes of urban blight that had already appeared in the Progressive Period. Furthermore, the Great Depression of the 1930's left most cities without financial resources to develop large scale urban planning projects, because they had to cope with staggering burdens of relief and welfare. At this point, the federal government began to play an important role in urban planning through the financing of public housing projects.

Franklin D. Roosevelt's New Deal administration has long been regarded by many historians as one of the most vigorous periods of reform in American history. It was at this time that the federal government became actively involved in programs for housing and urban renewal. The selection which follows examines the assumptions and methods of these projects of urban renewal.

Source: Charles Abrams, *The City is The Frontier* (New York: Harper and Row, Publishers, 1965), pp. 71–80.

In the Depression of the 1930s, when the central cities were wincing under the spasms of economic crisis, some of the New Deal experimenters milling in and out of the White House calculated that spending for public works and propping up the house-building industry were two good ways of lubricating the ailing economy. Their main interest was centered on helping the private builder and mortgagee. Though the time was also opportune for a major program of city rebuilding, the only interest in this sort of proposal was shown by Secretary of Labor Frances Perkins, who suggested that the clearance of slums might perform the dual purpose of stirring up building activity while incidentally improving the living conditions of the city's poor. Public housing thereafter gained a small experimental appropriation as a part of a huge public works program.

The interest in reviving the building industry was not hard to understand. It had long been the bellwether of economic activity. When buildings go up, so do employment, purchasing power, and local revenues. When construction dwindles, the economy suffers.

One trouble with the effort to help the building industry was that home building was then generated by a disparate and undercapitalized group of little builders who put up—on the average—only about four houses a year. But though they were small fry in the big pool of American enterprise, it was their small-fry operations that fortified local economies and started things moving in the bigger workshops and rolling mills of America. Some means had to be found, therefore, to expand their operations into the larger-scale deals that would be economically meaningful.

House-building was then a creature of the market in which this little builder put up the equity money and took the risks until a customer accepted his product. The builder needed capital that could be frozen for long periods, and lending institutions were chary of advancing more than two-thirds of the building value. He therefore built cheaper or costlier buildings, bad or better ones, depending on what his customers could afford and how much capital he could raise to finance his operations.

The federal government could have spurred the builder's operations either in the cities or on their fringes. But if building operations were activated in the cities, it would have been necessary to acquire contiguous sections of land, and this could be done on a large scale only through compulsory land acquisitions, which could be undertaken only by public agencies for clearly public purposes. It seemed simpler to help expand private building operations on open land. While a trickle of building found its way into the still-vacant land of cities, most of the building thereafter went to the suburbs.

To stimulate the small builder and help him finance larger operations, the Federal Housing Administration undertook to insure mortgages up to 90 per cent of the cost of land and building. At first, FHA's emphasis was on small homes, but it was not long before it embraced speculative multiple dwellings as well. Not only would the builder now require only a nominal investment in the operation—about equal to his building fee—but the government-insured lenders, it was thought, would no longer hesitate to advance all the money he needed for his larger undertakings. To stem the mounting foreclosures, but also to provide the lending institutions with added capital, the government set up the Home Owners Loan Corporation, which bailed the institutions out of their sour mortgages to the extent of more than $3 billion.

Once started on its course, federal ministrations to the building industry continued even after a full recovery had begun to set in. The government scattered its credit assistance over a widening terrain, and as it did so, the number of fresh claimants upon its generosity grew. Not only were builders and lenders now the beneficiaries but also home buyers and the new suburban jurisdictions in which they settled. Soon army personnel, war veterans, nursing home operators, prefabricators, cooperatives, farmers, the mobile homes industry, middle-class families, and colleges in need of dormitories also filed their claims and Congress sought to satisfy them too. After the initial public housing experiment, Congress in 1937 also passed a United States Housing Act under which it provided loans and subsidies to help cities house their low-income families. By 1950, hardly a phase of home building and improvement remained unaided. The little builder gradually became a bigger-time operator who could swing a million-dollar deal with no more than a little front money. The federal government became the shaft and spoke of the building wheel, the brace of the mortgage business, the buttress of home ownership, and the prop under new rental housing. It also became the destroyer of the nation's slums, an activity which at first had been a social operation but in 1949 also became a tool of the private building enterprise.

By 1963, Federal Housing Administration insurance had soared to $88 billion. From 1938 to 1963, the Federal National Mortgage Association had spent $12.5 billion to buy 1.2 million mortgages, while a host of new federal agencies had sprung up to busy themselves with innumerable private ventures drawing upon the federal largess or credit. Simultaneously, federal credit and insurance of their deposits made the savings and loan associations the nation's largest mortgage lenders on homes and one of the most influential lobbies in Washington.

The government assistance to building was not without its benefits for the five million families who in 1963 owned FHA-aided homes; the millions of war veterans who became home owners; the 940,000 families in aided multifamily projects; the more than 27 million home owners who were helped to repair their dwellings; the 540,000 families in low-rent public housing; and the countless others who borrowed from the burgeoning savings and loan associations. Many little folk who bought homes with thin equities saw their values rise to twice or three times their original cost, and many joined the middle class, thanks to their going into debt at the right time.

Once the federal government had admitted the private operator into the fraternity of enterprises enjoying federal gratuities, it found itself continuously revising the formula for the aided undertakings. Either the private entrepreneur felt he was not getting enough profit or the federal agencies thought they were being too liberal. A golden mean had to be found under which the amount of gold assigned to the entrepreneur would not be too mean. Thanks to federal credit, the former small-time operator was soon able to build large apartment houses as well as hundreds of suburban houses in a single operation.

By 1949, however, federal housing ventures had grown so discrepant that Congress thought all the housing programs should be harnessed to a goal. The goals of a government are the ends toward which the public purpose is directed. Goals express aspirations, but, like campaign oratory, they are too often promissory notes with no fixed amount and no due date. The goal in the 1949 act was put as follows:

The general welfare and security of the Nation and the health and living standards of its people require housing production and related community development sufficient to remedy the serious housing shortage, the elimination of substandard and other inadequate housing through the clearance of slums and blighted areas, and the realization as soon as feasible of the goal of a decent home and a suitable living environment for every American family thus contributing to the development and redevelopment of communities and to the advancement of the growth, wealth, and security of the Nation.

This was no mean national dedication. But it was in the subsequent portions of the act that the clue to how the goal was to be met was revealed. The law said:

1. Private enterprise was to be encouraged to serve as large a part of the need as possible.

2. Government aid was to spur private enterprise to serve more of the total need.

3. Local public bodies were to be stimulated into sponsoring programs for better neighborhoods as well as providing homes at lower costs but again only through the medium of the entrepreneur-builder.

4. Slums and blighted areas were to be cleared and low-income families rehoused by public agencies but only where private enterprise was not functioning.

The 1949 legislation was called an "omnibus" housing act. It presumably included something for everybody. It was clear, too, that the time was not yet ripe for scuttling the public housing program in cities where it had been going on fitfully since it had been ventured as an experiment fifteen years before. But despite the Congressional curtsy to the problems of urban low-income families and to the "advancement of communities" the general aim was becoming patent. Under the terms of the act, Congress was no longer to view the federal function as a direct operation (as in federal slum clearance and public housing, the Tennessee Valley Authority, or road building). Instead, housing programs and community improvement were to be carried out to respect the private enterprise process. The entrepreneur was to be the main artery through which federal slum clearance money and credit were thereafter to be channeled. General welfare in housing was to be served by entrepreneurial welfare. This applied both to FHA programs as well as to the new urban renewal program which the 1949 act authorized.

* * *

If public welfare and private welfare were to find common cause in a common effort, it could be justified politically only if it also brought some dividends to the common man, i.e., the "people" at the base of the social and economic pyramid whose "health and living standards" required the government intervention essential to assure "the growth, wealth and security of the nation."

The people, under the new formula, however, were now to be mostly the remainder-men, the residual legatees after the direct beneficiaries had had theirs. It was presumed and, it is fair to say, hoped, that the residuum would not be insubstantial. The full credits to the builder and the federal insurance of mortgages would provide the builder with more, longer, and higher credits and speed his production of homes. Since FHA-insured mortgages would be larger, the home buyer, by borrowing more, would be putting in less. He would also be given a good lifetime within which to liquidate his debt. With all these attractions, it was anticipated that the portion of the rank and file who could afford to buy dwellings would expand. Indeed it did expand—mainly on the open land outside the cities. With improved conditions and easier terms, the proportion of home ownership soared from a low of 43 per cent of all occupied units in the 1940s to 63 per cent in 1963.

While federal aid to FHA and the savings and loan associations boomed the suburbs and the newer cities of the West, it somehow fell short in the older urban centers. Of the 58.3 million units constituting the national housing stock in 1960, about 20 per cent were classified as unsound (8.4 million required repairs to make them livable, 3 million were dilapidated, of which some 2.3 million were inhabited). Of the occupied units, 6.2 million lacked private toilets, baths, or running water. Within the metropolitan areas, most of these deficiencies were found in the central cities which had experienced their fitful and distorted growth during the first ascent of industrialization and the first influx of cheap labor from the world's hinterlands.

The urban renewal formula launched by the 1949 act was thought to take care of both the slum-bound cities and their slums. If the slums could be razed and the sites rebuilt, the cities could be restored as rightful competitors for the good life and the good taxpayer. Though the federal government itself had cleared slums and built public housing from 1934 to 1937 and in 1937 had transferred the operational responsibility to the cities, the 1949 urban renewal formula turned over house production on slum-cleared sites to private entrepreneurs. The cities would buy the land or condemn it for them. The cities would clear the sites of tenants and write down the land costs to make the price attractive to the entrepreneurs. The entrepreneurs, not the public, would own the product, and for all practical purposes, they could pocket whatever profits the projects would net. Projects built for those who could pay the going price of the new dwellings would have higher assessed values and yield the cities more taxes. Mortgage insurance or direct federal loans would sweeten the entrepreneur's profit and inspire him to bid for the cheap land. The loss resulting from the sale of the land would be shared two-thirds by the federal government and one-third by the cities. Given such federal impetus and municipal cooperation, new buildings would supplant the slums, new revenues at least five times more than the old sites yielded would pour into the slack city treasuries, slums would disappear, the cities would begin to convalesce, and the general welfare would be served all around.

* * *

While renewing cities was long accepted as a national prerogative in the Old World, the assumption of national responsibility in America was a revolutionary concept, for under the doctrine of state sovereignty, the condition of the nation's cities was not a federal concern. This concept held fast even after the nation had become 70 per cent urbanized. That the state was never *concerned* about renewing its cities did not unbind the constitutional straitjacket.

It was apparent from the nature of the legislation that the main motivation that prompted the new national involvement was not the creation of the city beautiful, the city efficient, or the city solvent. It simply sought to expand slum clearance— already a national purpose—but it would now become another vehicle for private investment supported by new forms of federal assistance.

There was at least one questionable aspect of the new formula. The "serious housing shortage" which Congress's goal had promised to remedy was most serious for those city folk who occupied the slums marked for destruction. These slums may have been eyesores to the city officials,

but they were shelters for the families who could afford nothing better. And so they occupied the several million homes that were ramshackle or dilapidated, and the millions of houses lacking toilets, baths, and running water or needing major repairs to make them livable.

It was indeed hard to see how removing the urban slum dwellers' houses, bad as they might be, could either cure the serious housing shortage to which the 1949 act dedicated itself or provide these people with homes they could afford. Congress's answer, however, seemed simple: (1) Some public housing moneys would continue to be earmarked for the cities under the original slum clearance formula to rehouse the families displaced, and (2) the evicted families could be moved into other quarters in the existing urban stock. The act authorized payment of the families' moving expenses to speed their departure.

There was another complication. As the economy expanded and as FHA aid and savings and loan mortgages were speeding the move of white families to the suburbs, millions of Negroes, Puerto Ricans, and Mexicans poured into the cities. These people moved into the slums vacated by many of those who were now buying suburban homes under the easier terms. Of the minority families moving into the cities, the Negroes were the most numerous. The faster the Negro family filled the vacancies in the cities, the faster was the white exodus from the sections he entered. Urban renewal's steam shovel functioned mainly in the areas where the minorities had secured their footholds. About 70 per cent of those scheduled for urban renewal evictions were nonwhite, and a substantial

number of the rest were poorer folk, including elderly families. Since the Negro's income was only about half that of the whites, FHA-aided homes and those financed by the savings and loan associations were beyond his means; even if he could afford them, the new white suburbs would not allow him to come in.

The most home-hungry portion of the population now scurried about from one slum to another in search of more enduring footholds. Although the Housing Act of 1949 had authorized 135,000 public housing units annually, Congress after 1954 cut the authorization to 35,000–45,000 annually. The frittered public housing program became more a pretext than a refuge, for the program was hardly big enough to accommodate its own displacees, much less those displaced by road programs, code enforcement, and urban renewal as well. Surprisingly, not many of the displaced were either eligible, able, or anxious to move into the public housing projects. This was particularly true of the white displacees, many of whom looked upon them as institutionalized havens for the impoverished.

Despite its subventions, the renewal program for some reason could not get off the ground from 1949 to 1954. One reason was that it was new and untried. Regulations had to be framed, sites selected, land assembled and appraised, and builders found who were willing to invest in drawing plans and making estimates in the hope they would land the jobs. In areas with housing shortages, tenant resistance to eviction slowed the city's hand. Elsewhere private redevelopers seemed not too keen to bid for projects that would not bring the high rents required to pay the going charges. It seemed simpler to build in the suburbs than to brave the tedious routines. Besides, the federal financing terms for mortgages were not as lush as they were in the city's outskirts where the "Section 608" formula, which will be discussed later, was providing bonanza opportunities. ■

Regional Shopping Centers

Housing and urban renewal projects were soon followed by another significant change in the organization of urban life. This was the concept of the regional shopping center. In the selection which follows, urban planner Victor Gruen describes this phenomenon and states why he thinks shopping centers play a role far more significant than merely that of a place where one can buy goods readily and conveniently.

Source: Victor Gruen, *The Heart of Our Cities* (New York: Simon and Schuster, Inc., 1964), pp. 186–191.

The reason for the emergence of the regional shopping center is identical to that which has created many a great city in the past: commercialism. Let us follow the path of its development through the experiences of one individual merchandising enterprise, John Doe's Fashion Emporium. It had been founded by John Doe toward the end of the nineteenth century and was established successfully in the heart of the core area of Middle City, U.S.A. Business was fine and when John, Jr., who preferred to lead a life of leisure, took over, he could do so without hurting the success of the store. John III inherited the business in the 1920s, and he was quite an ambitious young man. He felt that the old store had become run-down and needed a face-lifting as well as a complete overhauling of the interior, but just about the time when he was ready to begin the work of renovation, business started to drop off. Attempting to elicit the reasons for bad business from his manager, he discovered that his best customers had left the area and fled to the suburbs. Mrs. Fox had moved to Lake Valley, Mrs. Wolf to Beauty Acres, Mrs. Badger to Sunnyside, and so on. True enough, new people had moved into their apartments, but they were not the type of customers whom the Fashion Emporium was seeking. John III postponed the alterations and business went downhill fast. Being an able and energetic young man, John III decided that action was needed, so he rented stores along some of the main highways in Lake Valley, Beauty Acres and Sunnyside, giving up the downtown lease. John III's enterprise and daring paid off, and he used to stand smiling in front of one or the other of his three stores, counting the ever-increasing number of automobiles on the highways along which they were located, with unconcealed satisfaction.

The story of John III's success spread like wildfire; on both sides of the highway, stores and all kinds of other retail enterprises were opened by fugitives from the center of the city—until there was a mile-long stretch, fully developed, lining the highway. In true cooperative spirit, the merchants got together in order to promote their common welfare. At both ends of the strip they erected large signs with the words *Miracle Mile*—which, however, they found they had to move out a little farther every few months. In a second session of the *Miracle Mile* Association, business conditions were discussed and the various members confessed to each other that in spite of the fact that more automobiles than ever could be counted going by their stores, they now moved rather slowly and sometimes not at all. The other trouble was that because of the growing traffic congestion, the municipality had forbidden curb parking so that suddenly no customers were able to park their cars in front of any of the stores. The decision was made to acquire land areas behind the stores and to build parking lots there. The result was not quite what was hoped for. John III found that the ladies who would be likely customers for the Fashion Emporium did not appreciate the fact that they had to walk in through the narrow rear door, through which deliveries also moved in and trash moved out. And thus, in spite of the great expenditure for the acquisition of land and the construction of parking lots, business diminished markedly.

John III, never slow to act, said to himself that the area in which he had been located for five years had obviously gone to hell and that he had better move still farther out, to highways in the new suburban developments to which Mrs. Fox, Mrs. Wolf and Mrs. Badger in the meantime had moved. (They had become disgusted with traffic congestion and cheap commercialism.) But like his first move, the second was also copied by many, and after another five years John III was faced with the identical difficulties, in spite of the fact that in the new location he had made one significant improvement: placing his parking areas in front of the store instead of behind it.

One of the reasons for the new trouble was that public authorities, reacting to the popular complaints about unbearable traffic congestion between the rows of suburban stores, had constructed a six-lane freeway bypassing the traffic-ridden area. On the morning when the freeway opened, merchants along the highway strip noticed that traffic congestion had indeed disappeared—but so had all their customers. A sign which they persuaded the authorities to erect along the freeway reading *Exit for Roadside Business* was of little help.

Now John III heard about three regional shopping centers, then in the planning stage, strategically located near the freeway ramps and within easy reach of his most desirable customers in the northern, eastern and southern areas of the metropolitan region. He negotiated leases and in spite of the somewhat surprising conditions imposed in these leases, John III, being a pioneering character, established his stores. At first he was quite upset about

the manner in which he, a desirable tenant, was treated by the shopping center management. He was told not only where he should locate his store within the shopping center but also how much space would be allotted to him. He was told to arrange his main entrance doors along interior courts, malls or lanes in which no automobiles would be permitted and only after it was convincingly put to him that his customers were actually people and not cars could he reconcile himself to that idea. He was told that he could receive and load merchandise only in specified areas in the basement, and that the loading areas would have to be approached by his trucks over an underground road especially reserved for this purpose. His greatest shock came when he was informed that his storefronts and signs would be subject to approval by the shopping center management and that the letters used to advertise his firm could not be higher than three feet and could be affixed only to a certain portion of the storefront. When he was reassured, however, that the same regulations would be imposed on everybody else he shrugged his shoulders and said, "Well, in that case I can save myself a lot of money. As long as nobody else can yell louder than I, I certainly don't mind."

Thus John III opened his three new stores in three well-planned regional shopping centers, and for the first time in his business life he was able to relax and abandon the continuous search for suitable locations.

Planned regional shopping centers, like those into which John III moved, are one of the few new building types created in our time and in the United States. Their history goes back to the village type of shopping environment, which made its appearance in the 1920s. An outstanding example of this, the Country Club Plaza, built in 1925 in Kansas City, Missouri, is still flourishing. This was a pioneering act in the sense that it moved the shopping environment away from arterial highways, that it formed an integral part of a large new residential district consisting of apartment buildings and single houses, and that it established a high degree of architectural unity through exterior treatment and the preplanned location of major stores. The Country Club Plaza found many imitators all over the country, most of them (for example, Westwood Village in Los Angeles) not living up to the quality of the original. Though some of these shopping districts of the village type are still doing reasonably well, they are suffering from automobile congestion and parking problems generated by the local shopping traffic because the idea of separating pedestrians from automobiles had then not been part of this shopping area concept.

Decisive progress, however, was made after World War II. In the 1950s the first of the large regional shopping centers attempting to bring into being a new orderly pattern opened their doors. Northgate, near Seattle, designed by John Graham & Co.; Shopper's World in Framingham, near Boston, designed by Ketchum, Giná and Sharp; Northland, near Detroit, designed by our office, were put into operation. Since then, dozens of regional shopping centers have made their appearance in every metropolitan area. Let us first analyze the features which these regional shopping centers have in common.

They are usually constructed on large tracts of land, anywhere from 60 to 120 acres, frequently former cow pastures or farmland. The land is selected with an eye on good surrounding highways, favorable physical characteristics, and a location within reach of a sufficient number of people (anywhere between 200,000 and 500,000) in a driving-time distance of about twenty minutes.

What is novel and revolutionary is the manner in which the store buildings are placed. Instead of being arranged conventionally, directly bordering the surrounding highways, they are located in the space theoretically least visible from the public roads and least directly accessible to automobiles: in the center of the site. There the buildings form a cluster of great compactness, with spaces between them reserved for pedestrian use only and equipped with such amenities and improvements as landscaping, rest benches, fountains and even, in some cases, works of the creative arts. The ring-shaped area around the building cluster is then utilized as a storage area for automobiles, offering between 3,000 and 10,000 car spaces. The car storage area is ringed by an internal distribution road, which, at various points, is connected with the public road network. In order to eliminate interference by delivery and service vehicles with the customers' cars or foot traffic (created by those who, after leaving their cars, enter the shopping center or, after leaving the stores, return to their cars), special roads for service traffic are arranged. These, in the larger shopping centers, dip underground and enter the basements of the stores, where loading docks and

utility lines are located. In some of the shopping centers special roads are also constructed for public transportation, with bus terminals and taxi stands provided.

Thus the regional shopping center has actually implemented the concept of separation of utilitarian and human activities, and through the general popularity and economic success of this arrangement has proved that the concept is feasible and practical. Separation is achieved in a horizontal sense, as far as automobile storage and automobile movement are concerned, by relegating these functions to the fringe of the core development; and it is achieved in a vertical sense, with regard to the transportation of goods and the provision of services and utilities, by relegating them to an underground level.

All the regional shopping centers have created superior environmental qualities within the building core. In many of them we find weather protection achieved through the introduction of colonnades and crosswalks, and some of them are esthetically as pleasing and as busy as the long-lost town square of our urban past.

Thus they represent a great step forward. They are clearly defined urban organisms, either constructed from the beginning in their ultimate size or preplanned for inner growth. Their developers, architects and planners have decided from the beginning on their optimal shape, form and size, with full knowledge that any planless future sprawl would destroy their usefulness. The attitude of enlightened shopping center developers is that if population in the area should markedly increase, this event would necessitate the construction of a new nucleus and not the *de*struction, through sprawl, of the old one.

None of these shopping centers, however, has treated successfully the appearance of the area immediately surrounding the building core, which appears like an asphalt desert occupied fully or partially by thousands of automobiles. And even where some attempts at beautification through the introduction of trees in the parking area have been made, the walk from the parked car to the building core, which might be as long as 600 feet, is not an enjoyable one. Because one of the attractions of the regional shopping center is the provision of ample and free parking, car storage is, for cost reasons, arranged only on the ground level, and thus an extremely land-wasting concept is created. In the average regional shopping center, four to five times as much land is devoted to parking and interior roads as to buildings and pedestrian areas. The wide ring of parking and transportation area surrounding the building core makes it undesirable to approach the shopping center on foot from the outside—even for those who might be living or working nearby. This is very much in contrast to the Swedish shopping centers in Vällingby and Farsta, where surface parking areas are comparatively small because many of the shoppers arrive by public transportation and where, at least on two sides of the shopping center's site, intimate contact between the building core and surrounding high-rise apartment houses is achieved; footpaths and bicycle paths lead directly from the residential area to the central building group.

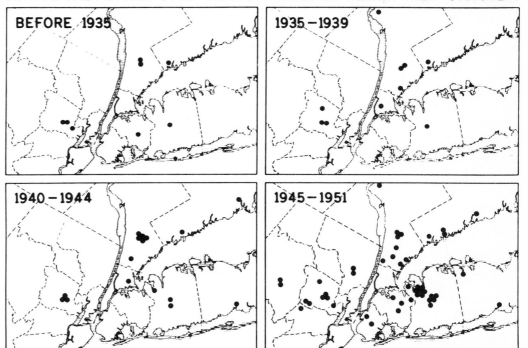

CENTRAL AREA STORES BUILD SUBURBAN BRANCHES NEARER THEIR CUSTOMERS

BEFORE 1935

1935–1939

1940–1944

1945–1951

Yet the regional shopping center represents an important and significant step in the right direction. It has proved that it is able to play the role not merely of a commercial center but of a social, cultural and recreational crystallization point for the up-to-then amorphous, sprawling suburban region. Shopping center planners and developers, recognizing the importance of this function, have year by year increased the number and types of facilities that would enable the regional shopping center to play more fully its role as a new heart area. Medical office buildings, general office buildings, hotels, theaters, auditoria, meeting rooms, children's play areas, restaurants, exhibit halls have been added to an environment that originally served only retail activities. ∎

CONCEPTIONS OF
URBAN RENEWAL

These two pages show photographs of urban conditions in areas that were destined for urban renewal. What kinds of problems seem prevalent in these areas? From your perspective, are there any positive aspects of city living illustrated in these photographs?

In the post-World War II era, urban renewal was born and sought to reverse the "decay" of the central city. On the following pages are plans, sketches, and actual photographs of urban renewal projects.

1 What particular problems do you think each project was trying to alleviate? How did the architect propose to solve these problems?

392 **2** How does the overall conception of an urban environment in the plans take account of technology, the "natural" environment, and the social needs of people? How does *this* conception of an urban environment compare with the conception inherent in the urban planning undertaken during the Progressive Era?

3 Judging from the photographs portraying each blighted area after its renewal, do you think the planner's hopes for his project were fulfilled? How do the sites compare in this respect and in terms of your own sense of what effective urban revitalization might accomplish?

4 What other kinds of evidence would you need to assess the success or failure of these urban renewal plans? ■

ATLANTA: Butler Street Project
Photos courtesy of the Housing Authority of the
City of Atlanta

Model depicting proposed redevelopment in Butler Street Area.

Commercial redevelopment projects in Butler
Street Project.

The 21-story Landmark Apartments, luxury housing in the Butler Street Project.

Low and moderate priced housing in the Butler Street Project, built by a non-profit corporation.

BOSTON: Government Center Project
Photos courtesy of the Boston Redevelopment Authority

Government Center project
nearing completion.

1 City Hall (New)
2 John F. Kennedy
  Federal Building (New)
3 Government Center Plaza (New)
4 Motor Hotel (New)
5 Parking Garage (New)
6 Private Office Building (New)
7 Police Station (New)
8 Chapel (New)
9 Sears Crescent (Rehabilitated)
10 State Service Center (New)
11 One Center Plaza (New
   Private Office Building)
12 20 State Street (New
   Private Office Building)
13 Jewish Family and Children's
   Service Building (New)

City Hall Plaza, looking across to Sears Crescent.

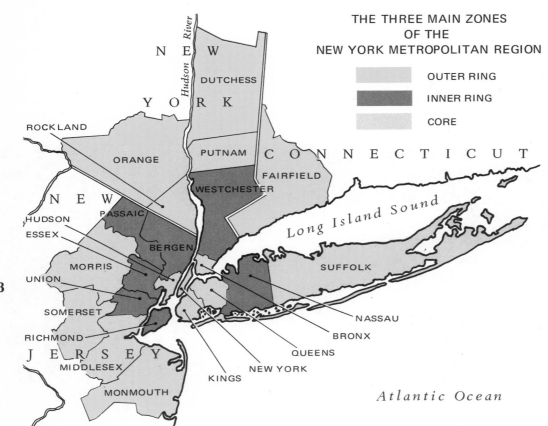

THE THREE MAIN ZONES
OF THE
NEW YORK METROPOLITAN REGION

OUTER RING

INNER RING

CORE

THE CRISIS OF THE MODERN METROPOLIS

DEMOGRAPHIC SHIFTS IN URBAN AMERICA

As the table below indicates, there has been a shift in population within metropolitan areas. Urban sociologists and geographers are in the process of analyzing this shift, which seems to be occurring in most major urban areas. In some senses New York represents an extreme of the trend, but it has been the subject of careful quantitative studies and may enhance our understanding of the nature and importance of this population shift. Examine the data from New York.

1 What does each table, map, or chart indicate about who is moving into the central city and who is moving out?

2 What hypotheses might explain the patterns of race, ethnicity, occupation, age, and income in these population shifts? ■

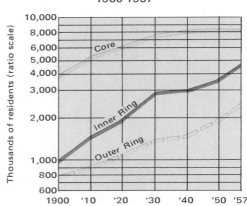

DISTRIBUTION OF POPULATION IN
NEW YORK METROPOLITAN REGION,
1900-1957

398

EMPLOYMENT IN COUNTIES OF NEW YORK METROPOLITAN REGION BY CATEGORIES OF INDUSTRIES, MARCH 1956 (IN THOUSANDS)

	Total employment	Manufac- turing	Wholesale trade	Financial community	Other office workers in office buildings	Consumer trades and services	Contract construction	Other employees
Region, total	6,699.3	1,889.9	453.5	320.2	895.6	1,244.0	241.8	1,654.8
New York City	4,051.2	947.5	344.3	251.4	683.5	729.6	115.3	979.6
Core, total	4,301.5	1,072.5	357.9	255.1	701.8	763.2	122.2	1,028.8
Inner Ring, total	1,572.3	518.4	70.5	51.3	133.1	319.8	78.5	400.7
Outer Ring, total	826.0	299.0	25.1	13.8	60.7	161.0	41.1	225.3

PERCENT OF THE DECENNIAL INCREASE IN STANDARD METROPOLITAN AREAS AND OTHER AREAS: 1900 TO 1955

[Minus sign (—) denotes decrease]

Year and type of area		1900 to 1950					
	Total	1900 to 1910	1910 to 1920	1920 to 1930	1930 to 1940	1940 to 1950	1950 to 1955
United States	100.0	100.0	100.0	100.0	100.0	100.0	100.0
Standard metropolitan area	73.2	61.6	75.0	80.9	61.6	80.6	97.3
Central cities	40.6	43.7	52.5	46.4	24.8	31.6	16.0
Remainder of areas	32.7	17.9	22.6	34.5	36.8	49.0	81.3
Urban	18.7	13.2	17.6	24.5	13.2	21.5	38.3
Rural	14.0	4.7	5.0	9.9	23.5	27.4	43.1
Areas outside standard metropolitan areas	26.7	38.4	25.0	19.1	38.4	19.4	2.7
Urban	19.3	17.2	18.5	15.7	23.5	23.0	9.7
Rural	7.4	21.2	6.5	3.4	15.0	—3.7	—7.0

Source: Based on U. S. Housing and Home Finance Agency, *Population Growth in Standard Metropolitan Areas, 1900–1950*, by Donald J. Bogue, table 3; U. S. Bureau of the Census, *Current Population Reports*, Series P-20, No. 63, "Civilian Population of the United States, by Type of Residence: April 1955 and 1950" (1955), with rural and urban areas as in 1950.

RELATIVE LEVELS OF PER CAPITA PERSONAL INCOME IN NEW YORK METROPOLITAN REGION, BY COUNTIES, 1939, 1947, 1956

	Per capita income as percentage of average for entire Region		
	1939	1947	1956
New York City	109	106	99
Core	108	105	98
Manhattan	163	149	114
Rest of Core	91	91	93
Queens	79	93	106
Bronx	84	93	89
Brooklyn	101	91	89
Hudson	88	88	84
Inner Ring	88	97	111
Nassau	74	78	125
Westchester	93	103	124
Bergen	85	79	109
Union	85	85	109
Essex	102	121	104
Richmond	80	83	87
Passaic	72	102	86
Outer Ring	81	84	86
Fairfield	90	119	114
Morris	81	68	92
Somerset	73	58	89
Middlesex	69	68	83
Monmouth	86	74	82
Suffolk	76	73	72
Rockland	75	65	70
Orange	88	88	69
Dutchess and Putnam	75	83	62

Source: Estimates by New York Metropolitan Region Study.

THE UNHEAVENLY CITY

Source: Jane Jacobs, *The Death and Life of Great American Cities* (New York: Random House, 1961), pp. 4–13.

Despite the reforms of the Progressive and New Deal eras, it is obvious to even the most casual observer that American cities are today in a state of crisis. Indeed, the crisis seems so severe that we wonder if our urban ills can be cured at all.

Even those urban reform projects which were once regarded as providing genuine hope and relief for the city have come under attack. This is evidenced by the following two selections. The first was written by Jane Jacobs, a social critic whose work on the deterioration of the American city has attracted wide attention. The second was written by the sociologist Herbert Gans, another widely respected authority on the American city. The final selection was written by Edward Banfield, a noted political scientist who specializes in urban politics.

The City Planning Myth

There is a wistful myth that if only we had enough money to spend—the figure is usually put at a hundred billion dollars —we could wipe out all our slums in ten years, reverse decay in the great, dull, gray belts that were yesterday's and day-before-yesterday's suburbs, anchor the wandering middle class and its wandering tax money, and perhaps even solve the traffic problem.

But look what we have built with the first several billions: Low-income projects that become worse centers of delinquency, vandalism and general social hopelessness than the slums they were supposed to replace. Middle-income housing projects which are truly marvels of dullness and regimentation, sealed against any buoyancy or vitality of city life. Luxury housing projects that mitigate their inanity, or try to, with a vapid vulgarity. Cultural centers that are unable to support a good bookstore. Civic centers that are avoided by everyone but bums, who have fewer choices of loitering place than others. Commercial centers that are lack-luster imitations of standardized suburban chain-store shopping. Promenades that go from no place to nowhere and have no promenaders. Expressways that eviscerate great cities. This is not the rebuilding of cities. This is the sacking of cities.

Under the surface, these accomplishments prove even poorer than their poor pretenses. They seldom aid the city areas around them, as in theory they are supposed to. These amputated areas typically develop galloping gangrene. To house people in this planned fashion, price tags are fastened on the population, and each sorted-out chunk of price-tagged populace lives in growing suspicion and tension against the surrounding city. When two or more such hostile islands are juxtaposed the result is called "a balanced neighborhood." Monopolistic shopping centers and monumental cultural centers cloak, under the public relations hoohaw, the subtraction of commerce, and of culture too, from the intimate and casual life of cities.

That such wonders may be accomplished, people who get marked with the planners' hex signs are pushed about, expropriated, and uprooted much as if they were the subjects of a conquering power. Thousands upon thousands of small businesses are destroyed, and their proprietors ruined, with hardly a gesture at compensation. Whole communities are torn apart and sown to the winds, with a reaping of cynicism, resentment and despair that must be heard and seen to be believed. A group of clergymen in Chicago, appalled at the fruits of planned city rebuilding there, asked,

Could Job have been thinking of Chicago when he wrote:

Here are men that alter their neighbor's landmark . . . shoulder the poor aside, conspire to oppress the friendless.

Reap they the field that is none of theirs, strip they the vineyard wrongfully seized from its owner . . .

A cry goes up from the city streets, where wounded men lie groaning. . . .

If so, he was also thinking of New York, Philadelphia, Boston, Washington, St.

Louis, San Francisco and a number of other places. The economic rationale of current city rebuilding is a hoax. The economics of city rebuilding do not rest soundly on reasoned investment of public tax subsidies, as urban renewal theory proclaims, but also on vast, involuntary subsidies wrung out of helpless site victims. And the increased tax returns from such sites, accruing to the cities as a result of this "investment," are a mirage, a pitiful gesture against the ever increasing sums of public money needed to combat disintegration and instability that flow from the cruelly shaken-up city. The means to planned city rebuilding are as deplorable as the ends.

Meantime, all the art and science of city planning are helpless to stem decay—and the spiritlessness that precedes decay—in ever more massive swatches of cities. Nor can this decay be laid, reassuringly, to lack of opportunity to apply the arts of planning. It seems to matter little whether they are applied or not. Consider the Morningside Heights area in New York City. According to planning theory it should not be in trouble at all, for it enjoys a great abundance of parkland, campus, playground and other open spaces. It has plenty of grass. It occupies high and pleasant ground with magnificent river views. It is a famous educational center with splendid institutions—Columbia University, Union Theological Seminary, the Juilliard School of Music, and half a dozen others of eminent respectability. It is the beneficiary of good hospitals and churches. It has no industries. Its streets are zoned in the main against "incompatible uses" intruding into the

preserves for solidly constructed, roomy, middle- and upper-class apartments. Yet by the early 1950's Morningside Heights was becoming a slum so swiftly, the surly kind of slum in which people fear to walk the streets, that the situation posed a crisis for the institutions. They and the planning arms of the city government got together, applied more planning theory, wiped out the most run-down part of the area and built in its stead a middle-income cooperative project complete with shopping center, and a public housing project, all interspersed with air, light, sunshine and landscaping. This was hailed as a great demonstration in city saving.

After that, Morningside Heights went downhill even faster.

Nor is this an unfair or irrelevant example. In city after city, precisely the wrong areas, in the light of planning theory, are decaying. Less noticed, but equally significant, in city after city the wrong areas, in the light of planning theory, are refusing to decay.

Cities are an immense laboratory of trial and error, failure and success, in city building and city design. This is the laboratory in which city planning should have been learning and forming and testing its theories. Instead the practitioners and teachers of this discipline (if such it can be called) have ignored the study of success and failure in real life, have been incurious about the reasons for unexpected success, and are guided instead by principles derived from the behavior and appearance of towns, suburbs, tuberculosis sanatoria, fairs, and imaginary dream cities—from anything but cities themselves.

If it appears that the rebuilt portions of cities and the endless new developments spreading beyond the cities are reducing city and countryside alike to a monotonous, unnourishing gruel, this is not strange. It all comes, first-, second-, third- or fourth-hand, out of the same intellectual dish of mush, a mush in which the qualities, necessities, advantages and behavior of great cities have been utterly confused with the qualities, necessities, advantages and behavior of other and more inert types of settlements.

There is nothing economically or socially inevitable about either the decay of old cities or the fresh-minted decadence of the new unurban urbanization. On the contrary, no other aspect of our economy and society has been more purposefully manipulated for a full quarter of a century to achieve precisely what we are getting. Extraordinary governmental financial incentives have been required to achieve this degree of monotony, sterility and vulgarity. Decades of preaching, writing and exhorting by experts have gone into convincing us and our legislators that mush like this must be good for us, as long as it comes bedded with grass.

Automobiles are often conveniently tagged as the villains responsible for the ills of cities and the disappointments and futilities of city planning. But the destructive effects of automobiles are much less a cause than a symptom of our incompetence at city building. Of course planners, including the highwaymen with fabulous sums of money and enormous powers at their disposal, are at a loss to make automobiles and cities compatible with one another. They do not know what to do with automobiles in cities because they do not know how to plan for workable and vital cities anyhow—with or without automobiles.

The simple needs of automobiles are more easily understood and satisfied than the complex needs of cities, and a growing number of planners and designers have come to believe that if they can only solve the problems of traffic, they will thereby have solved the major problem of cities. Cities have much more intricate economic and social concerns than automobile traffic. How can you know what to try with traffic until you know how the city itself works, and what else it needs to do with its streets? You can't.

It may be that we have become so feckless as a people that we no longer care how things do work, but only what kind of quick, easy outer impression they give. If so, there is little hope for our cities or probably for much else in our society. But I do not think this is so.

Specifically, in the case of planning for cities, it is clear that a large number of good and earnest people do care deeply about building and renewing. Despite some corruption, and considerable greed for the other man's vineyard, the intentions going into the messes we make are, on the whole, exemplary. Planners, architects of city design, and those they have led along with them in their beliefs are not consciously disdainful of the importance of knowing how things work. On the contrary, they have gone to great pains to learn what the saints and sages of modern orthodox planning have said about how cities *ought* to work and what *ought* to

be good for people and businesses in them. They take this with such devotion that when contradictory reality intrudes, threatening to shatter their dearly won learning, they must shrug reality aside.

Consider, for example, the orthodox planning reaction to a district called the North End in Boston. This is an old, low-rent area merging into the heavy industry of the waterfront, and it is officially considered Boston's worst slum and civic shame. It embodies attributes which all enlightened people know are evil because so many wise men have said they are evil. Not only is the North End bumped right up against industry, but worse still it has all kinds of working places and commerce mingled in the greatest complexity with its residences. It has the highest concentration of dwelling units, on the land that is used for dwelling units, of any part of Boston, and indeed one of the highest concentrations to be found in any American city. It has little parkland. Children play in the streets. Instead of super-blocks, or even decently large blocks, it has very small blocks; in planning parlance it is "badly cut up with wasteful streets." Its buildings are old. Everything conceivable is presumably wrong with the North End. In orthodox planning terms, it is a three-dimensional textbook of "megalopolis" in the last stages of depravity. The North End is thus a recurring assignment for M.I.T. and Harvard planning and architectural students, who now and again pursue, under the guidance of their teachers, the paper exercise of converting it into super-blocks and park promenades, wiping away its nonconforming uses, transforming it to

an ideal of order and gentility so simple it could be engraved on the head of a pin.

Twenty years ago, when I first happened to see the North End, its buildings—town houses of different kinds and sizes converted to flats, and four- or five-story tenements built to house the flood of immigrants first from Ireland, then from Eastern Europe and finally from Sicily—were badly overcrowded, and the general effect was of a district taking a terrible physical beating and certainly desperately poor.

When I saw the North End again in 1959, I was amazed at the change. Dozens and dozens of buildings had been rehabilitated. Instead of mattresses against the windows there were Venetian blinds and glimpses of fresh paint. Many of the small, converted houses now had only one or two families in them instead of the old crowded three or four. Some of the families in the tenements (as I learned later, visiting inside) had uncrowded themselves by throwing two older apartments together, and had equipped these with bathrooms, new kitchens and the like. I looked down a narrow alley, thinking to find at least here the old, squalid North End, but no: more neatly repainted brickwork, new blinds, and a burst of music as a door opened. Indeed, this was the only city district I had ever seen—or have seen to this day—in which the sides of buildings around parking lots had not been left raw and amputated, but repaired and painted as neatly as if they were intended to be seen. Mingled all among the buildings for living were an incredible number of splendid food stores, as well as such enterprises as upholstery making, metal

working, carpentry, food processing. The streets were alive with children playing, people shopping, people strolling, people talking. Had it not been a cold January day, there would surely have been people sitting.

The general street atmosphere of buoyancy, friendliness and good health was so infectious that I began asking directions of people just for the fun of getting in on some talk. I had seen a lot of Boston in the past couple of days, most of it sorely distressing, and this struck me, with relief, as the healthiest place in the city. But I could not imagine where the money had come from for the rehabilitation, because it is almost impossible today to get any

appreciable mortgage money in districts of American cities that are not either high-rent, or else imitations of suburbs. To find out, I went into a bar and restaurant (where an animated conversation about fishing was in progress) and called a Boston planner I know.

"Why in the world are you down in the North End?" he said. "Money? Why, no money or work has gone into the North End. Nothing's going on down there. Eventually, yes, but not yet. That's a slum!"

"It doesn't seem like a slum to me," I said.

"Why, that's the worst slum in the city. It has two hundred and seventy-five

dwelling units to the net acre! I hate to admit we have anything like that in Boston, but it's a fact."

"Do you have any other figures on it?" I asked.

"Yes, funny thing. It has among the lowest delinquency, disease and infant mortality rates in the city. It also has the lowest ratio of rent to income in the city. Boy, are those people getting bargains. Let's see . . . the child population is just about average for the city, on the nose. The death rate is low, 8.8 per thousand, against the average city rate of 11.2. The TB death rate is very low, less than 1 per ten thousand, can't understand it, it's lower even than Brookline's. In the old days the North End used to be the city's worst spot for tuberculosis, but all that has changed. Well, they must be strong people. Of course it's a terrible slum."

"You should have more slums like this," I said. "Don't tell me there are plans to wipe this out. You ought to be down here learning as much as you can from it."

"I know how you feel," he said. "I often go down there myself just to walk around the streets and feel that wonderful, cheerful street life. Say, what you ought to do, you ought to come back and go down in the summer if you think it's fun now. You'd be crazy about it in summer. But of course we have to rebuild it eventually. We've got to get those people off the streets."

Here was a curious thing. My friend's instincts told him the North End was a good place, and his social statistics confirmed it. But everything he had learned as a physical planner about what is good for people and good for city neighbor-

403

hoods, everything that made him an expert, told him the North End had to be a bad place.

The leading Boston savings banker, "a man way up there in the power structure," to whom my friend referred me for my inquiry about the money, confirmed what I learned, in the meantime, from people in the North End. The money had not come through the grace of the great American banking system, which now knows enough about planning to know a slum as well as the planners do. "No sense in lending money into the North End," the banker said. "It's a slum! It's still getting some immigrants! Furthermore, back in the Depression it had a very large number of foreclosures; bad record." (I had heard about this too, in the meantime, and how families had worked and pooled their resources to buy back some of those foreclosed buildings.)

The largest mortgage loans that had been fed into this district of some 15,000 people in the quarter-century since the Great Depression were for $3,000, the banker told me, "and very, very few of those." There had been some others for $1,000 and for $2,000. The rehabilitation work had been almost entirely financed by business and housing earnings within the district, plowed back in, and by skilled work bartered among residents and relatives of residents.

By this time I knew that this inability to borrow for improvement was a galling worry to North Enders, and that furthermore some North Enders were worried because it seemed impossible to get new building in the area except at the price of seeing themselves and their community

wiped out in the fashion of the students' dreams of a city Eden, a fate which they knew was not academic because it had already smashed completely a socially similar—although physically more spacious—nearby district called the West End. They were worried because they were aware also that patch and fix with nothing else could not do forever. "Any chance of loans for new construction in the North End?" I asked the banker.

"No, absolutely not!" he said, sounding impatient at my denseness. "That's a slum!"

Bankers, like planners, have theories about cities on which they act. They have gotten their theories from the same intellectual sources as the planners. Bankers and government administrative officials who guarantee mortgages do not invent planning theories nor, surprisingly, even economic doctrine about cities. They are enlightened nowadays, and they pick up their ideas from idealists, a generation late. Since theoretical city planning has embraced no major new ideas for considerably more than a generation, theoretical planners, financers and bureaucrats are all just about even today.... ■

Source: Herbert Gans, in *Commentary*, vol. XXXIX, no. 4 (April 1965), pp. 29–37.

The Failure of Urban Renewal

Suppose that the government decided that jalopies were a menace to public safety and a blight on the beauty of our highways and therefore took them away from their drivers. Suppose, then, that to replenish the supply of automobiles, it gave these drivers a hundred dollars each to buy a good used car and also made special grants to General Motors, Ford, and Chrysler to lower the cost—although not necessarily the price—of Cadillacs, Lincolns, and Imperials by a few hundred dollars. Absurd as this may sound, change the jalopies to slum housing, and I have described, with only slight poetic license, the first fifteen years of a federal program called urban renewal.

Since 1949, this program has provided local renewal agencies with federal funds and the power of eminent domain to condemn slum neighborhoods, tear down the buildings, and resell the cleared land to private developers at a reduced price. In addition to relocating the slum dwellers in "decent, safe, and sanitary" housing, the program was intended to stimulate large-scale private rebuilding, add new tax revenues to the dwindling coffers of the cities, revitalize their downtown areas, and halt the exodus of middle-class whites to the suburbs.

For some time now, a few city planners and housing experts have been pointing out that urban renewal was not achieving its general aims, and social scientists have produced a number of critical studies of individual renewal projects. These critiques, however, have mostly appeared in academic books and journals; otherwise there has been remarkably little public discussion of the federal program. Slum dwellers whose homes were to be torn down have indeed protested bitterly, but their outcries have been limited to particular projects; and because such outcries have rarely been supported by the local press, they have been easily brushed aside by the political power of the supporters of the projects in question. In the last few years, the civil-rights movement has backed protesting slum dwellers, though again only at the local level, while rightists have opposed the use of eminent domain to take private property from one owner in order to give it to another (especially when the new one is likely to be from out of town and financed by New York capital).

Slum clearance has also come under fire from several prominent architectural and social critics, led by Jane Jacobs, who have been struggling to preserve neighborhoods like Greenwich Village, with their brownstones, lofts, and small apartment houses, against the encroachment of the large, high-rise projects built for the luxury market and the poor alike. But these efforts have been directed mainly at private clearance outside the federal program, and their intent has been to save the city for people (intellectuals and artists, for example) who, like tourists, want jumbled diversity, antique "charm," and narrow streets for visual adventure and aesthetic pleasure. (Norman Mailer carried such thinking to its furthest point in his recent attack in *The New York Times* magazine section on the physical and social sterility of high-rise housing; Mailer's attack was also accompanied by an entirely reasonable suggestion—in fact, the only viable one

that could be made in this context—that the advantages of brownstone living be incorporated into skyscraper projects.)

But if criticism of the urban-renewal program has in the past been spotty and sporadic, there are signs that the program as a whole is now beginning to be seriously and tellingly evaluated. At least two comprehensive studies, by Charles Abrams and Scott Greer, are nearing publication, and one highly negative analysis—by an ultraconservative economist and often free-swinging polemicist—has already appeared: Martin Anderson's *The Federal Bulldozer*. Ironically enough, Anderson's data are based largely on statistics collected by the Urban Renewal Administration. What, according to these and other data, has the program accomplished? It has cleared slums to make room for many luxury-housing and a few middle-income projects, and it has also provided inexpensive land for the expansion of colleges, hospitals, libraries, shopping areas, and other such institutions located in slum areas. As of March 1961, 126,000 dwelling units had been demolished and about 28,000 new ones built. The median monthly rental of all those erected during 1960 came to $158, and in 1962, to $192— a staggering figure for any area outside of Manhattan.

Needless to say, none of the slum dwellers who were dispossessed in the process could afford to move into these new apartments. Local renewal agencies were supposed to relocate the dispossessed tenants in "standard" housing within their means before demolition began, but such vacant housing is scarce in most cities and altogether unavailable in some.

And since the agencies were under strong pressure to clear the land and get renewal projects going, the relocation of the tenants was impatiently, if not ruthlessly, handled. Thus, a 1961 study of renewal projects in 41 cities showed that 60 per cent of the dispossessed tenants were merely relocated in other slums; and in big cities, the proportion was even higher (over 70 per cent in Philadelphia, according to a 1958 study). Renewal sometimes even created new slums by pushing relocatees into areas and buildings which then became overcrowded and deteriorated rapidly. This has principally been the case with Negroes who, for both economic and racial reasons, have been forced to double up in other ghettos. Indeed, because almost two-thirds of the cleared slum units have been occupied by Negroes, the urban-renewal program has often been characterized as Negro clearance, and in too many cities this has been its intent.

Moreover, those dispossessed tenants who found better housing usually had to pay more rent than they could afford. In his careful study of relocation in Boston's heavily Italian West End, Chester Hartman shows that 41 per cent of the West Enders lived in good housing in this so-called slum (thus suggesting that much of it should not have been torn down) and that 73 per cent were relocated in good housing—thanks in part to the fact that the West Enders were white. This improvement was achieved at a heavy price, however, for median rents rose from $41 to $71 per month after the move.

According to renewal officials, 80 per cent of all persons relocated now live in good housing, and rent increases were justified because many had been paying unduly low rent before. Hartman's study was the first to compare these official statistics with housing realities, and his figure of 73 per cent challenges the official claim that 97 per cent of the Boston West Enders were properly rehoused. This discrepancy may arise from two facts: renewal officials collected their data after the poorest of the uprooted tenants had fled in panic to other slums; and officials also tended toward a rather lenient evaluation of the relocation housing of those actually studied in order to make a good record for their agency. (On the other hand, when they were certifying areas for clearance, these officials often exaggerated the degree of "blight" in order to prove their case.)

As for the substandard rents paid by slum dwellers, these are factual in only a small proportion of cases, and then mostly among whites. Real-estate economists argue that families should pay at least 20 per cent of their income for housing, but what is manageable for middle-income people is a burden to those with low incomes who pay a higher share of their earnings for food and other necessities. Yet even so, low-income Negroes generally have to devote about 30 per cent of their income to housing, and a Chicago study cited by Hartman reports that among non-white families earning less than $3,000 a year, median rent rose from 35 per cent of income before relocation to 46 per cent afterward.

To compound the failure of urban renewal to help the poor, many clearance areas (Boston's West End is an example) were chosen, as Anderson points out, not because they had the worst slums, but because they offered the best sites for luxury housing—housing which would have been built whether the urban-renewal program existed or not. Since public funds were used to clear the slums and to make the land available to private builders at reduced costs, the low-income population was in effect subsidizing its own removal for the benefit of the wealthy. What was done for the slum dwellers in return is starkly suggested by the following statistic: *only one-half of 1 per cent* of all federal expenditures for urban renewal between 1949 and 1964 was spent on relocation of families and individuals, and 2 per cent if payments to businesses are included.

Finally, because the policy has been to clear a district of all slums at once in order to assemble large sites to attract private developers, entire neighborhoods have frequently been destroyed, uprooting people who had lived there for decades, closing down their institutions, ruining small businesses by the hundreds, and scattering families and friends all over the city. By removing the structure of social and emotional support provided by the neighborhood, and by forcing people to rebuild their lives separately and amid strangers elsewhere, slum clearance has often come at a serious psychological as well as financial cost to its supposed beneficiaries. Marc Fried, a clinical psychologist who studied the West Enders after relocation, reported that 46 per cent of the women and 38 per cent of the men "give evidence of a fairly severe grief reaction or worse" in response to questions about leaving their tight-knit community. Far from "adjusting" eventually to this trauma, 26 per cent of the women remained sad or depressed even two years after they had been pushed out of the West End.

People like the Italians or the Puerto Ricans who live in an intensely group-centered way among three-generation "extended families" and ethnic peers have naturally suffered greatly from the clearance of entire neighborhoods. It may well be, however, that slum clearance has inflicted yet graver emotional burdens on Negroes, despite the fact that they generally live in less cohesive and often disorganized neighborhoods. In fact, I suspect that Negroes who lack a stable family life and have trouble finding neighbors, shopkeepers, and institutions they can trust may have been hurt even more by forcible removal to new areas. This suspicion is supported by another of Fried's findings: that the socially marginal West Enders were more injured by relocation than those who had been integral members of the old neighborhood. Admittedly, some Negroes move very often on their own, but then they at least do so voluntarily and not in consequence of a public policy which is supposed to help them in the first place. Admittedly also, relocation has made it possible for social workers to help slum dwellers whom they could not reach until renewal brought them out in the open, so to speak. But then only a few cities have so far used social workers to make relocation a more humane process.

These high financial, social, and emotional costs paid by the slum dwellers have generally been written off as an unavoidable by-product of "progress," the price of helping cities to collect more taxes, bring back the middle class, make better use of downtown land, stimulate private investment, and restore civic pride. But as Anderson shows, urban renewal has hardly justified these claims either. For one thing, urban renewal is a slow process: the average project has taken twelve years to complete. Moreover, while the few areas suitable for luxury housing were quickly rebuilt, less desirable cleared land might lie vacant for many years because developers were—and are—unwilling to risk putting up high- and middle-income housing in areas still surrounded by slums. Frequently, they can be attracted only by promises of tax write-offs, which absorb the increased revenues that renewal is supposed to create for the city. Anderson reports that, instead of the anticipated four dollars for every public dollar, private investments have only just matched the public subsidies, and even the money for luxury housing has come forth largely because of federal subsidies. Thus, all too few of the new projects have produced tax gains and returned suburbanites or generated the magic rebuilding boom.

Anderson goes on to argue that during the fifteen years of the federal urban-renewal program, the private housing market has achieved what urban renewal has failed to do. Between 1950 and 1960, twelve million new dwelling units were built, and fully six million substandard ones disappeared—all without government action. The proportion of substandard housing in the total housing supply was reduced from 37 to 19 per cent, and even among the dwelling units occupied by nonwhites, the proportion of substand-

ard units has dropped from 72 to 44 per cent. This comparison leads Anderson to the conclusion that the private market is much more effective than government action in removing slums and supplying new housing and that the urban-renewal program ought to be repealed. ∎

Boston Redevelopment Authority

Source: Edward Banfield, "The Unheavenly City" in *The Conscience of the City*, ed. Martin Meyerson (New York: George Braziller, 1970), pp. 37–51.

Our Unsolvable Urban Ills

I shall argue, first, that all of the serious problems of the cities are largely insoluble now and will be for the foreseeable future and, second, that insofar as it is open to government (federal, state, and local) to affect the situation, it tends to behave perversely—that is, not to do the things that would make it better, but instead to do those that will make it worse. These two arguments prepare the way for the question with which I shall be mainly concerned: What is there about our politics that accounts for this perversity?

I

By the serious problems of the cities I mean those that affect, or may affect, the essential welfare (as opposed to the comfort, convenience, and business advantage) of large numbers of people or the ability of the society to maintain itself as a "going concern," to be in some sense free and democratic, and to produce desirable human types. As examples of serious problems I will cite chronic unemployment, poverty, ignorance, crime, racial and other injustice, and civil disorder. To my mind, these problems are of a different order of importance than, say, the journey to work, urban sprawl, or the decline of department store sales.

What I am calling serious problems exist mainly in the inner parts of the central cities and of the older larger suburbs. The large majority of city dwellers do not live in these places and have little or no first-hand knowledge of these problems; most city dwellers have housing, schools, transportation, and community facilities that are excellent and getting better all the time. If

there is an urban crisis, it is in the inner city. The lowest-skilled, lowest-paid, and lowest-status members of the urban work force have always lived in the highest-density districts of the inner city, that being where most of the jobs for the low-skilled have always been. Improvements in transportation have in the last thirty years or so hastened a process of outward growth that has always been going on. Most of those who could afford to do so have moved from the central city to the suburbs and from inlying suburbs to outlying ones. Much manufacturing and commerce has done the same thing. The inner city still employs most of the unskilled, but the number (and proportion) that it employs is declining, and considerable numbers of the unskilled are in a sense stranded in the inner city. The presence there of large concentrations of people who have relatively little education and income accounts for—perhaps I should say constitutes—the so-called urban crisis. Most of these people are black. From an objective standpoint, this is of less importance than most people suppose: If all Negroes turned white overnight, the serious problems of the city would still exist and in about the same form and degree; it is the presence of a large lower class, not of Negroes as such, that is the real source of the trouble.

Government can change the situation that I have just described only marginally; it cannot change it fundamentally. No matter what we do, we are bound to have large concentrations of the unskilled, of the poor, and—what is by no means the same thing—of the lower class in the inner parts of the central cities and the larger older

suburbs for at least another twenty years. Rich as we are, we cannot afford to throw the existing cities away and build new ones from scratch. The decentralization of industry and commerce and of residential land use is bound to continue, leaving ever larger semi-abandoned and blighted areas behind.

If government cannot change fundamentally the pattern of metropolitan growth, neither can it solve any of the serious problems associated with it. To be specific, it cannot eliminate slums, educate the slum child, train the unskilled worker, end chronic poverty, stop crime and delinquency, or prevent riots. Of course, I do not mean that it cannot eliminate a single slum, educate a single slum child, or prevent a single riot. What I mean is that it cannot put a sizable dent in the problem as a whole. These problems may all become much less serious, but if they do, it will not be because of the direct efforts of government to bring about reforms.

We cannot solve these problems or even make much headway against them by means of government action not because, as many seem to suppose, we are selfish, callous, or stupid, but rather because they are in the main not susceptible to solution. For one reason or another, solving them is beyond the bounds of possibility. In the largest class of cases, solution depends upon knowledge that we do not and perhaps cannot possess. Consider, for example, the problem of educating the lower-class child. In recent years, there has been a vast outpouring of effort on this, and a great many well-thought-out and plausible ideas have been tried, some of them, like Operation Head Start, on a very large scale. So far none of these efforts can be said to have succeeded, and most of them have clearly failed. After surveying the various efforts at compensatory education, the U.S. Commission on Civil Rights said in *Racial Isolation in the Public Schools* that "none of the programs appear to have raised significantly the achievement of participating pupils, as a group, within the period evaluated by the Commission." It is probably safe to say that if the leading educators of this country were given first call on all of the nation's resources and told that they could do whatever they liked, they would not succeed in giving what any of us would consider an adequate education to a substantial number of slum children.

The nature of some problems is such that even if we knew how to solve them, we probably could not make use of the knowledge because the cure would be worse than the disease. However attractive they may otherwise be, all "solutions" that are incompatible with the basic principles of our political system must be considered unavailable—that is, beyond the bounds of possibility. If, for example, it were found to be possible to educate the lower-class child by taking him from his family shortly after birth and in no other way, we should have to give up the idea of educating those lower-class children whose parents refused to give them up; a free society cannot even consider taking children from their parents on the mere presumption—indeed not even on the certainty—that otherwise they will grow up ignorant, dependent, lower class.

Incompatibility with the basic principles of the political system is by no means the only ground on which a "solution" may be judged worse than the disease. Consider, for example, the police "crackdown" as a method of reducing crime on the streets. I do not know how well this method really works, but suppose for the sake of argument that it works very well. Even so, it is not a solution because, rightly or wrongly, a "crackdown" would be regarded by Negroes as an affront to the race. What is accomplished if crime is reduced slightly at the cost of deepening the cleavage between the Negro and the rest of society?

It is only because we seldom pay any attention to the indirect, unintended, and unwanted consequences of government actions that we fail to see that they are often worse than the diseases that the actions are supposed to cure. The usual assumption seems to be that a desirable consequence in hand offsets two undesirable ones in the bush. This may be reasonable. But what if the bush is full of extremely undesirable consequences?

II

Although government cannot cure the serious ills of the city, it might make the patient more comfortable and enable it to lead a somewhat more useful life despite its ills. I will list what I think are the more important things that it might do to improve the situation. In general, these are not the things that one would most like to have done (those being in most cases beyond the bounds of possibility for the reasons indicated), but they are all ones that it is possible in principle for government to do and that would make a more than trivial contribution to the improvement of the situation. Some of the items on the list may strike the reader as highly implausible, but this is not the place to try to justify them.

The list is as follows:

1 Use fiscal policy to keep unemployment below 3 per cent even though this would entail undesirable inflation. (The possibility of this for more than a few years was denied by Milton Friedman in his Presidential Address to the American Economics Association in 1967. Other leading economists assert it, however, and the question must be considered unsettled.)

2 Eliminate impediments to the free working of the labor market, particularly that for low-skilled labor. This implies removing legal and other barriers to the employment of the young, the unschooled, women, and Negroes. It implies repeal of minimum wage laws and of laws that enable unions to exercise monopolistic powers. It also implies improving the information available to workers about job opportunities in other places.

3 If the second recommendation is not carried into effect, suspend immigration of the unskilled. Also, by bringing about expansion of the rural southern and Puerto Rican economies and by setting welfare allowances so as to favor rural and small-town residence, discourage migration of unskilled Americans to the large cities.

4 Pay the poor to send infants and small children to nursery and pre-schools. Create a competitive school system by giving vouchers for use in any private (including parochial) school to parents of children who do not go to public school. Lower the compulsory attendance age to twelve and the normal school-leaving age to fourteen (grade twelve). Give boys and girls who leave school the choice between taking a job and going into a youth corps. Make it possible for all who qualify to get higher education subject to later repayment.

5 Define poverty in terms of "hardship" (as opposed to "inconvenience" or "relative deprivation") and bring all incomes up to this nearly fixed level. With respect to those competent to manage their own affairs (that is, all but the insane, the severely retarded, the senile, and unprotected children), make the income transfer by means of a negative income tax, leaving the recipients free to spend their money as they please. Public housing, public hospital care, "rehabilitation," and other welfare services in kind rather than in cash should go only to those requiring institutional or semi-institutional care.

6 Allow police officers wider latitude to deal out "curbstone justice" to petty offenders, especially juveniles. Repeal laws against gambling and usury. Change insurance and police practices (for example, free recovery of stolen cars) so that potential victims of crime will not be deprived of incentive to take precautions to prevent loss.

7 Eliminate impediments to the free working of the housing market. Establish building codes, uniform for the whole of a metropolitan area, that will permit the widest latitude for innovation and economizing consistent with safety. Assure that some part of every suburb is zoned in a manner that does not prevent low-income occupancy.

8 Prohibit "live" television coverage of riots.

9 Avoid rhetoric tending to create demands and expectations that cannot possibly be fulfilled or to excite alarm about nonexistent crises. Above all, stop attributing more importance to racial factors, including discrimination, than the facts warrant. Explain nothing on racial grounds that can be explained as well or better on income or class grounds.

I trust I do not need to say again that this is not a list of "consummations devoutly to be wished." Rather it is one of things that government could do and the doing of which would contribute more than trivially to the amelioration of the serious problems of the city. But even if all of these things were done, the situation would not be fundamentally changed; the improvements would be ones of degree rather than of kind.

III
Although the measures listed are possible, they are not politically feasible. It is safe to say that none of them will be tried in the near future. A politician with a heterogeneous constituency probably could not support any of them vigorously. Indeed, with respect to most of the items on the list, the politically feasible thing is the exact opposite of what has been recommended: for example, to raise the minimum wage, to raise the normal school-leaving age, to encourage immigration of the unskilled, to define poverty as relative deprivation rather than as hardship, to emphasize racial factors while denying the existence of class ones, and so on.

Why this perversity in the choice of policies? Before offering an answer to this question, I should acknowledge that its premises are questionable. Perhaps the recommendations made above are unsound; perhaps, too, the things that I said were beyond the bounds of possibility are not beyond them. Even if the recommendations are sound, the system may not be perverse in rejecting them for their opposites. It may be that "problems" arise only in those instances—which may be a very small proportion of the whole—where the system fails to select a right policy and by so doing fails to prevent a problem from arising. To explain an occasional visible failure on the grounds that the system is perverse is like explaining the presence of a few men in death row on grounds that the threat of capital punishment is not a deterrent. For all we know tens of thousands of men may *not* be in death row precisely because they *were* deterred. Space does not permit me to deal with these objections. All I can do is say that I am aware of them.

Perhaps the most palpable reason for the political infeasibility of most of the items on the list is that they would be instantly squashed by some interest group (or groups) if they were ever put forward. The founding fathers went to great pains to distribute power so widely that "factions" would check one another and prevent the growth of tyranny. This arrangement has the defects of its virtues, of course; one of the defects is that a very small group can often veto a measure that would be of great benefit to a large public. It is laughable, for example, to talk about eliminating impediments to the free working of the labor market so long as labor unions are politically powerful. New York City cannot employ unskilled laborers to repair the slum housing that they live in because to do so it would first have to get them into the building trades unions and then pay them union wages.

There are well-armed and strategically placed "veto groups" (as David Riesman calls them in *The Lonely Crowd*) for almost every item on the list. The organized teachers would veto a proposal to lower the school-leaving age. The organized social workers would veto the substitution of a negative income tax for the traditional arrangements. Civil rights organizations would veto giving policemen more latitude to deal out "curbstone justice." The television industry would veto the prohibition of "live" TV coverage of riots. And so on.

Although interest groups most often exercise their power by vetoing measures that might be injurious to them, they sometimes initiate ones that they think will benefit them. Why, it may be asked, do not the putative beneficiaries of the measures on the list above organize and apply pressure counter to that of the veto groups? The answer (as Mancur Olson has explained in *The Logic of Collective Action*) is that in most instances the benefits are in the nature of what economists call "public goods"—that is, they are such that if anyone benefits, all must benefit. This being the case, no individual has any incentive to support an organization to bring them into existence. TV stations find

it to their advantage to maintain an organization that can influence the F.C.C. not to prohibit "live" coverage of riots, but the ordinary citizen, even if he were very much in favor of prohibiting it, would not pay much of anything to have his view urged upon the F.C.C. because he would be sure that his small contribution would not affect the outcome. In a certain sense, therefore, it would be irrational for him to contribute, since he would have the same chance of getting the benefit (prohibition of "live" coverage) if he kept his money in his pocket. For most of the items on the list, the logic of collective action is of this sort.

In the last analysis, however, what makes the items on the list politically infeasible is that promising them would not help anyone to get elected. To some extent this is because public opinion does not favor them. (It is not for this reason entirely, however. As Anthony Downs has explained, candidates and parties offer combinations of measures—"budgets"— that confer on voters large benefits in terms of their primary interests and, at worst, small costs in terms of their secondary and tertiary interests. Thus, in principle, a winning coalition may be built around a "budget" no single item of which is favored by more than a few voters.)

It is pertinent to inquire, therefore, why *public opinion* is perverse. An answer sometimes given is that in matters such as these it is generally dominated by the opinion of the well educated and well off. These people (so the argument runs) are indifferent or downright hostile to the interest of the less well off and the poor. In short, the "masses" are against the recom-

mended measures because they have been misled by an elite that is looking after its own interests.

This explanation does not fit the facts. The perversity of policy does not benefit the well off; on the contrary, it injures them. The well off are not benefited by the minimum wage or by other laws and practices that price low-value labor out of the market and onto the welfare rolls. They are not benefited by laws that keep hundreds of thousands of children who cannot or will not learn anything in schools that they (the well off) must support. They are not benefited by an official rhetoric tending to persuade everyone that the society is fundamentally unjust.

I want to argue that public opinion (which I agree is decisively influenced in many matters by the opinion of the relatively well off) tends to be altruistic and that it is precisely because of its altruism that it opposes the recommendations on the list and favors instead ones that are the reverse of those recommended as well as ones that are beyond the bounds of possibility.

The American cultural ideal, which is most fully exemplified in the upper-middle and upper classes (and within those classes in people of dissenting—Protestant and Jewish—traditions), is oriented toward the future and toward progress. It sees the individual as perfectible by his own effort and society as perfectible by collective effort. Accordingly, it feels a strong obligation to engage in efforts at improvement of self and community. Americans tend to believe that all problems can be solved if only one tries hard enough, and they acknowledge a responsibility to im-

411

prove not only themselves, but everything else—community, society, the whole world. Ever since the days of Cotton Mather, whose *Bonifacius* was a "how to do it" book on the doing of good, service has been our motto. I do not mean to say that our practice has corresponded to our principles. The principles, however, have always been influential and often decisive. For present purposes they can be summarized in two very simple rules: first, DON'T JUST SIT THERE. DO SOMETHING; and, second, DO GOOD.

It is the application of these two rules that produces most of the perversity that I claim characterizes our choice of policies. Believing that any problem can be solved if only we try hard enough, we do not hesitate to attempt what we do not have the least idea how to do and what may even be impossible in principle. Not recognizing any bounds to what is possible, we are not reconciled to, indeed we do not even perceive, the necessity for choosing among courses of action all of which are unsatisfactory, but some of which are less unsatisfactory than others. That some children simply cannot or will not learn anything in school and that we do not know how to change this are facts that the American mind will not entertain. Our cultural ideal demands that we give everyone a good education whether or not he wants it and whether or not he is capable of receiving it. This ideal also tells us that if at first we don't succeed, we must try, try again. To suggest lowering the normal school-leaving age is, in terms of this secular religion, out-and-out heresy.

The recommendations listed above are unacceptable—indeed, downright repellent

—to public opinion because what they call for does not appear to be morally improving either to the doer or to the object of his doing. It does not appear to be improving to the child to send him to work rather than to school, especially as that is what it is to one's interest as a taxpayer to do. It does not appear to be improving to the delinquent to let the policeman "slap him around a little," especially as that accords with one's feelings of hostility toward the juvenile. It does not appear to be improving to the slum dweller to tell him that if his income is adequate and if he prefers to spend it for other things than housing, that is his affair, especially as that is in one's "selfish" interest. From the standpòint of the cultural ideal, the doing of good is not so much for the sake of those to whom the good is done as it is for that of the doers, whose moral faculties are activated and invigorated by the doing of it, and also for that of the community, the shared values of which are ritually asserted and vindicated by the doing of it. For this reason good done otherwise than by intention, especially good done in the pursuance of motives that are selfish or even "non-tuistic," is not really "good" at all. For this reason, too, actions taken from good motives count as good even when, in fact, they do harm. By far the most effective way of helping the poor is to maintain high levels of employment. This, however, is not a method that affords upper-middle- and upper-class people the chance to flex their moral muscles or the community the chance to dramatize its commitment to the values that hold it together. The way to do these things is by a War on Poverty. Even if the War should

turn out to have precious little effect on the incomes of the poor—indeed, even if it should *lower* their incomes—the undertaking would be justified as a sort of secular religious revival that affords the altruistic classes opportunities to bear witness to the cultural ideal and, by so doing, to strengthen society's adherence to it. One recalls the wisecrack about the attitude of the English Puritans toward bear-baiting: that they opposed the sport not for the suffering it caused the bear, but for the pleasure that it gave the spectators. Perhaps it is not farfetched to say that the present-day outlook is similar: The reformer wants to reform the city not so much to make the poor better off materially as to make himself and the society as a whole better off morally.

There is something to be said for this attitude. The old Puritans were certainly right in thinking it worse that people should enjoy the sufferings of animals than that animals should suffer. And the reformers are certainly right in thinking it more important that society display a concern for what is right and just than that the material level of living of the poor (which is already well above the level of physical hardship) be raised somewhat higher. There are problems here however. One is to keep the impulse for doing good from gushing incontinently into mass extravaganzas (Domestic Marshall Plans, for example) in which billions are pledged for no one knows what or how; surely if it is to be morally significant, good must be done from motives that are not contrived for the individual by people with big organizations to maintain and foisted upon him by the mass media. Another is to find ways of doing good that are relatively harmless—that do not unduly injure those to whom the good is done (as, for example, children who cannot or will not learn are injured by long confinement in a school), that are not unfair to third parties (tax-payers), and that do not tend to destroy the consensual basis of the society (as headline-catching official declarations about "white racism" may).

Looking toward the future, it is impossible not to be apprehensive. The frightening fact is that vast numbers of people are being rapidly assimilated to the ethos of the altruistic classes and are coming to have incomes—time as well as money—that permit them to indulge their taste for "serving" and "doing good." Television, even more than the newspapers, tends to turn the discussion of public policy questions into a branch of the mass entertainment industry. "Doing good" is becoming—has already become—a growth industry, like other forms of mass entertainment. This is the way it is in the affluent society. How will it be in the super-affluent one? How preoccupied can a society be with reform without thereby loosening the bonds that hold it together? If there is an urban crisis, perhaps this is its real basis. ∎

413

William B. Finch, Boston

URBAN AND SUBURBAN
ATTITUDES AND VALUES
IN ADVERTISING

Advertising is one of the largest industries in America. Billions of dollars are spent each year to make people aware of and favorably inclined toward products, services, and ideas. The gimmicks that advertisers employ vary widely but always they aim to make use of people's own attitudes and values to create a favorable image for whatever it is they are "pushing." The advertisements on these pages all appeared in the early 1950's.

1 What attitudes toward social position, work, life style, housing patterns, and so forth are appealed to in these ads? What kind of people are being addressed? Why?

2 How would different types of people in the central city and the suburban ring respond to these ads? Why?

3 Assuming that these ads have stated what "the good life" should be, how would you describe this life style?

4 Compare this image of life with the image currently presented in advertisements and commercials. What are the similarities and differences? ∎

414

415

THE PLIGHT
OF MODERN MAYORS

Source: *Look*, April 1, 1967, pp. 11–18.

Our generation, like the Progressive Era, has produced reform-minded mayors. But the burdens that face these elected officials seem overwhelming compared to those faced by the urban reformers of earlier periods.

In this section we look at analytic profiles of three contemporary mayors and their cities. The first is Mayor John V. Lindsay of New York.

John V. Lindsay of New York

"There are 1.6 million cars in New York," says Sanitation Commissioner Moeller, "and every car has to be somewhere. But we've got 6,000 miles of streets—that's 12,000 miles of curbs—to sweep." Why does the ghetto look so filthy? "Insufficient containerization" is the Commissioner's answer. He means that garbage overflows the cans; absentee landlords and floating janitors don't empty dumbwaiters. Stuff on the sidewalk gets kicked or swept into the street and left for the city to clean. Stripped and abandoned cars befoul streets for months. Sanitation people think they could win the battle against filth if they had more men, more efficient machines, and if cars did not obstruct street sweepers. What about cleaning vacant lots, abandoned stores, buildings? The law requires the property owners to clean them. "They can't even find him, how can they force him to clean the place?" says a black man.

Slum housing is another sign of urban decay. A critic of the Lindsay Administration blames City Hall for the failure to provide sufficient new housing. "When those people took over, they shunted aside a good bureaucracy. They don't have enough old pros in housing. They haven't taken advantage of all the available Federal money. They were slow in taking advantage of the 'turn key' approach—a private builder puts up middle-income housing, and when he completes the job, the city buys it. Private builders don't have to endure red-tape delays."

City Hall claims that the housing pipeline went dry during the last years of the preceding administration. Public housing requires several years of planning and approvals before the first shovel bites dirt. "We've cut the typical three-year lead time in housing to two," says Jason Nathan, Lindsay's Housing Commissioner. "What you have to remember is that what went into the ground in 1966 and 1967 depended upon what was done in 1963 and 1964," says Nathan. More important in his view was the decision to consolidate all aspects of city government relating to housing under one super-agency. "Reorganization was political idiocy in the short run," says Nathan. "Anybody who knows anything would know it would be a real crunch. But if you have enough guts, reorganization gets at the goddam cancer. Until we did this, there were six different routes by which a problem building came to the city. It was possible for one agency to slap a penalty on a landlord while another agency was offering him an incentive. Restrictions and penalties don't work. We haven't solved the problem of maintaining housing, but at least we're working on it. It's worse in other cities."

Part of the Lindsay-Nathan approach involves community participation in planning in place of back-room decisions. The Housing Commissioner boasts, "When people arrive by the busload at a hearing for a model-cities application and raise hell if it isn't passed, even though it involves relocating thousands of people, you know the system is working."

A garble of statistics supports and condemns the Lindsay Administration. Actual additions to the housing inventory of the city in the last three years are puny compared with those of previous periods, even allowing for tighter mortgage money and boom years spurred by the coming of

Wide World Photos

zoning restrictions. Publicly assisted housing for the last three years surpasses that of any other comparable era, but a big drop-off in private construction keeps the housing supply short.

Community involvement in housing means outfits like the Upper Park Avenue Community Association. Mrs. Margaret Jenkins, a small round woman who has spent most of her life in Harlem, was a founder. "In 1965, a group of housewives wanted to do something for the community. Everyone wasn't speaking to one another. We had American blacks, Puerto Ricans, a few Jewish families, Italian, Irish, even some Chinese. We planned a barbecue on East 119th Street. Store owners contributed hamburgers, hot dogs, and we had a steel band playing music to attract people. The money we got was enough to rent a storefront. We had no heat in the place, we were burning lights on the QT, you know," Mrs. Jenkins smiled. "The floor was all tore up; but before, we had to meet in hallways and houses, even empty lots.

"We went to the city to ask for money for fixing up some of the buildings, but we got pushed around quite a bit. We sat in at the anti-poverty agency for 26 hours when they kept telling us our proposals had something wrong with them." The Housing Rehabilitation office told the group to get a cosponsor. The New York Federation of Reform Synagogues agreed to be cosponsors.

"We've never had a problem with them. They've loaned us their expertise, showed us how to cut red tape, and we've kept our own ideas," says Mrs. Jenkins. *UPACA* has rehabilitated 35 units in two Harlem tenements into attractive modern apartments. Some tenants will have a rent subsidy, others will pay a surcharge when their income rises above a certain level. Every tenant takes a course in consumer education.

From back windows of one *UPACA* product, you look at burned-out corpses of buildings. "There's no such thing as an abandoned building when you want to acquire it," says Mrs. Jenkins. Meanwhile, the cadavers house junkies and winos, continue to be fire hazards and death-traps for exploring kids. *UPACA* is now building new housing, with black architect Roger Glasgow in charge. "I think the city is concerned about design, as it wasn't before," says Glasgow.

Corporations sponsored by the late Sen. Robert F. Kennedy have also had some

417

effect in Bedford-Stuyvesant, where there are more blacks than in Harlem and where, in 18 years after the Housing Act of 1949, not one dime went to put up housing. The first sprouts from the seed planted by RFK include an IBM factory that hired more than 100 people who live within a mile of it. Most of them had trouble finding work before. Bedford-Stuyvesant now has the first new-car dealership in the state of New York that is black-owned. Another 28 businesses have received assistance in money and management. The Bedford-Stuyvesant corporations hope to stabilize home mortgages through a $100 million consortium of banks and insurers.

Gibbon blamed barbarians and Christians in part for Rome's decline, but ghettos like Bedford-Stuyvesant suffer from the shifting native population. Herman Badillo says, "The difficulty of New York is that it has national problems with the limited resources of a municipality. You can't speak of New York City as just the eight million who live here. The population is affected by national trends, the movement of people from the South and Puerto Rico. And it's no longer possible to move up just through hard work. This isn't a blue-collar town; it's service-directed."

"Unbelievable changes occurred in neighborhoods," says Jason Nathan. "In nine years, one went from 90 percent white and 10 percent black to the opposite. Tenant-landlord relationships disappeared. The new population had different values, different patterns of living."

What will destroy New York eventually is what Gibbon described as the domestic quarrels of the citizens. The two major quarrels are those of labor vs. management, and the animosities among the various ethnic groups. For the union squabbles, Norman Frank, the spokesman of the Patrolmen's Benevolent Association, blames a lack of "sophistication" on the part of City Hall: "There's no fundamental understanding of the labor force's ambitions." In his opinion, Lindsay "lacks the courage to tell citizens they'll have to pay for better services. At the very beginning of his administration, he made constant reference to power brokers. There are a myriad of group and self-serving causes. It's the order of the day. For protection, you must devote yourself to your own group."

Theodore Kheel, who has built a national reputation as a mediator in settling strikes affecting New York City, declares, "In fairness to Lindsay, this is a period of inflationary pressures. Besides, all over the country, rank and file have been rejecting settlements," says Kheel. "What you have to do is avoid a sense of take-it-or-leave-it bargaining. Give credit and save cash, support the leadership of your adversary.

"A mayor dealing with city employees is in an ambivalent position. He's the employer and at the same time chief magistrate, with a responsibility for settling disputes. You can't be both a party to the bargaining and the mediator. Either accept the role of employer and use an outside mediator or be the mediator. But then you need some sort of city-manager type of government. The ambivalence probably leads to some of Lindsay's impatience with the labor-bargaining ritual."

Asked if he behaved with stiff-necked righteousness in the 1968 garbage strike, Lindsay retorts that he saved the city office of collective bargaining. "I can't see settling at any price. The public cries for leadership that stands for something; that's what's needed in this country."

The volcano beneath New York rumbled loudly in the school-decentralization controversy. The fight over who should have the right to assign and transfer teachers in the Ocean Hill-Brownsville experimental school district in Brooklyn erupted into overt anti-black, anti-white and anti-Semitic incidents. "You cannot change the institutions of the city without clear guidelines. Otherwise, confrontations in the street must settle the issues," says Herman Badillo, putting the blame for the teachers' strike on the Board of Education, which set up Ocean Hill-Brownsville, and the Ford Foundation, which helped finance the project and issued a school-decentralization plan without clear guidelines.

Other critics think a little good faith would have avoided a strike. But the union believed compromise would weaken job security and the school board felt it could not function effectively without the right to hire and fire or at least transfer. At best, the Mayor failed to soften an inevitable confrontation; and at worst, he appeared on TV announcing an agreement that did not exist.

"School decentralization," says the Mayor (who thinks "community control" is too emotional a label for the concept), "means parents have a meaningful voice in education. Decentralization would end a 25-year decline, particularly for the disadvantaged."

Integration of education in New York

City is now meaningless. More than 50 percent of the public-school population is nonwhite. Whether decentralization and community control will improve education has not been proved. "Decentralization doesn't mean anything," says Badillo, "unless you're going to spend more per pupil." Charles Wilson, the administrator of IS 201, an experimental decentralized school district, insists: "Those who have the power don't have the knowledge, and those who have the knowledge don't have the power."

The decentralization confrontation unmasked more than union-management antagonism. Less than a week after the teachers struck in September, 1968, Jacques Torezyner, president of the Zionist Organization of America, warned that "thousands of Jewish school teachers" faced expulsion because black extremists played a major role in decentralized school boards in New York. "We have a new brand of anti-Semitism," said he. Several black proponents of decentralization later attacked the Jewish leadership of the teachers union. A teacher at Ocean Hill, who claimed he only wanted to demonstrate the depth of feeling on the subject, read a pupil's anti-Semitic poem on the radio. A consultant to the Metropolitan Museum misedited an introduction to the catalog of its Harlem exhibition. Several paragraphs originally intended to explain the roots of black anti-Semitism were distorted into sounding anti-Semitic themselves. The Anti-Defamation League rushed out a poorly researched study on the rise of black anti-Semitism. Newspapers helped to raise the temperature of the Jewish community. White anti-Semites sat back and enjoyed the conflict of their enemies, Jews and blacks.

Reform Rabbi Balfour Brickner of the Union of American Hebrew Congregations says: "The ordinary Jew in New York has developed a sort of muscular response. It reflects what I call the Bruno Bettelheim-Hannah Arendt accusations, that the Jews went like lambs to the Nazi slaughterhouse. Jews here are absolutely determined that that charge will never be made against the American Jewish community.

"The danger is that the fabric of American democracy may come apart at the seams if blacks and Jews can't work together. Then the extremists will take over."

William Booth, a black man, served as Lindsay's Commissioner of Human Rights for three years. Jewish groups clamored that Booth lacked sensitivity to the question of anti-Semitism, and Lindsay nominated him out of the Human Rights Commission up to the Criminal Courts.

Says Booth: "I don't see the classic anti-Semitism here. The anti-Semitism is part of the anti-white feeling and results in very little action and nothing involving religion. Negro people are not using it to further their cause. There was a teacher in Harlem working a mimeograph machine, and he put out 8,000 pieces of anti-Semitic literature. We asked him to stop. The Commission doesn't have the power to ban slurs. We use persuasion. He stopped. But the teachers union took that piece of literature, printed 500,000 copies and distributed it.

"The most persistent institutional and individual racism is practiced against blacks and Puerto Ricans. When I went out to Francis Lewis High School in Queens, the striking teachers yelled, 'Sieg heil, Booth.' " An aide to Booth adds, "I heard teachers yell 'nigger lover' at those who crossed the picket lines."

At Franklin K. Lane High School in Brooklyn, a site of recent racial skirmishes, young whites passed out printed literature: "Victims of Jungle Savagery, Awake! Are you next? In 1967, Lane High School was only 40 percent jungle. Now due to liberal treachery your school is 65 percent jungle controlled. Will cannibalism be practiced in the school cafeteria?"

There are those who see the fight in terms of the Mayor. "He's the uptight white knight," says Jack Newfield, an editor at The Village Voice. "He's played Gary Cooper in a High Noon with the blacks and thrilled the people in the suburbs. It took guts, but he hasn't done anything for the youth: he hasn't solved the problems."

"I never heard anyone here speak against the Mayor," defends a UPACA member. "He's done a lot for people. I hope he runs again."

"Lindsay's doing the best he can, but he's a man with ten fingers, and there are 16 holes in the dike," worries Charles Wilson.

"The city is not going downhill. It's impacted," argues Rabbi Brickner. "Every city is going to have the problems of New York. It's just that they show up here first."

And so the dream struggles against the nightmare. Fun City against Fear City. Neither label is real, but people do not necessarily live and act on facts. What counts is what people believe, and New York's crisis has become one of crumbling faith in the city. ■

Source: *Newsweek*, April 5, 1971, pp. 80–84.

Richard Daley of Chicago

One of the most controversial of all America's central city mayors is Richard J. Daley of Chicago. The following is a profile of Daley done by *Newsweek*.

Wide World Photos

420

Head high, shoulders braced and wattles aquiver, the mayor of Chicago strode down the hallway toward the city council chambers, four plain-clothes men and two young aides half-trotting in his wake. "Good mornin', Mister Mare," called a broguish voice from the jostling mob of politicians, City Hall employees, policemen and photographers that thronged the corridor. "How are ya," Mayor Richard J. Daley grunted, but the ice-blue eyes remained fixed straight ahead as he marched toward the door of the chamber. "Clear a path, clear a path," shouted several policemen in unison, ignoring the fact that the crowd had already parted. A black alderman, his hands filled with petitions, edged into the open pathway as a dozen of his constituents watched nervously. "Mister Mayor, Mister Mayor," he shouted as Daley approached. "Here are some people who . . ." Daley didn't break stride. "How are ya," he mumbled over his shoulder as he and his entourage plunged through the doorway.

At precisely 10 a.m. the mayor took his seat in the council president's chair, slightly below the great seal of the city of Chicago and well above the heads of the 50 aldermen who compose the body. By Daley's standards, the session was a fairly sedate one. A third of the time was devoted to passing memorial resolutions ("Whereas God in his infinite wisdom has seen fit to call our dear colleague to his eternal reward . . ."). And for once there were no flowery accolades to the man who has gazed down impassively on these conclaves for sixteen years (until he died recently, one alderman often interrupted the city-council sessions by crying out exuberantly, "God bless our mayor, the greatest mayor in the world!").

Aloof: The only potentially sticky piece of business—a controversial plan to put up public housing in white ethnic neighborhoods—was quickly shunted to a committee. And when one of the council's tiny band of twelve Republican and Independent aldermen tried to protest, the mayor's paunchy floor leader silenced him by shouting, "Sit down or I'll knock ya down." Later, a second dissident sought to press a point and received an equally explicit warning from Thomas Buchanan, one of Daley's most ardent loyalists. "My Irish heritage tells me there's something I can do about you," bellowed Buchanan, shaking a clenched fist. "And I just may be tempted to do it before this day is out." At precisely 1:15, Daley banged his gavel and charged from the room before anyone but his bodyguards had realized that the council was adjourned.

The entire performance was quintessential Daley, and what lent it an extra dimension of improbability, at least to the casual visitor, was the fact that the star performer himself remained completely aloof from the tentative squabblings of the councilmen—a haughty, imperious figure who came, presided and departed, apparently not caring a whit whether the audience or the cast approved of the show or not.

Chicago's Mayor Daley is a curious, almost fathomless figure. He directs the affairs of the nation's second-largest city like a Caesar. To the vast majority of the country's liberal Democrats, and particularly to the young and the militant, he looms as a figure of near-Satanic evil—this last chiefly the result of his role in the riotous days of the 1968 Democratic National Convention. His goodwill and good offices are usually vital to the aspirations of any Democratic Presidential hopeful, a situation the late Robert F. Kennedy acknowledged laconically enough with the observation: "Daley's the ball game." And even after the Democratic convention, the mayor is a good man to have on one's side in the election, though he ignores the standing accusation that his organization regularly steals vast blocs of votes and withholds reporting them until Daley determines if they are needed to swing the election his way. . . .

Mayor Daley may strike many as outrageously dictatorial, congenitally devious and linguistically inept (his most cherished malapropism: "Together we must rise to ever higher and higher platitudes"). But in an age when *Homo urbanis* is surrounded by proliferating dissolution and decay, the tough, pragmatic Daley continues to operate one of the last efficient big-city governments left on the planet. This is not to suggest, reports *Newsweek* Chicago correspondent Frank Maier, that Daley's Chicago enraptures every resident or inspires every visitor to leave his heart behind. But it is a demonstrable fact that Chicago is that most wondrous of exceptions—a major American city that actually works.

While breakdowns in essential services have become an almost daily event elsewhere, Chicagoans enjoy a virtually uninterrupted supply of urban amenities. They commute to work on the nation's most ingeniously integrated transportation system—expressways fanning out from the central core with rapid-transit trains running down their median strips (or as Daley calls them, "medium strips"). Chicago's streets are probably the cleanest and best-illuminated on the metropolitan scene; its police and fire departments are ranked by professionals as among the most effective in the world. Indeed, while the number of major crimes in the U.S. jumped 11 per cent last year, Chicago actually witnessed a slight dip (.4 per cent) in its crime rate. Daley sees to it that his cops are rewarded with top pay and, as a result of this, Police Superintendent James Conlisk finds himself with ten applicants for every job opening.

Under Daley, liberal zoning laws and flexible tax policies have kept giant industrial firms happily within the city limits. The corporate exodus that is plaguing New York is unknown in Chicago. In the last five years, private investors have poured more than $5 billion into the downtown area, where the world's tallest building— the 110-story headquarters of Sears, Roebuck & Co.—will soon begin rising not far from the 100-story John Hancock Center. The Daley administration has thrown up a record 45,000 low-income housing units in the Near North, West and South Side ghettos (a policy that critics assail roundly as being designed deliberately to perpetuate the ghettos). Daley has also virtually transformed one of the city's most decayed neighborhoods by investing it with a major branch of the University of Illinois. Perhaps the most miraculous aspect of all this growth is that it rests on a rock-solid fiscal foundation. Chicago hasn't had a budget deficit in sixteen years; it issues municipal bonds with the highest rating awarded by Standard & Poor's and boasts one of the few expanding tax bases among U.S. metropolises.

Hurts: But there is another side of the Chicago story, and a less cheering one. Unhappily, Dick Daley's finesse in dealing with the housekeeping side of his job has not been matched in less visible areas. Inveterate Daley watchers such as Studs Terkel, the award-winning chronicler of the Depression and host of a local radio show, speaks for most of Daley's disparagers when he contends: "He's marvelous when it comes to building things like highways, parking lots and industrial complexes. But when it comes to healing the aches and hurts of human beings, Daley comes up short."

No amount of civic drumbeating, for example, can conceal the fact that Chicago's infant-mortality rate among blacks is one of the worst in the U.S., averaging almost 20 per cent higher than New York's. Nor do the city's peripatetic boosters like to discuss why 51 of Chicago's 57 high schools have fallen below the national average in IQ achievement. Most embarrassing of all, the Federal government is currently holding up some $55 million in urban-renewal and model-cities money because Chicago has failed to draw up an adequate blueprint for the construction of public-housing projects in its all-white enclaves.

'Why Us?' Daley has angrily defied a Federal court decision ordering the Chicago Housing Authority to produce such a plan posthaste. After blue-collar homeowners from Polish, Irish and Italian neighborhoods recently marched on their aldermen's offices with signs that read

"Never!" the mayor publicly vowed: "We're only going to build houses where people want them." That sort of standing-in-the-schoolhouse-door position prompted The Chicago Daily News to take an uncharacteristic swipe at the mayor. "A Daley with a deep sense of social justice," the News editorialized, "would have used his prestige long since to help the black people break out of their ghettos."

City Hall apologists like press aide Earl Bush counter such charges by employing a sort of "Why us?" rationale. "When people say, 'Daley's not solving the problems of race, housing and education'," growls Bush, "I simply say, 'Dammit, who the hell is?'" A somewhat more thoughtful defense of the mayor is offered by Prof. Louis Masotti, a sociologist at Northwestern University's Center for Urban Affairs. "The people who criticize Daley the most have never had to live in New York or Los Angeles," says Masotti. "What everyone wants is a philosopher-king, a mayor with both the power to govern and the wisdom to do right. But most cities end up with neither a philosopher nor a king. Take New York, for example. John Lindsay may have the wisdom, but he doesn't have the power. I greatly admire Lindsay's intent, but he's like a guy rollerskating in a herd of buffalo —he's not in control of anything. Whatever else you say about Daley, he's got the clout."

The principal sources of Daley's clout, which in turn provides the driving muscle behind much of Chicago's unique workability, are best symbolized by the sides of a triangle. One is the city's business establishment, the merchants and the bankers of State and LaSalle Streets—most of them blue-blood Republicans and thus, theoretically at least, Richard Daley's natural enemies. On the opposite side is organized labor, a more likely ally for the tough-talking son of a sheet-metal worker. Comprising the triangle's base side is that vast and celebrated political apparatus commonly referred to as The Machine—a term that Daley abhors ("Organization, not machine," he once snapped to a reporter. "Get that. Organization, not machine.").

That Chicago's GOP fat cats should quadrennially troop into Democrat Daley's camp like conquered princes paying homage to Genghis Khan is attributable much more to Daley's power to reward them than to his power to punish. In exchange for their support, the mayor gives the city's investment and business communities just about everything they want, whether it be new superhighways to whisk suburbanites into the downtown shopping district or an honorable peace with labor. Indeed, Daley's success in using his office to avert prolonged labor disputes may rank as his finest monument. For during four terms, the mayor of Chicago has personally settled some twenty major strikes by everyone from the city's gravediggers to members of the Chicago Symphony Orchestra.

Pals: Part of the rationale underlying Daley's extraordinary peace-keeping performance lies in the incestuous nature of Chicago politics. A significant number of the city's top labor leaders are boyhood pals of the mayor, serving on his boards and commissions and receiving city jobs for their friends and relations. In a demonstration of the value of such relationships, striking Chicago teachers recently reached a quick settlement when Daley personally undertook negotiations between teachers' union president John Desmond, a longtime crony of the mayor, and school-board head John Carey, a Daley appointee. "Public strikes in Chicago have been short and symbolic," says Northwestern's Masotti. "Daley sometimes lets them start, but then he quickly steps in and shows everyone he can stop them."

But it should also be noted that much of labor's fealty to Daley springs from a natural empathy for his blend of crusty toughness and misty-eyed civic chauvinism. Only Richard Daley, for example, could have gotten away with the following extemporaneous exhortation to the garbage-truck drivers of Chicago: "You men, with the help of God, are going to make this the finest city. You are going to go out and make every street and every alley the finest street and the finest alley." And certainly only this of all America's mayors could have inspired the mammoth love-in for Daley that organized labor staged recently in McCormick Place. While some 10,000 union members and officials applauded between bites of filet mignon, the banquet was hailed by one speaker as "the biggest dinner ever served under one roof in the chronicle of mankind."

Machine: There is no secret at all as to the source of Daley's power: it rests in his dual role as both mayor and chairman of the Cook County Democratic Committee, a combination that allows him to have final say over the award of some 35,000 patronage positions. At least once a week, Daley meets with his "director of patronage" to peruse every application for every city job, right down to the lowliest ditch digger's. If and when the mayor stamps his approval, the successful job winner almost by definition joins The Machine (or organization) and assumes the responsibility of working one of Chicago's 3,412 voting precincts come election time. That sort of quasi-military arrangement continues to produce virtual blitzes at the ballot box. In fact, there were so few Republican levers pushed in one West Side ward in 1967 that one of the mayor's lieutenants felt obliged to transfer some votes from his own tally just to make things look authentic.

The remarkable diligence displayed by the Democrats' precinct captains and ward committeemen in getting out the vote can be traced to their acute awareness that Daley is continually deciding who can still deliver and who cannot. One of the most withering experiences in a ward boss's life comes on election night when he must bring his tally downtown to party headquarters at the Sherman House Hotel. Somewhat in the manner of a schoolboy presenting his report card to a stern father, each of the 50 meets alone with Daley to submit his precinct-by-precinct vote. According to one insider who has observed the ritual, Daley sits at a desk and silently studies the tallies. If they please him, he rises and vigorously pumps both of the successful committeeman's hands. If they displease him, Daley gives the miscreant a blistering tongue-lashing. On one such occasion, the mayor was so incensed with a nonproducer that he reached across his desk and began shaking him by his necktie.

Affront: The Machine, of course, must be fueled by money as well as manpower. But under Daley's stewardship, there have been none of the sweeping scandals that wrecked its counterparts elsewhere. This doesn't mean that there isn't a certain amount of "honest graft,"—the term invoked by Chicago politicians to explain to their wives that otherwise mysterious $1,000 fee from, say, a building contractor. But Dick Daley himself has never been touched by even a hint of financial hanky-panky, and he takes such a proprietary view of Chicago that few wrongdoers escape retribution. "The boss identifies himself so closely with this city," says one alderman, "that he takes it as a personal affront when someone misbehaves."

* * *

Unpretentious: Like all the old, hard-line Irish political autocrats, however, this last of the breed has his sentimental side. Daley still lives in Bridgeport, the same white, blue-collar community where he was born and which has produced the city's last three mayors. "My Dad, Mike, told me to always remember from whence I came," he explains. At about 8 a.m. each working day, a limousine bearing the license number 708 222—the number of votes Daley received when first elected mayor—glides up to his neat brick bungalow at 3536 S. Lowe Avenue, just a block from where he was born and down the street from the church where he once served as an altar boy. The mayor nods at the occupants of the police patrol car who maintain a 24-hour watch on his house, slips into the back seat and speeds to St. Peter's Church in the Loop, to attend Mass. Often he makes it home for lunch with at least one of his seven children and his wife, Eleanor, an unpretentious, bread-baking Bridgeport girl whom the neighbors still call by her nickname of "Sis."

Daley's personal proclivities remain sternly Victorian. He doesn't smoke, rarely drinks and has been known to stalk out of meetings after someone told an off-color story. Would-be womanizers among his staff have long since discovered that their boss considers adulterous conduct as mortally sinful as a failure to get out the vote. Indeed, Dick Daley grew up to be what every Bridgeport-Irish mother wished her boy to be—religious, hard-working, clean-living, family-oriented and successful.

Rough: As a Bridgeport "yout'," Daley held a job penning cattle at the Chicago stockyards while attending DeLaSalle High School under the stern tutelage of the Christian Brothers. Bridgeport was a rough place in those days, and the old-timers who still frequent the neighborhood saloons like to recall that their mayor earned his first victories as a tenacious street brawler. After taking a law degree at DePaul University through night courses, Daley got his start in politics as the secretary to a local ward boss named McDonough. The rest seemed to follow naturally for a bright, industrious operator—election to the state legislature, chairmanship of the county Democratic apparatus, and, in 1955, a successful campaign for mayor. Daley's most oft-quoted statement of that campaign came in response to charges that he represented a rascal-ridden element. "I would not unleash the forces of evil," he cried. "It's a lie. I will follow the training of my good Irish mother—and Dad. If I am elected, I will embrace mercy, love, charity and walk humbly with my God."

* * *

Pizzazz: No single event better epitomizes the royal quality of Dick Daley's regime than the city's St. Patrick's Day parade, and this election year's version was no exception. For once the weather was clear and dry (at least outside), the Chicago River flowed green with dye and the mayor seemed full of the old pizzazz as he led the marchers down State Street and took his place in the center of the jammed reviewing stand. True, there were a few discordant notes. A shaven-skulled, saffron-robed contingent from the youthful U.S. branch of the Hare Krishna sect drew hard looks as they weaved through the marchers, their singsong chant rising above the skirl of the bagpipers. And some signs borne by one militant black group seemed deliberately designed to test the other marchers' sense of humor. "God made the Irish perfect," one read. "And then He created whisky."

Yet nary a frown crossed Dick Daley's pink face as he dipped his emerald green fedora to the passing faithful. To lift his spirits higher, that very afternoon the city's two Marshall Field newspapers had hit the streets with glowing endorsements of Chicago's favorite son. "He is a man who knows how to keep the machinery running," said the Daily News, "how to maintain and extend and improve the city's superb physical plant, how to keep it prosperous and on the move. In these achievements, he stands unique among the mayors of the nation's great cities."

Not every Chicagoan would shout "Right on!" to that, of course, but few would quibble with the notion that Richard Daley's record, with all its imperfections, has at least lent credence to one of his

424

higher platitudes: "Good politics makes for good government." As for the reaction that Daley's Chicago evokes in visitors from some of the nation's less effectively run cities, it can best be summed up in an aphorism by one recent sojourner from New York. "I have seen the past," he said wistfully, "... and it works." ■

Richard G. Hatcher of Gary, Indiana

In the following selection black political scientist Alex Poinsett profiles Mayor Richard G. Hatcher of Gary, Indiana.

Wide World Photos

Source: Alex Poinsett, *Black Power, Gary Style* (Chicago: Johnson Publishing Co., Inc., 1970), pp. 16–17; 107–128.

The Gary to which Mayor Hatcher was newly elected had been built by the United States Steel Corporation sixty-one years earlier on the sandy, southern tip of Lake Michigan, then moulded into a company town. Soon its skyline was dominated by the huge smokestacks of mills bustling with Croats, Poles, Czechs, Slovaks, Serbs, Hungarians, Greeks, Italians, in short, some fifty-four different ethnic groups. The first blacks had come at the end of World War I. By 1968, 100,000 of them (56 percent of the population) had been squeezed into an area of only 6.6 square miles, though the city sprawls over 56.2 square miles. Throughout his campaign Hatcher had always said he wanted to become "mayor of all the people," that he would not show favoritism to blacks. Yet he had insisted his people had been "suffering, getting the short end of the stick in every phase of life." One proof was an Indiana State Civil Rights Commission study which revealed blacks accounted for only 28.2% of all city employees, despite their numerical dominance in Gary's population. They were in lower-paying jobs and held only two of thirty department-head posts. Of two hundred firemen, only sixty-two were blacks. Of two hundred and seventy-six policemen, only thirty-four were blacks and none held a captain's rank. Out of forty-two Indiana cities, Gary ranked thirty-fourth in the municipal employment of blacks. This situation represented the rankest kind of discrimination, despite any speeches the Katz administration could have made.

Moreover, the crime syndicate had found a cozy haven in Gary for years. Prostitutes, charging $20 to $100, worked in shifts to avoid occupational fatigue.

With the syndicate's gross topping a billion dollars a year in Lake County (according to Northwest Indiana Crime Commission estimates), some elected officials made corruption a way of life. A "cooperative" mayor could expect an extracurricular income during his four-year term of from $3 million to $6 million—for doing nothing. His only real mistake would be to fail to report his graft on his income tax as had two recent mayors later convicted of income-tax evasion. Hatcher's predecessor, A. Martin Katz, a reform candidate in 1963, had pleaded that "You can't change established patterns of ten, twelve, thirty or forty years overnight." And Gary's police had made little effort to do so. Before the 1967 mayoral election, a Roman Catholic priest said he felt sorry for whoever won. As far as he could see the city could not be cleaned up in one, five, or even ten years. Not only was crime and corruption rampant, Gary was a city whose natural beauty had been pillaged and natural elements polluted.

Into this sordid picture, then, stepped Richard Gordon Hatcher, unburdened by political deals, so Spartan he neither smoked, drank nor used profanity, so dedicated he worked fourteen to eighteen hours a day, so religious he prayed in church on New Year's Eve while others partied, so committed his Gary soul brothers saw him as "a beautiful, black 'together' cat." In his new job he would be working for $20,000 a year—a $12,000 drop from his 1966 law practice income. He had pleaded in his victory speech: "Let's now transfer our campaign slogan, 'Let's Get Ourselves Together,' into action and make Gary a new and human city."

Hatcher was mayor now of a city which in many ways was a microcosm of the problems besetting urban America. It was hampered in coping with these problems, partially because it could not strengthen and organize strategic administrative and policy functions fast enough. "We can never be what we must become until we face up unflinchingly to what we are," the new mayor would soon declare in his first State of the City address. "Not in self-pity, not in despair, but in the pragmatic spirit of those who examine the real world in order to change it. Let us take a good hard look at the magnitude of the problems we face."

The problems were complicated by several factors, some old and some new, some common to many communities, and some perhaps unique to Gary. In the first place, an intricate and confusing division of responsibilities among city officials prevented efficiency and confused accountability. Secondly, Gary had no civil service system. Instead, all local government positions, except elected ones, were filled by the patronage system. Thirdly, Gary's sordid history of organized and unorganized crime, graft and corruption so lowered the morale and so generated apathy among its citizens that most felt powerless to do anything about local problems. Fourthly, the city lacked strong citizens' or community groups directly focused on local good government needs or mobilized to provide support to new, improved governmental services. Fifthly, Gary's low salary scale made it difficult to recruit the sort of experienced, top-quality personnel necessary for efficient and flexible urban management. Finally, the highly industrialized city

425

was hamstrung by an archaic, agrarian-oriented state legislature. Thus, for example, Gary had limited taxation powers. In addition the local poverty program was administered by the county, complicating tremendously the city's ability to deal effectively with problems of the poor within the city. Furthermore, the inherent tensions between county and city were heightened by the political and racial frictions that arose out of Mayor Hatcher's turbulent election campaign struggles with John Krupa, the Lake County Democratic chairman.

These, then, were a sampling of the problems the new mayor faced when he moved into his City Hall office for the first time at 10:30 a.m. on January 2, 1968. The city's General Fund held a scant $15,000, a sharp contrast to the $400,000 to $500,000 year-end balances usually left to city administrations in the past and also a sharp contrast to the $95,000 that would be in that Fund a year later. Nevertheless, Hatcher had come to head an urban laboratory which, because of the limited size of its problems by comparison with say New York or Chicago, was ripe for experimentation and innovation which could be quickly evaluated.

Unfortunately, because a black mayor was now in City Hall, many blacks and whites expected miracles. Indeed, during his first week a visiting group of black citizens demanded to know why all blacks did not have jobs and why all of Gary's slums had not been eliminated. They were soon to learn that efforts to deliver services were severely hampered in the administration's early days because equipment was in deplorable condition, much of it having been deliberately sabotaged by de-

parting city employees. An intensive program of salvaging and rehabilitating equipment had to be instituted in several departments including most notably General Services (sanitation, etc.) and the Police Department.

While Mayor Hatcher was ill-equipped to perform miracles, his mayoral powers were such that he could hire and fire all city department heads and the deputies of certain other elected officials. As dispensers of all city jobs except those of policemen and firemen, previous mayors had been ruthless political bosses of self-serving political machines. If Mayor Hatcher wished to head such a machine, he was going to have to build it almost from scratch. A substantial number of his predecessor's City Hall staff left so abruptly, the new mayor had to find replacements immediately for tasks as routine as manning the switchboard. And these replacements, many with no prior administrative experience let alone City Hall know-how, had to learn on the job by trial and error.

Yet whenever Mayor Hatcher recruited personnel outside of Gary, he was subjected to bitter criticism. Many of his local supporters had expected him to turn over city jobs to them—the usual reward for political services. But he was forced to reckon with the grim fact that the sort of expertise he needed so desperately was not always available locally. And he was steadfast in his determination to appoint on the basis of occupational merit rather than meritorious services rendered during the election. He was also determined to retain employees from the previous administration who, in addition to wanting to remain on board, showed themselves to be

honest and competent. "Dead wood" had to go, however. Included among the deposed was a former mayor who had been kicked out of office for misuse of funds and promptly put back on the city payroll by his successor. Charged with determining the capabilities of staffers in each of the city's departments was a Department of Program Development, established for the first time in Gary's history and headed by a recent graduate of Yale University Law School, Edward Grier. His responsibility was to troubleshoot for weaknesses in the structure and personnel of each department and to make recommendations that might bring about uniform quality throughout city government.

The organization of Grier's Department of Program Development was only one of Mayor Hatcher's immediate administrative changes aimed at making Gary's government operate more efficiently. Perhaps his most important administrative innovation during his first year involved the reorganization of the chain of command within the city. A cabinet replaced an obsolete management system in which more than thirty department heads reported directly to the mayor. These departments now worked together under three "super-administrators" who were responsible for Gary's overall operations and problems in the areas of (1) public safety and law enforcement, (2) housing and community development and (3) fiscal and personnel administration. These super-administrators were broad policy makers who were answerable only to the mayor. In this way, Hatcher created a more orderly flow of work and priorities.

* * *

Mayor Hatcher had not expected to please everyone when he took office. He had, however, planned a vigorous attack on Gary's massive problems of unemployment, housing, crime, etc. For this purpose he received a series of special grants and consultative services. Among them:

Ford Foundation granted $70,000 for studies in law enforcement, housing, and air pollution and $100,000 more for employing three special assistants to the mayor to help in the areas of housing, law enforcement and personnel administration and finance.

Potomac Institute of Washington, D.C., loaned a top level administrator to the city for the first six months of 1968 to assist in establishing an administrative management system and developing program.

Metropolitan Applied Research Center (MARC) of New York gave technical assistance in setting up office procedures; established contacts with foundations and aided in several funding endeavors.

Field Foundation awarded a $34,000 grant to AFDC mothers to organize welfare recipients.

Office of Economic Opportunity gave a $32,000 planning grant to set up Metro Corps, Inc., Gary's anti-poverty agency.

University of Chicago Center for Urban Studies assisted in resolving special problems.

Gary Model Cities received consultation services from numerous government and private agencies and industries including the federal departments of Health, Education and Welfare, Housing and Urban Development, Transportation, and Agriculture; Indiana State Department of Health; Purdue, Indiana and Illinois Universities; Gary School City; United States Steel and Portland Cement Association.

Labor Department furnished a program-planning expert to lay the groundwork for the Concentrated Employment Program.

Cummins Engine Foundation financed a nationwide talent search to attract highly qualified individuals to positions with the city administration.

This mix of federal government, corporate, and private foundation assistance produced immediate changes in Gary. In his first few months in office Mayor Hatcher could point to the $2.6 million Concentrated Employment Program (CEP) sponsored by the Department of Labor to train the otherwise unemployable. A controversial spinoff from CEP was the now-defunct Soul Inc., a federally-funded organization designed to take youth gang members and channel their energies into constructive activities such as operating their skating rink and movie theater. One of the more controversial aspects of the program had been its use of persons with prison and jail records. "I tell critics that we really have a choice," Mayor Hatcher explained at the time. "We can ignore the youth gangs and leave them to their own destructive impulses or we can work with them and try to reform them. I prefer doing the latter."

When the new Mayor took office, more than 80 percent of Gary's housing was substandard. Indeed, 40 percent of it was so substandard it was condemned. Although blacks accounted for 56 percent of the city's population, they were jammed into one-fourth of its dwelling units. Of these units, one-fifth failed to meet existing city building codes. No public housing had been constructed in Gary between 1952 and 1968. Part of the problem involved the unavailability of land. Housing developments to the North were prohibited by the steel mills and Lake Michigan, to the East and West by corporate limits. Further growth to the South required annexation. To attack this situation, the city undertook more than $10.5 million worth of inner-city urban-renewal projects and the Federal Department of Housing and Urban Development set a target of $2.6 million for a model-city program in 1969.

Gary began constructing 1,600 low- and middle-income housing units. U.S. Steel financed 500 additional units of middle-income housing. At the same time the city building department began aggressive enforcement of building code statutes. Department inspectors checked 4,184 buildings in one month for possible violations. (The previous administration for the same period had only been able to check 331 buildings.) Formerly, many building contractors had not even bothered to obtain building permits. Large companies would simply pay one flat fee and the building department was unable to determine how many jobs were handled under the one payment. Hatcher stopped the practice. Henceforth, everyone had to comply with the law.

Absentee landlords who refused to repair their property soon found the city boarding up their buildings and billing them for the costs. Those landlords who failed to repair buildings that were dangerous or unsafe for occupants had their properties seized through city court suits. Their rents were collected and the monies used to make necessary repairs, their only concern being the mortgage payments.

In July, 1968, the Hatcher administration launched Operation Showcase, a project designed to take a city block and show what could be done with only local governmental resources. If it needed garbage pickup four or five times a week to keep its alleys clean, the service was granted. If the block's residents needed house paint and could not afford it, the city supplied it. City Hall's concentrated interest in the one block soon inspired residents to take better care of their property.

But more important, Operation Showcase demonstrated that the city government was not some remote abstraction. This lesson was reinforced by the Mayor's Access Program (MAP), a deliberate effort to dispel the cold image of an impersonal, uncaring and unresponsive government. Six MAP teams were organized—one for every district in the city. These teams held meetings in neighborhoods all over the city (1) to give citizens a vehicle for their grievances and (2) to give city department heads a chance to explain programs under way in their departments. Thus MAP helped citizens feel closer to government. One woman reported she had been complaining to her landlord about conditions in her apartment and he had always ignored her. And then she told him she was going the next day to a MAP meeting where the Mayor was going to be present, and she was going to bring it up on the floor. That next morning he had repairmen out to her apartment. . . .

Perhaps Mayor Hatcher's most important effort during his first year of office involved his intensive war on crime. Some gambling dens, after-hours drinking spots, and vice operations closed shop when he took office early in January 1968. Within a week after his inauguration there were police raids on gambling establishments and vice dens. Most of the crooks got the message and departed for friendlier environs. To convince the others, the athletic young mayor accompanied a police raid in February on the Venus Cafe, the most lavish and notorious brothel and gambling center in town. "We want the citizens of Gary to know where the mayor's office stands on this sort of thing." Hatcher said to explain his personal participation in the crackdown.

He ordered police guards on city buses which had suffered thirty-one holdups in eleven months. When the mayor took office, Gary had only eight squad cars in working condition. Resigning officers had cannibalized many cars for parts. Very quickly the police force was furnished with forty-five squad cars.

For unorganized crime—street robberies, muggings and the like—Chief Hilton formed a special, sixteen-man tactical unit headed by Assistant Police Chief Boone and operated like the task force. In addition, the mayor proposed purchase of a police helicopter to patrol larger areas of Gary. But he was aware that the city which heretofore had taken a rather permissive attitude toward certain types of behavior was not going to reform overnight.

Gary escaped two other possible crises in 1968. Following the April 4 assassination of Dr. Martin Luther King rioting erupted in 125 U.S. cities. At least forty-six persons were killed, all but five of whom were blacks. More than 3,500 persons were injured, more than $45 million worth of property was lost by fire or looting and more than 20,000 arrests were made. But the tornado passed over Gary. It could have hit there, when two hundred black high school students stormed out of classes. But Mayor Hatcher met them before they had gone two blocks and persuaded them to return to their studies.

In July, however, violence erupted early one Sunday morning when several Gary citizens were wounded by apparently indiscriminate gun fire. One of them, a Gary fireman, was hit while performing his duties and required hospitalization. The outburst of lawlessness, during which three stores were set afire, was contained within two hours. The next night, however, there were some close calls although the end results were only broken windows and a damaged street light. Gary had not had a full-scale riot. The 550 National Guardsmen who were alerted remained outside the city at Mayor Hatcher's request. Looting, though evident, had not been conducted on a wholesale basis. Some 127 arrests had been made. It was clear that the city had not been made immune to violence and civil disorder by the election of a black mayor. ■

THE FUTURE OF THE CITY

Source: William H. Whyte, *The Last Landscape* (New York: Doubleday and Co., 1968), pp. 331–339.

Although the current writings of social scientists reveal a considerable amount of pessimism about the prospect of solving our critical urban problems, there are still a number of imaginative men and women who refuse to accept defeat. The next two selections are by men who believe that there is a viable future for American cities if only the right kind of planning takes place. William H. Whyte, the author of several widely read books on American social problems, argues that existing cities can be transformed, while Athelstan Spilhaus, president of the Franklin Institute in Philadelphia, envisions a bright future through the building of completely new cities. The visual materials which follow provide further evidence of imaginative conceptions for improving the quality of life in the city.

The Case for Urban Concentration

The net of what I have been saying about landscape action is that we are going to have to work with a much tighter pattern of spaces and development, and that our environment may be the better for it. This somewhat optimistic view rests on the premise that densities are going to increase and that it is not altogether a bad thing that they do. It is a premise many would dispute. Our official land policy is dead set against higher densities. It is decentralist, like official policies in most other countries. The primary thrust of it is to move people outward; reduce densities, loosen up the metropolis, and reconstitute its parts in new enclaves on the fringe.

I do not think it is going to work out this way. Certainly, outward movement will continue, but if our population continues to grow, the best way to accommodate the growth will be by a more concentrated and efficient use of the land within the area. The big "if" is whether or not intensity of use will be coupled with efficiency of use. It may not be. But it can be. Europe is the proof of this. Many of those who ask why we cannot take care of the landscape like Europeans do fail to realize that these landscapes, both urban and rural, accommodate far more people per acre than do ours. The disparity is not due primarily to our averages being weighted by the vast open spaces of the West. Even in our most urban states the metropolitan areas average out to lower densities than their counterparts in Europe—indeed, to some entire European countries.

* * *

The case for higher densities cannot rest on a shortage of land. There is none. It is true that top-grade agricultural lands are being overrun by urban expansion, that open space in the right places is increasingly difficult to save. The fact remains, however, that if we wish to go the expansion route, there is room for it. Expand the diameter of a metropolitan area by only a few miles and enough land will be encompassed to take care of a very large population increase. This may be a poor way to do it, but the option exists.

Nor are our cities running into each other. Metropolitan areas are being linked more tightly, but this is not the same thing as collision. Consider, for example, the great belt of urban areas along the Eastern Seaboard from Boston to Norfolk. It is well that we are paying more attention to the continuities of this megalopolis, as Jean Gottman has done so well, but to call it a "strip city," as many are doing, is misleading.

There is no such city, and the proposition can be easily tested. Fly from Boston to Washington and look out the window. Here and there one suburbia flows into another—between Baltimore and Washington, for example—but the cities retain their identities. This is especially apparent at night when the lights beneath simplify the structure so vividly: the brilliantly lit downtowns, the shopping centers, the cloverleafs, the spine of freeways that connect it all. But just as striking is what is dark—the forests of Massachusetts and Connecticut, the pine barrens of New Jersey, the farmlands of the Eastern Shore, the tidewater of Virginia. For many miles along the great urban route you can look down and see only the scattered lights of farms and small towns.

Urbanized sectors in others parts of the country—excepting, always, Los Angeles—show much the same characteristics. They are systems of cities, tied by high-speed rail and road networks, but they have not yet congealed into an undifferentiated mass. There is room outside them for expansion. There is room inside them. Whichever way is best, a measure of choice is still open to us.

The choice is by no means an either-or one, for there are forces working in both directions, and there is only so much we can do by planning and public policy to shape these forces to our liking. But this margin is important. Our government programs for transportation, for new housing and urban development have a great leverage, and a shift of emphasis one way or the other could have a considerable effect on the metropolis of not too many years hence.

Decentralize or concentrate? Most of the prescriptions for the ideal metropolis opt for decentralization. Expansion of the metropolis is to continue, only this time the expansion will be orderly. Instead of a sprawl of subdivisions, new development is to be channeled into planned new communities, with rapid transit linking them and green belts separating them. Some proposals would place the new communities outside the metropolitan areas altogether.

* * *

Obviously, the limits of suburbia are going to expand some in any event, and obviously there are going to be new com-

munities. But the main show is not going to be out on the perimeter. Outward expansion looks easiest, but it is the least efficient way of taking care of an increased population. As development moves further outward from the core, returns diminish and costs increase, and at an accelerating rate. Water distribution is an example. If you double the population within a given area, you can service it by enlarging the diameter of the present pipe system; if you try to take care of the population by doubling the area, however, you not only have to enlarge the present pipes, you have to lay down a prodigious amount of new ones, and as they poke out into the low density areas costs become progressively steeper. The new residents may be charged an extra sum to help foot these capital costs, but the rest of the community bears most of it.

The same is true with mass transit and other utilities and services. A disproportionate amount of capital investment is needed to provide urban services for people out in the low density areas out on the periphery, but because of the rate structures that usually apply to these services, the fact is masked that other people have to pay more than they should to make up the difference. The other people are the ones in the high density areas that are easiest and most profitable to serve. We have made utilities, economist Mason Gaffney observes, "an agency for milking the center to feed the border, thus subsidizing decentralization."

* * *

Concentration provides efficiency; for the same reason it provides maximum

access to what people want. This is what cities are all about. People come together in cities because this is the best way to make the most of opportunities, and the more accessible the core, the more choice of opportunities there are, the more access to skills, specialized services and goods, and to jobs. By subsidizing new freeways and peripheral beltways we can make it easier for people to move about within the outer area, but vigorous centers are not the less vital for this but the more, and a policy for dispersing their functions will fail.

Business and industry talk decentralization but while firms may be dispersing their production units, they have been centralizing their office and managerial operations more than before. As I have noted earlier, the British tried to reverse this trend by doing everything possible to stop commercial growth in London and make it go somewhere else. Despite the constraints, commercial growth expanded mightily, and an office building boom of spectacular proportions took place.

For a while we also entertained notions of a commercial exodus. Right after the war it was widely predicted that corporations would be moving their headquarters to campuslike retreats in the suburbs, and there was much favorable publicity when several firms in New York did so. Executives, it was said, would be able to think more; the office force would be closer to home, and more content; space would cost less; the surroundings would be more pleasant in every way. But the movement never quite came off, and several firms who had moved quietly repatriated. New office buildings went up, and on the highest-cost land in the center of the city. Before long, in what seemed almost a frenzy of centralization, whole blocks of big buildings on Park Avenue were being torn down to put up bigger buildings.

The center of things attracts because it is the center of things. What the decentralists would like to do is to cut down the number of things, or, rather, put them somewhere else. They are for urban renewal, but at much lower density. They want to open up the center, disperse as many of its functions as possible, and reassemble them in subcenters out in the hinterland where, in miniature, will be all the advantages of the city—art, music, commerce, universities, urban excitement—but without the disadvantages.

A dull metropolis it would be. This kind of decentralization would not only be a very inefficient way to accommodate growth, it would go against the grain of all the forces that give a metropolis its vitality. Rather than pursue this ill-conceived provincialism, we must look inward as well as outward, to the strengths of the metropolis, and seek a much more intensive and efficient use of the land already within it.

* * *

One way is to raise housing densities—both by putting more people on acres developed for housing and by bringing into use acres now wasted or underused. Densities are, of course, relative. What would be considered a very high density for suburbia—twenty people to the acre—would be low for the core, and densities will probably always tend to diminish as the distance from the city grows. At almost any point, however, there could be some increase in density without a lowering of living standards. In some cases the standards would be higher if there was an increase.

This is particularly true in the city. The decentralists who bewail its insensate concentrations talk as though cities are bad because we have been compressing more and more people into them. But we have not been. The populations of our cities have remained static or have decreased. One of the big problems of the gray areas of the cities, indeed, is that they do not have a sufficiently large or varied population to support an urban concentration of services and stores. Instead of cutting down the densities still further, it would make more sense to raise them.

In the city, English architect Theo Crosby points out, high densities are needed for a high level of amenity. Transportation, for example. "The typical planners' compromise—between 100 and 200 people per acre," says Crosby, "makes the vehicle-pedestrian dilemma insoluble. It is only at reasonably high densities (200-300 people per acre is the minimum) that the car is downgraded to the status of a luxury. At this density you can choose to use a car; you don't have to use it. Such a density also means that the network of public transport can be afforded, for it is only at high densities that rapid-transit systems make economic sense."

Density also has an important bearing on the look and feel of a neighborhood. If it is urban it ought to be urban. Most of our redevelopment projects are too loose in fabric. They would look better, as well as being more economic, if the scale were tightened up. This is true even of one of the best; the Southwest redevelopment area in Washington. Some of the architects involved believe that there would be more life and style to it if they had been able to pull the components closer together.

This does not mean putting everybody up in towers. Unfortunately, the arguments for and against high density are usually presented in terms of towers versus anything else—either spread out or go up in the air. But this is a false choice. A well-knit pattern of low buildings can house a great many people, and often quite amenably. So, obviously, can towers; on any one acre, the maximum possible. But there are other acres to be counted. When towers are spaced out in rows, as in the conventional urban project, the density figures for the over-all project can be surprisingly low.

The usual redevelopment or public housing project generally houses less people per acre than the neighborhood that was torn down to make way for it. The design formulas call for lots of space, almost to a suburban scale, and a big point is made of how little ground is taken for the buildings themselves. The projects of the New York City Public Housing Authority, for example, cover some 2000 acres, an area almost a seventh the size of Manhattan Island. The Housing Authority proudly points out that only sixteen percent of the area is used for buildings.

What is gained? Open space, it is said. But the open space is drab and institutional and much of it is forbidden to human trespass. The open space is for the architects, so they can have enough ground to put up towers. But to what end? The de-

Elliott Erwitt, Magnum

sign does not pursue its logic. The towers are put up, presumably, for density's sake —to make up for the housing that was not built on the open space. But the net density remains low, and not just by slum standards. In the standard public housing project the number of people per net acre is lower than in many middle class neighborhoods of three and four story houses.

If we study the way people themselves live, we will find strong empirical evidence that they can do quite well in high-density areas. It depends on the area. Some neighborhoods with relatively low densities have high disease and crime rates. Conversely, some neighborhoods with higher densities have low disease and crime rates. Obviously, other factors are the determining ones. (Hong Kong, one of the most densely populated cities in the world, with up to 2800 people per acre, has relatively low disease and crime rates compared to congested areas in the U.S.)

This is an inefficient use of high cost land, and if we are to continue it, we ought to have some strong social reason for doing so. The stock justification is that lower densities mean healthier living, and planners of this persuasion make much of the correlation between the number of people per acre and the rate of crime and disease in slum neighborhoods. There is a correlation. But is it cause and effect? There is a distinction to be made between overcrowding—that is, the too many people per room—and a high number of people per acre. Overcrowding does make for an unhealthy environment; high density may or it may not.

A lot of nonsense is heard these days about the psychological effects of living too close together in cities, or of living in cities at all for that matter. Many of the stock criticisms are quite ancient— filing-cabinet apartments producing filing-cabinet minds, neuroses, tenseness, conformity, and so on. But now the accusations are being made more scientifically. There is a rash of studies underway designed to uncover the bad consequences of overcrowding. This is all very well as far as it goes, but it only goes in one direction. What about undercrowding? The researchers would be a lot more objective if they paid as much attention to the possible effects on people of relative isolation and lack of propinquity. Maybe some of those rats they study get lonely too.

Why is it, furthermore, that so many of our high-density neighborhoods are the most sought after? This is not just a matter of high-rise luxury apartments; in New York some of the tree-lined blocks of four- and five-story brownstones with interior gardens have net densities higher than nearby public housing projects. The latter average about 250 people per acre. Remodeled brownstone areas run from about 180 people to as high as 350 people per acre.

Brooklyn Heights is an example. The fine old homes there (which are about 25 feet wide by 50 feet deep, plus a 50-foot garden) have been lovingly rehabilitated into a neighborhood of outstanding charm. But densities are high. For each gross acre (including streets) there are about 13 houses, and, on the average, they provide a total of 65 units. The number of people per unit averages between 3 and $3^1/_2$ people, giving an over-all density of about 200 people per gross acre. On the basis

Source: Athelstan Spilhaus, "The Experimental City," *Science,* vol. 159, no. 3816 (Feb. 16, 1968), pp. 710–715.

of land use efficiency, let alone amenity, this beats many a high-rise collective.

Other attractive examples can be found in Washington, Chicago, San Francisco, and many other cities; areas that by orthodox planning standards should be hopelessly congested are among the most pleasant, and sought after, in the city. Too much should not be made of the correlation, but surely something is wrong with a planning policy which calls for density standards so out of whack with the marketplace.

The standards are the legacy of a utopian concept which was never originally intended for the city. It is the garden city ideal: difficult enough to achieve in suburbia, and wholly inapplicable to the city.

In some aspects the original model was more realistic in its specifications than the current standards. Ebenezer Howard's ideal garden city called for somewhere between 70-100 people per acre and this was to be out in the country. For rebuilding of our cities some planning standards call for densities not much greater—about 100 people per acre for ideal neighborhoods, rarely more than 150 people.

To do away with congestion, these plans would do away with concentration. But concentration is the genius of the city, its reason for being. What it needs is not less people, but more, and if this means more density we have no need to feel guilty about it. The ultimate justification for building to higher densities is not that it is more efficient in land costs, but that it can make a better city. ■

The Case for Urban Dispersal

A federal commissioner recently expressed an opinion typical of the "hopelessness approach" to city problems when he said, "We cannot, even if we would, dismantle the urban complex." I disagree completely. The overgrown urban complex must be selectively dismantled and dispersed if we are to cure the ills of the megalopolis.

Half of the people in the United States live on 1 percent of the land, and there is a continual drift to the big cities. Urban renewal encourages the increase in the size of the cities. Two- or three-story slum buildings are torn down, and sterile, high-rise, so-called low-cost housing brings more people into the center of the city than ever before, compounding the problem.

Secretary of the Interior Stewart Udall, in an article which appeared in the September 1967 issue of the *Saturday Review,* addressed himself to the fundamental problem, that of controlling the population, and took a stand that must be considered courageous for a man in his position. If we consider that *any* excess that is harmful to decent living is a pollutant, then the prime pollutant on earth is too many people. But until we have the sense to control population, something has to be done for all these people, and here I discuss the question of what is to be done.

In his article, Udall goes on to say:

Our annual population growth of 4,000,000 people increases the physical and social pressures, causes us to seek quick remedies, leads us to waste too much wealth on quick-fix projects that provide at best a temporary respite from yesterday's mistakes. The razing of tenements, their instant replacement by high-rise slums, changes the facade—not the features—of the ghetto.

I agree completely, and propose, as a corrective, development of a system of dispersed cities of controlled size, differing in many respects from conventional cities, and surrounded by ample areas of open land. . . .

People like to live in cities. *Dispersal* does not mean that the whole United States is to become a single sprawling suburb, such as California is becoming. *Dispersal* refers to cities big enough to offer the advantages of city living yet small enough not to be subject to unplanned overgrowth. Each, with its surrounding reserved land, would be a separate unit. According to the Minnesota plan there would ultimately be many of these units, spread across the United States.

If the present 200 million people in the United States were living in 800 cities with a population of a quarter of a million each, and if these cities were scattered evenly across the United States, we would not have the pollution, the traffic congestion, the riots, and many of the other ills that develop when cities become too large.

In industry we already see trends toward dispersal. Industries are leading the way, by seeking small-town locations away from the large cities. Unfortunately, this migration has created a competition between Chambers of Commerce to retain industry or attract it to their present jurisdictions. Chambers of Commerce are strongest in the great overgrown cities.

433

They are, therefore, a powerful force against urban dispersal. In large urban complexes two Chambers of Commerce may operate within one metropolitan area, with divided municipal responsibilities. Thus, if the competitor across the river brings in something big, the other side must do likewise, and the result is continual growth of the oversized city.

Buckminster Fuller, architect and imaginative member of our Experimental City Steering Committee, feels that industry of the future, largely automated, will be located outside the cities, and that the many functions of the city which in the past were directed toward facilitating the exchange of physical goods will in the future be directed toward the exchange of what he calls metaphysical values—ideas, learning, and culture.

Planning, constructing, populating, and managing a dispersed city highly suitable for industry, commerce, and human occupation will require the leadership, imagination, and enthusiasm of scientists, industrialists, and educators alike. We must be prepared to discard convention and to experiment with new and radical ideas. We must utilize the most advanced methods of construction, transportation, communications, waste removal, and city management.

The project simply could not be accomplished through any attempt to rebuild a present city, regardless of its size or location, for, without exception, our cities are bound by tradition, outmoded building codes, restrictive legislation, and the consequences of unplanned, unhealthy growth.

*   *   *

The problems of our large cities indicate an urgent need to move toward the dispersal concept immediately. If the need is urgent in the United States, it is even more urgent in the world as a whole, especially in those countries where the birthrate is much higher than ours.

Let us look ahead and suppose that the world population, if we do nothing about population control, reaches 15 billion by A.D. 2068. And let us assume that our technology permits us to build cities on any solid land, from Antarctica to the tropics, from desert to rain forest. The area of all the continents is about 2.3 billion acres. If we built cities of controlled size, dispersed throughout the world, there would be 60 thousand cities of a quarter of a million people each, and each such city would be surrounded by 40 thousand acres, or 64 square miles, of open land. The alternative of allowing the present big cities to grow unplanned, or to accelerate their growth through so-called urban renewal, would mean that vast tracts of the earth's surface would be uninhabited and the urban complexes would be intolerable.

(There is no magic in the figure of a quarter of a million. It may be that a city of half a million would better provide the choices that people want, or it may be that cities of different sizes would be needed. The important thing is that the size be controlled and that the cities be kept within a small area, with bounds, so that they would remain surrounded by open land.)

The advent of atomic power opens up the possibility of building verdant cities even in desert areas, if these areas are near the sea. An atomic plant which would generate a million kilowatts of electricity could distill half a billion gallons of freshwater from seawater and, from the residue, make enough fertilizer to grow the food to feed the entire populations of ten cities the size of the proposed experimental city.

We must try these schemes and others that will emerge. The place to try them is in new experimental, dispersed cities, such as that envisioned in the Minnesota plan.

Early in planning the Minnesota Experimental City we set some guidelines. (i) The ultimate maximum population would be a quarter of a million. The community would be (ii) economically viable as a unit of the U.S. economy, (iii) truly experimental, (iv) at least 100 miles from any major existing urban center, and (v) a densely populated center surrounded by open land. This surrounding land, which would have an area perhaps 100 times that of the densely populated center, would be used for forests, outdoor museums, recreation, or agriculture, or just left as a rural area.

The idea would be to populate the experimental city in the shortest possible time by attracting people from the overcrowded urban complexes, in contrast to the past practice of letting the city slowly grow by drawing people from the immediately surrounding region. We must get away from what Fuller calls the "local focus" situation, wherein the city relates itself specifically to the needs, resources, and desires of people in its immediate vicinity.

Plans for building the Experimental City differ in many respects from plans for building other kinds of cities. Conventional cities grow above the ground, and as they grow, and as people demand transportation, power, water, gas, and sewers, the ground and rock underneath the city are tunneled for subways or the streets are dug up and the utility lines are buried. In the Experimental City the whole substructure will be planned and excavated, and the power lines and utility lines will be installed, before the city is built. Knowledge that the city is to be of a certain size will make this possible.

Costs of all city services will be part of the rental, occupancy charges—the "hotel bill"—for individuals, businesses, or industry in the city. Much of the equipment for servicing the city will be invisible and inaudible underground. Water and building materials can be stored there. Heating plants and cold-storage facilities can be located there. Underground pipelines can carry out solid wastes conventionally carried by trucks. Snow or rainwater from the streets can be channeled to underground reservoirs.

Pollution-producing vehicles can come in underground, and fume sewers can take the gases out to scrubbing and processing plants in the surrounding openland area. Air-burning vehicles that connect the city with the rest of the nation can be parked underground. Police, ambulance, and emergency vehicles will all have underground throughways. By eliminating the need for some service vehicles, restricting those that are needed to the substructure, and providing a free above-the-ground transportation system (discussed below), we hope to eliminate all vehicles from ground-level streets.

A lawyer at one of our planning sessions asked whether the Experimental City might not eventually disintegrate and become merely a more modern, but no more effective, city complex. "If Chicago, Minneapolis, New York, and St. Paul are willing to allow smoke to billow from new factories," he said, "if they permit automobiles to crowd their streets, and if they do not restrict building construction from occurring in illogical patterns, why should we expect anything different in the Experimental City?"

The answer is simple. Industries, before they are selected or approved for participation in the Experimental City, must agree to abide by the city's building programs. They will be required to conform to certain waste-disposal methods. Presumably they will be willing to do so because they will benefit from the City's central waste-processing facilities, smoke sewers, and other underground disposal facilities.

*   *   *

With new building materials and freedom from obsolete codes and building practices, both public buildings and commercial structures can be made extremely flexible, with adjustable floors, curtain-walls, and ceiling heights. It may even be possible to use inflatable buildings, which can be instantly deflated. Housing units may be precast, even prefurnished, in the manner of Expo's Habitat, with units put together like building blocks and arranged and rearranged as desired. Practical application of this idea is no dream. Precast rooms were used months ago in building San Antonio's Hilton Hotel.

*   *   *

Certain parts of the Experimental City probably will be domed, so that the advantages and disadvantages of totally enclosed cities can be determined. It is our current view that not all of the city should be domed. Doming only a part of it will enable us to determine the extremes of climate under which total enclosure is economical and acceptable.

In the domed portion of the Experimental City, which may enclose a medical complex, we can undertake experiments on allergy control, and studies of acoustics, ventilation, and maintenance of a clean atmosphere.

A dome 2 miles in diameter, made of glass, would cost an estimated $80 million, but it would eliminate the need for snow removal and would make heating more efficient and less costly. Savings equivalent to the cost of its construction could be achieved in a 10-year period.

With a controlled city, savings can be realized, too, through new methods of waste collection and through use, reuse, and recycling of wastes. It may not be possible to achieve complete recycling immediately, although the objective would always be borne in mind in our planning. Total recycling is the ultimate answer to the waste problem for a closed-system earth.

*   *   *

The very things we do today in our cities to dispose of wastes constitute pollution. Garbage cans litter the sidewalks, garbage trucks clog the streets, dumps of solid wastes insult our nostrils and esthetic sensibilities. The burning of land fills in municipal dumps pollutes the air, and green slime grows on the sewage- and detergent-filled waters.

In the pollution-free Experimental City the utility tunnels would carry away the liquid and gaseous wastes, and many of the solid wastes, to the processing plants. New systems for moving wastes may be used—pneumatic, hydraulic conveyors or unitized trains. If we can reduce the bulk of solid wastes and package them suitably, deadheading trains and trucks can take them away from the city to the open-land area, where they can be processed and then stored or reused, perhaps to build ski slopes, arenas, or other recreation facilities. Wastes that are not immediately reused can be sorted and stored in "mountains," to be mined when reuse becomes economically desirable.

In water-rich areas, water can be used first for drinking and then reused at least twice, for cooling and then for purposes of recreation. But if the Experimental City is to show the way for cities in arid areas, complete recycling of part of the water should be attempted.

One of the most pressing problems of our urban living is transportation and the use, care, parking, and garaging of the private automobile.

Doxiadis recognizes that it is a tragedy when our city buildings are primarily designed to accommodate cars, both stationary and moving, and to destroy the "human scale." Lewis Mumford recognizes that the private car no longer performs the role of "facilitating meeting and sociability" and that its "assumed right" is a "license to destroy a city."

How can we provide people with a transportation system that facilitates the desirable social relationships which constitute the joy of city living yet does not have undesirable side effects?

* * *

Now in the process of design are many systems that can move people in motorless, driverless, noiseless, semiprivate pods, computer-controlled so that the passengers travel from where they are to where they want to go without stopping. If you want to go to the store you don't go to the station and then walk to the store; your pod is sidetracked right into the store. The various systems have a common denominator: they are driven by a propulsion system built into the track. The pods are inexpensive, thus many of them can be used at the same time. Moving sidewalks, moving platforms, and other wheelless systems are all technically feasible. One important concept that has emerged in our discussions is this: if we are to use mass transportation in the Experimental City it should be free, like elevator service. You don't pay a fare to ride vertically in an elevator. Why should you pay a fare to ride horizontally? The cost can be embodied in the service costs of the city.

Eliminating the automobile by means of a modern transport system of this kind does away with the need for freeways and traffic control, eliminates smog, saves lives, lessens stress, and saves valuable space. Making the transit system free saves the costs otherwise associated with ticket-selling and ticket-taking. Because free transportation would reduce or eliminate the sale of automobiles, the parking-lot business, and other businesses basic to the economy of older cities, it can be introduced readily only in a newly planned, centrally governed city such as the Experimental City.

Among the greatest innovations that can be tried in the Experimental City are the new technologies in communications that have been developed but not yet put to practical use.

The current view is that radio frequencies should be reserved for purposes, such as communication to or from a vehicle in motion, where wires are not feasible. The substructure of the Experimental City would be wired, and coaxial cable would reach to every point where, conventionally, there would be a telephone. These wires and cables can be planned and located in the substructure even before we have a clear-cut idea of what terminals, picture-phones, computers, facsimile machines, and the like may ultimately be needed. (Because broad-band communications open up so many uses, the magnitude of the prospective network may be much greater than that required for ordinary telephone service. Consequently, special attention will have to be given to connection with the normal communication channels outside the Experimental City.)

Such a communication system can provide access from any point to large high-speed digital computers, for purposes of city management (on the basis of real information), crime prevention through the use of video monitors, and maintenance of up-to-the-minute data banks for the social experiment that the city constitutes. The same lines, in conjunction with smaller computers and other video terminals, can provide a means of decentralizing schools and hospitals and of bringing together electronically the now separated functions of shopping, charging, banking, credit, and business. Video terminals can even provide "tele-babysitting." The advanced system will provide an ideal laboratory for determining how to insure privacy of computer use yet insure that computers are used to the maximum benefit of society.

In the Experimental City we will have a large pilot plant in which to develop a modern library along the lines suggested by M.I.T.'s Project Intrex. The medical extensions of the advanced system may make it possible to set up a series of care centers providing different degrees of medical care, and thus to make available appropriate care at minimum cost. The various care centers would be in touch with each other through a communications system insuring instant access to specialists in case of emergency.

How will the Experimental City be populated? Politicians say you can't move people. Many sociologists who are more interested in studying what is happening and predicting doom than in taking the steps necessary to avert it, agree. But the fact is that, with our existing legal and governmental structure, we do move people. We push people around everywhere, always with the excuse that it is for their own good. We move them in wars; we displace them when we build highways; and we move them when we clear slums and build much larger buildings than were there before. We move them, but often in the wrong direction, into the already overgrown cities.

Urban renewal in its worst manifestations is the construction of the slums of the future. Many people in the present overgrown cities might like to move out into new complexes which provided the advantages of city life without the physical and social distress. Many others whom the authorities say they cannot move have never contemplated moving because they have been trapped, lacking the opportunity to go anywhere else. The fact is that most of those who can afford to do so have already fled the cities, to suburbs that will become the slums of tomorrow.

We must build a city for today's city-dwellers and suburb-dwellers to go to. We must provide people with a different choice, not just that between life in a dirty overgrown city with suburbs or a completely rural existence. We can provide a middle choice—clean cities of controlled size, with plenty of space and an exciting new environment.

Population balance for the Experimental City will be achieved through careful selection of the type of industry that will be invited to participate and of the commercial operations that will be established.

Now for two most important decisions: (i) Who will manage the Experimental City? (ii) How much will it cost?

The management of a typical city involves thousands of individuals. Many students of political science and law feel that this spreading of authority is basic to the democratic government of the city. There is, however, reason to believe that, with the changes in size of our cities and their merging together in huge complexes, this arrangement is no longer workable. For example, if one jurisdiction allows pollution, it will affect its neighbor. To resolve this conflict it has been necessary to establish federal standards and controls.

It would seem that the idea of running a city as a public utility by a quasi-public, quasi-private corporation should be tried. Present-day hotel complexes, with their associated shops, restaurants, transportation facilities, and so on, are growing larger and larger. Many of them are run very well. It is not much of a jump to think of experimental cities of controlled size as huge hotels. It seems to me that management of the city-hotel-corporation type should be tried.

Daniel Moynihan, director of the Harvard-M.I.T. Joint Center for Urban Studies, says realistically that the government cannot do everything well, and that many public services are best contracted to private enterprises. In the Experimental City, contracts for many such services would be let on a performance basis.

The federal government, too, is beginning to move in this direction. Agencies have let contracts to private enterprise for carrying out social work programs. Why not go the whole way and have responsible corporations provide all the services needed in the Experimental City?

As to the cost of building facilities for an Experimental City of a quarter of a million inhabitants, some simple arithmetic provides a reasonable estimate.

If we take 2.5 people as an average family unit, we will need 100,000 units. Taking $20,000 as the average cost per unit, we arrive at a figure of $2 billion. But because this city will be planned from scratch and have a large substructure housing all the equipment for city services, and because it will be experimental, we should prob-

The Rouse Corporation, Columbia, Maryland

ably double this figure. So we arrive at a guess of $4 billion.

It is important to stress that these costs are not an additional burden on the national economy. New housing and new factories and businesses will be built in any case, somewhere. We will merely concentrate the activity by attracting them to the Experimental City. The city must be built as any city is built. The plan must prove attractive to the industries that will come to the city to build new plants. If they are attracted to the Experimental City, they will bear part of the costs of construction and operation.

But it is realistic to recognize that a large sum of money is needed for planning and building the services substructure, which will utilize new technologies involving costly experimentation and research. Part of the construction costs could legitimately be funded by an FHA mortgage. Part of the costs of experimentation and research would be met by the private sector. Imaginative American industry needs a place, a city laboratory, in which to try out new technologies of waste management, communication, transportation, and construction. Industries are at present investing large sums in elements of these areas. Our plan for the Experimental City must show that it is the best place to do this research and to try out new developments.

At present, new systems for urban development must be tried piecemeal—a new transportation system here, a sewage system there, a communications system elsewhere. But a city is a complex system, and everything one does has an impact on other parts of the system. If we clean up the noise, take the waste heat out of the city, and control the filth of factories at the source, there will be no need for zoning. Factories, schools, and homes will all be in one complex. This will reduce the need for transportation. Reduced transportation further reduces pollution, and the combination of these technological improvements will have a profound influence on the city systems for health care, education, police surveillance, and other services.

I would expect that the Experimental City will be of interest as a laboratory to those of our industries that are getting heavily into the urban problem.

Other approaches to the problems of today's cities are being tried. The government's Model City program, an urban renewal program administered by the Department of Housing and Urban Development, is an attempt to alleviate the overwhelming problems of the overgrown cities. The objective is a most important one, but, in general, the means used are the tearing out of slums and their replacement with new construction. The government is becoming the new slum landlord.

Worthwhile experiments in the building of new cities are being made by private enterprise. Examples are Columbia, Maryland; Disneyworld's experimental prototype city in Florida; and Westinghouse's community proving ground in Florida. More than 200 "new cities" are either in the design stage or are under construction in the United States.

Some of the new towns are being built exclusively for the "senior citizen." In this country we are working hard at the problem of integrating people of different races, yet we segregate people of different ages. We must integrate people of all ages, income levels, and interests, to achieve the total mixture which makes up the stimulating society of a city.

These government-financed and privately financed "new cities" are similar to the Minnesota Experimental City in one respect: they are built from scratch. On the other hand they are, in the best meaning of the term, real estate developments, and consequently they tend to be satellites of existing urban complexes—communities where people live and from which they commute to work. That this is the case may be seen from the fact that almost all of the "new cities" are growing along the coastlines—East, West, and Gulf—where the overgrown cities already are. Generally their size is not controlled, and one can anticipate that even the best of them, such as Reston (Virginia) and Columbia, will be swallowed up as the nearby urban complexes—in this case Washington and Baltimore—expand. Because they do not have sufficient reserved open land around them, even the best of the "new cities" will become engulfed; moreover, since they are close to existing huge cities, they cannot develop with enough independence to try novel technologies.

It is obvious to me that we must use all of our land for living, not just tiny fractions of it. To do this we must look at solutions that envisage urban dispersal, and if we are to disperse into new planned cities, a national experimental cities program is an urgent must. ■

FUTURISTIC CONCEPTIONS OF THE AMERICAN CITY

Some architects and planners have sought to tackle the growing problems of the central city by envisioning completely new urban environments for the future. Some such futuristic conceptions are presented on the following pages.

1 How does each conception of an urban complex take account of technology, the natural environment and the social needs of people? How do these conceptions compare with each other in this respect?

2 What elements from the plans made during the Progressive Era and the post-World War II period recur in these futuristic plans? Which elements seem to be original? From where do you think these new elements are derived?

3 What values and attitudes toward urban life are expressed in each scheme? How do these compare with the values and attitudes expressed by Progressive urban planning and urban renewal?

4 How do these plans deal with the problems and potentialities of the modern city as you perceive them? Which of these futuristic plans seems best? On what basis did you make this decision, and what type of future does this suggest would be desirable for America? ■

RESIDENTIAL

CITY CENTER

COMMERCIAL

TER

ILITIES

PARK

GARDENS

CIRCU

LLINGS

LIVING-WORKING

PROMENADE

PUBLIC

FACTORIES AND UTILITIES

4.Babelnoah

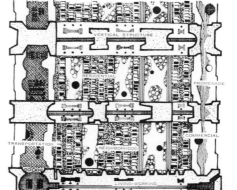

VERTICAL STRUCTURE

RESIDENTIAL

PROMENADE

TRANSPORTATION

NEIGHBORHOOD

COMMERCIAL

LIVING-WORKING

Soleri's cities are based on ecological considerations. They are condensed cities of giant geo-
metric shapes and self-contained units. They
grow up from the land, thus using as little of the
land as possible. They are surrounded by vast
open spaces. Within the city, which has a high
population density, automobiles are eliminated
and power is derived from solar or nuclear
energy.

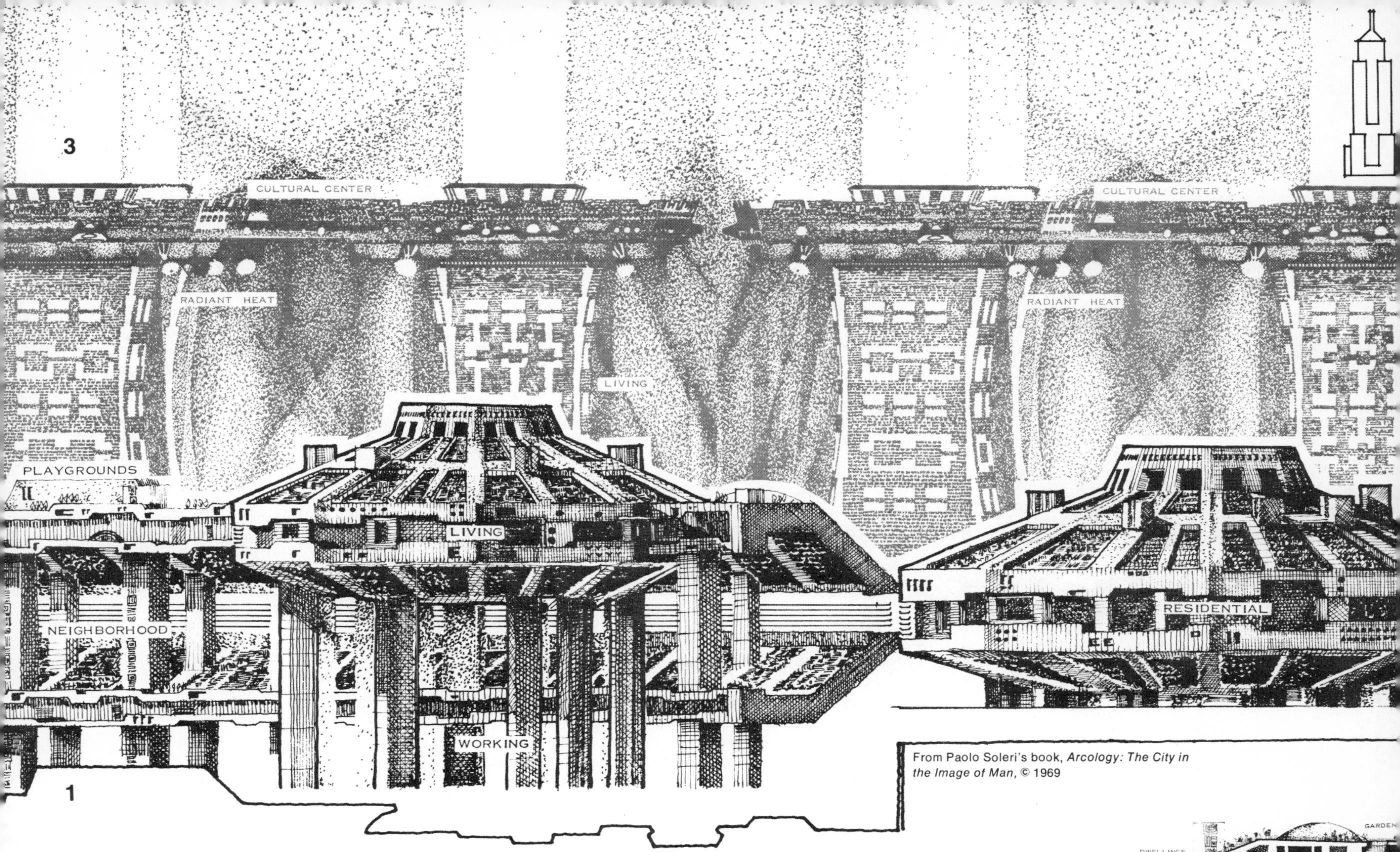

3

CULTURAL CENTER   CULTURAL CENTER

RADIANT HEAT   RADIANT HEAT

LIVING

PLAYGROUNDS

LIVING

NEIGHBORHOOD   RESIDENTIAL

WORKING

From Paolo Soleri's book, *Arcology: The City in the Image of Man,* © 1969

1

Babelnoah
(Coastal flat region)
Population   6,000,000
Density   822/hectare; 333/acre
Height   800–1,700 meters
Surface covered   7,300 hectares; 18,000 acres
Partial elevation: scale 1:10,000
Partial section and plan:
Scale   1:10,000

Comparative Arcology
Babel IIA
Population   800,000
Elevation: scale   1:10,000

DWELLINGS   GARDEN

TRANSPORTATION
CIRCULATION
LIVING-WORKING

PROMENADE

COMMERCIAL

WORKING

2

FACTORIES AND UTILITIES

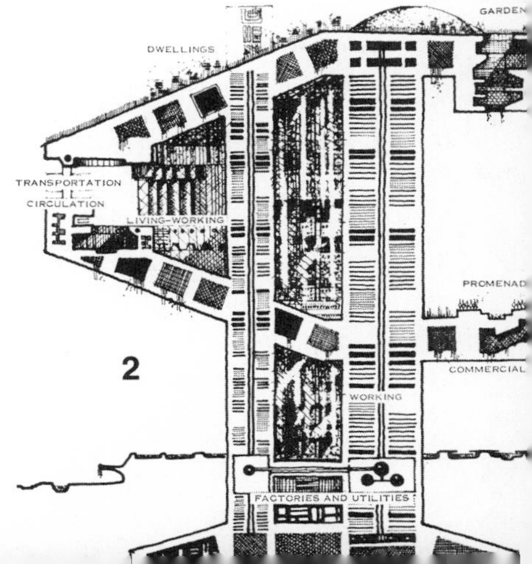

Movement in many aspects characterizes the walking city. It is a great 'heroic container' composed of self-sufficient units not unlike space capsules, which can detach themselves and go elsewhere. Since units are detachable, the composition of the city is temporary, ever changing. Within the city, whatever its composition, movement of people and things is via tube-like channels which extend between units.

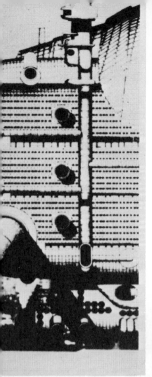

Herron: Cities Moving project 1964

The Plug-In city concept sees the city as made up of components designed for obsolesence, components which can be plugged in or pulled out from a fixed core to keep pace with the everchanging needs of the city. The fixed core is the part of the city structure which supplies the city with its basic communication needs.

444

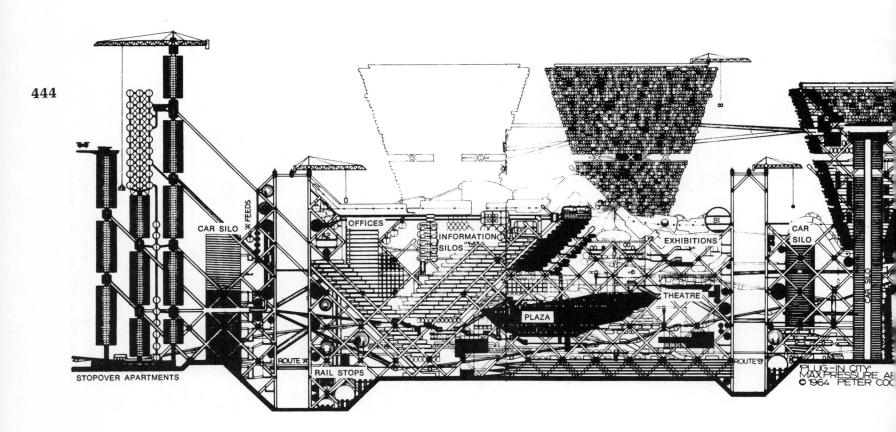

URBAN ECOLOGY

Throughout this unit we have sought to keep the relationship between the physical aspects of a city and its people and problems direct. As Roy Lubove stated, "The city, after all, is basically an artifact, a physical container within which complex human interactions occur; social organization and relationships are greatly influenced by land-use and housing patterns." The city, then, is a complex form of human ecology, as is any physical setting man has constructed.

We want to suggest a project in which you become involved in the analysis and/or planning of a man-made environment. This environment might range from your own home, to your school, to your city or town. Such a project should include:

A An analysis of how human relationships are influenced by the spatial environment in which they take place.

B Suggestions as to how this living space could be altered to make it more receptive to the kind of human interaction you think most desirable.

For this project you may make use of any photographic or graphic talents you have, or you can rely on a written report accompanied by rough sketches.

The following bibliography represents a selection of classic statements on the utilization of space in both the architectural and city planning areas. Some should prove useful as references or as sources of ideas and questions.

Eells, Richard, and Walton, Clarence, eds. *Man in the City of the Future.* London: The Macmillan Co., 1968. A collection of articles by prominent architects and urban philosophers who present their views of the city of the future.

Mumford, Lewis, *The City in History.* New York: Harcourt, Brace, and World, 1961. The classic study of the historical development of cities.

The following two books by noted architects are richly illustrated works which deal with cities of the future:

Cook, Peter. *Architecture: Action and Place.* New York: Reinhold Publishing Co., 1967.

Le Corbusier. *Toward a New Architecture.* New York: Praeger Publishers, 1970.

In recent years, there have been many treatments of the nature of tomorrow's cities in periodicals such as *Saturday Review, Life,* and the *New York Times Magazine.* ■

445

What have been the goals of American foreign policy since World War II?

How have Americans responded to the wars we have fought since 1914?

What aims have American foreign policy-makers pursued in their conduct of foreign affairs?

What is the relationship between public opinion and public policy on foreign affairs?

Can public opinion change the purposes of foreign policy?

THE UNITED STATES
AND GLOBAL POLITICS

5

THE UNITED STATES AND GLOBAL POLITICS

From the earliest days of our nation's history, the primary responsibility for the conduct of foreign relations has rested with the President. The Constitution provides him with an imposing set of powers: to negotiate treaties, to appoint ambassadors, to give diplomatic recognition to other nations and governments, to act as commander-in-chief of all the armed forces, and to exercise the authority that has been granted him by Congressional laws applying to foreign affairs. Little by little, these direct powers have been augmented by the implied powers resulting from the expectation that the President has both the power—and the duty—to act on behalf of the nation. It is no accident then that our major foreign policies have been presidential in origin and conception. We have even named many of these policies after the presidents who inaugurated them—Jefferson's Embargo, the Monroe Doctrine, Wilson's Fourteen Points, Franklin Roosevelt's Good Neighbor Policy, the Truman Doctrine, the Eisenhower Doctrine.

To be sure, the President does not have unlimited power in foreign affairs. Woodrow Wilson's failure to obtain the ratification of the Versailles Treaty and the League of Nations Covenant, the battles between President Roosevelt and Congress over neutrality legislation in the 1930's, or the more recent battles between President Nixon and the Senate over the withdrawal of American forces from Vietnam should remind us that the President shares his power over foreign relations with Congress. But even though he must ultimately obtain the advice and consent of the Senate for treaties, or appropriations from Congress to carry out some large policy in foreign affairs, the initiative in the making of foreign policy usually lies with the President.

The making of decisions in foreign policy has become a complex affair requiring a constant analysis of an enormous flow of information, much of it of a confidential nature. To make his decisions, the President can call upon the expertise of his White House staff, the State Department, the intelligence reports of the Central Intelligence Agency, the special military assessments of the Joint Chiefs of Staff, as well as the advice of the National Security Council. Congress, on the other hand, cannot match the President's resources for the rapid assembling and analysis of information. The Senate Foreign Relations Committee, for example, has a small staff to assist it in gathering information and it can obtain the testimony of specialists in foreign affairs in its investigations, but it rarely has ready access to the sources of information that would enable it to develop an initiative in foreign affairs which could supplant presidential leadership. This has been particularly true in the last twenty-five years when the threat of nuclear warfare has underscored the necessity for rapid responses to crisis situations.

Although a President has enormous power in the making of foreign policy—too much power in the estimation of many modern critics—he must constantly attend to public opinion. If a President can claim to speak for a larger constituency—the whole nation—than any member of Congress, he must also be more attentive to the very wide range of organized groups and politically significant values, attitudes and beliefs that affect electoral politics in the United States. An unpopular foreign policy can quickly undermine a President's popular support and weaken his political leverage in Congress. Hence even the most powerful President lives in a psychological atmosphere in which public opinion is a kind of brooding omnipresence—always there, always judging, always potentially dangerous to his political position.

Public opinion, however, does not speak with a single and well-defined voice. There are various kinds of publics that have an impact on presidents and other decision-makers. There is a "mass public" whose information about world affairs is taken mainly from newspaper headlines and television news reports and whose feelings and views are measured in polls, surveys, and analyses of voting behavior. There is an "informed public," rarely more than 10 per cent of the whole population, which takes a continuous interest in public policy and is aware of all the major issues in foreign affairs. Members of the "informed public" read books and magazines that contain thorough and competent analyses of policy alternatives and the detailed information on which they are based. Then there are the "self-interested publics" which are primarily interested in the particular advantages to be gained from one or another policy alternative, such as those affecting trade, investment, or the competition of foreign labor or foreign farm goods. "Self-interested publics" also include groups which react very strongly to foreign policies that affect the ethnic or religious groups with which they identify.

The President and his advisers are usually aware of the opinions of the "informed public" because they are often given expression by journalists, columnists, university professors, and other intellectuals in articles written for leading newspapers and magazines or in books which capture large audiences. Members of the "informed public" are more likely to write letters to the President or to their congressmen, to sign petitions, and to engage in public debates and demonstrations concerning foreign policy. Spokesmen for self-interested groups also seek to influence foreign policy by sustained lobbying efforts. But the great body of citizens in the "mass public"—unorganized, passive, uncertain in its moods and attitudes—is always present as a force that can be rallied to support or to frustrate the makers of foreign policy.

Every President, therefore, seeks to persuade and manipulate public opinion to support his foreign policy objectives. Similarly, his critics in Congress or among the spokesmen of the "informed public" seek to win wider public support for changes in policy. As a result, the media of mass communication—newspapers, radio, and television—become crucial mechanisms for influencing and manipulating public opinion. In the use of these mechanisms, especially television, the President has important advantages. He can dramatize his conception and interpretation of foreign policy by a news conference or an address to the nation which all television networks will feel obliged to carry because the head of the nation is speaking to the people. His ability to command a large audience provides the President with an opportunity to use his special sources of information to refute or to neutralize his critics. But the President's

resources are not overwhelming. His critics can also reach the public through sustained criticism of his policies, and this criticism may succeed in building up counter images and negative feelings in the consciousness of the mass public. Furthermore, the events that are the consequences of a President's foreign policy have a way of speaking for themselves. If a President wants to retain his credibility, the outcomes of foreign policy, reported as news events in the mass media, must have a palpable and positive relationship to the objectives that he has outlined to the people.

In this part of our inquiry into the challenge of change in American history, we shall examine the relationship between the making of foreign policy and public opinion in its various forms. We shall focus our attention particularly on the period since World War II when, because of the dramatic change in the structure of world politics, foreign policy questions rapidly moved to the center of the stage in American politics. ■

WORLD WAR II: "A Just War"

THE WAR AIMS OF POLITICAL LEADERS

On the following pages are statements made by three political leaders during World War II. The first two of these are presidential messages by Franklin Delano Roosevelt and the third is taken from a best-selling book written by Wendell Willkie, the Republican candidate for President in 1940. Although both men are speaking to the whole nation, they also represent the two largest political parties in the United States—whose combined support in the 1940 election amounted to 98.76 per cent of the total popular vote. Both leaders obviously believe that the war against the Axis powers is a just war and they set forth what they believe should be the policies of the United States in the postwar world. The fourth statement is taken from a speech by Norman Thomas, a pacifist and the leader of the Socialist Party, which polled less than 1 per cent of the popular vote in 1940. His views about the road to peace should be compared with those of Roosevelt and Willkie.

Source: Samuel I. Rosenman, ed., *The Public Papers and Addresses of Franklin D. Roosevelt* (New York: Random House, 1938–1950), 1942 volume, p. 35; 1944–1945 volume, pp. 496–497.

The Democratic President

The militarists of Berlin and Tokyo started this war. But the massed, angered forces of common humanity will finish it.

Destruction of the material and spiritual centers of civilization—this has been and still is the purpose of Hitler and his Italian and Japanese chessmen. They would wreck the power of the British Commonwealth and Russia and China and the Netherlands —and then combine all their forces to achieve their ultimate goal, the conquest of the United States.

They know that victory for us means victory for freedom.

They know that victory for us means victory for the institution of democracy— the ideal of the family, the simple principles of common decency and humanity.

They know that victory for us means victory for religion.

And they could not tolerate that. The world is too small to provide adequate "living room" for both Hitler and God. In proof of that, the Nazis have now announced their plan for enforcing their new German, pagan religion all over the world —a plan by which the Holy Bible and the Cross of Mercy would be displaced by *Mein Kampf* and the swastika and the naked sword.

Our own objectives are clear; the objective of smashing the militarism imposed by war lords upon their enslaved peoples— the objective of liberating the subjugated Nations—the objective of establishing and securing freedom of speech, freedom of religion, freedom from want, and freedom from fear everywhere in the world. ■

In the field of foreign policy, we propose to stand together with the United Nations not for the war alone but for the victory for which the war is fought.

It is not only a common danger which unites us but a common hope. Ours is an association not of Governments but of peoples—and the peoples' hope is peace. Here, as in England; in England, as in Russia; in Russia, as in China; in France, and through the continent of Europe, and throughout the world; wherever men love freedom, the hope and purpose of the people are for peace—a peace that is durable and secure.

It will not be easy to create this peoples' peace. We delude ourselves if we believe that the surrender of the armies of our enemies will make the peace we long for. The unconditional surrender of the armies of our enemies is the first and necessary step—but the first step only.

We have seen already, in areas liberated from the Nazi and the Fascist tyranny, what problems peace will bring. And we delude ourselves if we attempt to believe wishfully that all these problems can be solved overnight.

The firm foundation can be built—and it will be built. But the continuance and assurance of a living peace must, in the long run, be the work of the people themselves.

We ourselves, like all peoples who have gone through the difficult processes of liberation and adjustment, know of our own experience how great the difficulties can be. We know that they are not difficulties peculiar to any continent or any Nation. Our own Revolutionary War left behind it, in the words of one American

Source: Wendell Willkie, *One World* (New York: Simon and Schuster, 1943), pp. 173–175.

historian, "an eddy of lawlessness and disregard of human life." There were separatist movements of one kind or another in Vermont, Pennsylvania, Virginia, Tennessee, Kentucky, and Maine. There were insurrections, open or threatened, in Massachusetts and New Hampshire. These difficulties we worked out for ourselves as the peoples of the liberated areas of Europe, faced with complex problems of adjustment, will work out their difficulties for themselves.

Peace can be made and kept only by the united determination of free and peace-loving peoples who are willing to work together—willing to help one another—willing to respect and tolerate and try to understand one another's opinions and feelings. ■

The Republican Party's Titular Leader

If our withdrawal from world affairs after the last war was a contributing factor to the present war and to the economic instability of the past twenty years—and it seems plain that it was—a withdrawal from the problems and responsibilities of the world after this war would be sheer disaster. Even our relative geographical isolation no longer exists.

At the end of the last war, not a single plane had flown across the Atlantic. Today that ocean is a mere ribbon, with airplanes making regular scheduled flights. The Pacific is only a slightly wider ribbon in the ocean of the air, and Europe and Asia are at our very doorstep.

America must choose one of three courses after this war: narrow nationalism, which inevitably means the ultimate loss of our own liberty; international imperialism, which means the sacrifice of some other nation's liberty; or the creation of a world in which there shall be an equality of opportunity for every race and every nation. I am convinced the American people will choose, by overwhelming majority, the last of these courses. To make this choice effective, we must win not only the war, but also the peace, and we must start winning it now.

To win this peace three things seem to me necessary—first, we must plan now for peace on a world basis; second, the world must be free, politically and economically, for nations and for men, that peace may exist in it; third, America must play an active, constructive part in freeing it and keeping its peace.

When I say that peace must be planned on a world basis, I mean quite literally that it must embrace the earth. Continents and oceans are plainly only parts of a whole, seen, as I have seen them, from the air. England and America are parts. Russia and China, Egypt, Syria and Turkey, Iraq and Iran are also parts. And it is inescapable that there can be no peace for any part of the world unless the foundations of peace are made secure throughout all parts of the world.

This cannot be accomplished by mere declarations of our leaders, as in an Atlantic Charter. Its accomplishment depends primarily upon acceptance by the peoples of the world. For if the failure to reach international understanding after the last war taught us anything it taught us this: even if war leaders apparently agree upon generalized principles and slogans while the war is being fought, when they come to the peace table they make their own interpretations of their previous declarations. So unless today, while the war is being fought, the people of the United States and of Great Britain, of Russia and of China, and of all the other United Nations, fundamentally agree on their purposes, fine and idealistic expressions of hope such as those of the Atlantic Charter will live merely to mock us as have Mr. Wilson's Fourteen Points. The Four Freedoms will not be accomplished by the declarations of those momentarily in power. They will become real only if the people of the world forge them into actuality.

When I say that in order to have peace this world must be free, I am only reporting that a great process has started which no man—certainly not Hitler—can stop. Men and women all over the world are on the march, physically, intellectually,

451

and spiritually. After centuries of ignorant and dull compliance, hundreds of millions of people in eastern Europe and Asia have opened the books. Old fears no longer frighten them. They are no longer willing to be Eastern slaves for Western profits. They are beginning to know that men's welfare throughout the world is interdependent. They are resolved, as we must be, that there is no more place for imperialism within their own society than in the society of nations. The big house on the hill surrounded by mud huts has lost its awesome charm.

Our Western world and our presumed supremacy are now on trial. Our boasting and our big talk leave Asia cold. Men and women in Russia and China and in the Middle East are conscious now of their own potential strength. They are coming to know that many of the decisions about the future of the world lie in their hands. And they intend that these decisions shall leave the peoples of each nation free from foreign domination, free for economic, social, and spiritual growth. ■

Source: Norman Thomas, "Some Wrong Roads To Peace," *Vital Speeches of the Day,* **vol. IX, no. 23 (September 15, 1943), pp. 720–721.**

The Socialist Party's Titular Head

The radio carries thrilling news. More than once today you have snatched a few minutes to listen to the story of gallant deeds, perhaps of your sons and brothers, anyway of your fellow Americans, who press towards victory on land and sea and in the air, from the cold and fog of the Aleutians to the jungles of the South Seas; from Sicily to the convoy route to Murmansk. Victory is sweet and the tale of heroic deeds brings its own moments of exaltation. Yes, the radio brings thrilling news.

The radio brings terrible news. Victories are not won without sorrow and anguish. The finest of our young men must perforce be messengers of death and destruction, not merely to the enemy in arms, but to women and children. However carefully they may make military objectives their targets, they cannot altogether spare great cities and the noblest monuments in which men have written the record of their civilization.

Victory is sweet, but victory of itself is no compensation for those who mourn their husbands, sons and brothers. Victory *alone* is not worth the price of that last full measure of devotion which heroes, known and unknown, pay to win it. Victory—but for what?

Let the radio help me answer in terms not of the war but of the kind of peace, hope of which alone is compensation for the suffering and sorrow of those to whom glory is a poor return for the tragedy it costs. Men differ about many things. One thing more than all else unites us, Americans, British, Russians, Chinese, men of all the United Nations, yet, I think even of the enemy countries, and that is the hope that never again shall total war engulf the earth, that the little children who laugh and play about their mothers' knees shall never have to face what their fathers and older brothers are so heroically enduring tonight while I speak and you quietly listen. That means that we must seek not a peace, but a good peace, an intelligent peace, a peace that will last because it will deserve to last.

It is a sign of hope that the quest for the right kind of peace has enlisted so much thought and energy. Many are the roads which different guides tell us will lead to peace. I do not deny the sincerity or good faith of these guides when I say that some of the roads they urge upon us lead not to peace but to new and worse wars than our generation has known.

Tonight I want to describe some of the roads which I think lead away from peace and tell you briefly why. The first road to avoid is the road of vengeance against whole peoples. There is, indeed, a case for bringing before tribunals of justice the men particularly responsible in this war for cruelty exceeding even the bounds of war. There is no case that can stand the test of reason or of ethics for the kind of vengeance now preached against the German and the Japanese peoples. In a real sense they are the victims of their own warlords, and are paying with their own blood for accepting their rule. I do not hold them altogether guiltless, but if complete innocence is to be required for peace, who shall stand? Let us Americans reflect on three centuries of broken treaties with the Indians, on two and a half centuries of the bestial slave trade in human flesh and blood, on our continuing racial discrimination and our shameful race riots. If God or our fellow human beings should apply to us the judgments we are urged to visit upon enemy peoples, how grave would be our fate! There is no hope of peace except in a comradeship of forgiveness and nobler effort by the peoples of the earth.

* * *

Perhaps the greatest single danger to peace is that the victors will fall back on the ancient and discredited method of imperialism for reorganizing the world. Not all imperialisms are equally cruel. Not all measles are equally severe. But just as an efficient health department tries to get rid of all measles, not merely severe measles, so must we try to rid the world of all imperialism. Churchill pointed the road, not to peace but to war, when he had no answer for the problems of Southeastern Asia other than his famous declaration "We mean to hold our own." He was not talking about the white cliffs of Dover or the blue waters of Loch Lomond but of lands never England's own, save by right of conquest, never accepted by the conquered peoples. Many of those lands have been lost and cannot be recovered by England's might alone. It is time for us to say plainly that our boys shall not die to restore the British Empire in Burma and Malaya nor shall they die to become partners in it or to establish our own. The peoples of Asia redeemed from the Japanese warlords must work out their own destiny in cooperation with the Western world and not in subjection to it. The dogma of white supremacy in the world and in our own America is doomed. There are not enough of us

white folks to perpetuate it. The effort leads straight to new and tragic wars. ∎

AMERICANS will always fight for liberty

Brown Brothers

453

THE WAR AIMS OF SPECIFIC GROUPS

In the first cluster of selections in this section you examined certain statements made by American political leaders during World War II concerning the nation's war and peace objectives. On the following pages you will find statements made by citizens representing various sectors of public opinion during the same period. The remarks of a soldier, a black, a business leader, a labor leader, a woman, and an educator are included.

Source: Sgt. Thomas N. Pappas, United States Army, "What I Am Fighting For," *Saturday Evening Post*, July 10, 1943, p. 29.

A Soldier

I am fighting for that big white house with the bright green roof and the big front lawn, the house that I lived in before Hitler and the Japanese came into my life. I am fighting for those two big sycamore trees out there on the lawn where my brother and I spent so many happy and never-to-be-forgotten hours.

I am fighting for that little sister of mine, the one in the eighth grade, the one who shed so many tears when her brothers went marching off to war.

I am fighting for those two gray-haired grown-ups who live in that house right now. Those two hard-working and intelligent people who planned the lives of those two boys who went marching off to war. Those two people who fought so hard to give those boys a good education, to keep them well clothed, well fed and clean of body and mind.

I am fighting for that big stone church with its tall, stained-glass windows, its big organ with the magnificent tone, its choir, its people who were always so glad to see us. That big stone church with its great principles and ideals, its irreplaceable position in the community, its educational program for the young, its living testimony to the Creator of us all.

I am fighting for that big brick schoolhouse, that fine old college with all its tradition and its ivy-covered walls, that nice little roadster I used to have, my room at home with all the books, that radio in the living room, that phonograph with all its records, that piano, that tennis court back of the house, and that little black cocker spaniel with his big bright eyes and his funny walk.

I am fighting for my home and your home, my town and your town. I am fighting for New York and Chicago and Los Angeles and Greensboro and Hickory Flat and Junction City. And, above all, I am fighting for Washington. I am fighting for those two houses of Congress, for that dignified and magnificent Supreme Court, for that President who has led us so brilliantly through these trying years and for the man who succeeds him.

I am fighting for everything that America stands for. I am fighting for the rights of the poor and the rights of the rich. I am fighting for the right of the American people to choose their own leaders, to live their own lives, to pursue their own careers, to save their money if they like or to spend their money if they like.

I am fighting for that girl with the large brown eyes and the reddish tinge in her hair, that girl who is away at college right now, preparing herself for her part in the future of America and Christianity.

I am fighting for that freedom that so few of us seemed to realize we had before the war struck at us. I am fighting for that American belief in equality, in justice and in an Almighty God.

These are the things I am fighting for, and there are millions more in the Army fighting for them, too, and back on the home front the rest of the millions are buying the Bonds to help pay for the weapons of war and working day and night on the production lines to produce the weapons of war.

We cannot lose. ∎

Source: Nick Aaron Ford, "What Negroes Are Fighting For," *Vital Speeches of the Day,* vol. IX, no. 23 (September 15, 1943), pp. 720–721.

A Black

The bombs that fell on Pearl Harbor in the early hours of December 7, 1941, did more than kill three thousand Americans and demolish American property in that region. They shattered the very foundations of the world as we had known it—the world that had been in the making since the birth of Christ. And as that world lay teetering in the balance, ready to burst into a thousand pieces, three-fourths of the peoples of the earth joined hands with Uncle Sam to catch the broken pieces of that dying order in the hope of re-constructing them into a finer and nobler world of the future.

Since that memorable date twelve months ago, many revolutionizing events have occurred. A little colored nation, that Americans had always regarded as insignificant, inefficient, and incapable of engineering a successful war against a powerful white nation, astounded the world by winning every encounter with American forces for eight long months. Thus, for the first time in its history, the great American nation was faced with the folly of the white man's philosophy of racial superiority. Only through a tragic sacrifice of some of the best blood of its citizens did the nation finally learn that the color of a man's skin and the shape of his nose do not determine his capacity either for treachery, or courage, or calculating efficiency.

Since that memorable date American Negro troops for the first time have landed in the little Negro republic of Liberia, Africa, founded by American freedmen nearly a century and a quarter ago. When Private Napoleon Taylor led his black comrades down the gangplank of the great American transport that had brought them safely across 6,000 miles of submarine-infested waters, he greeted the Liberian officials in words similar to these:

We have come to join hands with you in the fight to keep your freedom and to win additional freedom for yourselves and for all oppressed peoples of the world.

These are only two of the revolutionary events that have thrust themselves upon a bleeding world since last December 7. But in the midst of these recollections, there comes a challenging question that is hurled at us from a hundred different quarters: What are Negroes fighting for? It is a question we cannot ignore, for it has been sarcastically asked by Hitler himself.

One can well visualize Mr. Hitler resting his satanic carcass upon a pile of his vile and slimy publication, *Mein Kampf,* which contains the statement by the Fuehrer himself that no person of African descent can ever become a citizen of Germany because he is too inferior to claim a heritage with a superior race. Yes, we can visualize this crafty hypocrite issuing orders from one corner of his mouth for the subjugation or total destruction of all non-Nordic races, and from the other corner asking, "What are you Negroes fighting for?"

"Aren't you segregated and discriminated against in America? Aren't you denied the right to work in defense industries and the right to fight on equal terms with your white countrymen? Aren't you insulted, and cheated, and oppressed by the very country for whom you are fighting? Aren't you lynched and burned at the stake and your bleeding or charred bodies left swinging in the breeze, as your tormentors march away singing, 'My country 'tis of Thee'?"

We are the first to admit that conditions are not ideal for Negroes in this country, not even during this all-out effort for national defense, but we cannot deny that powerful voices high in governmental circles are being raised in every section of the nation in behalf of equality and a full degree of democracy for our people. Where can you find in any Axis country a single voice of protest raised by a governmental official in behalf of mal-treated minorities?

America is the only country in the world whose written Constitution guarantees equal freedom and equal opportunity for all races, creeds, and religions. Certainly, there are injustices, but our *government* is committed to equal justice for all. Certainly, there are inequalities here, but our *government* is committed to the recognition of the essential equality of all men. As long as the ideal is before us, we can always have reason to hope that each new day will bring us nearer to that ideal. But if, like the Axis countries, the government acknowledges no responsibility for equality or justice, there can be no hope that they may ever be achieved.

Yes, Negroes are lynched in America, but never yet in the whole history of these shameful and barbarous episodes has any official of our national government publicly condoned such a crime. Every such incident has been vigorously condemned by our national government, by newspaper editorials, by state governors, and by many prominent white citizens in the very communities where the lynchers live. But what German, or Italian, or Japanese newspaper has dared to print a single line in con-

455

demnation of the brutal slaughter of thousands of innocent Jews on the streets of every German city? What Fascist governmental official has ever parted his lips in defense of scores of innocent hostages of minority groups that die before Fascist firing squads every day in every conquered nation of Europe?

It is true that injustices and mistreatment at home can never be excused by pointing to larger and graver injustices abroad. But the odious comparison can serve notice upon us that the Negro's only hope lies in victory for the United Nations and the complete destruction of totalitarian ideals. ◼

Source: Lewis H. Brown, President, Johns-Mansville Corp., "Change Is the Essence of Progress," *Vital Speeches of the Day*, vol. IX, no. 8 (February 1, 1943), pp. 240–241.

A Business Leader

As an industrial engineer, I visualize for comparison the free enterprise system and the totalitarian system, by imagining each to be a machine, and each propelled by a different kind of engine.

There is the totalitarian machine driven by a powerful, heavy steam engine familiar to those of us who are industrial engineers. Its motive power is sweat converted to steam by the heat of compulsion. It is lubricated by fear. Usually its control emanates from the central plant. It is large, cumbersome and complicated and needs an unusually expert man at the controls. It has real power, and after it gets going, can deliver lots of energy. Its operation and efficiency are strictly limited by the training, experience and capacity of its engineer and his assistant.

The free enterprise machine is activated by the compact, easy-to-operate, flexible gasoline engine. Its fuel is human aspiration ignited by self interest and it is lubricated by individual ambition and initiative. It possesses the power to do almost anything and goes wherever the people may guide it. The driver is the ordinary citizen who needs only a few rules to help him guide it so as not to endanger others. It needs no fettering central power plant. It needs no special tracks. It runs on the right-of-way of freedom available to all.

To win the war we have converted our governmental-economic machine over from a gasoline engine to a steam engine. After the war, we want the limitless advantages of the private enterprise gasoline engine.

As an industrial engineer, I believe the private enterprise machine—streamlined— is the best from all standpoints to propel the American nation to new heights of spiritual, cultural and material progress. I would recommend it as the basis of our design for the post-war model of the American Way. I believe the American people will prefer for peace the private enterprise machine controlled by the people. ◼

Source: Mathew Woll, Vice-President, American Federation of Labor, "Labor Looks at International Affairs," *Vital Speeches of the Day,* vol. XI, no. 15 (May 15, 1945), p. 488.

A Labor Leader

We entered this war because our democratic institutions and our political freedom were threatened by the Axis powers. German, Italian and Japanese aggression was on the march and until these powers were crushed on the field and at sea, America stood in mortal danger. It was as simple as that. We shall succeed in our task, of that I am certain. But whether we shall succeed in winning the peace and making our great country an oasis of democracy in a world of regimentation is an entirely different matter.

The kind of America which we shall inherit after the war will depend on what we do now. There is an old American saying to the effect that there is no time like the present. We must plan postwar America today, here and now. We must not wait for the outcome of world conferences or international debates. Churchill is not waiting for the conclusion of the war to determine the nature of postwar Britain. Postwar England is now in the making. And the same is true of postwar Russia. We, too, must lay the foundations of a postwar society that will endure in the difficult years that lie ahead.

But before attempting to outline a plan of a postwar America, perhaps it would not be amiss to take an inventory of our assets, to count our blessings, so to speak. We have seen, during the war, that modern American industry which operates by voluntary action through voluntary groups, has outproduced all the other countries of the world. Both Hitler and Mussolini thought that the solution of the American problem could not be solved. They thought that the enormous pressure of war would cause the American industrial machine to break down. They imagined that the need for profits by ownership and the desire for high wages and decent working conditions by labor would cause breakdowns in our industrial machines. But that erroneous concept has been bleeding to death on the battlefields of France, Belgium, Holland and Italy. American management and American labor have delivered every ton of war material that has been asked of them. If there are certain shortages, it is not the fault of American labor and industry; it is the fault of inadequate official planning.

This miracle of production is the result of our economic system of voluntarism—free enterprise, if you will. Our tremendous industrial plant, our vast shipyards, our Pittsburghs, our Willow Runs, all these are tangible evidences of American free enterprise. And let us never forget that an economic system, like a political system, can never be half-free. Free enterprise means free labor—and vice versa.

The most enlightened section of American industry and management are fully aware of this. Intelligent management knows that modern industrial society can grow only as the result of responsibilities equally shared by management and labor. This means that we shall all enjoy the fullest measure of independence and prosperity in ratio to the measure of the recognition and the granting of the rights and privileges of labor. But, it may be asked, if the existing relationship within the American industrial structure is free and voluntary, why must labor constantly insist upon its rights? Organized labor does this for several reasons, but the most obvious is that unless labor is free to demand higher standards of living, improved conditions of work, and greater opportunities for self-development, the inherently progressive nature of our industrial society will be halted. Labor demands these rights because to be free to demand is the very essence of voluntarism. In totalitarian countries like Germany and Russia to demand is tantamount to a request for liquidation. ∎

Source: Margaret A. Hickey, Chairman, Woman's Advisory Committee, War Manpower Commission, *Vital Speeches of the Day*, vol. IX, no. 8 (February 1, 1943), p. 51.

A Woman

Now many women are willing to take a job when necessity arises—personal or national, or the financial reward is high. And when the need disappears, they withdraw. But in the plans now being drawn for employment of people demobilized from the military and civilian industries, no attention is being given to the employment of women, even those in the labor market before the war. Actually the only consideration being given is to the disemployment of women. Quite casually it is estimated that five million women will return to their homes after the war is won. That's a dangerous assumption. Government and industry should not assume that women can be treated as a labor reserve, to be used during the war only. Women are an integral part of our great manpower resources. The right of the individual woman to work must be recognized and provided for just as the right of the individual man. Women who wish to stay in the labor market after the war should not be treated as usurpers of men's jobs. And if there is to be a weeding out process, let's make certain that it is done on the basis of ability rather than sex.

In the years immediately following this war, employment problems will overshadow every other issue on the American scene. In fact, if we cannot solve our re-employment problems at home, the peace of the entire world will be endangered. We must at all costs avoid a period of discrimination between men and women, between races, between older workers and younger workers, between native born and foreign born. Such antagonisms, the unrest and the bitter group feelings resulting would destroy our peace at home and abroad.

"We are bound for the future." Living on the home front so that we shall be ready for the peace when it comes will not be easy. Living for the peace while we are fighting a war requires that we fight defeatism about the peace. Walter Lippmann's book, "United States Foreign Policy" is a "must" for every business woman. In it he warns us that "We have had to wage war three times without being prepared to fight; and we have twice made peace without knowing what we wanted." We do not need to look backward very far to see the folly of such unpreparedness. This time, wisely, thoughtfully, unselfishly, women must help create a world view of faith and confidence in a just and durable peace. We have seen the evil results of a world view for war, the unchecked influence of an axis of hate and aggression and savagery—the world view of Berlin, Rome, and Tokyo. Women must create a new world view of the universal humanity.

The best peace will not be a perfect one. There will be conflicts in national interests; there will be dissimilarities in national temperament, in political methodology, but agreements can be reached. This is the task of statesmen, who perhaps will not please the idealists, who must have the kingdom of heaven on earth or nothing. On the other hand, the peace must not be that of the selfish reactionaries who even now menace the future, just as they have undermined efforts at world collaboration in the past.

There are difficulties ahead. In a world made intimate by invention, it isn't going to be easy to get along with our international neighbors without irritations that are certain to come with global propinquity. Then there are those evil potentials in triumph that we must prepare to meet. Modern science has made the whole world one neighborhood—women must help make it a good neighborhood.

"We are bound for the future. With no stars, the deep below, the snarl of danger above us." Perhaps no one has given us more inspiration and encouragement along the way to international understanding than Madame Chiang Kai-Shek. Those who dare to take off from this landing field in history might well imitate her selflessness, her honesty, her loyalty, and her humility. Ego, national or personal, with its petty prides and personal ambitions, will ground all of our plans. On the new Mayflower of the sky there are no outer decks where ego can expand in rude isolation and nurse its injured pride. We are all inside together. Each individual and each individual nation is going to need large reserves of tolerance and patience to fly past boundaries of race, religion, clique and party.

In quiet sanctuaries we must find inner shelter, so as to be ready for our place in this fellowship of struggle and sacrifice ahead. "We are bound for the future"—for a new age, a more spiritual age. The way to end wars and to prevent the recurrence of war is to build and keep on building a great peace through the discovery and the constant improvement of the spiritual resources of the nation. Ours must be the great unsecret weapon, the faith that will light up the life of the spirit and make it invincible in war and in peace. ■

Source: Robert M. Hutchins, President of the University of Chicago, "The New Realism," *Vital Speeches of the Day*, vol. XI, no. 19 (July 15, 1945), p. 602.

An Educator

The conquest of the United States by Hitler is revealed by our adoption of the Nazi doctrine that certain races or nations are superior and fit to rule, whereas others are vicious and fit only to be exterminated or enslaved. We are now talking about guilty races. We are saying about the Germans and the Japanese what Hitler said about the Jews. And we are saying about ourselves—or at least we are strongly hinting it—what Hitler said about the blond teutonic "Aryans." A graduate of the University of Chicago told me that he wished a dense cloud of poison gas would settle over the Japanese islands and destroy every man, woman, and child in them. He had the grace to add, "Maybe I'm not a Christian." Without debating the Christianity of declaring war on women and children, I merely point out the arrogance of the assumption that any American is fit to judge all Japanese.

Hitler's conquest of America proceeds apace as we succumb to the idea that social and political problems can be most effectively solved with the aid of a firing squad. I insist that criminals must be punished. Justice demands that none of the guilty escape. At the same time it must be clear that the characteristic of criminals is that they are individuals, not nations or races. They should be punished for what they individually did. What they did, to deserve punishment at the hands of human judges, must have been illegal at the time it was done. If the judgment is to command the respect of Americans, it must be shown that the act was one which a patriotic American would not have committed if he had been a patriotic German. Punishment for illegal acts must be meted out legally, with a fair trial and adherence to the Anglo-Saxon principle that every man is presumed innocent until he is proved guilty. We must remember the ancient doctrine that no man is a good judge in his own cause. And it would do us no harm to apply the maxim of equity that one must come into court with clean hands.

We should hesitate to punish Germans for acts which we have committed or may commit. For instance, are we prepared to stand trial ourselves for the violation of treaties and attacks on undefended places? Are we ready to say that in the face of the tommy guns of the SS we would have remained true to our ideals of democracy? Is the standard we intend to impose on the Germans the standard of heroes and saints, or that of the ordinary man, who throughout the world thinks first of the lives of his family and second about his principles? We could wish that all men were prepared to die for their principles in peace and in war. We do not expect Americans to do it except in war.

We may hesitate a little to punish Germans for crimes against Germans unless we are ready for a foreign investigation of American crimes against Americans. I should feel better about having Americans judge the anti-semitism and the concentration camps of Germany if I could forget the anti-semitism and the lynchings in the United States. Our religious and racial intolerance is unorganized, and violence is sporadic and illegal. We have not yet gone in for these things on the grand Nazi scale. But we are sufficiently vulnerable to lay ourselves open to some embarrassment if we set ourselves to pass judgment on the domestic conduct of other nations.

Of one crime the German people were certainly guilty, and that is the crime which the new realism sanctifies, the crime of indifference. The German people, all but a few million of them, were indifferent to the rights of man and indifferent to the violation of these rights by those in power. If any nation can be found which is not guilty of this crime, then it is qualified to judge the German people for their indifference to the crimes committed by Germans against Germans. As for ourselves, it is not unfair to say that the American people, except for a few million of them, are guilty of the crime of indifference in the face of race prejudice, economic exploitation, political corruption, and the degradation of oppressed minorities. This guilt does not assist our claim to judge and punish the German people for theirs. ∎

459

460

Library of Congress

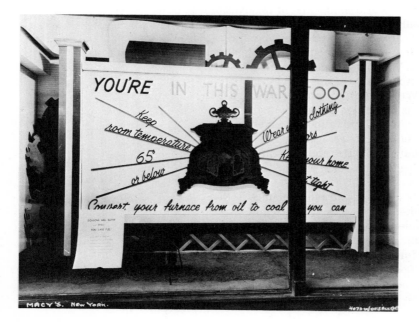

THE MASS MEDIA
AND WORLD WAR II

Not only did America's political leaders debate the causes and aims of the war, but the mass media also contributed continuously to this discussion. From 1941 to 1945, newspaper editorials and columns, political cartoons, and popular magazine articles were all heavily affected by the war. Even in the entertainment and commercial fields, the war became the dominant theme. The following political cartoons and comic strips are a sampling from the mass media during the war.

1 What emotional tone or moral stance concerning the causes and objectives of the war and toward America's enemies is taken in the comic strips? In the advertisements? In the political cartoons?

2 How do the attitudes expressed in these items from the mass media compare with the conceptions of the war enunciated by Roosevelt, Willkie, or Thomas?

3 Which items from the media are most supportive of the statements made by Roosevelt, Willkie, and Thomas? Explain why.

4 What hypotheses can you make, based on both the political leaders' statements and the samples from the mass media, concerning how Americans viewed the causes of the war, the objectives of the war, and the enemies the United States was fighting?

The following cartoons from MAD magazine indicate changes in movies which deal with World War II. Do you think the prediction has come true? ■

IT'S QUITE AN HONOR TO HAVE A FLYING FORTRESS NAMED AFTER CAPTAIN MARVEL, JR.! BUT IT ISN'T ALL HONOR-- WHEN A FAKE CAPTAIN MARVEL, JR. STREAKS ACROSS PACIFIC SKIES, LURING THE GREAT SHIP TOWARDS DESTRUCTION...

FAR IN THE SOUTH PACIFIC, A TROOP-LADEN JAP TRANSPORT SNEAKS TO THE AID OF A TRAPPED DIVISION...

SUDDENLY, OUT OF THE CONCEALING CLOUDS--

EEEEEOWIE! BULLSEYE! GIVE OUR LOVE TO YOUR ANCESTORS, BOYS! TELL HIROHITO THE CAPTAIN MARVEL JR. WAS HERE!

YIPPEE! LOOKIT THE NIPS SCAMPER! GIMME A RUN DOWN THE MIDDLE, MAC! WE'LL BLOW 'EM SKY-HIGH!

ACE BOMBER CREW SCORES AGAIN FOR NEW RECORD!

BACK IN AMERICA, AT THE NEWS-STAND OF CRIPPLED FREDDY FREEMAN---

GOSH, I'M SO PROUD! THE BOMBER THEY NAMED AFTER CAPT. MARVEL JR. IS CHAMP JAP-SINKER OF THE PACIFIC!

YES, SIR! IT'S CAPT. MARVEL JR. WHO GIVES US THE BREAKS EVERY TIME! HE'S OUR LUCK!

SSSOOO?

HIGH IN A NEARBY TREE, A JAP SNIPER OVER-HEARS!

MEANWHILE, BACK AT A PACIFIC ISLAND BASE---

CONGRATULATIONS, MEN! YOU'VE SET A NEW RECORD IN JAP TONNAGE SUNK BY ONE PLANE!

HERE'S THE BOY WHO DESERVES THE CREDIT, SIR! CAPT. MARVEL JR. IS OUR GOOD LUCK! WITHOUT HIM, WE COULDN'T DO HALF AS WELL!

A LITTLE LATER, IN A JAP POCKET ACROSS THE ISLAND, HE MAKES HIS REPORT!

AMERICAN FOOLS VERY SUPERSTITIOUS! BELIEVE THIS MARVEL JR. PERSON IS GOOD LUCK!

SO? THAT HONORABLE FOR DESTROYING DEVIL PLANE...

A FEW DAYS LATER, RETURNING FROM ANOTHER BOMBING MISSION---

WE'LL SAVE TIME AND GAS BY GOING THRU THE NORTH MOUNTAIN PASS!

MAC-- LOOK! AM I SEEING THINGS?

FOR TH--! IT'S HIM IT'S CAPT. MARVEL JR. HIMSELF AND HE'S MOTIONING US NOT TO ENTER THE PASS!

MUST BE AN AMBUSH-- WE'LL TAKE THE SOUTH PASS INSTEAD!

WHAT THE--? ACK-ACK! A HIDDEN ANTI-AIRCRAFT BATTERY! CAPT. MARVEL JR. SENT US RIGHT OVER THE TRAP!

IT WORKS LIKE A WATCH, BOYS! I'LL HELP YOU BOMB UP AND...

EEEYOW! GET A LOAD OF THIS, YOU GUYS---

THREE JAP SUPPLY BOATS ARE TRYING TO CUT AROUND BARAUL ISLAND! THEY'LL BE COLD MEAT FOR A U.S. BOMBER!

EEEOW! LEAD US TO IT! WE FLY AGAIN!

I'LL KEEP OUT OF SIGHT IN THE CLOUDS WHILE YOU COMPLETE YOUR MISSION! I HAVE A HUNCH THE JAPS WILL TROT OUT THEIR TRICK AGAIN WHEN THEY SEE YOU!

CAPTAIN MARVEL JR. HELPS LOAD UP THE BOMBER!

An hour later---

WOW! THREE JAPS WITH ONE BOMB-LOAD! NOW WE'LL SEE WHAT HAPPENS ON THEIR FLIGHT BACK TO BASE!

THEY GAVE THE SHIPS TIME TO IDENTIFY THEIR PLANE AND RADIO BASE! IF THE JAPS HAVE A TRICK, THEY'LL BE USING IT SOON!

At that moment---

READY, HONORABLE OGO! THIS TIME WE MAKE SURE AMERICAN DEVIL PLANE NEVER FLY AGAIN!

SA, IMATI! THIS TIME HONORABLE AMERICANS WILL FLY CLOSE TO HAVE BETTER LOOK AT MARVEL JR..

BEFORE THEY SEE HONORABLE MISTAKE, THIS ROCKET GUN WILL BLOW ALL INTO HONORABLE PIECES FOR GLORY OF EMPEROR! BANZAI!

AH-HA! HONORABLE BOMBER VERY CLOSE! WILL LET THEM GET CLOS SO NO POSSIBLE CHANCE TO MISS WITH MIGHTY ROCKET!

HOLY MOLEY, AS BILLY BATSON SAYS! IT IS A FIGURE DRESSED LIKE ME--AND FLYING THRU THE AIR! I'D BETTER INVESTIGATE--

BUT THE REAL CAPTAIN MARVEL JR.. ING PATROL, SPIES THE CUNNING JAP..

AIEEE! IS REAL CAPT. MARVEL JR.! WILL SHOOT PLANE! THEN PULL UP FAST!

AT THIS HONORABLE RANGE, IMPOSSIBLE TO MISS!

BANG!

YIIII! A ROCKET G WE CAN DODGE

WOW! I'VE GOT TO BEAT THAT ROCKET!

AWRRK! HE'LL BE BLOWN TO BITS! THOSE ROCKET SHELLS ARE TERRIBLE!

MADE IT!

SO THAT'S IT! A JAP SUSPENDED BY WIRE FROM A PLANE HIDDEN IN CLOUDS!

YIIII! PULL HONORABLE SELF UP!

LIKE ALL JAP IMITATIONS--- LOOKS REAL BUT MADE OF INFERIOR MATERIALS!

CAPTAIN MARVEL JUNIOR

BEFORE

The German Officer is evil and sinister. He shouts "Heil Hitler!" and "Schvienhundt!" He usually wears a monocle, and keeps vowing to destroy decadent American Democracy.

465

AFTER

The German Officer is honest and sincere, but confused. He says things like "Vere haf ve failed as human beinks?" He keeps vowing to destroy decadent Hitler-type fascism.

PUBLIC OPINION POLLS
AND WORLD WAR II

On the basis of statements made by three key political leaders and a few samples from the mass media you have made hypotheses concerning the attitude of Americans toward various aspects of World War II. For over thirty-five years a systematic effort has been made to measure public opinion on critical issues and events. Public opinion polling has sought to become a science which, through the process of carefully prepared questions and scientifically established samples, would accurately reflect the opinions of "the mass public." In the following selection of polls from the war years, Americans were questioned on the very issues about which you have formed hypotheses.

1 Do the public opinion polls confirm or deny the hypotheses you have made as to how Americans viewed their enemies and the war's causes and objectives? How would you modify each of your hypotheses on the basis of these polls?

2 Are there significant variations of opinion by sex, age, education, and so forth? How would you explain this?

3 Based on these polls, would you say that the American people accepted the intellectual and moral conceptions of the war and the war objectives set forth by their political leaders?

Robert Capa, Magnum

466

On the Enemy

US June 17 '42   If you were the one to decide, what would you do with Japan after she has been defeated? (OPOR)

Pious phrases	5%
Political change	4
Economic adjustment	2
Disarm them	13
League of Nations	6
Treat their leaders roughly	3
Territorial adjustment	7
Military rule	9
Eye for an eye	13
Annihilate	12
Don't know	24
No answer	2

US June 17 '42   If you were the one to decide, what would you do with Germany after she has been defeated? (OPOR)

Political change	6%
Economic adjustment	1
Disarm them	13
League of Nations	11
Treat their leaders roughly	6
Territorial adjustment	2
Military rule	6
Eye for an eye	19
Annihilate	10
Pious phrases	6
Don't know	19
No answer	2

From *Public Opinion, 1935–1946*, ed. Hadley Cantril (Princeton N. J.: Princeton University Press, 1951).

US Feb '42, June '43, Feb '44, Nov 26 '44,*
Dec '44, July '45, Nov '45, May '46 Which of
the following statements comes closest to
describing how you feel, on the whole, about
the people who live in Germany? Each respondent was handed a card bearing the following statements: (1) The German people
will always want to go to war to make themselves as powerful as possible. (2) The
German people may not like war, but they
have shown that they are too easily led into
war by powerful leaders. (3) The German
people are like any other people. If they could
really choose the leaders they want, they
would become good citizens of the world. The
wording of statement 3 was used only in
Feb '42. Subsequent questions used this statement: The German people do not like war. If
they could have the same chance as people
in other countries, they would become good
citizens of the world. (NORC)

	State- ment 1	State- ment 2	State- ment 3	Don't know
Feb '42	21%	30%	42%	7%
June '43	21	44	32	3
Feb '44	24	45	28	3
Nov 26 '44*	27	43	25	5
Dec '44	35	36	25	4
July '45	39	37	19	5
Nov '45	30	42	24	4
May '46	31	44	21	4

* Release date. Results have been re-percentaged to
include those who didn't know.

US Dec 23 '44 After the war, do you think
the Japanese military leaders should be
punished in any way? (AIPO)

Yes 88%   No 5%   No opinion 7%

In what way? Asked of 88% of the sample
who thought the Japanese military leaders
should be punished after the war.

Executed, shot, hung, firing squad, be-
headed, death, destroyed, murdered 47%
Imprisoned, concentration camp, sen-
tenced to hard labor 16
Trial, court martial, military tribunal .. 12
Punished (no specific means), punish
them short of death 7
Punished according to their crimes, as
they did to others 6
Tortured, death march, string them up
by their feet 3
Demote them, clean up military staff ... 4
Exiled, exiled as criminals 3
Justice accorded them, treated in a fair
Christian way, fair treatment unpun-
ished, handled by international law 1
Miscellaneous 1

467

Robert Capa, Magnum

HOW SHOULD WE TREAT THE GERMAN PEOPLE AFTER THE WAR
(A SURVEY OF U.S. PUBLIC OPINION)

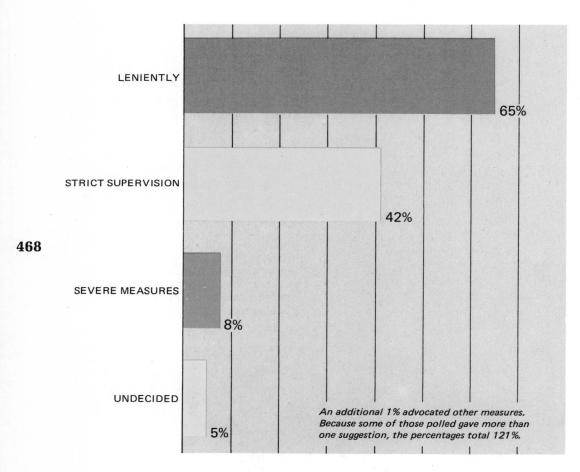

LENIENTLY 65%

STRICT SUPERVISION 42%

SEVERE MEASURES 8%

UNDECIDED 5%

An additional 1% advocated other measures. Because some of those polled gave more than one suggestion, the percentages total 121%.

468

US June 9 '42 After the war is over, how should we treat the Nazi leaders in Germany? (AIPO)

None of our affair—let their own people take care of them. We should stay out of European governments 2%
They won't be alive to be treated. They will have committed suicide or someone will have killed them 2
Be lenient, not too hard on them 2
Court martial them, give them a fair trial, face a military tribunal 2
Isolate them, exile them, same as Kaiser 2
Imprison them—confine them 31
Torture them, make them suffer mentally and physically, persecute them 2
Kill them 35
Treat them as they have treated others, an eye for an eye, give them some of their own medicine 5
Other answers 5
No opinion 12

Feb 20 '45
Kill them all 41%
Torture them 7
Exile them 2
Imprison them 13
Punish them severely 18
Bring them before a tribunal of the United Nations, try them and punish those found guilty 10
Be lenient with them, do unto them as we would have them do unto us 3
That's not our concern, leave it up to their own people 1
Undecided 5

US July 15 '42   From the words on this card, which seem to you to describe the German people best? Select as many as you wish and call off the letters and the words that go with them. (OPOR)

Hard-working 62%
Intelligent 41
Ordinary 9
Radical 23
Warlike 67
Practical 21
Artistic 8
Conceited 32
Quick-tempered 25
Lazy 1
Unimaginative 8
Sly 21
Treacherous 42
Aristocratic 8
Cruel 57
Ignorant 12
Rude 19
Dull 7
Brave 30
Religious 7
Arrogant 31
Progressive 32
Honest 10
Impossible to characterize 5
No answer 1

US Feb '42, June '43, Feb '44, Nov 26 '44*
Dec '44, July '45, Nov '45, May '46   Which of the following statements comes closest to describing how you feel, on the whole, about the people who live in Japan? Each respondent was handed a card bearing the following statements: (1) The Japanese people will always want to go to war to make themselves as powerful as possible. (2) The Japanese people may not like war, but they have shown that they are too easily led into war by powerful leaders. (3) The Japanese people are like any other people. If they could really choose the leaders they want, they would become good citizens of the world. The wording for statement 3 was used only in Feb '42. Subsequent questions used this statement: The Japanese people do not like war. If they could have the same chance as people in other countries, they would become good citizens of the world. (NORC)

469

	State-ment 1	State-ment 2	State-ment 3	Don't know
Feb '42	41%	27%	18%	14%
June '43	57	25	11	7
Feb '44	52	28	12	8
Nov 26 '44* ...	46	29	12	13
Dec '44	56	24	10	10
July '45	52	29	12	7
Nov '45	45	32	16	7
May '46	35	39	19	7

* Release date. Results have been re-percentaged to include those who didn't know.

HOW DO AMERICANS FEEL TOWARD THE PEOPLES OF GERMANY AND JAPAN?
HOW ABOUT THE WAR EFFORT?

QUESTION: "Which of the following statements comes closest to describing how you feel, on the whole, about the people who live in Germany (Japan)?"

(a) They will always want to go to war to make themselves as powerful as possible.

(b) They may not like war, but they have shown that they are too easily led into war by powerful leaders.

(c) They do not like war. If they could have the same chance as people in other countries, they would become good citizens of the world.

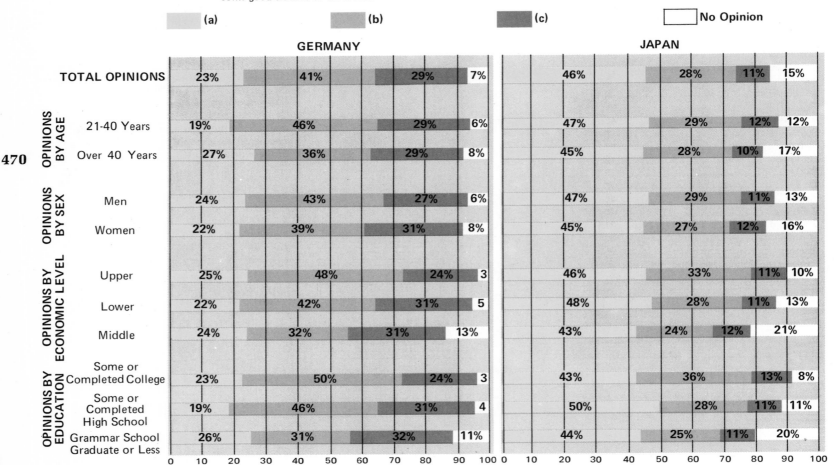

US July 15 '42 From the list of words on this card, which seem to you to describe the Japanese people best? Select as many as you wish and call off the letters and the words that go with them. (OPOR)

Hard-working	39%
Intelligent	25
Ordinary	6
Radical	12
Warlike	46
Practical	9
Artistic	19
Conceited	27
Quick-tempered	21
Lazy	3
Unimaginative	7
Sly	63
Treacherous	73
Aristocratic	4
Cruel	56
Ignorant	16
Rude	12
Dull	4
Brave	24
Religious	18
Arrogant	21
Progressive	19
Honest	2
Impossible to characterize	5
No answer	2

On War Aims

US Nov '42 What do you really think we are fighting this war for? Asked of a national cross-section of high-school students. (FOR)

	Want to keep on fighting	Want peace now
Liberty, freedom, democracy, American ideals, etc.	70.7%	49.3%
Because attacked, to stop Hitler and Japan, to protect our country	17.3	14.9
Peace	10.8	12.3
To get rid of dictatorship, Hitlerism, Nazi ideas	11.1	3.6
World freedom, to make world a better place, free conquered countries	10.9	2.0
For England, for power, territory, money interests	1.8	7.3
Other	10.8	17.9
Don't know	2.3	13.8

US Aug 25 '42 The United States is fighting this war because..... (AIPO)

Freedom and democracy throughout the world have been threatened	27%
Our freedom and democracy are endangered	32
We were attacked and must fight to defend our country and possessions	11
Germany and Japan must be defeated and their systems of government overthrown	6
We want to establish world peace	3
The capitalists got us into it	2
England needed our help—she could not win alone	2
The last war was not properly settled	1
The politicians got us into it	1
Miscellaneous reasons	7
Non-specific answers: we had to, forced into it	9
No opinion	5

On Peace Objectives

US Jan '43 People who think they've found out why the League fo Nations failed are now preparing for a new union of nations, if we win the war. Nobody can say for sure whether a new union would end all wars or only lead to worse ones. In order to try out a union of nations as a possible way of preventing wars, would you yourself be willing or not willing to do the following? (NORC)

	Willing	Not willing	Don't know
To stay on a rationing system in this country for about five years to help feed the starving people in other countries	81.6%	14.3%	4.1%
For part of the American army to remain overseas for several years after the war to help establish order	75.5	18.6	5.9
To consider most of our lend-lease materials as aid to the Allies and not expect any payment for them	41.3	48.8	9.9
To pay more taxes for a few years while the new union was being organized even if people in the other countries couldn't afford to pay much	63.5	28.0	8.5
To give up our army, navy and air force, if all other nations would do the same	41.1	54.6	4.3
To allow foreign goods to come into this country and compete with the things we grow or make here—even if the prices were lower	27.9	61.7	10.4
To forget reparations—that is, not try to collect any money from Germany or Japan to pay for what the war has cost us and our Allies	27.9	64.5	7.6

472

Robert Capa, Magnum

US Mar '44 If a general international organization should be set up, which of these things do you think it should and should not be organized to do? (FOR)

	Should	Should not	Don't know
Prevent any member country from starting a war of its own	79.0%	7.0%	14.0%
Decide which country is right if two members get into a dispute	75.9	8.2	15.9
Decide what taxes individual member nations must pay to support the organization	69.7	8.9	21.4
Decide what military strength each member nation can have	69.0	13.6	17.4
Regulate the rights of airplanes from one member nation to land on airfields in other member nations	61.1	14.0	24.9
Have a permanent military force of its own, stronger than any single nation	54.0	23.3	22.7
Decide what tariff rates should be charged by member nations	44.8	23.3	31.9
Decide which side is right if a civil war breaks out in a member nation, and support that side	43.0	31.7	25.3
Decide minimum standards for working conditions in member countries	32.0	44.7	23.3

US Mar 20 '45 What do you think would happen if we did not join a world organization? (AIPO)

Another war; peace wouldn't last; always fighting other nations 49%
Trouble start up everywhere; other countries turn against us; differences 13
We would lose out, be left in the cold; wouldn't get any advantages 10
No teeth in the organization, handicap it; league wouldn't mean anything 5
We would lose the present war and what we are fighting for; lose the peace; a step backwards 2
Our economic destruction; we can't live alone economically 1
Others; God's will; we would be selfish, etc. 3
Nothing; hard to tell, we won't have another war 6
Didn't say 11

473

Robert Capa, Magnum

US May 3 '45 Which one of these comes closest to expressing what you would like to have the United States do after the war? (NYHT)

Enter into no alliances and have as little as possible to do with other countries 9.7%

Depend only on separate alliances with certain countries 4.9

Take an active part in an international organization 71.8

Don't know 13.6

474

SHOULD THE UNITED STATES JOIN A POST-WAR WORLD UNION?

QUESTION: "After the war, if a union of nations that would try to solve world problems were formed, do you think it would be a good idea or a bad idea for the United States to join it?

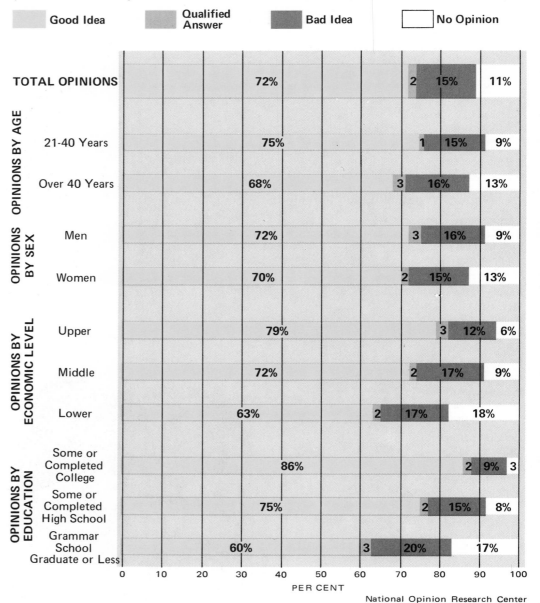

National Opinion Research Center

POSTER APPEALS TO
THE AMERICAN PEOPLE

Political leaders sought to convince the American people that there were basic reasons for the United States being in the war. But from another point of view, the United States was not only a nation with one overall cultural and social identity, it was also an amalgamation of many distinctive groups—young, old, laborers, businessmen, women, and innumerable minority groups. As you have seen, each one of these groups sought to identify its unique relationship to the war; at the same time, as evidenced by the following poll, the American public as a whole had opinions as to how some of these groups were cooperating with the war effort.

1 Which of these posters is making an appeal to a "self-interested" public; to a "mass public?" What interests and values are used to appeal to each?

2 What is the emotional tone and moral stance of these posters? How do they compare with the statements by the interest group spokesmen that you have read and with the statements of the three political leaders? How would you explain the similarities and differences in emotional tone and moral stance?

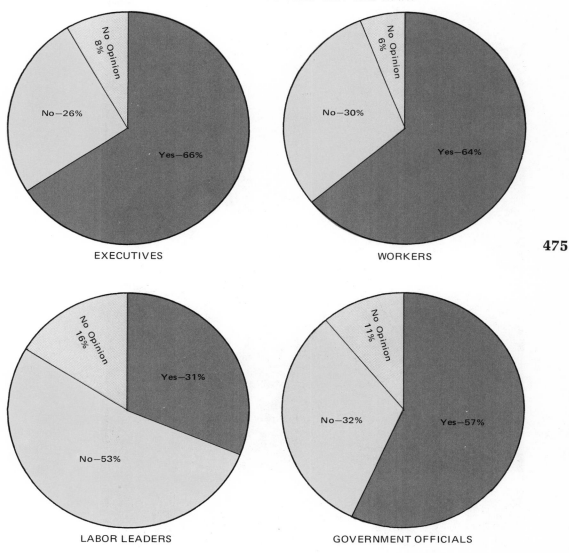

ARE EXECUTIVES . . . WORKERS . . . LABOR LEADERS . . . GOVERNMENT OFFICIALS DOING ALL THEY CAN TO HELP WIN THE WAR?

EXECUTIVES — No Opinion 8%, No—26%, Yes—66%

WORKERS — No Opinion 6%, No—30%, Yes—64%

LABOR LEADERS — No Opinion 16%, Yes—31%, No—53%

GOVERNMENT OFFICIALS — No Opinion 11%, No—32%, Yes—57%

National Opinion Research Center, August, 1942

475

THIS PAGE:
LEFT: Brown Brothers
ABOVE: Library of Congress

OPPOSITE PAGE:
LEFT: Brown Brothers
CENTER: Brown Brothers
RIGHT: Courtesy New York Historical Society,
New York City

477

THIS PAGE:
ABOVE: The Bettmann Archive
ABOVE RIGHT: Collection, The Museum of Modern Art, New York
Gift of the Office of Emergency Management
RIGHT: Collection, The Museum of Modern Art, New York
Gift of the Office of War Information

OPPOSITE PAGE:
ABOVE: All, Library of Congress
BELOW LEFT: Collection, The Museum of Modern Art, New York
CENTER AND RIGHT: Courtesy New York Historical Society, New York City

'Deliver Us...

...From Evil"

WORK TO KEEP FREE!

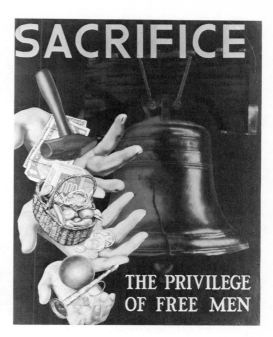

SACRIFICE

THE PRIVILEGE OF FREE MEN

This is the Enemy

ENEMY PLANES!

WILL YOU BE ASLEEP...
OR HELPING YOUR NEIGHBORS?

VOLUNTEER FOR VICTORY
REPORT CENTER AIDES
ARE URGENTLY NEEDED

BROOKLYN CIVILIAN DEFENSE VOLUNTEER OFFICE
131 LIVINGSTON STREET

Let's Finish the Job!

URGENT—
EXPERIENCED SEAMEN NEEDED!

WIRE COLLECT: Merchant Marine · Washington, D. C.

The high hopes for a new structure of world peace invested in the United Nations after World War II were quickly succeeded by a mood of suspicion and mistrust arising from the increasing tensions between the United States and Soviet Russia, the two strongest powers in the coalition that had defeated the Axis. Serious disagreements developed between the Russian and American leaders over the international control and inspection of atomic weapons by the United Nations, over the iron-handed political methods used by the Soviets in the Eastern European countries of Poland, Hungary, Rumania, and Bulgaria, over the question of continued American economic aid to war-devastated Russia, and over the amount of German reparations and the final peace settlements to be written for the defeated powers—Germany, Italy, and Japan. In February of 1946, Joseph Stalin, the leader of the Soviet Union, delivered an important speech to the Russian people warning them that they must prepare themselves industrially and militarily for an era in which there would be no real peace between the capitalist and Communist worlds. A month later, the wartime leader of Great Britain, Winston Churchill, delivered an address at Fulton, Missouri (with the apparent approval of his host, President Harry Truman) in which he declared that an "iron curtain" was descending between the free world and the totalitarian police states of the Communist world.

At almost the same time a civil war broke out in Greece, where Communist-supported guerrillas were seeking to oust the British-supported government. By early 1947 the British government, close to economic collapse because of the enormous costs of postwar economic recovery, informed the American government that it could no longer provide support, financial or military, for the Greek government. At the same time, the Russians were bringing pressure on the Turkish government for control of the Dardanelles. Fearful of the possibility of Russian expansion into the eastern Mediterranean and alarmed at the growing signs of economic collapse in the countries of Western Europe, President Truman called upon Congress to provide military and financial aid to Greece and Turkey and to embark upon a sustained program of massive economic aid to Europe. The assumption of Truman and his policy-planners was that such measures would "contain" the aggressive and expansionist aims of Soviet Russia. ■

The following statements are representative selections from the debate over the policy of containment which provided the basic rationale for the Greece-Turkey aid bill and the Marshall Plan (named after Truman's Secretary of State) for the economic recovery of Europe. The first statement is taken from an article written by George F. Kennan, who headed a policy planning staff created by the State Department to deal with the task of formulating a plan for the reconstruction of Europe. The second was written by Walter Lippmann, a widely syndicated newspaper columnist, whose writings carried considerable weight with the "informed public" in the United States. The third statement is taken from an address on foreign policy delivered by President Truman at the University of California in Berkeley. The final selection was written by Henry A. Wallace, who resigned from Truman's cabinet in protest over the policies associated with the growing "cold war."

Source: George F. Kennan, "The Sources of Soviet Conduct," *Foreign Affairs*, vol. 25, no. 4 (July 1947), pp. 573–582.

Soviet Pressures and American Policy

Of the original [Soviet] ideology, nothing has been officially junked. Belief is maintained in the basic badness of capitalism, in the inevitability of its destruction, in the obligation of the proletariat to assist in that destruction and to take power into its own hands. But stress has come to be laid primarily on those concepts which relate most specifically to the Soviet régime itself: to its position as the sole truly Socialist régime in a dark and misguided world, and to the relationships of power within it.

The first of these concepts is that of the innate antagonism between capitalism and Socialism. . . . It has profound implications for Russia's conduct as a member of international society. It means that there can never be on Moscow's side any sincere assumption of a community of aims between the Soviet Union and powers which are regarded as capitalist. It must invariably be assumed in Moscow that the aims of the capitalist world are antagonistic to the Soviet régime, and therefore to the interests of the peoples it controls. If the Soviet Government occasionally sets its signature to documents which would indicate the contrary, this is to be regarded as a tactical manœuvre permissible in dealing with the enemy (who is without honor) and should be taken in the spirit of *caveat emptor*. Basically, the antagonism remains. It is postulated. And from it flow many of the phenomena which we find disturbing in the Kremlin's conduct of foreign policy: the secretiveness, the lack of frankness, the duplicity, the wary suspiciousness, and the basic unfriendliness of purpose. These phenomena are there to stay, for the foreseeable future. There can be variations of degree and of emphasis. When there is something the Russians want from us, one or the other of these features of their policy may be thrust temporarily into the background; and when that happens there will always be Americans who will leap forward with gleeful announcements that "the Russians have changed," and some who will even try to take credit for having brought about such "changes." But we should not be misled by tactical manœuvres. These characteristics of Soviet policy, like the postulate from which they flow, are basic to the internal nature of Soviet power, and will be with us, whether in the foreground or the background, until the internal nature of Soviet power is changed.

This means that we are going to continue for a long time to find the Russians difficult to deal with. It does not mean that they should be considered as embarked upon a do-or-die program to overthrow our society by a given date. The theory of the inevitability of the eventual fall of capitalism has the fortunate connotation that there is no hurry about it. The forces of progress can take their time in preparing the final *coup de grâce*. Meanwhile, what is vital is that the "Socialist fatherland" —that oasis of power which has been already won for Socialism in the person of the Soviet Union—should be cherished and defended by all good Communists at home and abroad, its fortunes promoted, its enemies badgered and confounded. The promotion of premature, "adventuristic" revolutionary projects abroad which might embarrass Soviet power in any way would be an inexcusable, even a counter-revolutionary act. The cause of Socialism is the support and promotion of Soviet power, as defined in Moscow.

This bring us to the second of the concepts important to contemporary Soviet outlook. That is the infallibility of the Kremlin. The Soviet concept of power, which permits no focal points of organization outside the Party itself, requires that the Party leadership remain in theory the sole repository of truth. For if truth were to be found elsewhere, there would be justification for its expression in organized activity. But it is precisely that which the Kremlin cannot and will not permit.

The leadership of the Communist Party is therefore always right, and has been always right ever since in 1929 Stalin formalized his personal power by announcing that decisions of the Politburo were being taken unanimously.

On the principle of infallibility there rests the iron discipline of the Communist Party. In fact, the two concepts are mutually self-supporting. Perfect discipline requires recognition of infallibility. Infallibility requires the observance of discipline. And the two together go far to determine the behaviorism of the entire Soviet apparatus of power. But their effect cannot be understood unless a third factor be taken into account: namely, the fact that the leadership is at liberty to put forward for tactical purposes any particular thesis which it finds useful to the cause at any particular moment and to require the faithful and unquestioning acceptance of that thesis by the members of the movement as a whole. This means that truth is not a constant but is actually created, for all intents and purposes, by the Soviet leaders themselves. It may vary from week to week, from month to month. It is nothing absolute and immutable—nothing which flows from objective reality. It is only the most recent manifestation of the wisdom of those in whom the ultimate wisdom is supposed to reside, because they represent the logic of history. The accumulative effect of these factors is to give to the whole subordinate apparatus of Soviet power an unshakeable stubbornness and steadfastness in its orientation. This orientation can be changed at will by the Kremlin but by no other power. Once a given party line has been laid down on a given issue of current policy, the whole Soviet governmental machine, including the mechanism of diplomacy, moves inexorably along the prescribed path, like a persistent toy automobile wound up and headed in a given direction, stopping only when it meets with some unanswerable force. The individuals who are the components of this machine are unamenable to argument or reason which comes to them from outside sources. Their whole training has taught them to mistrust and discount the glib persuasiveness of the outside world. Like the white dog before the phonograph, they hear only the "master's voice." And if they are to be called off from the purposes last dictated to them, it is the master who must call them off. Thus the foreign representative cannot hope that his words will make any impression on them. The most that he can hope is that they will be transmitted to those at the top, who are capable of changing the party line. But even those are not likely to be swayed by any normal logic in the words of the bourgeois representative. Since there can be no appeal to com-

mon purposes, there can be no appeal to common mental approaches. For this reason, facts speak louder than words to the ears of the Kremlin; and words carry the greatest weight when they have the ring of reflecting, or being backed up by, facts of unchallengeable validity.

But we have seen that the Kremlin is under no ideological compulsion to accomplish its purposes in a hurry. Like the Church, it is dealing in ideological concepts which are of long-term validity, and it can afford to be patient. It has no right to risk the existing achievements of the revolution for the sake of vain baubles of the future. The very teachings of Lenin himself require great caution and flexibility in the pursuit of Communist purposes. Again, these precepts are fortified by the lessons of Russian history: of centuries of obscure battles between nomadic forces over the stretches of a vast unfortified plain. Here caution, circumspection, flexibility and deception are the valuable qualities; and their value finds natural appreciation in the Russian or the oriental mind. Thus the Kremlin has no compunction about retreating in the face of superior force. And being under the compulsion of no timetable, it does not get panicky under the necessity for such retreat. Its political action is a fluid stream which moves constantly, wherever it is permitted to move, toward a given goal. Its main concern is to make sure that it has filled every nook and cranny available to it in the basin of world power. But if it finds unassailable barriers in its path, it accepts these philosophically and accommodates itself to them. The main thing is that there should always be pressure, unceasing constant

pressure, toward the desired goal. There is no trace of any feeling in Soviet psychology that that goal must be reached at any given time.

These considerations make Soviet diplomacy at once easier and more difficult to deal with than the diplomacy of individual aggressive leaders like Napoleon and Hitler. On the one hand it is more sensitive to contrary force, more ready to yield on individual sectors of the diplomatic front when that force is felt to be too strong, and thus more rational in the logic and rhetoric of power. On the other hand it cannot be easily defeated or discouraged by a single victory on the part of its opponents. And the patient persistence by which it is animated means that it can be effectively countered not by sporadic acts which represent the momentary whims of democratic opinion but only by intelligent long-range policies on the part of Russia's adversaries —policies no less steady in their purpose, and no less variegated and resourceful in their application, than those of the Soviet Union itself.

In these circumstances it is clear that the main element of any United States policy toward the Soviet Union must be that of a long-term, patient but firm and vigilant containment of Russian expansive tendencies. It is important to note, however, that such a policy has nothing to do with outward histrionics: with threats or blustering or superfluous gestures of outward "toughness." While the Kremlin is basically flexible in its reaction to political realities, it is by no means unamenable to considerations of prestige. Like almost any other government, it can be placed by tactless and threatening gestures in a position where it cannot afford to yield even though this might be dictated by its sense of realism. The Russian leaders are keen judges of human psychology, and as such they are highly conscious that loss of temper and of self-control is never a source of strength in political affairs. They are quick to exploit such evidences of weakness. For these reasons, it is a *sine qua non* of successful dealing with Russia that the foreign government in question should remain at all times cool and collected and that its demands on Russian policy should be put forward in such a manner as to leave the way open for a compliance not too detrimental to Russian prestige.

In the light of the above, it will be clearly seen that the Soviet pressure against the free institutions of the western world is something that can be contained by the adroit and vigilant application of counter-force at a series of constantly shifting geographical and political points, corresponding to the shifts and manœuvres of Soviet policy, but which cannot be charmed or talked out of existence. . . .

It is clear that the United States cannot expect in the foreseeable future to enjoy political intimacy with the Soviet régime. It must continue to regard the Soviet Union as a rival, not a partner, in the political arena. It must continue to expect that Soviet policies will reflect no abstract love of peace and stability, no real faith in the possibility of a permanent happy coexistence of the Socialist and capitalist worlds, but rather a cautious, persistent pressure toward the disruption and weakening of all rival influence and rival power.

Balanced against this are the facts that Russia, as opposed to the western world in general, is still by far the weaker party, that Soviet policy is highly flexible, and that Soviet society may well contain deficiencies which will eventually weaken its own total potential. This would of itself warrant the United States entering with reasonable confidence upon a policy of firm containment, designed to confront the Russians with unalterable counter-force at every point where they show signs of encroaching upon the interests of a peaceful and stable world.

But in actuality the possibilities for American policy are by no means limited to holding the line and hoping for the best. It is entirely possible for the United States to influence by its actions the internal developments, both within Russia and throughout the international Communist movement, by which Russian policy is largely determined. This is not only a question of the modest measure of informational activity which this government can conduct in the Soviet Union and elsewhere, although that, too, is important. It is rather a question of the degree to which the United States can create among the peoples of the world generally the impression of a country which knows what it wants, which is coping successfully with the problems of its internal life and with the responsibilities of a World Power, and which has a spiritual vitality capable of holding its own among the major ideological currents of the time. To the extent that such an impression can be created and maintained, the aims of Russian Communism must appear sterile and quixotic, the hopes and enthusiasm of Moscow's sup-

porters must wane, and added strain must be imposed on the Kremlin's foreign policies. For the palsied decrepitude of the capitalist world is the keystone of Communist philosophy. Even the failure of the United States to experience the early economic depression which the ravens of the Red Square have been predicting with such complacent confidence since hostilities ceased would have deep and important repercussions throughout the Communist world.

By the same token, exhibitions of indecision, disunity and internal disintegration within this country have an exhilarating effect on the whole Communist movement. At each evidence of these tendencies, a thrill of hope and excitement goes through the Communist world; a new jauntiness can be noted in the Moscow tread; new groups of foreign supporters climb on to what they can only view as the band wagon of international politics; and Russian pressure increases all along the line in international affairs.

It would be an exaggeration to say that American behavior unassisted and alone could exercise a power of life and death over the Communist movement and bring about the early fall of Soviet power in Russia. But the United States has it in its power to increase enormously the strains under which Soviet policy must operate, to force upon the Kremlin a far greater degree of moderation and circumspection than it has had to observe in recent years, and in this way to promote tendencies which must eventually find their outlet in either the break-up or the gradual mellowing of Soviet power. For no mystical, Messianic movement—and particularly not that of the Kremlin—can face frustration indefinitely without eventually adjusting itself in one way or another to the logic of that state of affairs.

Thus the decision will really fall in large measure on this country itself. The issue of Soviet-American relations is in essence a test of the over-all worth of the United States as a nation among nations. To avoid destruction the United States need only measure up to its own best traditions and prove itself worthy of preservation as a great nation. . . . ■

Source: Walter Lippmann, *The Cold War* (New York: Harper and Row, 1947), pp. 18–20.

The Fallacy of Containment

I find it hard to understand how Mr. X could have recommended such a strategic monstrosity. For he tells us, no doubt truly, that the Soviet power "cannot be easily defeated or discouraged by a single victory on the part of its opponents," and that "the patient persistence by which it is animated" means that it cannot be "effectively countered" by "sporadic acts." Yet his own policy calls for a series of sporadic acts: the United States is to apply "counterforce" where the Russians encroach and when they encroach.

On his own testimony no single victory will easily defeat or discourage the patient persistence of the Kremlin. Yet Mr. X says that the United States should aim to win a series of victories which will cause the Russians to "yield on individual sectors of the diplomatic front." And then what? When the United States has forced the Kremlin to "face frustration indefinitely" there will "eventually" come "either the breakup or the gradual mellowing of the Soviet power."

There is, however, no rational ground for confidence that the United States could muster "unalterable counterforce" at all the individual sectors. The Eurasian continent is a big place, and the military power of the United States, though it is very great, has certain limitations which must be borne in mind if it is to be used effectively. We live on an island continent. We are separated from the theaters of conflict by the great oceans. We have a relatively small population, of which the greater proportion must in time of war be employed in producing, transporting and servicing the complex weapons and en-

gines which constitute our military power. The United States has, as compared with the Russians, no adequate reserves of infantry. Our navy commands the oceans and we possess the major offensive weapons of war. But on the ground in the interior of the Eurasian continent, as we are learning in the Greek mountains, there may be many "individual sectors" where only infantry can be used as the "counterforce."

These considerations must determine American strategy in war and, therefore, also in diplomacy, whenever the task of diplomacy is to deal with a conflict and a contest of power. The planner of American diplomatic policy must use the kind of power we do have, not the kind we do not have. He must use that kind of power where it can be used. He must avoid engagements in those "individual sectors of the diplomatic front" where our opponents can use the weapons in which they have superiority. But the policy of firm containment as defined by Mr. X ignores these tactical considerations. It makes no distinction among sectors. It commits the United States to confront the Russians with counterforce "at every point" along the line, instead of at those points which we have selected because, there at those points, our kind of sea and air power can best be exerted.

American military power is peculiarly unsuited to a policy of containment which has to be enforced persistently and patiently for an indefinite period of time. If the Soviet Union were an island like Japan, such a policy could be enforced by American sea and air power. The United States could, without great difficulty, impose a blockade. But the Soviet Union has to be contained on land, and "holding the line" is therefore a form of trench warfare.

Yet the genius of American military power does not lie in holding positions indefinitely. That requires a massive patience by great hordes of docile people. American military power is distinguished by its mobility, its speed, its range and its offensive striking force. It is, therefore, not an efficient instrument for a diplomatic policy of containment. It can only be the instrument of a policy which has as its objective a decision and a settlement. It can and should be used to redress the balance of power which has been upset by the war. But it is not designed for, or adapted to, a strategy of containing, waiting, countering, blocking, with no more specific objective than the eventual "frustration" of the opponent.

The Americans would themselves probably be frustrated by Mr. X's policy long before the Russians were.

* * *

At the root of Mr. X's philosophy about Russian-American relations and underlying all the ideas of the Truman Doctrine there is a disbelief in the possibility of a settlement of the issues raised by this war. Having observed, I believe quite correctly, that we cannot expect "to enjoy political intimacy with the Soviet regime," and that we must "regard the Soviet Union as a rival, not a partner in the political arena," and that "there can be no appeal to common purposes," Mr. X has reached the conclusion that all we can do is to "contain" Russia until Russia changes, ceases to be our rival, and becomes our partner.

The conclusion is, it seems to me, quite unwarranted. The history of diplomacy is the history of relations among rival powers, which did not enjoy political intimacy, and did not respond to appeals to common purposes. Nevertheless, there have been settlements. Some of them did not last very long. Some of them did. For a diplomat to think that rival and unfriendly powers cannot be brought to a settlement is to forget what diplomacy is about. There would be little for diplomats to do if the world consisted of partners, enjoying political intimacy, and responding to common appeals.

The method by which diplomacy deals with a world where there are rival powers is to organize a balance of power which deprives the rivals, however lacking in intimacy and however unresponsive to common appeals, of a good prospect of successful aggression. That is what a diplomat means by the settlement of a conflict among rival powers. He does not mean that they will cease to be rivals. He does not mean that they will all be converted to thinking and wanting the same things. He means that, whatever they think, whatever they want, whatever their ideological purposes, the balance of power is such that they cannot afford to commit aggression.

In our conflict with Russia a policy of settlement . . . would aim to redress the balance of power, which is abnormal and dangerous, because the Red Army has met the British and American armies in the heart of Europe. The division between east and west is at that military boundary line. The meeting of those armies caused the division. No state in eastern Europe can be independent of the Kremlin as long as the

Red Army is within it and all around it. No state in western Europe is independent while it is in effect in the rear of this military frontier. The presence of these non-European armies in the continent of Europe perpetuates the division of Europe. The Soviet government has been communist for thirty years. For more than a hundred years all Russian governments have sought to expand over eastern Europe. But only since the Red Army reached the Elbe River have the rulers of Russia been able to realize the ambitions of the Russian Empire and the ideological purposes of communism.

A genuine policy would, therefore, have as its paramount objective a settlement which brought about the evacuation of Europe. That is the settlement which will settle the issue which has arisen out of the war. The communists will continue to be communists. The Russians will continue to be Russians. But if the Red Army is in Russia, and not on the Elbe, the power of the Russian communists and the power of the Russian imperialists to realize their ambitions will have been reduced decisively.

Until a settlement which results in withdrawal is reached, the Red Army at the center of Europe will control eastern Europe and will threaten western Europe. In these circumstances American power must be available, not to "contain" the Russians at scattered points, but to hold the whole Russian military machine in check, and to exert a mounting pressure in support of a diplomatic policy which has as its concrete objective a settlement that means withdrawal.

Then we shall know what we are trying

to do. The Russians will know it. Europe will know it. We shall be trying to do a great thing which is simple and necessary: to settle the main actual consequences of this particular war, to put an end to the abnormal situation where Europe, one of the chief centers of civilization, though liberated from the Nazis, is still occupied by its non-European liberators.

We shall be addressing ourselves to an objective to which our own power is suited —be it in diplomacy or in war. We shall be seeking an end that all men can understand, and one which expresses faithfully our oldest and best tradition—to be the friend and the champion of nations seeking independence and an end to the rule of alien powers. ■

484

Source: Harry S. Truman, *Public Papers of the Presidents* (Washington, D.C.: U.S. Government Printing Office, 1964), 1948 volume, pp. 337–339.

American Measures For Peace

Anyone can talk peace. But only the work that is done for peace really counts.

I propose to describe the specific steps the United States has taken to obtain peace in the world. I propose, also, to discuss what further measures we must take, and what measures others must take, if our hopes for peace are to be fulfilled.

The United States has consistently done its part in meeting the requirements for a peaceful world.

We fought through World War II with only one purpose: to destroy the tyrants who tried to impose their rule on the world and enslave the people. We sought no territories; we asked for only token reparations. At the end of the war, we quickly dismantled the greatest military machine ever built by any nation. We withdrew and demobilized the American armies that had swept across Europe and the Pacific, leaving only minimum occupation forces in Germany, Austria, Japan, and Korea. The nations which our army had helped to liberate were left free to work out their postwar problems without interference from us.

That was not the course of a nation that sought to impose its will upon others. It was not the course of an aggressor.

Long before the fighting had ended, our Government began planning for a world organization which could provide security for all nations. At Dumbarton Oaks, at Yalta, at San Francisco, the United States led the way in preparing for a strong and useful United Nations. In the past 3 years we have taken a leading part in establishing the United Nations, and the related agencies—such as the World Bank and the Food and Agriculture Organization—which are fundamental to world peace and prosperity.

No action by the United States has revealed more clearly our sincere desire for peace than our proposal in the United Nations for the international control of atomic energy. In a step without precedent, we have voluntarily offered to share with others the secrets of atomic power. We ask only for conditions that will guarantee its use for the benefit of humanity—and not for the destruction of humanity.

To assist world economic recovery, we have contributed nearly $20 billion in loans and grants to other nations. American dollars have been invested generously in the cause of peace because we know what peace is worth.

This is a record of action in behalf of peace without parallel in history.

Many other nations have joined wholeheartedly with us in our work for peace. They share our desire for international control of atomic energy, for the early conclusion of peace treaties, for world economic recovery, and for the effective development of the United Nations.

Why then, after such great exertions and huge expenditures, do we live today in a twilight period, between war so dearly won and a peace that still eludes our grasp?

The answer is not hard to find.

It lies largely in the attitude of one nation—the Soviet Union.

Long before the war the United States established normal diplomatic and commercial relations with the Soviet Union. In doing so we demonstrated our belief that it was possible to get along with a nation whose economic and political system differs sharply from ours.

During the war we worked with the Soviet Union wholeheartedly in defeating the common enemy. In every way we could we tried to convince the Soviet Government that it was possible and necessary for allied unity to continue in the great task of establishing the peace. We hoped that the Soviet Union, secure in her own strength and doubly secure in respect of her allies, would accept full partnership in a peaceful world community.

The record, however, is clear for all to read. The Soviet Government has rejected the invitation to participate, freely and on equal terms, in a great cooperative program for reconstruction of Europe. It has constantly maneuvered for delay and for propaganda effect in every international conference. It has used the veto excessively and unreasonably in the Security Council of the United Nations. It has boycotted the "Little Assembly" and several special United Nations commissions. It has used indirect aggression against a number of nations in Eastern Europe and extreme pressure against others in the Middle East. It has intervened in the internal affairs of many other countries by means of Communist parties directed from Moscow.

The refusal of the Soviet Union to work with its wartime allies for world recovery and world peace is the most bitter disappointment of our time.

The great issues of world peace and world recovery are sometimes portrayed as disputes solely between the United States and the Soviet Union. This is not the case. The fact is that not a single one of the major unsettled questions of the postwar world is primarily a disagreement between

485

this country and the Soviet Union. We are not engaged in a struggle with the Soviet Union for any territory or for any economic gain. We have no hostile or aggressive designs against the Soviet Union or any other country. We are not waging a "cold war."

The cleavage that exists is not between the Soviet Union and the United States. It is between the Soviet Union and the rest of the world.

The great questions at stake today affect not only the United States and the Soviet Union; they affect all nations.

Whether it be the control of atomic energy, aggression against small nations, the German or the Austrian peace settlements, or any of the other questions, the majority of nations concerned have found a common basis for action. But in every case the majority agreement has been rejected, denounced, and openly attacked by the Soviet Union and her satellites whose policy she controls.

Let me repeat: the division has not been between the United States and the Soviet Union, but between the Soviet Union and the free nations of the world.

The United States is strongly devoted to the principle of discussion and negotiation in settling international differences. We do not believe in settling differences by force. There are certain types of disputes in international affairs which can and must be settled by negotiation and agreement.

But there are others which are not susceptible to negotiation.

There is nothing to negotiate when one nation disregards the principles of international conduct to which all the members of the United Nations have subscribed. There is nothing to negotiate when one nation habitually uses coercion and open aggression in international affairs.

What the world needs in order to regain a sense of security is an end to Soviet obstruction and aggression.

I will give you two clear illustrations of what I have in mind.

The situation in Greece has caused a great deal of uneasiness throughout the world. It has been the subject of a series of investigations on the part of commissions of the United Nations. The facts have been established over and over again by these investigations. They are clear beyond dispute. Some twenty thousand Greek guerrillas have been able to keep Greece in a state of unrest and to disrupt Greek recovery, primarily because of the aid and comfort they have been receiving from the neighboring countries of Bulgaria, Yugoslavia, and Albania.

Last October, the United Nations General Assembly adopted a resolution calling upon Bulgaria, Yugoslavia, and Albania to stop their illegal aid and comfort to the Greek rebels. This resolution was agreed to by more than two-thirds of the membership of the United Nations. But it has been boycotted by Russia.

The situation in Greece requires no special negotiation, or discussion, or conference.

On its own initiative the Soviet Government can cease its boycott of the United Nations recommendation. It can join with other nations in stopping illegal foreign support of the Greek guerrillas so that Greece may have an opportunity for peaceful reconstruction.

If the Soviet Union genuinely desires to make a contribution to the peace and recovery of the world, it can prove it in Greece.

The situation in Korea is also disturbing. There the Soviet Government has defied the clearly expressed will of an overwhelming majority of the United Nations, by boycotting the United Nations Temporary Commission on Korea. This commission was created last fall by the General Assembly to help set up a Korean national government based on free and democratic elections.

The Soviet boycott has prevented the residents of the northern zone of Korea from electing representatives to establish a unified national government for Korea.

The situation in Korea requires no special negotiation, or discussion, or conference.

On its own initiative, the Soviet Union can abandon its boycott of the United Nations Commission. It can permit the people of North Korea to work with their compatriots in the south in creating an independent and democratic nation.

If the Soviet Union genuinely desires to make a contribution to peace and recovery in the world, it can prove it in Korea.

In these questions, as in all others, there are practical ways for the Soviet Union to show its good faith by proper action.

The United States will always respond to an honest move by any nation to further the principles and purposes of the Charter of the United Nations.

But no nation has the right to exact a price for good behavior.

What is needed is a will for peace. What is needed is the abandonment of the absurd idea that the capitalistic nations will collapse and that the instability in international affairs will hasten their collapse, leaving the world free for communism. It is possible for different economic systems to live side by side in peace, one with the other, provided one of these systems is not determined to destroy the other by force.

I have said before and I repeat now: the door is always open for honest negotiations looking toward genuine settlements.

The door is not open, however, for deals between great powers to the detriment of other nations or at the expense of principle. We refuse to play fast and loose with man's hope for peace. That hope is too sacred to be trifled with for propaganda purposes, or selfish advantage, by any individual or nation. We are interested in peace—not in propaganda. ∎

Source: Henry A. Wallace, *New Republic*, January 12, 1948, pp. 13–14.

Peace Through the United Nations

In an address in Milwaukee, Wisconsin, on December 30, I laid down the principles which seem to me essential for a genuine plan for world recovery. I think the best use I can make of my space in the *New Republic* this week is to repeat what I said then, especially in view of the hostile reception and inadequate report given my ideas by most of the American press.

Yesterday I announced that there would be a new party, and to that end I announced that I am an independent candidate for the presidency in 1948.

My final decision was made solely on the basis of giving the American people a chance to vote for peace and security. I fear the die was cast when Truman came out for military aid to Greece and Turkey last March. Steadily during 1947 our help to foreign lands has been in the spirit of fighting Russia, not in the spirit of helping starving humanity. Steadily the military, the Wall Street press and the State Department have been waging psychological warfare against the American people to blind them to the fact that our unilateral help to Europe intervenes in the internal politics of nearly every Western European nation, that the ordinary European worker looks on it as naked imperialism—or even worse, in the case of Greece—and that in the end the cold war will end in bombs and expeditionary forces across Canada and the Scandinavian peninsula.

There are no more tragic victims of our insane policy, which will bankrupt us morally and financially, than the Greek people. Our first loan has been spent, Greek children still cry for milk, while the American-trained Greek army parades the severed heads of guerrillas through the streets, and a corrupt government decrees the death penalty for legitimate trade-union activities. The people of the world must see that there is another America than this Truman-led, Wall Street-dominated, military-backed group that is blackening the name of American democracy all over the world.

The original Marshall Plan speech sounded good to me when it was delivered. The principles of self-help, mutual aid and American support were the same that I had suggested on many occasions. The differences now are clear. They are fatal differences. When the Marshall Plan was announced, I declared that the Truman Doctrine would have to be scrapped to give it meaning. It has not been scrapped. With the Truman Doctrine as its core, the so-called European Recovery Program is a plan to interfere in the social, economic and political affairs of countries receiving aid. We are saying, "We will help you if you have our kind of government and subordinate your economy to ours."

We have invested $400 million in Greece and Turkey; $2 billion in China and $25 billion for our armed forces to support a foreign policy which leads to war, not peace. We *can* afford to invest in European reconstruction, *but* our policy must not require billions of dollars for arms, and millions of men in arms to back it up.

We can't stop communism or any other idea in Western Europe with military might or by supporting undemocratic governments. The bipartisan coalition has allied the American people with kings, fascists and reactionaries.

The Russians certainly aren't blameless for the cold war. But even if we should accept every charge made against the Russians, it does not excuse an American policy which runs contrary to American principles.

A practical policy must begin with genuine support for the United Nations. We have been ignoring the UN. We circumvented the UN in the name of "emergency" to send military help to Greece and Turkey. We killed UNRRA, which had Europe on the road to recovery. We ignored the UN in proposing the Marshall Plan. We must reaffirm our faith in the UN. It cannot succeed if the most powerful nation in the world destroys confidence in the principle of world organization and operates in direct violation of that principle. We can't talk the language of one world and use our economic and political power to split that one world in two.

Today, when there is almost unanimous agreement on the necessity for helping Europe, is the time to "get practical."

If we reject the Marshall Plan as it is now proposed to apply it, this does not mean that we are without a plan. We propose a plan based on world unity and friendship that will lay the foundation of peace, not a plan based on world division and conflict that sows the seeds of war. We propose a plan that will effectuate the fine words spoken by Secretary Marshall at Harvard last June—not a plan whose deeds contradict those words.

The experience of UNRRA proved that such a plan is eminently practical—that such a plan will work. That experience showed indeed that *only* such a plan will work for peace—not war.

In the past 15 months I have repeatedly indicated the elements of such a plan. Let me restate them in brief and concrete terms:

My plan calls for a proposal from the US to the UN for the establishment of a UN Reconstruction Fund, modeled after UNRRA, for the rehabilitation and reconstruction of the war-devastated lands in Europe and Asia to the end that their industry and agriculture may be restored and placed on a self-sustaining basis at the earliest possible moment.

I propose that this Reconstruction Fund be administered by an agency of the UN established for that purpose.

The Reconstruction Fund should be made up of contributions appropriated by our Congress and other nations possessed of the means, in an amount sufficient to finance an over-all five-year plan. A part of the fund may be in the form of loans and the balance in the form of a grant.

The UN agency should be directed to give priority in the allocation of funds to those nations which suffered most severely from Axis aggression. Allocations must be based solely on these considerations of merit and need, without regard to the character of the politics and social institutions of the recipient nations.

The allocation of funds by the UN agency must be made with scrupulous respect for the national sovereignty of all beneficiary countries. There must be no political or economic conditions attached to loans or grants. In particular, the UN agency must not make aid conditional

upon conformity by any nation with an over-all economic plan, but must leave each nation free fully to develop its own national economic plan. Aid must not be coupled with any restrictions upon the development by recipient nations of expanded or new industries, or any attempt made to require restrictions on full and free economic development as the price of assistance. Provision should be made that the funds, made available with due regard for sovereignty, are not wasted by graft and inefficiency, and that the expenditures are subject to review by a UN authority to make sure that there is not such graft and inefficiency.

The entire fund shall be used exclusively for peaceful purposes and no monies shall be available to finance the purchase of military supplies, armaments or war preparations.

Finally, the German industrial heartland in the Ruhr Valley should be placed under international administration and control by the Big Four, in order, first, that its resources may be made available to aid in the reconstruction of Europe and second, to guarantee that Germany shall never again be in a position to threaten the security of her neighbors or the peace of the world.

These are essentials for world peace. The greatest, richest, most powerful nation in the world can afford to take leadership on such constructive proposals. We must take leadership as well on a program of disarmament which will outlaw all mass methods of destruction and permit the efforts of workers and farmers the world over to be used in creating the abundance our resources, science and know-how make possible.

A sound, principled foreign policy is essential. It is not the whole story. The evidence of good faith which we must give in foreign affairs must be backed up with vigorous action here at home. I predict that unless our investments in foreign reconstruction are backed with sound domestic planning to control inflation, we shall witness a deadly resurgence of isolationism. The Greek, Turkish and Chinese programs have already created skepticism about the wisdom of foreign aid. Only a one-world policy of investment in peace can win continued support from the American people. A failure to protect the worker, farmer and consumer from the inflationary effects of huge appropriations for arms and unsound investments abroad will be tragic.

In addition to sound economic planning here at home, we must back a new foreign policy with demonstrations that when we speak of "democracy" we really mean it.

Jim Crow in all its forms must go.

The poll tax and restrictions to suffrage must go.

Civil liberties must be restored and protected.

The good name of American democracy must be strengthened. There is no room for continued feudalism in twentieth-century America. We must end Wall Street's colonial rule of the South and West.

These things are essential, not only to our national welfare, but to the cause of world peace.

We do not fool the peoples of the world when we maintain undemocratic practices within our own borders. Wall Street men find it expedient to use the language of humanitarianism but the peoples of the world know their records. They know that these men have opposed every domestic proposal for the health, education, social security and general welfare at home. The war lords and money changers must be driven from their places of power if the good name of American democracy is to be preserved the world around. It is that course upon which we have embarked.

Progressives by the millions voted for Franklin Roosevelt every time he ran for President. Conservatives and reactionaries from 1932 through 1944 voted for Republican presidential candidates. Until I announced for President, Americans who elected Franklin Roosevelt four times had no choice in 1948. We will never compromise with reaction. I call upon all progressive people in the United States—and you constitute the overwhelming majority of the American people—to work and vote for progress and peace in 1948 and at every election thereafter. I ask you to enlist for the duration of the war against privilege, against monopoly, against poverty. I ask you to join in the fight for peace. This is a great undertaking. Your first opportunity to stand up and be counted is 1948. We shall continue to fight as long as we live. We shall win.

The great hopes of the people here at home and throughout the world that the last war would begin a new era of progressive development are being dissipated by men who oppose progress and by those who compromise with the opponents of progress. During the war we said: "Strong in the faith of the Lord, we who fight in the people's cause will not stop fighting until that cause is won."

That cause has not yet been won. We are still fighting—we have, indeed, only started to fight. ■

ANALYZING THE DEBATE OVER THE CONTAINMENT POLICY

You have just read four views concerning the nature of the foreign policy the United States ought to adopt toward the U.S.S.R. in the postwar world. These statements, in essence, make up the debate over the "containment" policy formulated in the Truman Administration. Many disagreements are reflected in the different positions advanced. Some are value disagreements, that is, disagreements in belief about the rightness or wrongness of certain goals or means. Others are analytic disagreements, or disagreements over the assumptions about reality employed, over how data are used as evidence, and over how conclusions should be drawn. These methods of judging led the authors of the four statements to advocate different policies toward the Soviet Union.

490

1 Identify the dominant values, such as peace, justice, security, and so forth, expressed in each statement. What are the major differences? What are the major similarities? Are any of the values expressed common to all four spokesmen? If so, are these values applied differently to the specific situation?

2 What assumptions about reality do the writers make? What conclusions does each statement reach concerning United States foreign policy? What facts are used to support these? What are the major areas of agreement or disagreement in the way each writer analyzes the problem?

3 Two of the writers are political leaders, the other two, foreign policy analysts. Do you see any differences in the methods of analysis used or in the type of arguments employed? If so, what are they? ∎

THE PUBLIC'S RESPONSE TO THE CONTAINMENT POLICY

During the years immediately after World War II the central concern in global politics was the deterioration of relations between the United States and Communist Russia. The containment policy was the Truman Administration's response to this situation. The cartoons and opinion polls indicate the reactions of the American press and public to Russia and her leaders as well as to specific aspects of the United States' policy of containment.

1 What attitudes toward the Russians are expressed in the polls conducted prior to the end of World War II? Do these attitudes, as reflected in the polls, change or remain consistent between 1945 and 1952?

2 How do the attitudes toward Russia expressed in the political cartoons compare with the attitudes expressed in the polls?

3 Judging from the polls taken regarding specific Truman Administration policies toward Russia, what hypotheses can you make as to how Americans viewed the containment policy? ■

On The Russians

U.S. July 15, '42 Look at the list and select the words that you think describe the Russian people best. Each respondent was handed a card with descriptive terms. (OPOR)

Hard-working	61%*
Intelligent	16
Ordinary	25
Radical	25
Warlike	14
Practical	18
Artistic	10
Conceited	3
Quick-tempered	10
Lazy	5
Unimaginative	14
Sly	7
Treacherous	10
Aristocratic	3
Cruel	9
Ignorant	20
Rude	6
Dull	13
Brave	48
Religious	10
Arrogant	2
Progressive	24
Honest	19
Impossible to characterize	16
No answer	2

* Since respondents were asked to pick as many descriptive terms as they liked, percentages add to considerably more than 100.

U.S. Sept. '45 Would you describe Russia as a peace-loving nation, willing to fight only if she thinks she has to defend herself, or as an aggressive nation that would start a war to get something she wants? (FOR)

Peace-loving	38.6%
Aggressive	37.8
Both (volunteered)	8.4
Don't know	15.2

WILL RUSSIA COOPERATE AFTER THE WAR?
1942–1945

1942	Yes	No	Uncertain
February	38	37	25
June	41	33	26
November	52	26	22
1943			
January	46	29	25
June	48	27	25
December	51	27	22
1944			
January	40	37	23
June	47	36	17
November	47	35	18
1945			
February	55	31	14
May	45	38	17
August	54	30	16
October	41	43	16

Percentage Believing Russia "Out to Rule the World"

June, 1946	58
October, 1947	76
March, 1948	77
May, 1949	66
January, 1950	70

491

From *Public Opinion Quarterly* (Princeton, N. J.: Princeton University Press).

"EVERYTHING'S O.K.—I'M BACKING UP!"

Hutton, *Philadelphia Inquirer*

492

U.S. — AIPO — Mar. 28, '47 Would you favor sending American civilian experts over to Greece to help supervise the uses to which this money will be put?*

Yes	83%
No	14
No opinion	3

* Question asked of the 82% of a sample who had heard or read about Truman's speech to Congress asking for $400 million to help Greece and Turkey.

U.S. — AIPO — Mar. 28, '47 Would you favor sending American civilian experts over to Turkey to help supervise the uses to which this money will be put?*

Yes	77%
No	17
No opinion	6

U.S. — AIPO — Mar. 28, '47 Would you favor sending American military advisers to train the Greek army?*

Yes	37%
No	54
No opinion	9

U.S. — AIPO — Mar. 28, '47 Would you favor sending them [American military advisers] to train the Turkish army?*

Yes	33%
No	55
No opinion	12

U.S. — AIPO — Mar. 28, '47 Do you think that lending money to aid Greece and Turkey is or is not likely to get us into war?*

Is likely	30%
Not likely	54
No opinion	16

U.S. — AIPO — Mar. 28, '47 Do you think that the present Greek government has the backing of the majority — that is, more than half — of the Greek people?*

Yes	33%
No	25
No opinion	42

U.S. — AIPO — Mar. 28, '47 Do you think that the present Turkish government has the backing of the majority — that is, more than half — of the Turkish people?*

Yes	34%
No	14
No opinion	52

U.S. — AIPO — Mar. 28, '47 Suppose other nations find themselves in the same fix as Greece. Do you think the United States will have to do something about it?*

Yes	68%
No	20
No opinion	12

U.S. — AIPO — Mar. 28, '47 Generally speaking, should the United States take a strong stand in European affairs, or should we try to get out of European affairs?

Strong stand	58%
Get out	32
No opinion	10

* Questions asked of the 82% of a sample who had heard or read about Truman's speech to Congress asking for $400 million to help Greece and Turkey.

V FOR VICTORY

shop, *St. Louis Star-Times*

U.S. — AIPO — Mar. 28, '47 Do you approve or disapprove of the bill asking for 250 million dollars to aid Greece? Asked of a national cross-section of persons who had heard or read about the issue of aid to Greece.

	Yes	No	No opinion
National total	56%	32%	12%
World War II veterans*	57	36	7
BY POLITICS**			
Democrats	56%	32%	12%
Republicans	56	31	13
BY EDUCATION**			
College	65%	26%	9%
High school	57	30	13
Grade or no school	48	36	16

* Veterans' figures released for publication Apr. 2, '47.
** Additional breakdowns released for publication Apr. 4, '47.

U.S. — AIPO — Apr. 13, '47 Do you think the problem of aid to Greece and Turkey should be turned over to the United Nations organization?

IN COMPARISON WITH MAR. 28		
	Mar. 28	Today
Yes	56%	63%
No	25	23
No opinion	19	14

AIPO — Feb. 8, '48 What is your understanding of the purpose of this [Marshall] Plan? Asked of 71% of a U.S. sample familiar with the plan at this date.

To help Europe	56%
To curb Communism	8
To foster better understanding with Europe	2
Other answers	8
No opinion	26
	100%*

* 100% of those familiar with the plan.

AIPO — Feb. 8, '48 and Mar. 3, '48 Have you heard or read about the Marshall Plan?

IN COMPARISON WITH OTHER COUNTRIES

	Have heard	Have not
England	89%	11%
France	91	9
Italy	78	22
U.S. — July, '47	49	51
U.S. — Oct., '47	49	51
U.S. — Nov., '47	61	39
U.S. — Dec., '47	64	36
U.S. — Feb., '48	71	29
U.S. — Mar., '48	79	21

AIPO — Feb. 8, '48 and Mar. 3, '48 What is your opinion of the [Marshall] Plan? Asked of those who had heard or read of the plan.

IN COMPARISON WITH OTHER COUNTRIES

	Favor	Oppose	No opinion
England	60%	20%	20% = 100%*
France	60	13	27
Italy	65	14	21
U.S. — Nov., '47	47	15	38
U.S. — Feb., '48	56	17	27
U.S. — Mar., '48	57	18	25

U.S. OPINION IN MARCH BY GEOGRAPHICAL SECTION

New England and Mid-Atlantic	61%	16%	23%
East Central	50	25	25
West Central	56	18	26
South	57	14	29
Far West	58	16	26

* 100% of those familiar with the plan.

NORC — Sept. 15, '48 Would you approve or disapprove of President Truman going to Europe to talk with Stalin to try to settle the differences between the United States and Russia? Asked in April and again in June.

	Approve	Disapprove	Undecided
April '48	52%	40%	8%
June '48	53	41	6

494

JUMPING-OFF PLACE

I REALLY DON'T CARE ABOUT GOING SWIMMING HERE, BUT SINCE YOU'VE BUILT IT I SUPPOSE I SHOULD USE IT!

arrish, *Chicago Tribune-New York News* Syndicate, Inc.

40% of the April sample and 41% of the June sample who disapproved the idea of Truman trying to settle matters with Stalin were asked to give their reasons. Following is a tabulation based on the number of disapproving respondents.

	April '48	June '48
Oppose meeting under any circumstances	35%	27%
It won't do any good; Russia won't compromise, can't be trusted	16%	9%
It won't do any good (no specific blame of Russia)	16	12
It isn't necessary, can agree without special meeting	3	6
Oppose meeting as stated, but don't necessarily object to idea	54	60
Truman is not man to send; criticisms of Truman	23	30
Let them come here, Truman should not go there	18	16
It would be a sign of weakness, appeasement	13	14
Other reasons	9	11
Don't know, just disapprove	2	2
	100%	100% of those questioned

NORC — Sept. 15, '48 In what way should we be firmer [with Russia]? Asked in June of 53% of the sample who believed we should be even firmer than at present.

State our position clearly; warn Russia of our attitude	13%
Be firmer in economic matters; don't send them anything	12
Be firm about aggression; stop spreading Communism	9
Be firmer militarily; strengthen our armed forces	6
Be firmer in UN; eliminate veto power; make UN work	5
Be firm about Germany, Japan, Korea, Berlin, peace treaties	5
Fight her now; declare war; drop an atom bomb on her	2
Other suggestions	10
Don't know; just be firm; vague, irrelevant answers	42

THE SPEAKER'S PLATFORM

Marcus © 1949 by the *New York Times*

496

AIPO — May 18 and July 8, '49 The United States and various North Atlantic countries, such as Canada, England, France, Norway, and Holland have signed a mutual defense pact — that is, each country has agreed to come to the defense of any of the other countries if it is attacked. Do you think the U.S. Senate should or should not ratify (approve) the North Atlantic Security Pact.

	Should	Should not	No opinion
May '49	67%	12%	21%
July '49	67	15	18

OPINION IN MAY BY EDUCATION

	Should	Should not	No opinion
College	80%	12%	8%
High school	73	11	16
Grammar school	58	12	30

JULY OPINION BY GEOGRAPHICAL SECTION

	Should	Should not	No opinion
New England and Mid-Atlantic	67%	17%	16%
East central	64	14	22
West central	69	10	21
South	68	13	19
Far West	72	14	14

AIPO — May 18, '49 Do you think that the U.S. should or should not supply arms and war materials to the North Atlantic nations if they agree to provide us with air bases and any other help that they may be able to give?

	Should	Should not	No opinion
National total	65%	16%	19%

BY EDUCATION

	Should	Should not	No opinion
College	75%	17%	8%
High school	71	14	15
Grade school	55	18	27

AIPO — June 5, '49 Some people say that the North Atlantic Security Pact is a plan for the United States and other member nations to get ready for an attack on Russia. Other people say that the North Atlantic Pact is a plan only for defense in case the U.S. or any member nation is attacked. Which do you agree with? Asked only of those who had heard or read about the Atlantic Pact.

	Defense	Ready to attack	No opinion	Unfamiliar with pact
National total	53%	5%	7%	35%

BY EDUCATION

	Defense	Ready to attack	No opinion	Unfamiliar with pact
College	79%	6%	7%	8%
High school	60	6	6	28
Grade school	39	4	8	49

RUDE AWAKENING

Shoemaker, *Chicago Daily News*

AIPO — **June 26, '49** Do you think Russia will cooperate with us in world affairs?

Yes	20%
No	62
No opinion	18

AIPO — **Feb. 2, '51** In general, who do you think is winning the cold war — Russia or the United States? Asked only of those who were able to give a generally correct definition in answer to the question: Will you tell me what the term "cold war" means?

	IN COMPARISON WITH EARLIER DATES				
	Russia	U.S.	Neither	No opinion	Unfamiliar
Current survey	30%	9%	12%	4%	45%
March 1950	23	16	5	14	42
December 1948	15	17	16	6	46
	CURRENT OPINION BY EDUCATION				
College	55%	11%	17%	2%	15%
High school	34	7	14	4	41
Grade school	19	9	10	4	58

UNINTENTIONAL CUPID

Yardley, *The Sun*, Baltimore, Maryland

ASIA: Containment Becomes Global

By 1948 the tensions of the cold war had reached a very high pitch. A Communist coup in Czechoslovakia in February seemed to underscore the dangers of the further expansion of Russian influence in central Europe. A few months later the Russians blockaded all overland traffic from West Germany to the Allied zones of occupation in Berlin. The United States responded with a spectacular airlift of supplies to Berlin, and the Western European nations formed the North Atlantic Treaty Organization in 1949 to coordinate the military defense of Western Europe. The Senate of the United States, after a sharp debate, ratified the treaty which made the United States a member of NATO. Indeed, the United States provided the major contributions of troops, naval vessels, and air forces to the new organization.

Meanwhile, the Chinese civil war between Chiang Kai-shek's Nationalist government and the Chinese Communist forces, which had been renewed with full fury after the defeat of Japan, reached a climax in 1949. The corrupt and inefficient government of Chiang Kai-shek began to crumble before the sustained and well-organized attacks of Mao Tse-tung's forces, despite large infusions of American military and financial aid. Convinced that the Chiang Kai-shek government lacked the will and capacity to prevail, Truman's new Secretary of State, Dean Acheson, issued a White Paper to the effect that the United States would not intervene any longer and that the Chinese political situation would have to be settled by the Chinese people themselves. Acheson's White Paper produced a vigorous debate over the policies

that the United States should pursue in Asia—a debate that became even more bitter when the United States went to the aid of South Korea in June 1950, after that country had been attacked by North Korean forces supplied with Soviet Russian tanks and other military weapons. And within six months, the American and United Nations forces in Korea found themselves fighting the Chinese army, which had been sent across the Yalu River to aid the North Koreans. Thus Asia was drawn into the conflict between the free-world nations and the Communist bloc of nations, and for the United States the containment policy became a global rather than merely a European policy.

The following statements are representative selections from the debate over Asian policy that took place during the cold war period. The first was prepared by Secretary of State Dean Acheson, a key figure in the Truman Administration. Acheson's summary of American-Chinese relations was prepared at the request of President Truman and became known as the White Paper on China.

The second selection was written by Owen Lattimore, an American official who spent more than twenty years in China, Japan, and the borderland between China and Russia. In 1943 and 1944, Mr. Lattimore was Deputy Director of the Office of War Information in charge of the Far East Division. Largely because of his views on Asian policy, Mr. Lattimore was later subjected to considerable harassment by a Senate investigatory committee headed by Senator Joseph McCarthy.

The final statement included in this section was made by Walter H. Judd, who

was a United States representative from Minnesota during the cold war years. ∎

Dean Acheson's White Paper on China, *Department of State Bulletin*, Department of State Publication 3573, Far Eastern Series Item 913, 1949.

China Policy Re-examined

In accordance with your wish, I have had compiled a record of our relations with China, special emphasis being placed on the last five years. This record is being published and will therefore be available to the Congress and to the people of the United States.

Although the compilation is voluminous, it necessarily covers a relatively small part of the relations between China and the United States. Since the beginning of World War II, these relations have involved many Government departments and agencies. The preparation of the full historical record of that period is by no means yet complete. Because of the great current interest in the problems confronting China, I have not delayed publication until the complete analysis could be made of the archives of the National Military Establishment, the Treasury Department, the Lend-Lease Administration, the White House files and many other official sources. However, I instructed those charged with the compilation of this document to present a record which would reveal the salient facts which determined our policy toward China during this period and which reflect the execution of that policy. This is a frank record of an extremely complicated and most unhappy period in the life of a great country to which the United States has long been attached by ties of closest friendship. No available item has been omitted because it contains statements critical of our policy or might be the basis of future criticism. The inherent strength of our system is the responsiveness of the Government to an informed and critical public opinion. It is precisely this informed and critical public opinion which totalitarian governments, whether Rightist or Communist, cannot endure and do not tolerate.

The interest of the people and the Government of the United States in China goes far back into our history. Despite the distance and broad differences in background which separate China and the United States, our friendship for that country has always been intensified by the religious, philanthropic and cultural ties which have united the two peoples, and has been attested by many acts of good will over a period of many years, including the use of the Boxer indemnity for the education of Chinese students, the abolition of extraterritoriality during the Second World War, and our extensive aid to China during and since the close of the war. The record shows that the United States has consistently maintained and still maintains those fundamental principles of our foreign policy toward China which include the doctrine of the Open Door, respect for the administrative and territorial integrity of China, and opposition to any foreign domination of China. It is deplorable that respect for the truth in the compilation of this record makes it necessary to publish an account of facts which reveal the distressing situation in that country. I have not felt, however, that publication could be withheld for that reason.

The record should be read in the light of conditions prevailing when the events occurred. It must not be forgotten, for example, that throughout World War II we were allied with Russia in the struggle to defeat Germany and Italy, and that a prime object of our policy was to bring Russia into the struggle against Japan in time to be of real value in the prosecution of the war. In this period, military considerations were understandably predominant over all others. Our most urgent purpose in the Far East was to defeat the common enemy and save the lives of our own men and those of our comrades-in-arms, the Chinese included. We should have failed in our manifest duty had we pursued any other course.

In the years since V-J Day, as in the years before Pearl Harbor, military considerations have been secondary to an earnest desire on our part to assist the Chinese people to achieve peace, prosperity and internal stability. The decisions and actions of our Government to promote these aims necessarily were taken on the basis of information available at the time. Throughout this tragic period, it has been fully realized that the material aid, the military and technical assistance, and the good will of the United States, however abundant, could not of themselves put China on her feet. In the last analysis, that can be done only by China herself.

Two factors have played a major role in shaping the destiny of modern China.

The population of China during the eighteenth and nineteenth centuries doubled, thereby creating an unbearable pressure upon the land. The first problem which every Chinese Government has had to face is that of feeding this population. So far none has succeeded. The Kuomintang attempted to solve it by putting many land-reform laws on the statute books. Some of these laws have failed, others have been ignored. In no small measure, the predicament in which the National Government finds itself today is due to its

failure to provide China with enough to eat. A large part of the Chinese Communists' propaganda consists of promises that they will solve the land problem.

The second major factor which has shaped the pattern of contemporary China is the impact of the West and of Western ideas. For more than three thousand years the Chinese developed their own high culture and civilization, largely untouched by outside influences. Even when subjected to military conquest the Chinese always managed in the end to subdue and absorb the invader. It was natural therefore that they should come to look upon themselves as the center of the world and the highest expression of civilized mankind. Then in the middle of the nineteenth century the heretofore impervious wall of Chinese isolation was breached by the West. These outsiders brought with them aggressiveness, the unparalleled development of Western technology, and a high order of culture which had not accompanied previous foreign incursions into China. Partly because of these qualities and partly because of the decay of Manchu rule, the Westerners, instead of being absorbed by the Chinese, introduced new ideas which played an important part in stimulating ferment and unrest.

By the beginning of the twentieth century, the combined force of overpopulation and new ideas set in motion that chain of events which can be called the Chinese revolution. It is one of the most imposing revolutions in recorded history and its outcome and consequences are yet to be foreseen. Out of this revolutionary whirlpool emerged the Kuomintang, first under the leadership of Dr. Sun Yat-sen, and later

Generalissimo Chiang Kai-shek, to assume the direction of the revolution. The leadership of the Kuomintang was not challenged until 1927 by the Chinese Communist party which had been organized in the early twenties under the ideological impetus of the Russian revolution. It should be remembered that Soviet doctrine and practice had a measurable effect upon the thinking and principles of Dr. Sun Yat-sen, particularly in terms of economics and party organization, and that the Kuomintang and the Chinese Communists cooperated until 1927 when the Third International demanded a predominant position in the Government and the army. It was this demand which precipitated the break between the two groups. To a large extent the history of the period between 1927 and 1937 can be written in terms of the struggle for power between the Kuomintang and the Chinese Communists, with the latter apparently fighting a losing battle. During this period the Kuomintang made considerable progress in its efforts to unify the country and to build up the nation's financial and economic strength. Somewhere during this decade, however, the Kuomintang began to lose the dynamism and revolutionary fervor which had created it, while in the Chinese Communists the fervor became fanaticism.

Perhaps largely because of the progress being made in China, the Japanese chose 1937 as the departure point for the conquest of China proper, and the goal of the Chinese people became the expulsion of a brutal and hated invader. Chinese resistance against Japan during the early years of the war compelled the unqualified admiration of freedom-loving peoples throughout the world. Until 1940 this resistance was largely without foreign support. The tragedy of these years of war was that physical and human devastation to a large extent destroyed the emerging middle class which historically has been the backbone and heart of liberalism and democracy.

In contrast also to the unity of the people of China in the war against Japan were the divided interests of the leaders of the Kuomintang and of the Chinese Communists. It became apparent in the early forties that the leaders of the Government, just as much as the Communist leaders, were still as preoccupied with the internal struggle for power as they were with waging war against Japan. Once the United States became a participant in the war, the Kuomintang was apparently convinced of the ultimate defeat of Japan and saw an opportunity to improve its position for a show-down struggle with the Communists. The Communists, for their part, seemed to see in the chaos of China an opportunity to obtain that which had been denied them before the Japanese war, namely, full power in China. This struggle for power in the latter years of the war contributed largely to the partial paralysis of China's ability to resist.

It was precisely here that two of the fundamental principles of United States policy in regard to China—noninterference in its internal affairs and support of its unity and territorial integrity—came into conflict and that one of them also conflicted with the basic interests of the Allies in the war against Japan. It seemed highly probable in 1943 and 1944 that, unless the Chinese could subordinate their

Robert Capa, Magnum

internal interests to the larger interest of the unified war effort against Japan, Chinese resistance would become completely ineffective and the Japanese would be able to deprive the Allies of valuable bases, operating points and manpower in China at a time when the outcome of the war against Japan was still far from clear. In this situation and in the light of the paramount necessity of the most vigorous prosecution of the war, in which Chinese interests were equally at stake with our own, traditional concepts of policy had to be adapted to a new and unprecedented situation.

After Pearl Harbor we expanded the program of military and economic aid which we had inaugurated earlier in 1941 under the Lend-Lease Act. That program, described in Chapter I of the attached record, was far from reaching the volume which we would have wished because of the tremendous demands on the United States from all theaters of a world-wide war and because of the difficulties of access to a China all of whose ports were held by the enemy. Nevertheless it was substantial.

Representatives of our Government, military and civilian, who were sent to assist the Chinese in prosecuting the war soon discovered that, as indicated above, the long struggle had seriously weakened the Chinese Government not only militarily and economically, but also politically and in morale. The reports of United States military and diplomatic officers reveal a growing conviction through 1943 and 1944 that the Government and the Kuomintang had apparently lost the crusading spirit that won them the people's loyalty during

the early years of the war. In the opinion of many observers they had sunk into corruption, into a scramble for place and power, and into reliance on the United States to win the war for them and to preserve their own domestic supremacy. The Government of China, of course, had always been a one-party rather than a democratic government in the Western sense. The stresses and strains of war were now rapidly weakening such liberal elements as it did possess and strengthening the grip of the reactionaries who were indistinguishable from the war lords of the past. The mass of the Chinese people were coming more and more to lose confidence in the Government.

It was evident to us that only a rejuvenated and progressive Chinese Government which could recapture the enthusiastic loyalty of the people could and would wage an effective war against Japan. American officials repeatedly brought their concern with this situation to the attention of the Generalissimo and he repeatedly assured them that it would be corrected. He made, however, little or no effective effort to correct it and tended to shut himself off from Chinese officials who gave unpalatable advice. In addition to a concern over the effect which this atrophy of the central Chinese administration must have upon the conduct of the war, some American observers, whose reports are also quoted in the attached record, were concerned over the effect which this deterioration of the Kuomintang must have on its eventual struggle, whether political or military, with the Chinese Communists. These observers were already fearful in 1943 and 1944 that the National

Government might be so isolating itself from the people that in the postwar competition for power it would prove itself impotent to maintain its authority. Nevertheless, we continued for obvious reasons to direct all our aid to the National Government.

This was of course the period during which joint prosecution of the war against Nazi Germany had produced a degree of cooperation between the United States and Russia. President Roosevelt was determined to do what he could to bring about a continuance in the postwar period of the partnership forged in the fire of battle. The peoples of the world, sickened and weary with the excesses, the horrors, and the degradation of the war, shared this desire. It has remained for the postwar years to demonstrate that one of the major partners in this world alliance seemingly no longer pursues this aim, if indeed it ever did.

When Maj. Gen. Patrick J. Hurley was sent by President Roosevelt to Chungking in 1944 he found what he considered to be a willingness on the part of the National Government and the Chinese Communists to lay aside their differences and cooperate in a common effort. Already they had been making sporadic attempts to achieve this result.

Previously and subsequently, General Hurley had been assured by Marshal Stalin that Russia had no intention of recognizing any government in China except the National Government with Chiang Kai-shek as its leader. It may be noted that during the late war years and for a time afterwards Marshal Stalin reiterated these views to American officials. He and Molotov expressed the view that China should look to the United States as the principal possible source of aid. The sentiments expressed by Marshal Stalin were in large part incorporated in the Sino-Soviet treaty of 1945.

From the wartime cooperation with the Soviet Union and from the costly campaigns against the Japanese came the Yalta Agreement. The American Government and people awaited with intense anxiety the assault on the main islands of Japan which it was feared would cost up to a million American casualties before Japan was conquered. The atomic bomb was not then a reality and it seemed impossible that the war in the Far East could be ended without this assault. It thus became a primary concern of the American Government to see to it that the Soviet Union enter the war against Japan at the earliest possible date in order that the Japanese Army in Manchuria might not be returned to the homeland at the critical moment. It was considered vital not only that the Soviet Union enter the war but that she do so before our invasion of Japan, which already had been set for the autumn of 1945.

At Yalta, Marshal Stalin not only agreed to attack Japan within two or three months after V-E Day but limited his "price" with reference to Manchuria substantially to the position which Russia had occupied there prior to 1904. We for our part, in order to obtain this commitment and thus to bring the war to a close with a consequent saving of American, Chinese and other Allied lives, were prepared to and did pay the requisite price. Two facts must not, however, be lost sight of in this connection. First, the Soviet Union, when she finally did enter the war against Japan,

could in any case have seized all the territories in question and considerably more regardless of what our attitude might have been. Second, the Soviets, on their side in the Sino-Soviet Treaty arising from the Yalta Agreement, agreed to give the National Government of China moral and material support and moreover formalized their assurances of noninterference in China's internal affairs. Although the unexpectedly early collapse of Japanese resistance later made some of the provisions of the Yalta Agreement seem unnecessary, in the light of the predicted course of the war at that time they were considered to be not only justified but clearly advantageous. Although dictated by military necessity, the Agreement and the subsequent Sino-Soviet Treaty in fact imposed limitations on the action which Russia would, in any case, have been in a position to take.

For reasons of military security, and for those only, it was considered too dangerous for the United States to consult with the National Government regarding the Yalta Agreement or to communicate its terms at once to Chungking. We were then in the midst of the Pacific War. It was felt that there was grave risk that secret information transmitted to the Nationalist capital at this time would become available to the Japanese almost immediately. Under no circumstances, therefore, would we have been justified in incurring the security risks involved. It was not until June 15, 1945, that General Hurley was authorized to inform Chiang Kai-shek of the Agreement.

In conformity with the Russian agreement at Yalta to sign a treaty of friendship and alliance with Nationalist China, nego-

tiations between the two nations began in Moscow in July 1945. During their course, the United States felt obliged to remind both parties that the purpose of the treaty was to implement the Yalta Agreement—no more, no less—and that some of the Soviet proposals exceeded its provisions. The treaty, which was signed on August 14, 1945, was greeted with general satisfaction both in Nationalist China and in the United States. It was considered that Russia had accepted definite limitations on its activities in China and was committed to withhold all aid from the Chinese Communists. On September 10, however, our embassy in Moscow cautioned against placing undue confidence in the Soviet observance of either the spirit or letter of the treaty. The subsequent conduct of the Soviet Government in Manchuria has amply justified this warning.

When peace came the United States was confronted with three possible alternatives in China: (1) it could have pulled out lock, stock, and barrel; (2) it could have intervened militarily on a major scale to assist the Nationalists to destroy the Communists; (3) it could, while assisting the Nationalists to assert their authority over as much of China as possible, endeavor to avoid a civil war by working for a compromise between the two sides.

The first alternative would, and I believe American public opinion at the time so felt, have represented an abandonment of our international responsibilities and of our traditional policy of friendship for China before we had made a determined effort to be of assistance. The second alternative policy, while it may look attractive theoretically and in retrospect, was wholly impracticable. The Nationalists had been unable to destroy the Communists during the 10 years before the war. Now after the war the Nationalists were, as indicated above, weakened, demoralized, and unpopular. They had quickly dissipated their popular support and prestige in the areas liberated from the Japanese by the conduct of their civil and military officials. The Communists on the other hand were much stronger than they had ever been and were in control of most of North China. Because of the ineffectiveness of the Nationalist forces which was later to be tragically demonstrated, the Communists probably could have been dislodged only by American arms. It is obvious that the American people would not have sanctioned such a colossal commitment of our armies in 1945 or later. We therefore came to the third alternative policy whereunder we faced the facts of the situation and attempted to assist in working out a *modus vivendi* which would avert civil war but nevertheless preserve and even increase the influence of the National Government.

As the record shows, it was the Chinese National Government itself which, prior to General Hurley's mission, had taken steps to arrive at a working agreement with the Communists. As early as September 1943 in addressing the Kuomintang Central Executive Committee, the Generalissimo said, "we should clearly recognize that the Communist problem is a purely political problem and should be solved by political means." He repeated this view on several occasions. Comprehensive negotiations between representatives of the Government and of the Communists, dealing with both military cooperation and civil admin-

istration, were opened in Sian in May 1944. These negotiations, in which Ambassador Hurley later assisted at the invitation of both parties between August 1944 and September 1945, continued intermittently during a year and a half without producing conclusive results and culminated in a comprehensive series of agreements on basic points on October 11, 1945, after Ambassador Hurley's departure from China and before General Marshall's arrival. Meanwhile, however, clashes between the armed forces of the two groups were increasing and were jeopardizing the fulfillment of the agreements. The danger of widespread civil war, unless the negotiations could promptly be brought to a successful conclusion, was critical. It was under these circumstances that General Marshall left on his mission to China at the end of 1945.

As the account of General Marshall's mission and the subsequent years in chapters V and VI of the underlying record reveals, our policy at that time was inspired by the two objectives of bringing peace to China under conditions which would permit stable government and progress along democratic lines, and of assisting the National Government to establish its authority over as wide areas of China as possible. As the event proved, the first objective was unrealizable because neither side desired it to succeed: the Communists because they refused to accept conditions which would weaken their freedom to proceed with what remained consistently their aim, the communization of all China; the Nationalists because they cherished the illusion, in spite of repeated advice to the contrary from our military representatives,

that they could destroy the Communists by force of arms.

The second objective of assisting the National Government, however, we pursued vigorously from 1945 to 1949. The National Government was the recognized government of a friendly power. Our friendship, and our right under international law alike, called for aid to the Government instead of to the Communists who were seeking to subvert and overthrow it. The extent of our aid to Nationalist China is set forth in detail in chapters V, VI, VII and VIII of the record and need not be repeated here. The National Government had in 1945, and maintained until the early fall of 1948, a marked superiority in manpower and armament over their rivals. Indeed during that period, thanks very largely to our aid in transporting, arming and supplying their forces, they extended their control over a large part of North China and Manchuria. By the time General Marshall left China at the beginning of 1947, the Nationalists were apparently at the very peak of their military successes and territorial expansion. The following year and a half revealed, however, that their seeming strength was illusory and that their victories were built on sand.

The crisis had developed around Manchuria, traditional focus of Russian and Japanese imperialism. On numerous occasions, Marshal Stalin had stated categorically that he expected the National Government to take over the occupation of Manchuria. In the truce agreement of January 10, 1946, the Chinese Communists agreed to the movement of Government troops into Manchuria for the purpose of restoring Chinese sovereignty over this

504

area. In conformity with this understanding the United States transported sizable government armies to the ports of entry into Manchuria. Earlier the Soviet Army had expressed a desire to evacuate Manchuria in December 1945, but had remained an additional two or three months at the request of the Chinese Government. When the Russian troops did begin their evacuation, the National Government found itself with extended lines of communications, limited rolling stock and insufficient forces to take over the areas being evacuated in time to prevent the entry of Chinese Communist forces, who were already in occupation of the countryside. As the Communists entered, they obtained the large stocks of matériel from the Japanese Kwantung Army which the Russians had conveniently "abandoned." To meet this situation the National Government embarked on a series of military campaigns which expanded the line of its holdings to the Sungari River. Toward the end of these campaigns it also commenced hostilities within North China and succeeded in constricting the areas held by the Communists.

In the spring of 1946 General Marshall attempted to restore peace. This effort lasted for months and during its course a seemingly endless series of proposals and counterproposals were made which had little effect upon the course of military activities and produced no political settlement. During these negotiations General Marshall displayed limitless patience and tact and a willingness to try and then try again in order to reach agreement. Increasingly he became convinced, however, that twenty years of intermittent civil war

between the two factions, during which the leading figures had remained the same, had created such deep personal bitterness and such irreconcilable differences that no agreement was possible. The suspicions and the lack of confidence were beyond remedy. He became convinced that both parties were merely sparring for time, jockeying for military position and catering temporarily to what they believed to be American desires. General Marshall concluded that there was no hope of accomplishing the objectives of his mission.

Even though for all practical purposes General Marshall, by the fall of 1946, had withdrawn from his efforts to assist in a peaceful settlement of the civil war, he remained in China until January 1947. One of the critical points of dispute between the Government and the Communists had been the convocation of the National Assembly to write a new constitution for China and to bring an end to the period of political tutelage and of one-party government. The Communists had refused to participate in the National Assembly unless there were a prior military settlement. The Generalissimo was determined that the Assembly should be held and the program carried out. It was the hope of General Marshall during the late months of 1946 that his presence in China would encourage the liberal elements in non-Communist China to assert themselves more forcefully than they had in the past and to exercise a leavening influence upon the absolutist control wielded by the reactionaries and the militarists. General Marshall remained in China until the Assembly had completed its work. Even though the proposed new framework of government appeared satis-

factory, the evidence suggested that there had been little shift in the balance of power.

In his farewell statement, General Marshall announced the termination of his efforts to assist the Chinese in restoring internal peace. He described the deep-seated mutual suspicion between the Kuomintang and the Chinese Communist Party as the greatest obstacle to a settlement. He made it clear that the salvation of China lay in the hands of the Chinese themselves and that, while the newly adopted constitution provided the framework for a democratic China, practical measures of implementation by both sides would be the decisive test. He appealed for the assumption of leadership by liberals in and out of the Government as the road to unity and peace. With these final words he returned to Washington to assume, in January 1947, his new post as Secretary of State.

As the signs of impending disaster multiplied, the President in July 1947, acting on the recommendation of the Secretary of State, instructed Lt. Gen. Albert C. Wedemeyer to survey the Chinese scene and make recommendations. In his report, submitted on September 19, 1947, the General recommended that the United States continue and expand its policy of giving aid to Nationalist China, subject to these stipulations:

1. That China inform the United Nations of her request for aid.

2. That China request the United Nations to bring about a truce in Manchuria and request that Manchuria be placed under a Five-Power guardianship or a trusteeship.

3. That China utilize her own resources,

Henri Cartier-Bresson, Magnum

reform her finances, her Government and her armies, and accept American advisers in the military and economic fields.

General Wedemeyer's report, which fully recognized the danger of Communist domination of all China and was sympathetic to the problems of the National Government, nevertheless listed a large number of reforms which he considered essential if that Government were to rehabilitate itself.

It was decided that the publication at that time of a suggestion for the alienation of a part of China from the control of the National Government, and for placing that part under an international administration to include Soviet Russia, would not be helpful. In this record, the full text of that part of General Wedemeyer's report which deals with China appears as an annex to chapter VI.

The reasons for the failures of the Chinese National Government appear in some detail in the attached record. They do not stem from any inadequacy of American aid. Our military observers on the spot have reported that the Nationalist armies did not lose a single battle during the crucial year of 1948 through lack of arms or ammunition. The fact was that the decay which our observers had detected in Chungking early in the war had fatally sapped the powers of resistance of the Kuomintang. Its leaders had proved incapable of meeting the crisis confronting them, its troops had lost the will to fight, and its Government had lost popular support. The Communists, on the other hand, through a ruthless discipline and fanatical zeal, attempted to sell themselves as guardians and liberators of the people. The Nationalist armies did not have to be defeated; they disintegrated. History has proved again and again that a regime without faith in itself and an army without morale cannot survive the test of battle.

The record obviously cannot set forth in equal detail the inner history and development of the Chinese Communist Party during these years. The principal reason is that, while we had regular diplomatic relations with the National Government and had the benefit of voluminous reports from our representatives in their territories, our direct contact with the Communists was limited in the main to the mediation efforts of General Hurley and General Marshall.

Fully recognizing that the heads of the Chinese Communist Party were ideologically affiliated with Moscow, our Government nevertheless took the view, in the light of the existing balance of forces in China, that peace could be established only if certain conditions were met. The Kuomintang would have to set its own house in order and both sides would have to make concessions so that the Government of China might become, in fact as well as in name, the Government of all China and so that all parties might function within the constitutional system of the Government. Both internal peace and constitutional development required that the progress should be rapid from one party government, with a large opposition party in armed rebellion, to the participation of all parties, including the moderate non-communist elements, in a truly national system of government.

None of these conditions has been realized. The distrust of the leaders of both the Nationalist and Communist Parties for each other proved too deep-seated to permit final agreement, notwithstanding temporary truces and apparently promising negotiations. The Nationalists, furthermore, embarked in 1946 on an over-ambitious military campaign in the face of warnings by General Marshall that it not only would fail but would plunge China into economic chaos and eventually destroy the National Government. General Marshall pointed out that though Nationalist armies could, for a period, capture Communist-held cities, they could not destroy the Communist armies. Thus every Nationalist advance would expose their communications to attack by Communist guerrillas and compel them to retreat or to surrender their armies together with the munitions which the United States has furnished them. No estimate of a military situation has ever been more completely confirmed by the resulting facts.

The historic policy of the United States of friendship and aid toward the people of China was, however, maintained in both peace and war. Since V-J Day, the United States Government has authorized aid to Nationalist China in the form of grants and credits totaling approximately 2 billion dollars, an amount equivalent in value to more than 50 percent of the monetary expenditures of the Chinese Government and of proportionately greater magnitude in relation to the budget of that Government than the United States has provided to any nation of Western Europe since the end of the war. In addition to these grants and credits, the United States Government has sold the Chinese Government large quantities of military and civilian war surplus property with a total procurement cost of over 1 billion dollars, for which the agreed realization to the United States was 232 million dollars. A large proportion of the military supplies furnished the Chinese armies by the United States since V-J Day has, however, fallen into the hands of the Chinese Communists through the military ineptitude of the Nationalist leaders, their defections and surrenders, and the absence among their forces of the will to fight.

It has been urged that relatively small amounts of additional aid—military and economic—to the National Government would have enabled it to destroy communism in China. The most trustworthy military, economic, and political information available to our Government does not bear out this view.

A realistic appraisal of conditions in China, past and present, leads to the conclusion that the only alternative open to the United States was full-scale intervention in behalf of a Government which had lost the confidence of its own troops and its own people. Such intervention would have required the expenditure of even greater sums than have been fruitlessly spent thus far, the command of Nationalist armies by American officers, and the probable participation of American armed forces—land, sea, and air—in the resulting war. Intervention of such a scope and magnitude would have been resented by the mass of the Chinese people, would have diametrically reversed our historic policy, and would have been condemned by the American people.

It must be admitted frankly that the American policy of assisting the Chinese people in resisting domination by any foreign power or powers is now confronted with the gravest difficulties. The heart of China is in Communist hands. The Communist leaders have foresworn their Chinese heritage and have publicly announced their subservience to a foreign power, Russia, which during the last 50 years, under czars and Communists alike, has been most assiduous in its efforts to extend its control in the Far East. In the recent past, attempts at foreign domination have appeared quite clearly to the Chinese people as external aggression and as such have been bitterly and in the long run successfully resisted. Our aid and encouragement have helped them to resist. In this case, however, the foreign domination has been masked behind the facade of a vast crusading movement which apparently has seemed to many Chinese to be wholly indigenous and national. Under these circumstances, our aid has been unavailing.

The unfortunate but inescapable fact is that the ominous result of the civil war in China was beyond the control of the government of the United States. Nothing that this country did or could have done within the reasonable limits of its capabilities could have changed that result; nothing that was left undone by this country has contributed to it. It was the product of internal Chinese forces, forces which this country tried to influence but could not. A decision was arrived at within China, if only a decision by default.

And now it is abundantly clear that we must face the situation as it exists in fact. We will not help the Chinese or ourselves by basing our policy on wishful thinking. We continue to believe that, however tragic may be the immediate future of China and however ruthlessly a major portion of this great people may be exploited by a party in the interest of a foreign imperialism, ultimately the profound civilization and the democratic individualism of China will reassert themselves and she will throw off the foreign yoke. I consider that we should encourage all developments in China which now and in the future work toward this end.

In the immediate future, however, the implementation of our historic policy of friendship for China must be profoundly affected by current developments. It will necessarily be influenced by the degree to which the Chinese people come to recognize that the Communist regime serves not their interests but those of Soviet Russia and the manner in which, having become aware of the facts, they react to this foreign domination. One point, however, is clear. Should the Communist regime lend itself to the aims of Soviet Russian imperialism and attempt to engage in aggression against China's neighbors, we and the other members of the United Nations would be confronted by a situation violative of the principles of the United Nations Charter and threatening international peace and security.

Meanwhile our policy will continue to be based upon our own respect for the Charter, our friendship for China, and our traditional support for the Open Door and for China's independence and administrative and territorial integrity. ■

Source: Owen Lattimore, "Rebuilding Our Policy in Asia," *Atlantic Monthly,* vol. 185, no. 1 (January 1950), pp. 21–23.

Toward A New China Policy

When the White Paper on China was published last summer, one of its main purposes, beyond a doubt, was to shock the public into realization that an era of policy in Asia had closed. The Department of State has been in search of a new policy ever since. The search has been headed by a top-drawer committee consisting of Dr. Raymond B. Fosdick of the Rockefeller Foundation and President Everett N. Case of Colgate University, under the chairmanship of Ambassador-at-Large Philip C. Jessup. It has held conferences and consultations which prove that it realizes that in launching a major new policy it is as essential to take soundings of opinion at home as it is to calculate the forces abroad with which the policy must deal.

In clearing the way for a fresh approach, it is well to remember that it is never possible to sit down and draft an "ideal" policy as if no previous policy had existed. There is always the problem of disentangling the new policy from the lingering effects of whatever it was that went wrong with the old policy.

The White Paper has documented the reasons why the type of policy represented by support for Chiang Kai-shek has, in recent months, done more harm than good to the interests of the United States. Nor is there any modification of this type of policy that promises well for the future. In face of the temper of Asia today, to force any American nominee into the role of a Chiang Kai-shek is to condemn him in the eyes of his own people. To try to line up a team of little Chiang Kai-sheks, when support of the once great Chiang has failed, would be a confession of futility.

For the Chiang Kai-shek whose fall dragged American prestige with it had been in his time a unique figure in Asia, who had captured the imagination of his people as a leader during the war, but failed to hold their confidence as the builder of a new social and political structure after the war.

The eclipse of Chiang has not even left behind the moral prestige of a good but losing fight in defense of a weak cause. On the contrary, the Kuomintang, under the increasingly jealous and narrow leadership of Chiang, put up the worst possible defense of a cause that was originally good and should have won.

It is not probable that the new China can be brought into line by economic coercion. The Chinese Communists need to achieve only a minimum level of economic stability in order to make their regime politically tolerable enough to the majority of the Chinese people to prevent widespread risings. It would be exceedingly unwise to assume that they will fail to achieve this minimum. The record shows that during the years when their strongholds were in the worst regions of chronic famine in China they handled with competence the elemental problems of food and distribution.

A quick survey shows that there is no country in Asia that can serve as a substitute for China under the Kuomintang, as an instrument of the kind of American policy that tried, through support of the Kuomintang, to control the balance of power in Asia.

India, in spite of Communist accusations, is not under a "Kuomintang" type of government, nor is Nehru a Chiang Kai-shek.

India is anti-Communist, and wary of Russia, but it is not anti-Russian to the extent of being willing to serve in the front line against Russia. Nor will India offer to the United States the economic ascendancy that Kuomintang China was willing to offer. The bankers and industrialists of India are stronger than those of China. Having thrown off British political control, they will not willingly come under American control.

Japan, though docile in defeat, cannot be made a satisfactory instrument of American policy. There are only two alternatives in Japan. The first is for the United States to keep Japan alive by "blood transfusions" of raw materials and credits. Under heavy enough subsidy—the cost is currently estimated at half a billion dollars a year—Japan can be given the surface appearance of a willing ally; but the reality will be overcommitment of American resources to a distant and vulnerable region.

Under the second alternative, Japan can keep itself alive by coming to terms, economically and politically, with its neighbors in Asia, and especially with Communist-controlled China, which is Japan's natural supplier of iron ore and coking coal. Under this alternative, Japan cannot become a trusted American ally. Its own interests will compel it to balance and bargain between what it can get out of Asia and what it can get out of America. The best that Japan can hope for in the way of true independence is independence of maneuver; and it is the honestly patriotic Japanese who will insist on a national policy of maneuver.

Southeast Asia is a region of no supreme

power. Europe cannot possibly recover the power that it once exercised in its colonial domains. The power lost by Europe has not fallen to America, and cannot be created afresh by America. Yet, at the same time, no nation in Southeast Asia has yet won its own revolution, as China has, and not one has the power to direct its own future regardless of friendly relations with Europe and America. The region as a whole demands three-way European-American-Asian compromises, the basis of which must be the restoration of economic activity. Europe must make greater political concessions than it has yet been willing to make. The United States must, for the sake of Europe, make economic grants to Southeast Asia and not simply grants to finance recovery of European economic control over Southeast Asia. The nationalist leaders of Southeast Asia must be persuaded that any sacrifices they are asked to make are not designed to give priority to the interests of Europe, but to bring joint benefits to Asia and Europe, on terms that advance, even if they do not completely satisfy, the Asian aspiration to equality.

Such minor countries as the Philippines and Korea cannot be made major bases of American action. South Korea, especially, is an American liability. It is doubtful how long the present regime in South Korea can be kept alive. The mere effort to keep it alive is a bad advertisement which continually draws attention to a band of little and inferior Chiang Kai-sheks who as a barrier against the Communists have the backing of the hated, Japanese-trained police but not the people, and have lost the respect of groups and movements throughout Asia which would like, with American backing, to move toward a future democracy.

Great wariness is needed in American handling of the relationship between China and Russia. The United States cannot assume that Russia will move in and take over direct control in China, and will thus become subject to heavy economic and strategic strains. It is dangerous to assume that there will be a diversion of Russian resources toward Asia that will limit Russia's ability to maneuver in Europe. Recent developments in the Far East have been favorable to Russia, but not in a way that lessens the resources that Russia can deploy toward Europe.

When such a move as an economic *cordon sanitaire* around China is considered, policy toward Russia is also involved. Blockade would increase Chinese dependence on Russia, but probably would not force Russia to undertake a large program in China. It is possible for China to get along for years at a more comfortable subsistence level than that which prevailed during the long years of the war with Japan and the civil war.

When an old policy will no longer work, it is a fundamental error to try to make it work by simply "turning on more juice." Fortunately, however, a new policy can attain positive objectives.

Policy in Asia and policy toward Russia, whether the future holds peace or war, have a bearing on each other. It certainly cannot yet be said, however, that regional wars in Asia to stop the spread of Communism, involving a major over-all commitment of American resources, have become either inevitable or desirable for their own sake. Nor can it be said that, in the event of an armed conflict undertaken for the purpose of forcing Russia back from Europe, the Far East would be a decisive or even an advantageous field of operation.

Long-range policy must always keep in sight both alternatives—war and peace. If there is to be war, Russia can be defeated only in Russia—not in North Korea, Viet Nam, or even China. Sound policy should therefore avoid premature or excessive strategic deployment in the Far East. If peace can be maintained for a long period, it will be possible primarily because of stabilization of the relations between the United States and Russia. Sound policy should therefore aim at the maximum flexibility. If mutually acceptable agreements with Russia should become possible, American policy in Asia should be in a position to contribute to the necessary negotiations. It should not be so mired down in local situations that major American-Russian negotiations are actually hampered.

At the same time, any new departure in United States policy in Asia must be proof against the accusation of "appeasing" Communism as a doctrine or Russia as a state. At this point, politics at home interact on policy abroad. Any proposed United States policy in Asia that is attacked in America itself as a bid for better relations with Russia runs the danger of being defeated.

On the other hand, any United States policy that is interpreted in various countries in Asia as a maneuver to create a league against Russia will merely increase the ability of those countries to bargain with Russia, as well as with the United States. It will also increase the identification, in those areas, between nationalism and Communism.

There is only one way to escape this dilemma. United States policy should aim to increase the ability of countries in Asia to do without Russia, by encouraging a steady improvement of the three-way economic relationship between Asia, Europe, and America, including the resumption of the supply of raw materials from Asia, the sale of Europe's manufactures in Asia, and American financing both of industrialization in Asia and recovery in Europe. The American financing should be undertaken as a sound enterprise in increasing production and consumption, not as a doling out of subsidies to keep the economies of Asia and Europe stagnantly alive.

Even China is within reach of this kind of policy, because many of the things that China needs can be got in better quality and greater quantity from the United States than from Russia. Such a policy is much more modest in aim than a policy of organizing hostility to Russia on a grand scale; but the aim is at least attainable, whereas the aim of a unified and organized hostility to Russia throughout Asia is unattainable.

In organizing non-dependence on Russia as an alternative to hostility against Russia, United States policy in Europe and Asia must be coördinated. Europe cannot become healthy by accepting American subsidy as a permanent "new order," replacing world trade. America is not strong enough to subsidize Europe, coerce Asia, stockpile against Russia, and maintain a prosperous democracy in the United States, all four at the same time. Most of Asia is strong enough to resist reconquest by Eu-

rope, but with the exception of China is not strong enough to threaten to close its doors entirely to European and American trade.

The grounds for compromise therefore exist. They are: less control over Asia than Europe wants; less political independence in some countries, and less economic independence in most countries, than Asia wants; more socialism, more state enterprise, and more neighborly relations with Russia than America wants.

On these grounds of compromise, United States policy in Asia can be rebuilt successfully enough not only to stabilize Asia, but to contribute to the stabilization of the world.

To implement a policy of this general character, the first step should be to channel all the necessary agreements through the United Nations. There has been an increasing tendency to make agreements, when they can be made, outside of the United Nations, in order to enhance national prestige, and to bring to the United Nations chiefly those debates that end in stalemate. There is no better way to mobilize American public opinion afresh than to bring to the United Nations negotiations that end in agreement.

For the problem of the recognition of the new government of China, the United Nations offers the ideal avenue to a solution. If, with no pressure against China from the United States, a majority of non-Communist countries in Europe, Latin America, and Asia should vote to seat new Chinese representatives to the United Nations, the United States should not vote against that verdict. Deferment to the majority among the non-Communist nations

would come gracefully from the United States, and would be a blow to the Russian propaganda that the United States seeks to dictate to the block that it leads.

After recognition in the United Nations, it should be made clear that direct relations between Washington and Peking depend on the friendliness or unfriendliness of Peking, not Washington. For the United States to penalize the Chinese people for having a government not approved in advance by Washington would be a diplomatic mistake that would have repercussions throughout Asia. For the Chinese government to inflict hardship on the Chinese people by denying them trade with America would be a mistake that would register instantly throughout Asia, and most deeply of all in the minds of the Chinese people.

It would be foolish to think that the United States could ever win the real friendship of a Communist government. It would be equally foolish to go on neglecting the fact that people under a Communist government can only bring real pressure to bear on their government when it is the people, rather than the government, who benefit from friendly relations with the United States. ∎

Source: Speech Delivered by Walter H. Judd to the United States House of Representatives.

Our Blundering Asian Policy

I should like to approach the problems we face today as a result of the Korean invasion much as a doctor approaches a body at the autopsy table: to make an honest examination of our mistakes. In the present crisis, we need to discover how we made the miscalculations that have brought us for the second time in one decade to the brink of a world war. Both times it began with the very same error: failure to realize how important it is to our own security that the opposite shores of the Pacific as well as of the Atlantic be in the hands of friends instead of enemies; failure to understand that it is imperative to U. S. security that the nations of Asia be independent and friendly to ourselves and the other democratic free nations of the world, instead of organized and controlled either by Japan's totalitarian militarism or by the Soviet Union's imperialism.

For almost 100 years our forefathers did not make the mistake we have made. They supported whatever government was in China, whether good, bad or indifferent, rather than let China's potential might come under any outside power that might be hostile to ourselves.

That was our basic policy and it was sound. We got into trouble in Asia only when we abandoned it in 1931 after Japan invaded Manchuria. To the credit of President Hoover and Secretary of State Stimson, they saw the danger and recommended that the League of Nations take a strong stand, pledging our support. But the free world refused to take strong action against that aggression.

By 1940 and 1941 President Roosevelt and Secretary of State Hull reawakened to the fact that it was essential to our security to keep Japan from getting control of the manpower, territory and resources of China and then of the rest of Asia. So they took a belated stand against Japan's further expansion, which, after we had systematically built her up to the point where she was strong enough to attack us, led of course to Pearl Harbor.

But our Government's return to the principle of maintaining the independence of China was short-lived. As we approached the end of the war in 1945, the desire to get the Soviet Union to join us against Japan and to coöperate in forming the United Nations led our leaders to sell out the principles they themselves had declared in the Atlantic Charter. They invited the Soviet Union into Manchuria and gave her control of its major ports and railroads although at Cairo they had promised unequivocally that Manchuria would be returned to China. Thus was set up the situation which has led us in five years to the brink of another world war.

So the first finding in the autopsy is that twice in little more than a decade we made the same mistake of imagining that what was happening in Europe was more likely to get us into war than what was happening in Asia.

The second finding is that in both wars we ourselves helped bring on the trouble by putting expediency ahead of principle. In the '30's we helped the aggressor, Japan, instead of the victim, China.

In the '40's we bribed Russia by giving her China's territory and then appeased Communism in China while denouncing those who were resisting it.

In Europe we insisted that in order to get our help the governments must keep the Communists out, but in China we insisted that in order to get our help the government must take the Communists in.

We had better begin to recognize the potentialities in Asia. It has great undeveloped natural resources and human resources. More than half the people of the world live in Asia. Which way they go is likely to be the decisive question of this century.

At the end of the last war the Soviets had about 200,000,000 people under their control. Now, with their satellites in Europe and what they have seized in Asia, they have almost 800,000,000. We of the free Western world are almost 800,000,000 people. The two roughly balance. Who determines which way the balance is to tip? The remaining 700,000,000, of course. And where do they live? On the periphery of China—in Korea, Japan, Formosa, the Philippines, Indonesia, Indo-China, Siam, Malaya, Burma, India, Pakistan. These 700,000,000 people, who can tip the balance of power between the Soviet world and the free world, are still on the fence. Which way are they to go—with us or with the Soviets? All the other problems on the international front depend on that.

And in determining which way they are to go, China has always been and still is the crucial area. The Communists have always realized this fact. Back in 1927 Earl Browder was in China with other leaders of the Communist hierarchy to help the Reds seize complete control of China as the Bolsheviks had done in Russia ten years before. Chiang Kai-shek was scheduled to be in China what Kérensky had been in Russia—an interim leader to be overthrown by the Reds as soon as they had defeated the war lords in southern and central China. But Chiang was strong enough to block the 1927 Red rebellion in China.

If the Communists had succeeded in their plans, it would have advanced their program of world conquest by at least a decade. Naturally they have hated Chiang fiercely, working always to weaken and discredit him and the Chinese Government until they could take over China.

It will be incomprehensible to historians why some in the U. S. State Department should also have made it a major project for the last seven years to discredit and destroy the one man who more than all others bought us years of time in this fight to the death with an enemy which he knew and has warned all along was our enemy as much as China's.

Here is a sentence from a 1937 letter by Mao Tse-tung, now president of the so-called People's Democratic Republic in Peking:

"We feel that, when we achieve victory, this victory will be of considerable help to the struggle of the American people for liberation."

You see, after they have conquered and subdued China, then they will be in a position to help liberate us too from our capitalistic tyranny. They understood correctly what our Government refused to see, that Communist victory in China would gravely weaken our position in the world, would make us vulnerable to attacks like that in Korea, would increase the burdens and drains on our strength.

In the Communist *Daily Worker* for December 2, 1945, are the official instructions given by William Z. Foster, head of the Communist Party in this country, to the national committee of the Party:

"On the international scale, the key task is to stop American intervention in China."

Which is Communist lingo for "stop American assistance to China."

The Communists and their stooges both inside and outside our Government knew, as everyone else should have known, that without outside assistance the Chinese Government could not possibly recover from the strains of war. They knew that, if they could persuade us to withdraw our support from China, its power to resist would be worn down and the country at last be taken over.

The success of the Communists in beguiling us into stopping effective assistance to China led of course not to peace but to war—first in China and now in Korea. So the third finding in the autopsy is that the Kremlin has been vastly smarter than our Government in understanding where the real keys to world power are.

However, some people besides the Communists have long understood this. In 1947 General MacArthur said to me:

"Our failure to help the government of China effectively at the end of the war, with its otherwise insuperable problems, particularly the Communist rebellion, will turn out, I fear, to be the greatest single blunder in the history of the United States. For the first time in our relations with Asia, we confused the paramount strategic interests of the United States in that area with an internal purification problem in China."

Let me pursue further the question of why the loss of China to Communist con-

Henri Cartier-Bresson, Magnum

trol is the key to present events in the Far East. It is due in large part to China's central geographical position in Asia. State Department spokesmen for years have talked almost casually of walling off China and then building up the countries around her. But if we let the hub of a wheel be chopped out, how can you hold together to make anything useful out of the individual spokes? Korea is just one of the spokes.

Among the mistakes that led to the Korean tragedy, the first was at Yalta, where we granted to Russia rights in Manchuria which did not belong to us and did so without even the knowledge of the Chinese to whom they did belong and to whom we had solemnly promised at Cairo that they would be returned.

There is no way we can build a world order that will be just and peaceful without international morality, and we cannot get international morality by breaking commitments. It was wrong when Hitler did it; it was wrong when Japan did it; it was wrong when the Kremlin did it; it was wrong when we did it. Most of our troubles today flow right from the expediencies of Yalta.

A second mistake was the decision by military men in Washington to divide Korea along the 38th parallel and assign the Russians to accept the Japanese surrender north of that parallel while we were moving our troops in to accept surrender south of it. The line chosen was just about the worst possible one that could have been picked. Division along the 38th parallel made it impossible for either side to survive without a lot of assistance from the outside. The best agriculture is south of the line; most of the good coal, water

power and industries are north of it. And there is no evidence that any division at all was necessary.

A third mistake was that for the first three years after V-J Day we refused to train armed forces to defend South Korea, although we knew the Russians were feverishly developing large forces in North Korea and had large and experienced units made up of Koreans in both Siberia and Manchuria.

One hears people ask, How did the North Korean armies become such fanatical fighters, such skillful warriors? First, because those who are actually North Koreans have been in training for as much as five years. Second, no one yet knows how many of them are not North Koreans but Siberian Koreans trained by the Russians. On top of that, there are somewhere between 50,000 and 100,000 Manchurian Koreans who have been trained and have fought with the Chinese Communists in Manchuria. They too have had battle experience and long indoctrination.

A fourth mistake was the withdrawal of our own troops in June of last year. On November 20, 1948, the Korean National Assembly passed a resolution urging that United States troops remain in Korea until the security forces of the republic became capable of maintaining national security. Instead, our Army decided that Korea was not of great strategic advantage to us— and it was not. So it pulled out before the South Koreans had had a chance to build the strength necessary to hold their own.

That brings us to the biggest error of all—the announcement by the President on last January 5 that we were not going to provide any military aid or advice to Chi-

nese forces on Formosa, those Chinese who have been fighting Communism for 23 years—most of the time alone—and who still have the courage to fight it. The Secretary of State enlarged upon the President's statement in a press conference:

"We are not going to get involved militarily in any way on the island of Formosa."

Those statements gave public notice to the Kremlin that the door to Formosa was open as far as we were concerned, and they could walk right in.

Then on January 12, 1950, the Secretary of State was reported as saying that our security line runs from the Aleutians through Japan and Okinawa to the Philippines. The occupants of the Kremlin looked at the map and found that Korea, like Formosa, was beyond our line and therefore would not be defended by us. So they moved in. Why should anyone be surprised?

In view of all this, why did the President reverse the previous policy and send troops back into Korea? It was not because Korea had strategic value to us, or because of any possible material gain to ourselves.

We had to do it, when it came to a showdown, because of the moral factors involved and the political objectives at stake. If we had failed to take a stand against this further and particularly bold and unprovoked Communist aggression, then not only Korea but the United Nations would have gone down just as the League of Nations did when it failed to act against aggression. Who in Asia—or Europe, for that matter—could again put any confidence in us or in the United Nations? Formosa would go. The Philippines would go. Indo-China and the rest of southeast Asia would go. Then Europe would go, because it cannot become self-supporting without Asia.

We had either to resist this aggression in Korea or withdraw to the North American continent. Those were the only choices we had.

The Kremlin embarked long ago on a vast program of world conquest. Never in history has such a military expansion stopped until it was checked. Our only choice has been whether we would check it early when we are still strong and have allies and most of the world is with us, or wait until we stand alone.

You ask, May this action lead to all-out war? Of course it may lead to war; but not to take it certainly would have led to war, and very possibly to our destruction. Great as are the risks of the decision that has been made, the risks of further indecision would be greater.

As a matter of fact, there are some grounds for encouragement. Our mistakes and miscalculations are being recognized and acknowledged. That is the first step toward their correction.

Moreover, we are arriving at last at a clear diagnosis: Communists in Asia are not likely to be accepted much longer as simple agrarian reformers. Communist movements are seen to be not spontaneous peasant uprisings but organized aggression completely subservient to and directed from the Kremlin.

And we have quit running backward. At last we are beginning to grapple with the problem instead of deluding ourselves that it does not exist, or at least is not serious.

For the first time, the doctrine of con-

taining Communism until it breaks from its inner weaknesses and cruelties has a chance to succeed, because for the first time we are to try it. Another favorable factor is that it is better to have the showdown over a case of naked premeditated aggression against the United Nations-sponsored Republic of Korea, with a government chosen in a supervised election in which a substantial percentage of the people voted, than to have the issue drawn over Hong Kong or Indo-China, for example. Our moral case is stronger because the issues in Korea are clear and uncompromised.

There are only two things to be afraid of in this whole world situation. One is that we might fail to understand the nature or underestimate the strength, the determination, the wide infiltration, the cruel ruthlessness of the forces of the enemy that are against us. Americans dare not fool themselves longer. It would be fatal.

The other is that we might fail to understand the nature or underestimate the size, the strength, the wide distribution, even behind the Iron Curtain, of the forces of freedom that are for us. That would be just as deadly a mistake.

If as a result of this cruel attack upon the free Republic of Korea we come to understand at last the full import of Communism's crusade for enslavement of the world, and rededicate ourselves to the crusade for freedom which has been America's historic mission, then what looks now like total disaster can conceivably bring some ultimate benefit; it can be the beginning of the end for the Kremlin's tyranny.

A lot of time has been lost; it is late, but I believe not yet too late. If we will mobilize fully and organize effectively the

moral, the material and the military resources of ourselves and of all free peoples under imaginative, courageous and inspiring leadership, then the tide of tyranny that threatens everything we count precious can be turned back. ■

OPINION POLLS AND THE KOREAN WAR

Ordinarily, public opinion polls are reported in an immediate context. However, increasing numbers of interpretative articles which compare the poll data on one event or issue over a period of time have appeared. These seek to summarize polling data in order to help the reader understand the fluctuations and trends of opinion. In the following article prepared by the Gallup Poll, conclusions are drawn from a number of polls taken on the question of the Korean War.

1 What does the trend of opinion indicate about the public's view of containment during the Korean War? Does this trend seem to favor the policies advocated by Acheson? By Lattimore? By Judd?

2 How does the insertion of news events into the summary influence the way the polls will be read and interpreted? How do events influence poll results?

3 Do you think the polls used as evidence for these conclusions are as sophisticated and complete as others you have seen earlier? Would you agree with the major conclusions stated or implied in the Gallup Poll? ■

516

Source: "Public Opinion and the Korean War," *Gallup Political Index* (American Institute of Public Opinion, August 1965), pp. 23–27.

Because there are many important parallels with the present war in Viet Nam, the Gallup Poll has prepared this review of public opinion as measured regularly during the period of the Korean War. Representative samples of the American people were asked to express their views on a wide array of issues which came up throughout this struggle.

The Korean War, it will be recalled, started June 25, 1950, when North Korean troops invaded South Korea.

As the findings here show, attitudes of people toward the war changed substantially after the Chinese Communists entered the fighting. In 1952, the war became one of the key factors in the presidential campaign and the election of President Dwight D. Eisenhower.

The start of the Korean War had an effect on the personal popularity of President Harry S. Truman. Although his popularity rating with the American people had declined steadily between 1945 and the time of the Korean invasion (primarily for reasons other than foreign policy), it received a slight boost following his decision to defend South Korea.

The question asked:

"Do you approve or disapprove of the way Truman is handling his job as President?"

Following are the results as measured before and after the Korean invasion:

	Just Before Korea Invasion	Just After Korea Invasion
Approve	37%	46%
Disapprove	45	37
No opinion	18	17

Did we make a mistake? In October, 1950, at a time when the U.S. had become completely involved in the Korean situation, the Gallup Poll had its interviewers ask this question of adults across the country:

"In view of the developments since we entered the fighting in Korea, do you think the U.S. made a mistake in deciding to defend Korea, or not?"

The findings:

Yes, we made a mistake	20%
No, we did not	65
No opinion	15

At this early stage in the Korean conflict, the public believed we should defeat the Communist forces and not just push them back over the 38th Parallel, to their pre-invasion position.

Sixty-four per cent, in October, 1950, favored continuing the fight into North Korea, until the Communist forces surrendered.

On the home front Back at home, President Truman announced curtailment of many essential lines of civilian production—along with price and credit controls, higher taxes, and reduced non-military government expenditures.

The public favored price controls on meats, butter, sugar, fats and oils, but opposed government rationing of any of these products.

As for paying the increased cost of defense, the public frowned on the idea of borrowing money for this increased cost. Here is the question asked and the results:

"How should the Federal Government pay the increased cost of defense— CHIEFLY by extra taxes, or CHIEFLY by borrowing more money?"

Taxes	60%
Borrowing	19
No opinion	21

Universal draft? The suggestion was raised by Gov. Thomas E. Dewey of New York late in 1950 that all men over 17 register for military service.

The public had long favored this proposal. In October of 1950, this question was put to a cross-section of Americans:

"In the future, do you think every able-bodied young man (who has not already been in the armed forces) should be required to take military or naval training for one year?"

The results:

Universal Military Training?	
Favor	78%
Oppose	17
No opinion	5

Chinese enter war On November 26, 1950, an army estimated at 200,000 Red Chinese "volunteers" began crossing the Yalu River into North Korea. By January 1, 1951, the Chinese had begun crossing the 38th Parallel into South Korea, and in an enormous onslaught had captured the strategic cities of Seoul and Inchon.

Public ignorant of Chinese strength Prior to Communist China's entry into the war, the American people had been baffled as to the population of that nation. In September, 1950, this question was asked:

"Just your best guess, what would you say the population of China is?"

The results:

Population of China	
Under 150 million	26%
150 – 399 million	20
400 – 499 million	12
500 million and over	13
"Very big," etc.	3
Don't know	26

In view of the public's lack of knowledge about the population of China, it was not surprising that evidence of general confusion appeared in the results of this second question asked:

"Just your best guess, about how many soldiers do you think Communist China could raise for an all-out war?"

How Many Soldiers Could China Raise?

3 million or less	31%
4 – 6 million	12
7 – 10 million	11
11 – 20 million	9
21 million or more	11
Miscellaneous	6
Don't know	20

Median Average — 5 million

518

The public's feelings about how the war was going changed drastically after the Communist Chinese entered the fighting.

In January, 1951, a cross-section of the public was asked this question:

"Now that Communist China has entered the fighting in Korea with forces far outnumbering the United Nations troops there, which one of these two courses would you yourself prefer that we follow: (A) Pull our troops out of Korea as fast as possible; (B) Keep our troops there to fight these larger forces?"

Here are the results:

Pull out	66%
Stay there	25
No opinion	9

At the same time, Americans were coming around to the view that the U.S. had made a mistake in deciding to defend Korea.

It will be recalled that several months earlier only 2 persons in 10 thought the U.S. had made a mistake, but the surprise entry of the Chinese into the war changed the complexion of U.S. public opinion. One month after China entered the war, almost half (49 per cent) held the view that the U.S. had blundered.

Here is the trend:

	After China Entered War	August, 1950
Yes, we made a mistake	49%	20%
No, we did not	38	65
No opinion	13	15

Peace conferences begin During the spring of 1951, as the tense fighting in Korea continued, the UN made numerous efforts to establish negotiations. But these attempts were in vain.

In June, 1951, the Soviet Deputy Foreign Minister, Jacob A. Malik, proposed that the Korean War be ended by a cease-fire along the 38th Parallel — where the war had begun. All nations involved immediately endorsed the proposal but rebuffed the demand by Peiping that all troops be pulled out of Korea.

Less than one month after Malik's proposal, the Gallup Poll asked this question:

"It has been suggested that the UN call for a truce at the 38th Parallel in Korea, with peace terms to be worked out later. Would you approve or disapprove of this?"

A narrow majority of the public (51 per cent) favored this proposal. Thirty-seven per cent expressed disapproval, with 12 per cent undecided.

The actual negotiations began in July, 1951, but were followed by a long stretch of bickering and failure.

Even though attempts at reaching a peace agreement in Korea were in vain for over a year, the public, at the time of these negotiations, solidly backed the UN's agreeing to such peace talks. Seventy-four per cent of persons in the United States held this view.

Some observers have held that no one really won the war in Korea, and that the whole situation was a "useless conflict."

Prior to the final peace settlement, the public was equally confused as to which side would come out best if the war in Korea ended at the 38th Parallel.

Thirty per cent said the UN forces would be better off, 33 per cent said the Communists, 23 per cent said "neither" and 14 per cent couldn't decide.

The final armistice was signed by the United Nations and Communist delegates on July 27, 1953. Hostilities ended 12 hours later and troops began to set up a buffer zone.

No formal treaty to end the conflict has been signed to date. ■

VIETNAM: The Crisis of American Foreign Policy

The Korean War ended in a stalemate and the heavy casualties that American soldiers had suffered left many American leaders and a large portion of the general public with the conviction that we should not allow ourselves to get drawn into another ground war in Asia. On the other hand, the policy-makers of every subsequent administration remained convinced that the spread of Communism and of Chinese influence in Asia must somehow be contained just as Soviet influence had to be contained in Europe. Hence, economic and military aid was offered to the small nations on the periphery of China, and a defense organization known as SEATO (Southeast Asia Treaty Organization) was established under American auspices. Included in this treaty organization were such nations as Australia, New Zealand, Thailand, Pakistan, and the Philippines.

The most serious problem faced by American policy-makers in Asia after the Korean War was the protracted civil war in Indochina. The United States had given its support to the French army in its efforts to suppress the guerrilla forces led by the Vietnamese Communist leader Ho Chi Minh. When the French withdrew from Indochina in 1954 after disastrous military defeats, the Indochina problem became an American problem. The Eisenhower Administration gave support to limited clandestine operations against the North Vietnamese after the Geneva Accords of 1954 had set forth conditions designed to bring about the political unification of North and South Vietnam. The Kennedy Administration expanded the American political and military commitment to the non-Communist government of South Vietnam; American military forces in Vietnam totaled 16,000 at the time of President Kennedy's assassination. But it was not until President Johnson took over that the American military commitment in Vietnam was expanded to a point where it equaled and even exceeded U.S. involvement in the Korean War. ■

THE DECISION TO ESCALATE

Five of the following selections are taken from the so-called "Pentagon papers," first published by the *New York Times* in the summer of 1971. They include some of the secret memoranda written by top government officials and presidential advisers during the year 1965, when the crucial decisions to expand the role of the United States in Vietnam were made. The sixth selection is taken from Lyndon Baines Johnson's memoirs of his presidential years, published under the title *The Vantage Point*. This selection gives Mr. Johnson's version of how the discussions of policy within his Administration led to the decision to expand the air and ground war in Vietnam.

Source: The Pentagon Papers As Published by the *New York Times* (Bantam Books, 1971), pp. 423–427; 432–441; 447–454.

Annex A, "A Policy of Sustained Reprisal," to memorandum to President Lyndon B. Johnson from McGeorge Bundy, Presidential assistant for national security, Feb. 7, 1965.

I INTRODUCTORY

We believe that the best available way of increasing our chance of success in Vietnam is the development and execution of a policy of *sustained reprisal* against North Vietnam—a policy in which air and naval action against the North is justified by and related to the whole Viet Cong campaign of violence and terror in the South.

While we believe that the risks of such a policy are acceptable, we emphasize that its costs are real. It implies significant U.S. air losses even if no full air war is joined, and it seems likely that it would eventually require an extensive and costly effort against the whole air defense system of North Vietnam. U.S. casualties would be higher—and more visible to American feelings—than those sustained in the struggle in South Vietnam.

Yet measured against the costs of defeat in Vietnam, this program seems cheap. And even if it fails to turn the tide—as it may —the value of the effort seems to us to exceed its cost.

II OUTLINE OF THE POLICY

1 In partnership with the Government of Vietnam, we should develop and exercise the option to retaliate against *any* VC act of violence to persons or property.

2 In practice, we may wish at the outset to relate our reprisals to those acts of relatively high visibility such as the Pleiku incident. Later, we might retaliate against the assassination of a province chief, but not necessarily the murder of a hamlet official; we might retaliate against a grenade thrown into a crowded cafe in Saigon, but not necessarily to a shot fired into a small shop in the countryside.

3 Once a program of reprisals is clearly underway, it should not be necessary to connect each specific act against North Vietnam to a particular outrage in the South. It should be possible, for example, to publish weekly lists of outrages in the South and to have it clearly understood that these outrages are the cause of such action against the North as may be occurring in the current period. Such a more generalized pattern of reprisal would remove much of the difficulty involved in finding precisely matching targets in response to specific atrocities. Even in such a more general pattern, however, it would be important to insure that the general level of reprisal action remained in close correspondence with the level of outrages in the South. We must keep it clear at every stage both to Hanoi and to the world, that our reprisals will be reduced or stopped when outrages in the South are reduced or stopped—and that we are *not* attempting to destroy or conquer North Vietnam.

4 In the early stages of such a course, we should take the appropriate occasion to make clear our firm intent to undertake reprisals on any further acts, major or minor, that appear to us and the GVN as indicating Hanoi's support. We would announce that our two governments have been patient and forebearing in the hope that Hanoi would come to its senses without the necessity of our having to take further action; but the outrages continue and now we must react against those who are responsible; we will not provoke; we will not use our force indiscriminately; but we can no longer sit by in the face of repeated acts of terror and violence for which the DRV is responsible.

5 Having once made this announcement, we should execute our reprisal policy with as low a level of public noise as possible. It is to our interest that our acts should be seen—but we do not wish to boast about them in ways that make it hard for Hanoi to shift its ground. We should instead direct maximum attention to the continuing acts of violence which are the cause of our continuing reprisals.

6 This reprisal policy should begin at a low level. Its level of force and pressure should be increased only gradually—and as indicated above should be decreased if VC terror visibly decreased. The object would not be to "win" an air war against Hanoi, but rather to influence the course of the struggle in the South.

7 At the same time it should be recognized that in order to maintain the power of reprisal without risk of excessive loss, an "air war" may in fact be necessary. We should therefore be ready to develop a separate justification for energetic flak suppression and if necessary for the destruction of Communist air power. The essence of such an explanation should be that these actions are intended solely to insure the effectiveness of a policy of reprisal, and in no sense represent any intent to wage offensive war against the North. These distinctions should not be difficult to develop.

8 It remains quite possible, however, that this reprisal policy would get us quickly into the level of military activity contemplated in the so-called Phase II of our

December planning. It may even get us beyond this level with both Hanoi and Peiping, if there is Communist counteraction. We and the GVN should also be prepared for a spurt of VC terrorism, especially in urban areas, that would dwarf anything yet experienced. These are the risks of any action. They should be carefully reviewed—but we believe them to be acceptable.

9 We are convinced that the political values of reprisal require a *continuous* operation. Episodic responses geared on a one-for-one basis to "spectacular" outrages would lack the persuasive force of sustained pressure. More important still, they would leave it open to the Communists to avoid reprisals entirely by giving up only a small element of their own program. The Gulf of Tonkin affair produced a sharp upturn in morale in South Vietnam. When it remained an isolated episode, however, there was a severe relapse. It is the great merit of the proposed scheme that to stop it the Communists would have to stop enough of their activity in the South to permit the probable success of a determined pacification effort.

III EXPECTED EFFECT OF SUSTAINED REPRISAL POLICY

1 We emphasize that our primary target in advocating a reprisal policy is the improvement of the situation in *South* Vietnam. Action against the North is usually urged as a means of affecting the will of Hanoi to direct and support the VC. We consider this an important but longer-range purpose. The immediate and critical targets are in the South—in the minds of the South Vietnamese and in the minds of the Viet Cong cadres.

2 Predictions of the effect of any given course of action upon the states of mind of people are difficult. It seems very clear that if the United States and the Government of Vietnam join in a policy of reprisal, there will be a sharp immediate increase in optimism in the South, among nearly all articulate groups. The Mission believes—and our own conversations confirm—that in all sectors of Vietnamese opinion there is a strong belief that the United States could do much more if it would, and that they are suspicious of our failure to use more of our obviously enormous power. At least in the short run, the reaction to reprisal policy should be very favorable.

3 This favorable reaction should offer opportunity for increased American influence in pressing for a more effective government —at least in the short run. Joint reprisals would imply military planning in which the American role would necessarily be controlling, and this new relation should add to our bargaining power in other military efforts—and conceivably on a wider plane as well if a more stable government is formed. We have the whip hand in reprisals as we do not in other fields.

4 The Vietnamese increase in hope could well increase the readiness of Vietnamese factions themselves to join together in forming a more effective government.

5 We think it plausible that effective and sustained reprisals, even in a low key, would have a substantial depressing effect upon the morale of Viet Cong cadres in South Vietnam. This is the strong opinion of CIA Saigon. It is based upon reliable reports of the initial Viet Cong reaction to the Gulf of Tonkin episode, and also upon

the solid general assessment that the determination of Hanoi and the apparent timidity of the mighty United States are both major items in Viet Cong confidence.

6 The long-run effect of reprisals in the South is far less clear. It may be that like other stimulants, the value of this one would decline over time. Indeed the risk of this result is large enough so that we ourselves believe that a very major effort all along the line should be made in South Vietnam to take full advantage of the immediate stimulus of reprisal policy in its early stages. Our object should be to use this new policy to effect a visible upward turn in pacification, in governmental effectiveness, in operations against the Viet Cong, and in the whole U.S./GVN relationship. It is changes in these areas that can have enduring long-term effects.

7 While emphasizing the importance of reprisals in the South, we do not exclude the impact on Hanoi. We believe, indeed, that it is of great importance that the level of reprisal be adjusted rapidly and visibly to both upward and downward shifts in the level of Viet Cong offenses. We want to keep before Hanoi the carrot of our desisting as well as the stick of continued pressure. We also need to conduct the application of force so that there is always a prospect of worse to come.

8 We cannot assert that a policy of sustained reprisal will succeed in changing the course of the contest in Vietnam. It may fail, and we cannot estimate the odds of success with any accuracy—they may be somewhere between 25% and 75%. What we can say is that even if it fails, the policy will be worth it. At a minimum it will damp down the charge that we did not do all that we could have done, and this charge will be important in many countries, including our own. Beyond that, a reprisal policy—to the extent that it demonstrates U.S. willingness to employ this new norm in counter-insurgency—will set a higher price for the future upon all adventures of guerrilla warfare, and it should therefore somewhat increase our ability to deter such adventures. We must recognize, however, that that ability will be gravely weakened if there is failure for any reason in Vietnam.

IV PRESENT ACTION RECOMMENDATIONS

1 This general recommendation was developed in intensive discussions in the days just before the attacks on Pleiku. These attacks and our reaction to them have created an ideal opportunity for the prompt development and execution of sustained reprisals. Conversely, if no such policy is now developed, we face the grave danger that Pleiku, like the Gulf of Tonkin, may be a short-run stimulant and a long-term depressant. We therefore recommend that the necessary preparations be made for continuing reprisals. The major necessary steps to be taken appear to us to be the following:

(1) We should complete the evacuation of dependents.

(2) We should quietly start the necessary westward deployments of [word illegible] contingency forces.

(3) We should develop and refine a running catalogue of Viet Cong offenses which can be published regularly and related clearly to our own reprisals. Such a catalogue should perhaps build on the foundation of an initial White Paper.

(4) We should initiate joint planning with the GVN on both the civil and military

Philip Jones Griffiths, Magnum

level. Specifically, we should give a clear and strong signal to those now forming a government that we will be ready for this policy when they are.

(5) We should develop the necessary public and diplomatic statements to accompany the initiation and continuation of this program.

(6) We should insure that a reprisal program is matched by renewed public commitment to our family of programs in the South, so that the central importance of the southern struggle may never be neglected.

(7) We should plan quiet diplomatic communication of the precise meaning of what we are and are not doing, to Hanoi, to Peking and to Moscow.

(8) We should be prepared to defend and to justify this new policy by concentrating attention in every forum upon its cause—the aggression in the South.

(9) We should accept discussion on these terms in any forum, but we should *not* now accept the idea of negotiations of any sort except on the basis of a stand down of Viet Cong violence. A program of sustained reprisal, with its direct link to Hanoi's continuing aggressive actions in the South, will not involve us in nearly the level of international recrimination which would be precipitated by a go-North program which was not so connected. For this reason the international pressures for negotiation should be quite manageable. ∎

Memorandum from Walt W. Rostow, chairman of the State Department's Policy Planning Council, for Secretary of State Rusk, "Victory and Defeat in Guerrilla Wars: The Case of South Vietnam," May 20, 1965, as provided in the body of the Pentagon's study.

In the press, at least, there is a certain fuzziness about the possibility of clear-cut victory in South Viet-Nam; and the President's statement that a military victory is impossible is open to misinterpretation.

1 Historically, guerrilla wars have generally been lost or won cleanly: Greece, China mainland, North Viet-Nam, Malaya, Philippines. Laos in 1954 was an exception, with two provinces granted the Communists and a de facto split imposed on the country.

2 In all the cases won by Free World forces, there was a phase when the guerrillas commanded a good part of the countryside and, indeed, placed Athens, Kuala Lumpur, and Manila under something close to siege. They failed to win because all the possible routes to guerrilla victory were closed and, in failing to win, they lost. They finally gave up in discouragement. The routes to victory are:

(a) Mao Stage Three: going to all-out conventional war and winning as in China in 1947–49;

(b) Political collapse and takeover: North Viet-Nam;

(c) Political collapse and a coalition government in which the Communists get control over the security machinery; army and/or police. This has been an evident Viet Cong objective in this [rest illegible].

(d) Converting the bargaining pressure generated by the guerrilla forces into a partial victory by splitting the country: Laos. Also, in a sense, North Viet-Nam in 1954 and the Irish Rebellion after the First World War.

3 If we succeed in blocking these four routes to victory, discouraging the Communist force in the South, and making the continuance of the war sufficiently costly to the North there is no reason we cannot win as clear a victory in South Viet-Nam as in Greece, Malaya, and the Philippines. Unless political morale in Saigon collapses and the ARVN tends to break up, case c), the most realistic hope of the VC, should be avoidable. This danger argues for more rather than less pressure on the North, while continuing the battle in the South in such a way as to make VC hopes of military and political progress wane.

4 The objective of the exercise is to convince Hanoi that its bargaining position is being reduced with the passage of time; for, even in the worst case for Hanoi, it wants some bargaining position (rather than simply dropping the war) to get U.S. forces radically reduced in South Viet-Nam and to get some minimum face-saving formula for the VC.

5 I believe Hanoi understands its dilemma well. As of early February it saw a good chance of a quiet clean victory via route c. It now is staring at quite clear-cut defeat, with the rising U.S. strength and GVN morale in the South and rising costs in the North. That readjustment in prospects is painful; and they won't, in my view, accept its consequences unless they are convinced time has ceased to be their friend, despite the full use of their assets on the ground in South Viet-Nam, in po-

Philip Jones Griffiths, Magnum

523

litical warfare around the world, and in diplomacy.

6 Their last and best hope will be, of course, that if they end the war and get us out, the political, social, and economic situation in South Viet-Nam will deteriorate in such a way as to permit Communist political takeover, with or without a revival of guerrilla warfare. It is in this phase that we will have to consolidate, with the South Vietnamese, a victory that is nearer our grasp than we (but not Hanoi) may think. ∎

First draft of "Annex—Plan for Action for South Vietnam," appended to memorandum from John T. McNaughton, Assistant Secretary of Defense for International Security Affairs, for Secretary of Defense Robert S. McNamara, March 24, 1965.

1 U.S. aims:

70%—To avoid a humiliating U.S. defeat (to our reputation as a guarantor).

20%—To keep SVN (and the adjacent) territory from Chinese hands.

10%—To permit the people of SVN to enjoy a better, freer way of life.

ALSO—To emerge from crisis without unacceptable taint from methods used.

NOT—to "help a friend," although it would be hard to stay in if asked out.

2 The situation: The situation in general is bad and deteriorating. The VC have the initiative. Defeatism is gaining among the rural population, somewhat in the cities, and even among the soldiers—especially those with relatives in rural areas. The Hop Tac area around Saigon is making little progress; the Delta stays bad; the country has been severed in the north. GVN control is shrinking to the enclaves, some burdened with refugees. In Saigon we have a remission: Quat is giving hope on the civilian side, the Buddhists have calmed, and the split generals are in uneasy equilibrium.

3 The preliminary question: Can the situation inside SVN be bottomed out (a) without extreme measures against the DRV and/or (b) without deployment of large numbers of U.S. (and other) combat troops inside SVN? The answer is perhaps, but probably no.

4 Ways GVN might collapse:

a VC successes reduce GVN control to enclaves, causing:

(1) insurrection in the enclaved population,

(2) massive defections of ARVN soldiers and even units,

(3) aggravated dissension and impotence in Saigon,

(4) defeatism and reorientation by key GVN officials,

(5) entrance of left-wing elements into the government,

(6) emergence of a popular-front regime,

(7) request that U.S. leave,

(8) concessions to the VC, and

(9) accommodations to the DRV.

b VC with DRV volunteers concentrate on I and II Corps:

(1) conquering principal GVN-held enclaves there,

(2) declaring Liberation Government,

(3) joining the I & II Corps areas to the DRV, and

(4) pressing the course in **a** above for rest of SVN.

c While in a temporary funk, GVN might throw in sponge:

(1) dealing under the table with VC,

(2) asking the U.S. to cease at least military aid,

(3) bringing left-wing elements into the government,

(4) leading to a popular-front regime, and

(5) ending in accommodations to the VC and DRV.

d In a surge of anti-Americanism, GVN could ask the U.S. out and pursue course otherwise similar to **c** above.

5 The "trilemma": U.S. policy appears to be drifting. This is because, while there is consensus that efforts inside SVN (para 6) will probably fail to prevent collapse, all three of the possible remedial courses of action have so far been rejected:

a Will-breaking strikes on the North (para 7) are balked (1) by flash-point limits, (2) by doubts that the DRV will cave and (3) by doubts that the VC will obey a caving DRV. (Leaving strikes only a political and anti-infiltration nuisance.)

b Large U.S. troop deployments (para 9) are blocked by "French-defeat" and "Korea" syndromes, and Quat is queasy. (Troops could be net negatives, and be besieged.)

c Exit by negotiations (para 9) is tainted by the humiliation likely to follow.

Effort inside South Vietnam: Progress inside SVN is our main aim. Great, imaginative efforts on the civilian political as well as military side must be made, bearing in mind that progress depends as much on GVN efforts and luck as on added U.S. efforts. While only a few of such efforts can pay off quickly enough to affect the present ominous deterioration, some may, and we are dealing here in small critical margins. Furthermore, such investment is essential to provide a foundation for the longer run.

a Improve spirit and effectiveness. (fill out further, drawing from State memo to the President)

(1) Achieve governmental stability.

(2) Augment the psy-war program.

(3) Build a stronger pro-government infrastructure.

b Improve physical security. (fill out)

c Reduce infiltration. (fill out)

STRIKES ON THE NORTH (PROGRAM OF PROGRESSIVE MILITARY PRESSURE)

a Purposes:

(1) to reduce DRV/VC activities by affecting DRV will.

(2) To improve the GVN/VC relative "balance of morale."

(3) To provide the U.S./GVN with a bargaining counter.

(4) To reduce DRV infiltration of men and materiel.

(5) To show the world the lengths to which U.S. will go for a friend.

b Program: Each week, 1 or 2 "mission days" with 100-plane high-damage U.S.-VNAF strikes each "day" against important targets, plus 3 armed recce missions—all moving upward in weight of effort, value of target or proximity to Hanoi and China.

ALTERNATIVE ONE: 12-week DRV-wide program shunning only "population" targets.

ALTERNATIVE TWO: 12-week program short of taking out Phuc Yen (Hanoi) airfield.

c Other actions:

(1) Blockade of DRV ports by VNAF/U.S.-dropped mines or by ships.

(2) South Vietnamese-implemented 34A MAROPS.

(3) Reconnaissance flights over Laos and the DRV.

(4) Daily BARREL ROLL armed recce strikes in Laos (plus T-28s).

(5) Four-a-week BARREL ROLL choke-point strikes in Laos.

(6) U.S./VNAF air & naval strikes against VC ops and bases in SVN.

(7) Westward deployment of U.S. forces.

(8) No de Soto patrols or naval bombardment of DRV at this time.

d Red "flash points." There are events which we can expect to imply substantial risk of escalation.

(1) Air strikes north of 17°. (This one already passed.)

(2) First U.S./VNAF confrontation with DRV MIGs.

(3) Strike on Phuc Yen MIG base near Hanoi.

(4) First strikes on Tonkin industrial/population targets.

(5) First strikes on Chinese railroad near China.

(6) First U.S./VNAF confrontation with Chicom MIGs.

(7) First hot pursuit of Chicom MIGs into China.

(8) First flak-suppression of Chicom or Soviet-manned SAM.

(9) Massive introduction of U.S. ground troops into SVN.

(10) U.S./ARVN occupation of DRV territory (e.g., Ile de Tigre).

(11) First Chi/Sov-U.S. confrontation or sinking in blockade.

e Blue "flash points." China/DRV surely are sensitive to events which might cause us to escalate.

(1) All of the above "red" flash points.

(2) VC ground attack on Danang.

(3) Sinking of a U.S. naval vessel.

(4) Open deployment of DRV troops into South Vietnam.

(5) Deployment of Chinese troops into North Vietnam.

(6) Deployment of FROGs or SAMs in North Vietnam.

(7) DRV air attack on South Vietnam.

(8) Announcement of Liberation Government in I/II Corps area.

f Major risks:

(1) Losses to DRV MIGs, and later possibly to SAMs.

(2) Increased VC activities, and possibly Liberation Government.

(3) Panic or other collapse of GVN from under us.

(4) World-wide revulsion against us (against strikes, blockades, etc.).

(5) Sympathetic fires over Berlin, Cyprus, Kashmir, Jordan waters.

(6) Escalation to conventional war with DRV, China (and USSR?)

(7) Escalation to the use of nuclear weapons.

g Other Red moves:

(1) More jets to NVN with DRV or Chicom pilots.

(2) More AA (SAMs?) and radar gear (Soviet-manned?) to NVN.

(3) Increased air and ground forces in South China.

(4) Other "defensive" DRV retaliation (e.g., shoot-down of a U-2).

(5) PL land grabs in Laos.

(6) PL declaration of new government in Laos.

(7) Political drive for "neutralization" of Indo-China.

h Escalation control. We can do three things to avoid escalation too-much or too fast:

(1) Stretch out. Retard the program (e.g., 1 not 2 fixed strikes a week).

(2) Circuit-breaker. Abandon at least temporarily the theory that our strikes are intended to break DRV will, and "plateau" them below the "Phuc Yen Airfield" flash point on one or the other of these tenable theories:

(a) That we strike as necessary to interdict infiltration.

(b) That our level of strikes is generally responsive to the level of VC/DRV activities in South Vietnam.

(3) Shunt. Plateau the air strikes per para (2) and divert the energy into:

(a) A mine—and/or ship-blockade of DRV ports.

(b) Massive deployment of U.S. (and other?) troops into SVN (and Laos?):

(1) To man the "enclaves," releasing ARVN forces.

(2) To take over Pleiku, Kontum, Darlac provinces.

(3) To create a [word illegible] sea-Thailand infiltration wall.

i Important miscellany:

(1) Program should appear to be relentless (i.e., possibility of employing "circuit-breakers" should be secret).

(2) Enemy should be kept aware of our limited objectives.

(3) Allies should be kept on board.

(4) USSR should be kept in passive role.

(5) Information program should preserve U.S. public support.

PROGRAM OF LARGE U.S. GROUND EFFORT IN SVN AND SEA

a Purposes:

(1) To defeat the VC on the ground.

(2) To improve GVN/VC relative "morale balance."

(3) To improve U.S./GVN bargaining position.

(4) To show world lengths to which U.S. will go to fulfill commitments.

b Program:

(1) Continue strike-North "crescendo" or "plateau" (para 7 above.); (2) Add any "combat support" personnel needed by MACV; and (3) Deploy remainder of the III Marine Expeditionary Force to Danang;

and (4) Deploy one U.S. (plus one Korean?) division to defeat VC in Pleiku-Kontum-Darlac area; and/or (5) Deploy one U.S. (plus one Korean?) division to hold enclaves (Bien Hoa/Ton Son Nhut, Nha Trang, Qui Non, Pleiku); and/or (6) Deploy 3-5 U.S. divisions (with "international" elements) across Laos-SVN infiltration routes and at key SVN population centers.

c Advantages:

(1) Improve (at least initially) manpower ratio vs. the VC.

(2) Boost GVN morale and depress DRV/VC morale.

(3) Firm up U.S. commitment in eyes of all Reds, allies and neutrals.

(4) Deter (or even prevent) coups in the South.

d Risks:

(1) Deployment will suck Chicom troops into DRV.

(2) Deployment will suck counter-balancing DRV/Chinese troops into SVN.

(3) Announcement of deployment will cause massive DRV/Chicom effort preemptively to occupy new SVN territory.

(4) U.S. losses will increase.

(5) Friction with GVN (and Koreans?) over command will arise.

(6) GVN will tend increasingly to "let the U.S. do it."

(7) Anti-U.S. "colonialist" mood may increase in and outside SVN.

(8) U.S. forces may be surrounded and trapped.

e Important miscellany:

(1) There are no obvious circuit-breakers. Once U.S. troops are in, it will be difficult to withdraw them or to move them, say, to Thailand without admitting defeat.

(2) It will take massive deployments

(many divisions) to improve the GVN/U.S.:VC ratio to the optimum 10+:1.

(3) In any event, our Project 22 planning with the Thais for defense of the Mekong towns must proceed apace.

EXIT BY NEGOTIATIONS

a Bargaining counters.

(1) What DRV could give:

a/Stop training and sending personnel to SVN/Laos.

b/Stop sending arms and supplies into SVN/Laos.

c/Stop directing military actions in SVN/Laos.

d/Order the VC/PL to stop their insurgencies.

e/Stop propaganda broadcasts to South Vietnam.

f/Remove VM forces and cadres from SVN and Laos.

g/See that VC/PL stop incidents in SVN and Laos.

h/See that VC/PL cease resistance.

i/See that VC/PL turn in weapons and bases.

j/See that VC/PL surrender for amnesty/expatriation.

(2) What GVN/U.S. could give:

a/Stop (or not increase) air strikes on DRV.

b/Remove (or not increase) U.S. troops in SVN.

c/Rice supply to DRV.

d/Assurance that U.S./GVN have no designs on NVN.

e/Assurance that U.S./GVN will not demand public renunciation by the DRV of Communist goals.

f/Assurance that "peaceful coexistence" (e.g., continuation of Red propaganda in SVN) is acceptable.

g/Capitulation: Leftists in GVN, coalition government, and eventual incorporation of SVN into DRV.

b Possible outcomes.

(1) Pacified non-Communist South Vietnam.

(2) "Laotian" solution, with areas of de facto VC dominion, a "government of national unity," and a Liberation Front ostensibly weaned from DRV control.

(3) Explicit partition of SVN, with each area under a separate government.

(4) A "semi-equilibrium"—a slow-motion war—with slowly shifting GVN-VC lines.

(5) Loss of SVN to the DRV.

c Techniques to minimize impact of bad outcomes. If/when it is estimated that even the best U.S./GVN efforts mean failure ("flash" or defeat), it will be important to act to minimize the afterdamage to U.S. effectiveness and image by steps such as these:

(1) Publicize uniqueness of congenital impossibility of SVN case (e.g., Viet Minh held much of SVN in 1954, long sieve-like borders, unfavorable terrain, no national tradition, few administrators, mess left by French, competing factions, Red LOC advantage, late U.S. start, etc.).

(2) Take opportunity offered by next coup or GVN anti-U.S. tantrum to "ship out" (coupled with advance threat to do so if they fail to "shape up"?)

(3) Create diversionary "offensives" elsewhere in the world (e.g., to shore up Thailand, Philippines, Malaysia, India, Australia; to launch an "anti-poverty" program for underdeveloped areas).

(4) Enter multi-nation negotiations calculated to shift opinions and values.

d Risks. With the physical situation and the trends as they are the fear is overwhelming that an exit negotiated now would result in humiliation for the U.S.

Evaluation: It is essential—however badly SEA may go over the next 1-3 years—that U.S. emerge as a "good doctor." We must have kept promises, been tough, taken risks, gotten bloodied, and hurt the enemy very badly. We must avoid harmful appearances which will affect judgments by, and provide pretexts to, other nations regarding how the U.S. will behave in future cases of particular interest to those nations —regarding U.S. policy, power, resolve and competence to deal with their problems. In this connection, the relevant audiences are the Communists (who must feel strong pressures), the South Vietnamese (whose morale must be buoyed), our allies (who must trust us as "underwriters") and the U.S. public (which must support our risk-taking with U.S. lives and prestige).

Urgency: If the strike-North program (para 7) is not altered: we will reach the MIG/Phuc Yen flash point in approximately one month. If the program is altered only to stretch out the crescendo: up to 3 months may be had before that flash point, at the expense of a less persuasive squeeze. If the program is altered to "plateau" or dampen the strikes: much of their negotiating value will be lost. (Furthermore, there is now a hint of flexibility on the Red side: the Soviets are struggling to find a Gordian knot-cutter; the Chicoms may be wavering (Paris 5326).

POSSIBLE COURSE

(1) Redouble efforts inside SVN (get better organized for it).

(2) Prepare to deploy U.S. combat troops in phases, starting with one Army division at Pleiku and a Marine MEF at Danang.

(3) Stretch out strike-North program, postponing Phuc Yen until June (exceed flash points only in specific retaliations).

(4) Initiate talks along the following lines, bearing in mind that formal partition, or even a "Laos" partition, is out in SVN; we must break the VC back or work out an accommodation.

PHASE ONE TALKS:

(A) When: Now, before an avoidable flash point.

(B) Who: U.S.-USSR, perhaps also U.S.-India. (Not with China or Liberation Front; not through UK or France or U Thant; keep alert to possibility that GVN officials are talking under the table.)

(C) How: With GVN consent, private, quiet (refuse formal talks).

(D) What:

1/Offer to stop strikes on DRV and withhold deployment of large U.S. forces in trade for DRV stoppage of infiltration, communications to VC, and VC attacks, sabotage and terrorism, and for withdrawal of named units in SVN.

2/Compliance would be policed unilaterally. If as is likely, complete compliance by the DRV is not forthcoming, we would carry out occasional strikes.

3/We make clear that we are not demanding cessation of Red propaganda nor a public renunciation by Hanoi of its doctrines.

4/Regarding "defensive" VC attacks— i.e., VC defending VC-held areas from encroaching ARVN forces—we take the public position that ARVN forces must be free to operate throughout SVN, especially

Philip Jones Griffiths, Magnum

in areas where amnesty is offered (but in fact, discretion will be exercised).

5/Terrorism and sabotage, however, must be dampened markedly throughout the country, and civilian administrators must be free to move and operate freely, certainly in so-called contested areas (and perhaps even in VC base areas).

PHASE TWO TALKS:
(A) When: At the end of Phase One.
(B) Who: All interested nations.
(C) How: Publicly in large conference.
(D) What:
1/Offer to remove U.S. combat forces from South Vietnam in exchange for repatriation (or regroupment?) of DRV infiltrators and for erection of international machinery to verify the end of infiltration and communication.

2/Offer to seek to determine the will of the people under international supervision, with an appropriate reflection of those who favor the VC.

3/Any recognition of the Liberation Front would have to be accompanied by disarming the VC and at least avowed VC independence from DRV control.

PHASE THREE TALKS: Avoid any talks regarding the future of all of Southeast Asia. Thailand's future should not be up for discussion; and we have the 1954 and 1962 Geneva Accords covering the rest of the area.

Special Points:
(1) Play on DRV's fear of China.
(2) To show good will, suspend strikes on North for a few days if requested by Soviets during efforts to mediate.
(3) Have a contingency plan prepared to evacuate U.S. personnel in case a para-9-type situation arises.
(4) If the DRV will not "play" the above game, we must be prepared (a) to risk passing some flash points, in the Strike-North program, (b) to put more U.S. troops into SVN, and/or (c) to reconsider our minimum acceptable outcome. ∎

Memorandum from John A. McCone, Director of Central Intelligence, to Secretary Rusk, Secretary McNamara, McGeorge Bundy and Ambassador Taylor, April 2, 1965, as provided in the body of the Pentagon's study. Paragraphs in italics are the study's paraphrase or explanation.

McCone did not inherently disagree with the change in the U.S. ground-force role, but felt that it was inconsistent with the decision to continue the air strike program at the feeble level at which it was then being conducted. McCone developed his argument as follows:

I have been giving thought to the paper that we discussed in yesterday's meeting, which unfortunately I had little time to study, and also to the decision made to change the mission of our ground forces in South Vietnam from one of advice and static defense to one of active combat operations against the Viet Cong guerrillas.

I feel that the latter decision is correct only if our air strikes against the North are sufficiently heavy and damaging really to hurt the North Vietnamese. The paper we examined yesterday does not anticipate the type of air operation against the North necessary to force the NVN to reappraise their policy. On the contrary, it states, "We should continue roughly the present slowly ascending tempo of ROLLING THUNDER operations——," and later, in outlining the types of targets, states, "The target systems should continue to avoid the effective GCI range of MIG's," and these conditions indicate restraints which will not be persuasive to the NVM and would probably be read as evidence of a U.S. desire to temporize.

I have reported that the strikes to date have not caused a change in the North Vietnamese policy of directing Viet Cong insurgency, infiltrating cadres and supplying material. If anything, the strikes to date have hardened their attitude.

* * *

We must look with care to our position under a program of slowly ascending tempo of air strikes. With the passage of each day and each week, we can expect increasing pressure to stop the bombing. This will come from various elements of the American public, from the press, the United Nations and world opinion. Therefore time will run against us in this operation and I think the North Vietnamese are counting on this.

Therefore I think what we are doing is starting on a track which involves ground force operations, which, in all probability, will have limited effectiveness against guerrillas, although admittedly will restrain some VC advances. However, we can expect requirements for an ever-increasing commitment of U.S. personnel without materially improving the chances of victory. I support and agree with this decision but I must point out that in my judgment, forcing submission of the VC can only be brought about by a decision in Hanoi. Since the contemplated actions against the North are modest in scale, they will not impose unacceptable damage on it, nor will they threaten the DRV's vital interests. Hence, they will not present them with a situation with which they cannot live, though such actions will cause the DRV pain and inconvenience.

I believe our proposed track offers great danger of simply encouraging Chinese Communists and Soviet support of the DRV and VC cause, if for no other reason than the risk for both will be minimum. I envision that the reaction of the NVN and Chinese Communists will be to deliberately, carefully, and probably gradually, build up the Viet Cong capabilities by covert infiltration on North Vietnamese and, possibly, Chinese cadres and thus bring an ever-increasing pressure on our forces. In effect, we will find ourselves mired down in combat in the jungle in a military effort that we cannot win, and from which we will have extreme difficulty in extracting ourselves.

Therefore it is my judgment that if we are to change the mission of the ground forces, we must also change the ground rules of the strikes against North Vietnam. We must hit them harder, more frequently, and inflict greater damage. Instead of avoiding the MIG's, we must go in and take them out. A bridge here and there will not do the job. We must strike their airfields, their petroleum resources, power stations and their military compounds. This, in my opinion, must be done promptly and with minimum restraint. . . . ■

Memorandum, "A Compromise Solution in South Vietnam," from Under Secretary of State George W. Ball for President Johnson, July 1, 1965.

1 A Losing War: The South Vietnamese are losing the war to the Viet Cong. No one can assure you that we can beat the Viet Cong or even force them to the conference table on our terms, no matter how many hundred thousand *white, foreign* (U.S.) troops we deploy.

No one has demonstrated that a white ground force of whatever size can win a guerrilla war—which is at the same time a civil war between Asians—in jungle terrain in the midst of a population that refuses cooperation to the white forces (and the South Vietnamese) and thus provides a great intelligence advantage to the other side. Three recent incidents vividly illustrate this point: (a) the sneak attack on the Da Nang Air Base which involved penetration of a defense perimeter guarded by 9,000 Marines. This raid was possible only because of the cooperation of the local inhabitants; (b) the B52 raid that failed to hit the Viet Cong who had obviously been tipped off; (c) the search and destroy mission of the 173rd Air Borne Brigade which spent three days looking for the Viet Cong, suffered 23 casualties, and never made contact with the enemy who had obviously gotten advance word of their assignment.

2 The Question to Decide: Should we limit our liabilities in South Vietnam and try to find a way out with minimal long-term costs?

The alternative—no matter what we may wish it to be—is almost certainly a protracted war involving an open-ended com-

mitment of U.S. forces, mounting U.S. casualties, no assurance of a satisfactory solution, and a serious danger of escalation at the end of the road.

3 Need for a Decision Now: So long as our forces are restricted to advising and assisting the South Vietnamese, the struggle will remain a civil war between Asian peoples. Once we deploy substantial numbers of troops in combat it will become a war between the U.S. and a large part of the population of South Vietnam, organized and directed from North Vietnam and backed by the resources of both Moscow and Peiping.

The decision you face now, therefore, is crucial. Once large numbers of U.S. troops are committed to direct combat, they will begin to take heavy casualties in a war they are ill-equipped to fight in a non-cooperative if not downright hostile countryside.

Once we suffer large casualties, we will have started a well-nigh irreversible process. Our involvement will be so great that we cannot—without national humiliation—stop short of achieving our complete objectives. *Of the two possibilities I think humiliation would be more likely than the achievement of our objectives—even after we have paid terrible costs.*

4 Compromise Solution: Should we commit U.S. manpower and prestige to a terrain so unfavorable as to give a very large advantage to the enemy—or should we seek a compromise settlement which achieves less than our stated objectives and thus cut our losses while we still have the freedom of maneuver to do so.

5 Costs of a Compromise Solution: The answer involves a judgment as to the cost to the U.S. of such a compromise settle-

ment in terms of our relations with the countries in the area of South Vietnam, the credibility of our commitments, and our prestige around the world. In my judgment, if we act before we commit substantial U.S. troops to combat in South Vietnam we can, by accepting some short-term costs, avoid what may well be a long-term catastrophe. I believe we tended grossly to exaggerate the costs involved in a compromise settlement. An appreciation of probable costs is contained in the attached memorandum.

6 With these considerations in mind, I strongly urge the following program:

(a) Military Program

1/Complete all deployments already announced—15 battalions—but decide not to go beyond a total of 72,000 men represented by this figure.

2/Restrict the combat role of the American forces to the June 19 announcement, making it clear to General Westmoreland that this announcement is to be strictly construed.

3/Continue bombing in the North but avoid the Hanoi-Haiphong area and any targets nearer to the Chinese border than those already struck.

(b) Political Program

1/In any political approaches so far, we have been the prisoners of whatever South Vietnamese government that was momentarily in power. If we are ever to move toward a settlement, it will probably be because the South Vietnamese government pulls the rug out from under us and makes its own deal *or* because we go forward quietly without advance prearrangement with Saigon.

2/So far we have not given the other side

a reason to believe there is *any* flexibility in our negotiating approach. And the other side has been unwilling to accept what *in their terms* is complete capitulation.

3/Now is the time to start some serious diplomatic feelers looking towards a solution based on some application of a self-determination principle.

4/I would recommend approaching Hanoi rather than any of the other probable parties, the NLF—or Peiping. Hanoi is the only one that has given any signs of interest in discussion. Peiping has been rigidly opposed. Moscow has recommended that we negotiate with Hanoi. The NLF has been silent.

5/There are several channels to the North Vietnamese but I think the best one is through their representative in Paris, Mai Van Bo. Initial feelers of Bo should be directed toward a discussion both of the four points we have put forward and the four points put forward by Hanoi as a basis for negotiation. We can accept all but one of Hanoi's four points, and hopefully we should be able to agree on some ground rules for serious negotiation—including no preconditions.

6/If the initial feelers lead to further secret, exploratory talks, we can inject the concept of self-determination that would permit the Viet Cong some hope of achieving some of their political objectives through local elections or some other device.

7/The contact on our side should be handled through a non-governmental cut-out (possibly a reliable newspaper man who can be repudiated).

8/If progress can be made at this level a basis can be laid for a multinational con-ference. At some point, obviously, the government of South Vietnam will have to be brought on board, but I would postpone this step until after a substantial feeling out of Hanoi.

9/Before moving to any formal conference we should be prepared to agree once the conference is started:

(a) The U.S. will stand down its bombing of the North,

(b) The South Vietnamese will initiate no offensive operations in the South, and

(c) the DRV will stop terrorism and other aggressive action against the South.

10/The negotiations at the conference should aim at incorporating our understanding with Hanoi in the form of a multi-national agreement guaranteed by the U.S., the Soviet Union and possibly other parties, and providing for an international mechanism to supervise its execution.

PROBABLE REACTIONS TO THE CUTTING OF OUR LOSSES IN SOUTH VIETNAM

We have tended to exaggerate the losses involved in a complete settlement in South Vietnam. There are three aspects to the problem that should be considered. First, the local effect of our action on nations in or near Southeast Asia. Second, the effect of our action on the credibility of our commitments around the world. Third, the effect on our position of world leadership.

A. Free Asian Reactions to a Compromise Settlement in South Vietnam Would Be Highly Parochial.

With each country interpreting the event primarily in terms of (a) its own immediate interest, (b) its sense of vulnerability to Communist invasion or insurgency, and (c) its confidence in the integrity of our commitment to its own security based on evidence other than that provided by our actions in South Vietnam.

Within this framework the following groupings emerge:

1/The Republic of China and Thailand: staunch allies whose preference for extreme U.S. actions including a risk of war with Communist China sets them apart from all other Asian nations;

2/The Republic of Korea and the Philippines: equally staunch allies whose support for strong U.S. action short of a war with Communist China would make post-settlement reassurance a pressing U.S. need;

3/Japan: it would prefer wisdom to valor in an area remote from its own interests where escalation could involve its Chinese or Eurasian neighbors or both;

4/Laos: a friendly neutral dependent on a strong Thai-U.S. guarantee of support in the face of increased Vietnamese and Laos pressures.

5/Burma and Cambodia: suspicious neutrals whose fear of antagonizing Communist China would increase their leaning toward Peiping in a conviction that the U.S. presence is not long for Southeast Asia; and

6/Indonesia: whose opportunistic marriage of convenience of both Hanoi and Peiping would carry it further in its overt aggression against Malaysia, convinced that foreign imperialism is a fast fading entity in the region.

JAPAN

Government cooperation [words illegible] essential in making the following points to the Japanese people:

(1) U.S. support was given in full

measure as shown by our casualties, our expenditures and our risk taking;

(2) The U.S. record in Korea shows the credibility of our commitment so far as Japan is concerned.

The government as such supports our strong posture in Vietnam but stops short of the idea of a war between the U.S. and China.

THAILAND

Thai commitments to the struggle within Laos and South Vietnam are based upon a careful evaluation of the regional threat to Thailand's security. The Thais are confident they can contain any threats from Inochina alone. They know, however, they cannot withstand the massive power of Communist China without foreign assistance. Unfortunately, the Thai view of the war has seriously erred in fundamental respects. They believe American power can do anything, both militarily and in terms of shoring up the Saigon regime. They now assume that we really could take over in Saigon and win the war if we felt we had to. If we should fail to do so, the Thais would initially see it as a failure of U.S. will. Yet time is on our side, providing we employ it effectively. Thailand is an independent nation with a long national history, and unlike South Vietnam, an acute national consciousness. It has few domestic Communists and none of the instability that plague its neighbors, Burma and Malaysia. Its one danger area in the northeast is well in hand so far as preventive measures against insurgency are concerned. Securing the Mekong Valley will be critical in any long-run solution, whether by the partition of Laos with Thai-U.S. forces occupying the western half or by some

[word illegible] arrangement. Providing we are willing to make the effort, Thailand can be a foundation of rock and not a bed of sand in which to base our political/military commitment to Southeast Asia.

—With the exception of the nations in Southeast Asia, a compromise settlement in South Vietnam should not have a major impact on the credibility of our commitments around the world . . . Chancellor Erhard has told us privately that the people of Berlin would be concerned by a compromise settlement of South Vietnam. But this was hardly an original thought, and I suspect he was telling us what he believed we would like to hear. After all, the confidence of the West Berliners will depend more on what they see on the spot than on [word illegible] news or events halfway around the world. In my observation, the principal anxiety of our NATO Allies is that we have become too preoccupied with an area which seems to them an irrelevance and may be tempted in neglect to our NATO responsibilities. Moreover, they have a vested interest in an easier relationship between Washington and Moscow. By and large, therefore, they will be inclined to regard a compromise solution in South Vietnam more as new evidence of American maturity and judgment than of American loss of face . . . On balance, I believe we would more seriously undermine the effectiveness of our world leadership by continuing the war and deepening our involvement than by pursuing a carefully plotted course toward a compromise solution. In spite of the number of powers that have—in response to our pleading—given verbal support from feeling of loyalty and dependence, we cannot ignore the fact that

the war is vastly unpopular and that our role in it is perceptively eroding the respect and confidence with which other nations regard us. We have not persuaded either our friends or allies that our further involvement is essential to the defense of freedom in the cold war. Moreover, the more men we deploy in the jungles of South Vietnam, the more we contribute to a growing world anxiety and mistrust.

[Words illegible] the short run, of course, we could expect some catcalls from the sidelines and some vindictive pleasure on the part of Europeans jealous of American power. But that would, in my view, be a transient phenomenon with which we could live without sustained anguish. Elsewhere around the world I would see few unhappy implications for the credibility of our commitments. No doubt the Communists will stand to gain propaganda value in Africa, but I cannot seriously believe that the Africans care too much about what happens in Southeast Asia. Australia and New Zealand are, of course, special cases since they feel lonely in the far reaches of the Pacific. Yet even their concern is far greater with Malaysia than with South Vietnam, and the degree of their anxiety would be conditioned largely by expressions of our support for Malaysia.

[Words illegible] Quite possibly President de Gaulle will make propaganda about perfidious Washington, yet even he will be inhibited by his much-heralded disapproval of our activities in South Vietnam.

South Korea—As for the rest of the Far East the only serious point of concern might be South Korea. But if we stop pressing the Koreans for more troops to Vietnam (the Vietnamese show no desire for addi-

Philip Jones Griffiths, Magnum

533

tional Asian forces since it affronts their
sense of pride) we may be able to cushion
Korean reactions to a compromise in
South Vietnam by the provision of greater
military and economic assistance. In this
regard, Japan can play a pivotal role now
that it has achieved normal relations with
South Korea. ■

Source: Lyndon B. Johnson, *The Vantage Point: Perspectives of the Presidency, 1963–1969* (New York: Holt, Rinehart and Winston, 1971), pp. 119–149 *passim*.

The Decision Defended

The idea of hitting North Vietnam with air power, either on a reprisal basis or in a sustained campaign, had been discussed inside the Government, in Saigon, and in the American press for a long time.

However, during my first year in the White House no formal proposal for an air campaign against North Vietnam ever came to me as the agreed suggestion of my principal advisers. Whenever the subject came up, one or another of them usually mentioned the risk of giving Communist China an excuse for massive intervention in Vietnam. Rusk was concerned that putting direct pressure on North Vietnam might encourage the Soviets to raise the level of tension around Berlin, in the Middle East or elsewhere. I fully concurred. Our goals in Vietnam were limited and so were our actions. I wanted to keep them that way.

Many advisers in my Administration, in both State and Defense, were concerned that heavy air strikes against the North might cause Hanoi to launch a massive outright invasion of the South or at least to step up significantly the level of the guerrilla war. American officials in Washington and in Saigon agreed that the political and military machinery in South Vietnam was then much too fragile to survive that kind of hammer blow.

Pessimistic reports continued to come to me from my advisers and from the field. Early in January, 1965, Maxwell Taylor sent in a report concluding that "we are presently on a losing track and must risk a change. . . . To take no positive action now is to accept defeat in the fairly near future." That was the view of every responsible military adviser in Vietnam and in Washington. Painfully and reluctantly, my civilian advisers were driven to the same conclusion by the hard facts.

On Jan. 27, 1965, Mac Bundy sent me a memo saying that he and Bob McNamara were "pretty well convinced that our current policy can lead only to disastrous defeat."

Bundy and McNamara saw two alternatives: either to "use our military power in the Far East and to force a change of Communist policy" or to "deploy all our resources along a track of negotiation, aimed at salvaging what little can be preserved with no major addition to our present military risks." They said that they were inclined to favor the first alternative— use of more military power—but they believed that both courses should be studied carefully and that alternative programs should be developed and argued out in my presence.

The memo concluded by pointing out that Dean Rusk did not agree with the McNamara - Bundy assessment. Rusk knew things were going badly and he did not claim that the deterioration could be stopped. "What he does say," the memo stated, "is that the consequences of both escalation and withdrawal are so bad that we simply must find a way of making our present policy work. This would be good if it was possible. Bob and I do not think it is."

Word came on the afternoon of Feb. 6 that the Communists had carried out major attacks on the U.S. Army advisers' barracks at Pleiku and on a U.S. Army helicopter base about four miles away, as well as on several Vietnamese targets. Eight Americans had been killed outright in the attacks, one died later, and more than a hundred had been wounded. Five U.S. aircraft had been destroyed and 15 damaged.

My advisers strongly urged that we answer the attacks by striking four targets in North Vietnam immediately. United States planes would handle three: the South Vietnamese Air Force would strike the fourth. The targets were Army barracks associated with North Vietnam's infiltration system into the South.

After long discussion I authorized the strikes, provided the South Vietnamese Government agreed. There was little doubt about the latter, since Saigon had been urging retaliation against the North for some time. I also ordered the prompt evacuation of our dependents from Vietnam.

We met again the next morning to review the situation. Three of the four authorized targets had been fogged in; only one had been struck. Should we go back after the other three? The consensus was "no," and I agreed. We all felt that a second-day strike by U.S. planes might give Hanoi and Moscow the impression that we had begun a sustained air offensive. That decision had not been made. However, we all agreed that the South Vietnamese Air Force should go back after its target. The Vietnamese concurred emphatically.

That night Mac Bundy and his specialists returned to Washington from Saigon. About 11 P.M. Bundy came to the White House to see me. He left with me the report he and his group had developed on their tour of Vietnam.

"The situation in Vietnam is deteriorating," the report began, "and without new U.S. action defeat appears inevitable —probably not in a matter of weeks or perhaps even months, but within the next year or so. There is still time to turn around, but not much."

The annex to the Bundy report, prepared mainly by Assistant Secretary of Defense John McNaughton, stated at the outset:

"We believe that the best available way of increasing our chance of success in Vietnam is the development and execution of a policy of sustained reprisal against North Vietnam—a policy in which air and naval action against the North is justified by and related to the whole Vietcong campaign of violence and terror in the South."

The idea of attacking North Vietnam with air power had been a feature of several planning exercises and position papers in 1964. But now, I knew, we were at a turning point. Though the Bundy report proposed a course of action we had considered and turned down only three months before, I was impressed by its logic and persuaded strongly by its arguments. I cabled Taylor in Saigon. I told him I wanted him to know that I had decided to carry out a plan for "continuing action" against North Vietnam "with modifications up and down in tempo and scale in the light of your recommendations . . . and our own continuing review of the situation."

On Feb. 13 we notified Taylor and the military command in Saigon that I had approved a three-point program of immediate actions. First, we would intensify the pacification program by all available means. Second, we would carry out "measured and limited air action jointly with the GVN" [Government of (South) Vietnam] against military targets in the North below the 19th parallel. Finally, we would go to the U.N. Security Council and detail the case against Hanoi's aggression.

My advisers had long argued that a weak government in Saigon would have difficulty surviving the pressures that might be exerted against the South if we bombed the North. I now concluded that political life in the South would soon collapse unless the people there knew that the North was paying a price in its own territory for its aggression. There were strong military reasons for our action, as the Joint Chiefs had long argued. Now the weight of the political argument as well had shifted to support intensified action.

From the time our planes hit the first military target in North Vietnam early in February, we were subjected to an increasingly heavy propaganda barrage from Hanoi, Peking and Moscow. Before long some American public figures began to repeat the theme. They all ignored the vital fact that we were bombing the North because Hanoi was stepping up its war in the South.

I decided it was time to make another major statement on Vietnam to the American people. For this purpose I accepted a long-standing invitation from President Milton Eisenhower of Johns Hopkins University in Baltimore to speak there on April 7, 1965. I listed the essential elements of a just peace: an independent South Vietnam that was "securely guaranteed and able to shape its own relationships to all others— free from outside interference—tied to no alliance—a military base for no other country."

I then looked forward, beyond war and the coming of peace, to what could happen in that troubled and underdeveloped region of the world.

"For our part," I said, "I will ask the Congress to join in a billion-dollar American investment in this effort as soon as it is under way. And I would hope that all other industrialized countries, including the Soviet Union, will join in this effort to replace despair with hope, and terror with progress."

The Communists' answer came quickly. On April 9 Radio Peking said my offer was "full of lies and deceptions." The following day Moscow called the proposal "noisy propaganda." Two days after that Hanoi's Communist party newspaper described the Johns Hopkins offer as "bait."

Although the bombing of the North remained at a fairly low level during the first few months of what was called the Rolling Thunder campaign, the level of criticism was high.

I had discussed halting the bombing with various advisers. An inter-agency working group was developing a plan for such a pause. Late in April Bobby Kennedy came to see me in the White House. The newly elected Senator from New York had several things on his mind, and one of them was a possible bombing pause. We sat in the small private study next to the Oval Office. I told him that we had been considering a pause for some time and were giving the matter careful study. He suggested that we try it for a few days, even one or two. A brief pause would do no harm, he said, and maybe something useful would come of it. I repeated that we had been discussing such a move and he could rest assured it was receiving very serious consideration.

On May 10 I decided to end the bombing for a limited period. We informed the Russians of our position and asked them to pass the information along to the North Vietnamese. But the Soviets refused to act as intermediaries. We delivered a message to the North Vietnamese Embassy in Moscow for their Ambassador. The note was returned to our embassy the next day in a plain envelope. We later arranged for direct delivery to Hanoi through another government, but that message was also returned.

Hanoi never answered directly but infiltration into the South continued, as did Vietcong attacks. Then Hanoi denounced the pause, and Peking even alleged there was no pause. Once again we had tried to open the door; once again Hanoi had slammed it shut. In the face of Hanoi's continued hostility, we resumed bombing on May 18.

Once sustained bombing of the North began, my advisers and I were convinced that the Communists would make the air base near Danang a high-priority target since many air strikes were launched there. The Vietnamese authorities shared our conviction. In March I agreed to General Westmoreland's request that we land two Marine battalions to provide security for the Danang air base. This released for offensive action against the Vietcong some of the Vietnamese troops who had been protecting the base.

In March our estimate of Communist troop strength rose to 37,000 in main-force units and 100,000 in regional forces and local guerrillas. That represented a 33 per

536

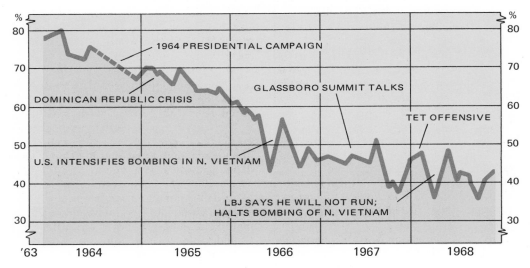

LBJ'S APPROVAL RATING — 5 YEAR TREND

1964 PRESIDENTIAL CAMPAIGN

DOMINICAN REPUBLIC CRISIS

GLASSBORO SUMMIT TALKS

TET OFFENSIVE

U.S. INTENSIFIES BOMBING IN N. VIETNAM

LBJ SAYS HE WILL NOT RUN; HALTS BOMBING OF N. VIETNAM

'63 1964 1965 1966 1967 1968

President Johnson's first popularity rating, recorded in Dec., 1963, was 79 per cent approval. During the roughly five years between then and now, the President's rating has slipped 36 percentage points, to 43 per cent today.

cent increase over 1964. In a few months the over-all estimate was raised to 153,000. In real combat strength the South Vietnamese had at best about 133 maneuver battalions, and their enemy had 72. That was a ratio of less than 2 to 1, and specialists in guerrilla warfare had long maintained that success against a determined guerrilla enemy called for a ratio of about 10 to 1 in favor of the defense forces.

Among the specific military actions I approved in April were:

An 18,000-to-20,000-man increase in U.S. logistic and support forces.

Deployment of two additional Marine battalions (for a total of four) and one Marine air squadron to the Danang-Hue area, with one of the battalions to go to

Phubai, near Hue, to protect communications facilities and an airfield in that area.

A change in mission for the marines to permit "their more active use" under rules to be approved by the Secretaries of State and Defense. This did not mean, as has been frequently interpreted, that the Marines were to have an unlimited combat role. It did mean more aggressive patrolling and limited counterinsurgency combat operations in the vicinity of the Marine bases.

The basic mission of the U.S. forces in Vietnam up to mid-May had been to secure the base areas to which they were assigned. This mission had been broadened somewhat to permit active and aggressive patrolling near those bases. In May General

Westmoreland asked permission to use his forces in combat support if it became necessary to assist a Vietnamese unit in serious trouble. I granted that permission and announced it in a White House press statement on June 9.

Later in June General Westmoreland requested and received additional authority. This permitted him to commit U.S. troops to combat "independently of or in conjunction with" Vietnamese forces if asked by the Vietnamese and if Westmoreland himself judged that their use was "necessary to strengthen the relative position of GVN forces."

Meanwhile, another political crisis was boiling up in Saigon. Prime Minister Phan Huy Quat was feuding with Vietnam's Catholics and was also at odds with the Vietnamese chief of state, Phan Khac Suu. On June 12 Quat resigned, announcing that he was turning power back to the military. The generals set up a National Leadership Committee chaired by Gen. Nguyen Van Thieu, thus making him chief of state. They also selected an Executive Council, which they called their "war cabinet," and picked Marshal Nguyen Cao Ky, chief of the Vietnamese Air Force, to head it with the powers of Prime Minister.

One of the first things General Thieu and Prime Minister Ky told McNamara, who was in Vietnam on a visit, was that they were convinced that American and perhaps other foreign forces would be needed to hold back the Communist attackers. When McNamara asked for their estimate of how many might be needed, the Vietnamese leaders said they thought that in addition to the 44 battalions they had already requested, there should be another combat division. Their total estimate called for about 200,000 American men in all categories.

There were then 15 American combat battalions either in Vietnam or en route, and a total force level of 75,000. McNamara recommended that the number of battalions be increased to 34. The Koreans had promised to send nine battalions; if they failed to do so, we should make up the difference—a total in that case of 43 battalions. That would raise the level of our forces to 175,000 men, or 200,000 if the Koreans failed to come through as promised.

I wanted to go over this proposal with the greatest care. I realized what a major undertaking it would be. The call-up of large numbers of reserves was part of the package. I summoned my top advisers to the White House on July 21, the day after McNamara returned.

We considered many alternatives. Under Secretary of State George Ball had been less enthusiastic about some aspects of our involvement in Southeast Asia. At the afternoon session I asked Ball to outline his views. His basic thesis was that we could not win a protracted war against local guerrillas in Asian jungles. He thought there was great danger of intrusion by the Chinese Communists. In his opinion, we were losing friends and influence in Europe and elsewhere because of our commitment in Asia. The best thing to do, he thought, was to cut our losses and pull away.

Dean Rusk expressed one worry that was much on my mind. It lay at the heart of our Vietnam policy. "If the Communist world finds out that we will not pursue our commitments to the end," he said, "I don't know where they will stay their hand."

I felt sure they would *not* stay their hand. If we ran out on Southeast Asia, I could see trouble ahead in every part of the globe—not just in Asia but in the Middle East and in Europe, in Africa and in Latin America. I was convinced that our retreat from this challenge would open the path to World War III.

I told the N.S.C. there were five possible choices available to us.

"We can bring the enemy to his knees by using our Strategic Air Command," I said describing our first option. "Another group thinks we ought to pack up and go home.

"Third, we could stay there as we are—and suffer the consequences, continue to lose territory and take casualties. You wouldn't want your own boy to be out there crying for help and not get it.

"Then, we could go to Congress and ask for great sums of money; we could call up the reserves and increase the draft; go to a war footing; declare a state of emergency. There is a good deal of feeling that ought to be done. We have considered this. But if we go into that kind of land war, then North Vietnam would go to its friends, China and Russia, and ask them to give help. They would be forced into increasing aid. For that reason I don't want to be overly dramatic and cause tensions. I think we can get our people to support us without having to be too provocative and warlike.

"Finally, we can give our commanders in the field the men and supplies they say they need."

I had concluded that the last course was the right one. ∎

THE PUBLIC CONTROVERSY OVER VIETNAM

The largely secret debate over Vietnam policy that took place within the Johnson Administration was paralleled by a vigorous debate carried on in the press, in the halls of Congress, on college campuses, and by way of demonstrations and counterdemonstrations throughout the country. The political cartoons, bumper stickers, placards, news summaries, headlines, and posters presented here partially describe the intensity of the public controversy over the Vietnam War.

All photos from Magnum

1 Are there conflicting assumptions about the facts of the Vietnamese situation in the public debate? Do the same conflicts exist in the interior debate among Johnson's advisors?

2 What value conflicts are expressed in the public debate? How do these compare with the value conflicts expressed in the interior debate?

3 How do those engaged in the public debate seek to influence the direction of the interior debate? Does the interior debate reflect concern over the impact of public opinion? What does this indicate about the influence of public opinion on foreign policy? ■

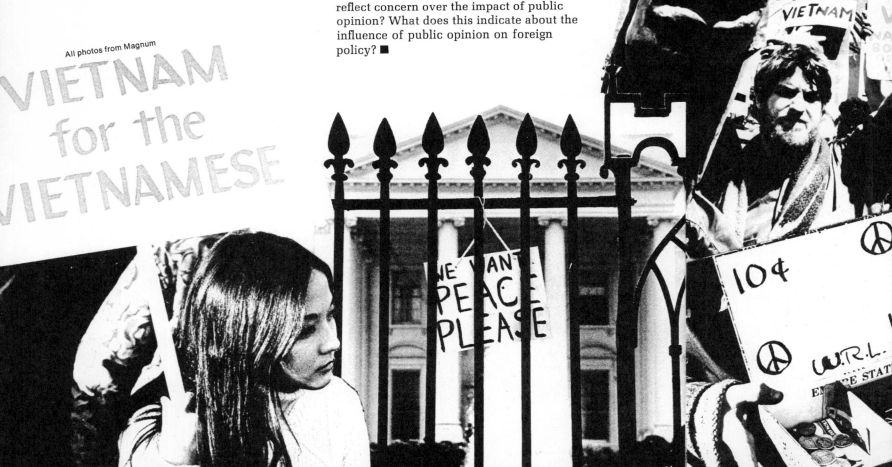

VIETNAM for the VIETNAMESE

WE WANT PEACE PLEASE

VIETNAM

10¢

W.R.L.

REPENT
ASIA IS
NONE OF OUR
BUSINESS

HE JUST STARTED AS A LITTLE DRAGON WE
WERE JUST ADVISING

Yardley, *The Sun*, Baltimore, Md.

I WON'T FIGHT
IN VIETNAM

RADCLIFFE

Source: *Facts on File,* vol. XXVII, no. 1375 (March 2–8, 1967).

News Summary of the
Vietnam Controversy.

Pres. Johnson replied in a speech at Princeton University May 11 to a charge that the U.S. was "succumbing to the arrogance of power" by equating "its power with virtue and its major responsibilities with a universal mission." The charge had been made by Sen. J. W. Fulbright (D., Ark.) in the 3d of 3 lectures he had delivered at the School of Advanced International Studies of the Johns Hopkins University.

In the May 5 lecture, Fulbright said he had "not the slightest doubt" of the sincerity of Pres. Johnson and Administration officials in pursuing U.S. policy in Vietnam. But he expressed doubt that the U.S. could "go into a small, alien, undeveloped Asian nation and create stability where there is chaos, the will to fight where there is defeatism, democracy where there is no tradition of it and honest government where corruption is almost a way of life." He declared that in Vietnam "we are still acting like boy scouts dragging reluctant old ladies across streets they do not want to cross." "If America has a service to perform in the world," Fulbright said, "it is in large part the service of its own example" in its "domestic life."

The President went to Princeton, N.J. May 11 to speak at dedication ceremonies for the Woodrow Wilson School of Public & International Affairs and to accept an honorary LL.D. Rebutting Fulbright's charge, without mentioning Fulbright's name, Mr. Johnson urged "responsible" intellectuals, "in the language of the current generation, to 'cool it'—to bring what my generation called 'not heat but light' to public affairs." "The exercise of power in this century," he said, "has meant for all of us in the United States not arrogance but agony. We have used our power not willingly and recklessly ever, but always reluctantly and with restraint." Referring to Vietnam, Mr. Johnson asked: "What nation has announced such limited objectives or such willingness to remove its military presence once those objectives are secured and achieved? What nation has spent the lives of its sons and vast sums of its fortune to provide the people of a small, striving country the chance to elect a course that we might not ourselves choose?"

The President said America was "a nation whose might is not her master but her servant," "a nation conscious of lessons so recently learned that security and aggression as well as peace and war must be the concerns of our foreign policy; that a great power influences the world just as surely when it withdraws its strength as when it exercises its strength; that aggression must be deterred where possible and met early when undertaken; that the application of military force when it becomes necessary must be for limited purposes and must be tightly controlled."

(In a speech in Washington May 12 at a $100-a-plate party dinner attended by more than 6,000 Democrats, Pres. Johnson said: "If we were to turn our backs on freedom in South Vietnam—if Vietnam were to fall to an aggressor's force—what an empty thing our commitment to liberty would really turn out to be.")

Sen. Jacob K. Javits said in a Senate speech May 5 that the U.S. had been motivated by "an acceptance of power" rather than "an arrogance of power" in its foreign policy since World War II.

Fulbright was attacked May 5 by ex-Sen. Barry Goldwater, who said Fulbright should resign as chairman of the Senate Foreign Relations Committee for giving "aid and comfort to the enemy." "No American has the right or the justification to level such charges against his own country," Goldwater said. "And that goes double for doing it in a time of war. . . ."

Fulbright expressed regret May 17 that he had made the statement about the "arrogance of power" because it "lent" itself to misinterpretation. Referring to his Apr. 28 charge about America's "fatal presumption" of power, Fulbright said: "I regret that I neglected to make it clear that I was talking about the extent, not the character, of a nation's aspirations." He said the next sentence in the speech—stating that the process had hardly begun but that the Vietnam war could hasten it—had been generally ignored in news accounts. He stressed that in his May 5 lecture he "did not charge any American official with arrogance in the exercise of power" but rather was critical of the tendency of powerful nations, "of which the United States is the current example, to get puffed up about all the terrific things they think they ought to be doing with their power." Fulbright also said he regretted his statement May 5 that "Saigon had become an American brothel." "I had not thought I was maligning the brave young Americans in Vietnam," he said. "What I was referring to was the inevitable impact on a fragile Asian society of Western soldiers" with money to spend "behaving in the way that is to be expected of men of war."

Goldwater May 5 also attacked the Administration as waging a limited war "to curry favor with a domestic political group to whom the word 'escalation' is the greatest of all evils." In an interview published Apr. 18 in *U.S. News & World Report,* Goldwater advocated U.S. bombing of "the petroleum depots around Hanoi" and the closing of the port of Haiphong by "sinking light ships in its very shallow and narrow channel."

House minority leader Gerald R. Ford (Mich.) said in a statement issued Apr. 18 that the U.S. would have to use more air and sea power or send as many as 200,000 more GIs to Vietnam "to achieve even a stalemate . . . in a war that now looks like a war without end."

Vice Pres. Humphrey continued his defense of U.S. policy in Vietnam by saying at the Democratic Women's Campaign Conference in Washington Apr. 18: "We are not in Vietnam because of geography or who is in charge of a government. We are there because America has given a pledge to future generations to preserve law and order." In a CBS-TV interview Apr. 19, Humphrey called the Honolulu Declaration "a pledge . . . to defeat aggression, to defeat social misery, to build viable, free political institutions and to achieve peace." "I think there is a tremendous new opening here for realizing the dream of the great society in the great area of Asia, not just here at home," he said.

Sen. Wayne L. Morse (D., Ore.) questioned Defense Secy. Robert S. McNamara May 11 about whether the loss of 3,234 U.S. troops killed and 15,000 wounded had brought the Vietnamese war closer to victory or negotiated settlement. The con-frontation occurred at a Senate Foreign Relations Committee hearing on the foreign aid program. McNamara replied: "The first step in a negotiated peace is the avoidance of a loss, and that step has been taken as a direct result of the introduction of United States forces." "Had the men not been introduced, the Viet Cong and North Vietnam would have won. They would have slaughtered thousands and probably tens of thousands of South Vietnamese, and all of Southeast Asia would be in turmoil."

Asserting that he "disagree[d] completely," Morse said: "We must find some way to get some other forces to come in and try to settle the thing" or put a resolution for a cease-fire before the UN Security Council. "I would put France and Russia right on the spot, and if that didn't work I would push for the resolution before the General Assembly."

McNamara said that "even the UN secretary general," U Thant, "seems to have despaired of the ability of the UN to act in this situation." Morse replied: "That's why we should have a new secretary general."

McNamara also told the committee that: (a) The U.S. bombing had had a "noticeably adverse effect on Viet Cong morale and expectation of victory" (the observation was based on intelligence reports of increases in desertions and defections among Communists and of Communist drafting of youths 15–17 years old); (b) "it appears that the Viet Cong is losing what support it had from the rural population"; (c) these comments should not lead to undue optimism since the dominant theme was the "deliberate decision" of the North Vietnamese to continue and intensify the war; (d) the political upheaval in South Vietnam had reduced the level of military operations. ■

PUBLIC OPINION POLLS
AND THE VIETNAM WAR

Reprinted below is a section from a Gallup Poll pamphlet entitled *Public Opinion and the Vietnam War*. This report was based on more than sixty nationwide surveys and interviews having to do with the Vietnam War. The introduction to the report states:

Important news events have been listed chronologically to provide background information and to show how the trend of public opinion relates in general terms to the trend of events. The dates given for the summaries are the publication dates of the full reports in client newspapers; it is important to bear in mind that these reports are based on interviewing conducted one to three weeks prior to publication date.

Only one year—1965—covered by this report is included. This year was selected because it was at this time that the debate within the government over Vietnam policy was taking place.

1 What do the polls indicate about the public's knowledge or lack of knowledge concerning the major issues at stake in the debate over the Vietnam War?

2 In what ways do specific polls or the trend of the polls indicate that Americans are being influenced by the public debate? In what way do the polls suggest that Americans are being influenced by the statements or actions of the Johnson administration?

3 How do news events appear to influence the results of the polls?

4 How would you compare the quality and sophistication of this summary of public

opinion on the Vietnam War with the quality of the summary of public opinion during the Korean War? ■

Source: *Gallup Opinion Index* (Princeton, N. J.: Gallup International, Inc., December 1967), pp. 13–18.

1965
Jan. 31
SEE SOUTH VIETNAMESE LOSING WAR: The majority of persons who have followed developments in Vietnam are pessimistic about the trend of events. By the ratio of 4-to-1, they believe the South Vietnamese are losing to the communist Vietcong. In addition, the public believes by the ratio of 2-to-1 that the different groups in South Vietnam will not be able to form a stable government.

At the same time, the prevailing opinion holds that the U.S. has a responsibility to keep independent nations from being overrun by the communists. Half (50 per cent) think our country was right to have become involved in Southeast Asia; 28 per cent say we should not have become involved.

Eight persons in ten favor the suggestion that President Johnson try to set up talks with leaders of Southeast Asia and China to see if a peace agreement can be reached.

Widespread interest is found in reaching some kind of acceptable and peaceful compromise. But if such a compromise cannot be worked out, and it comes to a question of our either being pushed out of the country or forced into a military crisis, sentiment is 4-to-3 in favor of sending in more men.

Feb. 7
Communist guerrillas stage attack on U.S. outpost. U.S. planes strike targets in North Vietnam.

Feb. 8
President Johnson indicates that further developments depend on Communist response.

544

Feb. 8

Premier Kosygin announces Soviet willingness to aid North Vietnam if she is invaded.

Feb. 11

Secretary General U Thant calls for international negotiations on Vietnam inside or outside of the U.N.

Feb. 15

Chinese Communists threaten to enter the war if American troops enter North Vietnam.

Feb. 17

RETALIATORY AIR STRIKES SUPPORTED: Two out of every three Americans who have followed the recent developments in Vietnam voice approval of the action taken by the U.S. in making retaliatory air strikes against North Vietnam.

At the same time, a majority (64 per cent) believes that the U.S. should continue its present efforts there, but 18 per cent think the U.S. should withdraw its forces from Vietnam. Another 18 per cent are undecided.

When the 64 per cent who say the U.S. should continue its present efforts were asked if the U.S. should do so at the risk of nuclear war, about half—or 31 per cent—said yes.

Feb. 17

WILL CRISIS LEAD TO BIGGER WAR? Forty-five per cent of those persons who have followed recent developments think the situation in Vietnam is likely to lead to a bigger war. Almost exactly the same proportion—44 per cent—think it will not.

At the same time, a majority of 62 per cent of adults think the U.S. is doing as well as can be expected in handling affairs in South Vietnam. The proportion who hold this view is far greater at this time than those who think the U.S. is handling affairs poorly—22 per cent.

Six out of ten persons who have followed developments favor a proposal to have a United Nations army deal with the problems of Southeast Asia and Vietnam.

Feb. 25

North Vietnamese officials state negotiations would be considered if American troops were withdrawn.

Feb. 27

State Department issues white paper detailing charges of aggression on the part of North Vietnam.

Feb. 28

United States and South Vietnamese officials declare that President Johnson has decided to open continuous limited air strikes against North Vietnam in order to bring about a negotiated settlement.

Mar. 12

SUPPORT FOR U.S. POLICY STAYS HIGH: Events of recent weeks have had little impact on the public's views concerning the Vietnam crisis. Immediately following the first major U.S. retaliatory air strikes on North Vietnam over a month ago, a nationwide survey showed that the public had backed the President's policy. In the days since this first action, there has been considerable argument for both carrying the war on and for pulling our forces

out of Vietnam. The public, however, still is in favor of continuing our present military program. The results of the earlier survey found 64 per cent of those persons following the situation saying that the U.S. should continue its present program. Today, the comparable figure is 66 per cent.

Opinion is still sharply divided about the possibility of this crisis leading to a bigger war. Results of the earlier survey showed that 45 per cent believed that the situation in Vietnam would lead to a bigger war; 44 per cent held the opposite view, with 11 per cent undecided. The results of today's survey show that there has been virtually no change.

Mar. 28

RED CHINA REPLACES RUSSIA AS NO. 1 FOE: One of the major shifts in public opinion in recent years has been the transference of the worries of many Americans about Russia and her intentions to worries about Communist China.

Apr. 2

United States announces intention of sending several thousand more troops to South Vietnam.

Apr. 7

PUBLIC DIVIDED BETWEEN ESCALATION, NEGOTIATIONS: Although the American public has followed the events in Vietnam, nothing approaching a consensus has yet developed in their ideas of what the U.S. should do next there. When asked what future steps the U.S. should take in Vietnam, the public's views are widely diversified—ranging from immediate withdrawal of our armed forces to the bombing of Communist China. Only small minorities, however, accept either of these extreme views. When asked to choose between trying to start peace negotiations or sending more troops and airplanes, the public is evenly divided in their opinions.

The public, of course, is not fully aware of all the "behind the scenes" actions now taking place in the capitals of the world, nor are they cognizant of the complexities of the military situation in Vietnam. Their views, however, are still important to our government policy makers, even if only to make sure that the public is kept informed about present policies in Southeast Asia.

Apr. 16

CIVIL RIGHTS ISSUE SEEN AS TOP PROBLEM: Despite the widespread concern of the American public over the situation in Southeast Asia, the domestic issue of civil rights is currently most often cited as the top problem facing the nation. Fifty-two per cent of persons interviewed in the latest survey name racial problems, compared to 37 per cent who cite international problems.

Apr. 23

JOHNSON TAKING "MIDDLE-OF-ROAD" IN VIET POLICIES: As many people in the United States say that we should take an even more aggressive stand in Southeast Asia as say we should stop our present fighting and withdraw our troops. Based on this evidence, it would appear that President Johnson is pursuing a "middle-of-the-road" course in dealing with Vietnam.

WHAT SHOULD U.S. DO NEXT IN VIETNAM?

Withdraw completely from
  Vietnam 17%

Start negotiations, stop fighting $\underline{12}$
                                   29%

Continue present U.S. policy
  (continuing military action,
  but remaining ready for
  negotiations) 14%
Step up military activity 12%
Go all out, declare war .... $\underline{19}$
                                   31%

A total of 28 per cent had no definite view as to what the U.S. should do next about Vietnam, and another 5 per cent gave a variety of responses, which could not be classified in the above categories. The total of percentages add to more than 100 per cent since some persons gave more than one response.

By a ratio of more than 2-to-1, the public currently approves of the Government's handling of the situation.

May 6

Two U.S. Marine battalions sent to Vietnam; first combat units to be deployed to South Vietnam.

May 13

United States halts bombing missions on North Vietnam.

May 19

United States resumes air attacks on North Vietnamese targets.

June 7

U.S. military authorities disclose that number of American military personnel in South Vietnam has passed 50,000 mark.

June 7

By vote of 42 to 26 Senate adopts amendment adding $89 million to foreign aid bill in accordance with President's request of June 1.

June 16

Secretary McNamara announces new troop movements to Vietnam which will bring total there to over 70,000.

June 28

American troops participate in their first major attack of the Vietnamese war.

July 12–18

The United States begins a large-scale buildup of its forces in South Vietnam.

July 20

Secretary McNamara leaves Vietnam after receiving request for additional U.S. troops. He states that "in many respects there has been a deterioration" in the Vietnam war since his last visit 14 months ago.

Aug. 11

VIETNAM IS CHIEF WORRY OF AMERICANS: The Vietnam situation has moved into the forefront of the public's consciousness as a source of worry, far overshadowing even the civil rights issue. At the same time, concern about the Dominican crisis has virtually disappeared.

Aug. 19

The Defense Department reports that 561 Americans had been killed, 3,024 wounded, and 44 missing in Vietnam between January 1, 1961, and August 16, 1965.

Aug. 26

PUBLIC SUPPORT GROWING FOR VIET-NAM POLICY: The program to educate the public about the Vietnam policies of the Johnson Administration is making progress. Evidence that the policy is paying off in terms of public support is provided by the latest Gallup survey. Since June, the percentage of people who say they approve of the way President Johnson is dealing with the situation in Vietnam has increased from 48 per cent to 57 per cent. In the latest survey, a clear majority of America's adults approve of the way the Johnson Administration is handling the situation in Vietnam.

Aug. 29

'ANOTHER KOREA': Relatively few Americans today are looking for the war in Vietnam to end in a military victory for our side. The thinking of the American public today parallels attitudes of people found in the latter part of the Korean War: they expect the war to end in some kind of compromise or negotiated peace. Significantly, 39 per cent of the people are unwilling to hazard even a guess as to the outcome. This is in sharp contrast to the views of the people as gauged during World War II when most Americans looked forward confidently to "total victory."

With many persons believing that the war will end in some sort of negotiated peace, and many others taking frankly pessimistic views, it is to be expected that they are willing to listen to proposals for a negotiated peace. Eight persons in ten approve of the move to ask the United Nations to try to work out its own formula for peace in Vietnam.

Oct. 14

The Defense Department orders a military draft call of 45,224 men for December, the biggest quota since the Korean War.

Oct. 15–16

The student-run National Coordinating Committee to End the War in Vietnam sponsors a series of nationwide demonstrations.

Oct. 21

U. S. Defense Department casualty report states: Vietcong deaths in 1965 totaled about 25,000; 830 U. S. military personnel had been killed between January 1961 and October 18, 1965.

Oct. 22

STUDENT DEMONSTRATIONS DO NOT REFLECT U.S. VIEWS: Doubts about the American public's attitudes have been heightened by recent student demonstrations in many areas throughout the country, but as the survey figures reveal, the public is solidly behind present efforts:

1) The American people support President Johnson and approve of the way the Johnson Administration is handling the situation in Vietnam. In the current survey, those who approve of the Administration's actions outnumber those who disapprove by a ratio of more than two and a half to one. The majority of people not only approve, but the percentage voicing their approval has risen steadily since mid-June, when the military buildup had begun to accelerate.

2) By a majority of two-to-one, as reported in an earlier survey, the public has

held that the Administration made the right decision in becoming involved with its military forces in Vietnam.

3) The public, by an even larger approval ratio, believes that we should continue to bomb North Vietnam.

4) At the same time, the country is eager to find a peaceful solution to the conflict there. An overwhelming majority (six-to-one) approves of the United Nations' efforts to seek a peace formula. Voters would like to have their Congressional representatives try harder to find a compromise peace settlement.

Oct. 23

U.S. military authorities in Saigon reported that U.S. forces in South Vietnam have reached a total of 148,300 men; 89,000 Army, 8,000 Navy, 37,000 Marine Corps, 14,000 Air Force, and 300 Coast Guard.

Nov. 11

Defense Secretary McNamara announces that the administration "believes it will be necessary to add further to the strength of U.S. combat forces in Vietnam."

Nov. 17

ONE IN TEN HAS FELT URGE TO PROTEST: Recent public demonstrations over U.S. policy in Vietnam and the continuing demonstrations for civil rights have raised the question of whether public protests are becoming the American way of expressing grievances. According to the results of a recent nationwide survey, only one person in ten (10 per cent) says that he has ever considered organizing or joining a protest demonstration. It is important to note, however, that this finding does not necessarily represent *active* participation. In terms of actual involvement or participation in a demonstration, the 10 per cent figure is undoubtedly on the high side.

About one in three who said at some time they had felt the urge to demonstrate about something singled out the movement for civil rights and racial equality as the goal of their protests. Another small group (less than 1 in 10) said they would like to demonstrate about the war in Vietnam and most of these, in support of U.S. policy.

Nov. 19
PUBLIC BELIEVES COMMUNISTS IN-VOLVED IN DEMONSTRATIONS: The American public believes that Communists have been involved in both the demonstrations protesting U.S. policy in Vietnam and also the civil rights demonstrations. Only about one person in twenty says that these public protests have been free of Communist involvement.

Nov. 18
A Defense Department casualty report states that 108 U.S. soldiers were slain in the week ending November 15, a weekly record total, bringing to 1,095 the number of Americans slain since January 1, 1961.

Nov. 28–29
It is reported that the U.S. military authorities request that U.S. forces in Saigon be increased to 350,000 to 400,000 men.

Nov. 29
Defense Secretary McNamara states in a press conference that the Vietcong's "expressed determination to carry on the con-

flict . . . . . can lead to only one conclusion —that it will be a long war."

Dec. 1
CONCERN GROWS OVER VIETNAM WAR: The proportion of Americans who name the war in Vietnam as the most important problem facing the nation is higher now than in any other previous measurement. More than one of every three persons (37 per cent) cite Vietnam as America's greatest concern. Mentioned next most often, by 17 per cent, is the civil rights issue. In a previous survey, conducted in the wake of the rioting in the Watts area of Los Angeles, 27 per cent named civil rights, compared with 19 per cent who named Vietnam.

Dec. 18
A North Vietnamese statement calls reports of Hanoi's peace feelers "sheer groundless fabrications."

Dec. 24–25
A 1-day Christmas truce is agreed to by the United States and the Vietcong. The United States also suspends air strikes as part of the short cease-fire.

Dec. 26
United States and South Vietnamese offensive operations are resumed in the face of a resumption of heavy Vietcong attacks; however, the suspension of air raids on North Vietnam is continued. ■

VIETNAM IN RETROSPECT

The materials in this section have focused upon private and public statements and opinions concerning American foreign policy in general and involvement in Vietnam in particular. Throughout this period of involvement, countless articles and books have been written and offered to the well-informed public.

Selections from two such pieces follow. The first, "The Lessons of Vietnam," was written by *New York Times* analyst Max Frankel. The second is taken from the book *Off Course: From Truman to Nixon*, by Rexford G. Tugwell.

Source: Max Frankel, "The Lessons of Vietnam," *New York Times*, July 6, 1971, pp. 1; 14.

The Tragedy of Vietnam

WASHINGTON, July 5—The Pentagon papers on how the United States went to war in Indochina probably mark the end of an era in American foreign policy—a quarter of a century of virtually unchallenged Presidential management and manipulation of the instruments of war and the diplomacy bearing on war. Yet the papers cannot be more than the beginning of reflection on that era and its climax, the nation's painful, disillusioning and still unresolved involvement in Vietnam.

Massive but incomplete, comprehensive but by no means exhaustive, remarkably honest but undoubtedly warped by perspective and experience, the papers are unlike any others ever composed in the midst of war and published within 3 to 10 years of the secret deliberations and calculations they describe.

They form a unique collection and they have been summarized under unique circumstances in nine installments in The New York Times—over unique legal challenge of the United States Government. The very novelty of the papers and the contest over their publication have tended to divert attention from the essential tale they bear. There has already been dispute not only about what they mean but also about what they say.

From the perspective of 1971, they could be read as an anatomy of failure: the misapplication of an earlier day's theories and techniques for containing Communism and the misfire of the political wisdom of that day that the United States would pay any price and bear any burden to prevent the loss of one more acre of ground to Communists anywhere.

Yet, paradoxically, the Pentagon papers tell the story of the successful application of those theories and they demonstrate the great and still-surviving force of those political convictions and fears.

But they could also be read as a chronicle of success: the tenacious collaboration of four—and now perhaps five—administrations of both major parties in the preservation of a commitment to an ally, the demonstration of American fidelity to an enterprise once begun and the denial of victory to Communist adversaries.

Yet the Pentagon papers show that despite the sacrifices of life, treasure and serenity to the Vietnam war, the predominant American objective was not victory over the enemy but merely the avoidance of defeat and humiliation.

How Did the Agony Begin?

In sum, the papers and the discussion now swirling about them command at least a preliminary appraisal—of what they are and what they are not, of what they reveal and what they neglect. Who really deceived whom? And how did all this agony really arise?

Essentially the Pentagon papers are raw material for history—an insiders' study of the decision-making processes of four administrations that struggled with Vietnam from 1945 to 1968. The papers embody 3,000 pages of often overlapping analyses and 4,000 pages of supporting documents. They were commissioned by Secretary of Defense Robert S. McNamara, in a period of frustration with a war that critics sardonically gave his name to. But they were written and compiled by 36 analysts, civilian and military, most of them still anonymous, and they were finally printed and bound into fewer than 20 sets in the early months of the Nixon Administration, which paid them no heed until they began to appear in The Times.

The study drew primarily upon Pentagon files that are still sealed and upon some of the most important Presidential orders and diplomatic materials of the time under review. The analysts did not have access to the most private White House documents bearing on the moods and motives of the Presidents. And in the form obtained by The Times, the study also lacked several of the 47 volumes, among them four devoted to the diplomacy that surrounded the war.

Many Draft Proposals

But the Pentagon papers also offer more than the most polished of histories. They present not only the directives, conclusions and decisions of government in an era of prolonged crisis, but also many of the loose memorandums, speculations, draft proposals and contingency plans composed by influential individuals and groups inside that government.

Whatever is missing, for lack of access or perception, is more than recompensed by the sheer sweep and drama of this contemporaneous record.

Unlike diary, which can never escape the moment, and unlike history, which must distill at a remote future, the Pentagon study was able to re-enact a fateful progression of attitudes and decisions while simultaneously viewing them from a perspective greater than that of any of the participants.

So whatever its shortcomings, the study

will stand as a vast trove of insights, hindsights and revelations about the plans and conceptions of small groups of men as they guided the nation into a distant but grievous venture, about how they talked and wrote to each other, to friend and foe, in public and in private. And the study is bound to stand as a new model for governmental analysis, raising questions normally reserved for literature: how powerful and sophisticated men take on commitments while they think themselves free, how they reach decisions while they see the mirage of choice, how they entrap themselves while they labor to induce or coerce others to do their will.

As the coordinator of the Pentagon study, Leslie H. Gelb, recently said of this story, "It was and is a Greek tragedy."

550

No Villains or Heroes

As written at the Pentagon and as recounted by The Times, the study found no villains or heroes. It made no historical value judgments. It argued no brief.

The portraits of the principal actors—especially those such as Secretary of State Dean Rusk, who were wary of betraying their views in interagency meetings and memorandums—are far from complete or satisfying. The portraits of the Presidents, even if their own files had been available, would remain inadequate until they were set against the political and international imperatives felt at the White House at every stage.

In the absence of a comparable study of the objectives and tactics of the Vietnam adversaries—notably the Government of North Vietnam and the coalition of insurgents in South Vietnam—the Pentagon papers could not presume to judge the morality or even the wisdom of the policies they record and describe.

And although many of the authors appear to have become disillusioned doves about the war, their study could stand almost as well as a brief for frustrated hawks; its central conclusion, that the nation simply pursued excessive aims with insufficient means, leaves entirely unresolved the central question of whether it would have been better to do more or to seek less.

Of all the revelations in the Pentagon papers, the most important deal with the patterns of thought and action that recur at almost every stage of the American involvement in Indochina:

This was a war not only decreed but closely managed by the civilian leaders of the United States. The military chiefs were in fact reluctant at the start, unimpressed by the strategic significance of Vietnam and worried throughout that they would never be allowed to expand the size and scope of the war to the point where they could achieve a clear advantage over the enemy.

This was not a war into which the United States stumbled blindly, step by step, on the basis of wrong intelligence or military advice that just a few more soldiers or a few more air raids would turn the tide. The nation's intelligence analysts were usually quite clear in their warnings that contemplated escalations of force and objective would probably fail.

Yet military considerations took precedence over political considerations at almost every stage. Since none of the Americans managing the Vietnam problem were prepared to walk away from it, they were forced to tolerate the petty political maneuvering in Saigon and Saigon's political and economic policies, even when Washington recognized them as harmful. As a result, even the military chiefs, and notably Gen. William C. Westmoreland, yielded to the temptation of seeking victory on the ground, although it was known that the enemy could always resupply just enough men to frustrate the American military.

The public claim that the United States was only assisting a beleaguered ally who really had to win his own battle was never more than a slogan. South Vietnam was essentially the creation of the United States. The American leaders, believing that they had to fight fire with fire to ward off a Communist success, hired agents, spies, generals and presidents where they could find them in Indochina. They thought and wrote of them in almost proprietary terms as instruments of American policy. Ineluctably, the fortunes of these distant, often petty men became in their minds indistinguishable from the fortunes of the United States.

The views of the world and the estimate of the Communist world that led the United States to take its stand in Indochina remained virtually static for the men who managed the Vietnam war. The "domino theory"—that all the other nations of Asia would topple if Indochina fell into Communist hands—moves robustly through the Pentagon papers, even by momentous events such as the split between the Soviet Union and Communist China, Peking's preoccupation with its Cultural Revolution or the bloody destruction of the Communist challenge in Indonesia.

The American objective in Vietnam, although variously defined over the years, remained equally fixed. Disengagement, no matter how artfully it might have been arranged or managed, was never seriously considered so long as a separate, pro-American and non-Communist government was not safely installed in Saigon.

The American Presidents, caught between the fear of a major war involving the Soviet Union or China and the fear of defeat and humiliation at the hands of a small band of insurgents, were hesitant about every major increase in military force. But they were unrestrained in both their public and private rhetorical commitments to "pay the price," to "stay the course" and to "do whatever is necessary."

The American military and civilian bureaucracies, therefore, viewed themselves as being on a fixed course. They took seriously and for the most part literally the proclaimed doctrines of successive National Security Council papers that Indochina was vital to the security interests of the nation. They thus regarded themselves as obligated to concentrate always on the questions of *what* to do next, not *whether* they should be doing it.

But the principal findings of the Pentagon papers cannot be fully understood without some recollection of the traditions, the training and the attitudes of the men who led the United States in the generation following World War II.

As The Economist of London has observed, these men were reared in the habits of the internationalist Presidents, notably Woodrow Wilson and Franklin D. Roosevelt, who also felt duty-bound to lead the nation into war after vowing to avoid it.

Philip Jones Griffiths, Magnum

551

The British Weekly goes so far as to suggest that secret maneuver and public deception may be the only way to take great democracies to war.

Moreover, as Senator Frank Church of Idaho, one of the early Congressional critics of the war in Vietnam, remarked in Washington the other day, Presidents Truman, Eisenhower, Kennedy and Johnson were all reared to the conviction that only Presidents and their experts can have the perspective and knowledge needed to define the national interest in a hostile world.

They lived with the memory of Congress destroying Wilson's League of Nations and hampering Roosevelt's quest for safety in alliances against Germany and Japan.

They lived with the memory of two costly world wars, both of which they judged avoidable if American power had been arrayed soon enough against distant aggression.

The Lesson of Munich

They lived with the nightmare that "appeasement" would only invite more aggression and lead directly to World War III, as the sacrifice of Czechoslovakia to Hitler at Munich led to World War II.

And they lived with the knowledge that another major war would be a nuclear war unless it were deterred with frequent demonstrations of American resolve and readiness to honor promises to friends and threats against adversaries.

These are the convictions that the men who made the Vietnam war carried into the post-world-war rivalry against the Soviet Union and against what they regarded for many years as a highly disciplined international Communist conspiracy, directed from Moscow and aimed at worldwide revolution and conquest.

After the "loss" of half of Europe to Communism, the American leaders set out to draw the line, wherever possible, to "contain" the Communists without major war.

They were imaginative and cold-blooded about the techniques they used in this effort. They broke the Berlin blockade without firing a shot. They poured $12-billion in economic aid into the revival of the economies of Western Europe. They led the United Nations into war in defense of South Korea. They sent military missions, military equipment, spies and agitators to all parts of the world. They sought to make and to destroy governments. They tried to "build" nations where none had existed before.

A Long Hunt at Home

But they paid a profound psychological price. Their summons to sacrifice at home gave the contest an uncontrollable ideological fervor. The "loss" of China to Communism in 1949 and the further frustration of war in Korea in 1950 inspired a long hunt at home for knaves and traitors, in the White House and below, from which American politics is only beginning to recover.

Politicians and the politicians who became Presidents goaded each other to the conclusion that they could not "lose" another inch of territory to Communism, anywhere. The Republicans took after Democrats by saying they had been weak or treacherous about China and had accepted less than total victory in Korea.

The Democrats took after Republicans by saying they had lost Cuba and dissipated American prestige and missile strength.

As President Eisenhower reached the end of his Administration, his greatest fear was the "loss" of Laos. And as President Kennedy assumed office, the Government's greatest ambition was the "liberation" of Cuba. No matter how small the nations or how marginal their threat to the United States, their "loss" came to be seen as an intolerable humiliation of American purpose and a dangerous invitation to aggression elsewhere.

Instinctive of Force

Thus whenever aid and intrigue had failed, the cold-war instinct was resort to overt force. And the failure of force in one place only magnified the temptation to use it elsewhere. The simultaneous fiasco at the Bay of Pigs in Cuba and dissolution of anti-Communist forces in Laos in 1961 was uppermost in the minds of the Kennedy men who then proceeded to raise the stakes in Vietnam.

As the Pentagon papers show, they were motivated by the desire to contain China and what they considered to be the Asian branch of "international Communism," to protect the "dominoes" of non-Communist Asia, to discredit the Communist theories of guerrilla war and "wars of national liberation" and to demonstrate to allies everywhere that the United States would honor its pledges and make good on its threats no matter how difficult the task or insignificant the terrain.

These objectives were widely supported in the United States throughout the nineteen-sixties. But the Presidents who progressively decided on an ultimate test in Vietnam never shared with the Congress and the public what is now seen to have been their private knowledge of the remoteness of success.

As the Pentagon papers show, every President from Truman to Johnson passed down the problem of Vietnam in worse shape than he had received it. The study gives special point to President Johnson's recently disclosed remark to his wife in the spring of 1965, at the very *start* of his massive commitment of troops:

"I can't get out. I can't finish it with what I have got. So what the hell can I do?"

What he and his predecessors did not do was to inform the country of the dilemma and invite it to help make the choice.

The Pentagon papers reveal that all the difficulties of defining the Indochina problem date from the very earliest American experiences there, under Presidents Truman and Eisenhower. They show that Gen. George C. Marshall, a Secretary of State for Mr. Truman, recognized the Vietnamese Communists to be also the leaders of a legitimate Vietnamese anti-colonialism. He thus recognized their challenge as different from any other Communist bid for power, but the distinction was soon lost.

The papers show that even after President Eisenhower reluctantly let the French go down to defeat in Indochina, his Administration refused to accept the compromise settlement of Geneva in 1954. It set out to supplant the French and to carry on the struggle, with hastily organized acts of sabotage, terror and psychological warfare against the new Communist Government in North Vietnam and with programs of aid and military training to establish a

rival anti-Communist nation of South Vietnam.

A Complicating Factor

The stories now revealed make vastly more complicated the official American version of Vietnam history, in which the Hanoi Communists alone were charged with aggression and a ruthless refusal to leave "their neighbors" alone. Clearly, the American commitment to save at least half of Vietnam from Communism antedates the whole succession of Saigon governments to which it was nominally given.

Even in these early years of American involvement, the Governments of South Vietnam were perceived as mere instruments of larger American objectives. It was Gen. J. Lawton Collins, acting as President Eisenhower's personal representative in Indochina, who first proposed the ouster of Ngo Dinh Diem. The Vietnamese leader was saved at the time by agents of the C.I.A., but several of those agents were still available to help arrange a coup against Mr. Diem eight years later.

Even in those early years, the Pentagon papers show, Washington's public optimism about the prospects for anti-Communists in Vietnam masked a private pessimism.

And even then the North Vietnamese Communists were being held responsible for the direction of the insurgency in the South, even though it was not for lack of trying that the Americans in the South failed to cause equal difficulty in the North.

Much More of the Same

In hindsight, with the benefit of the Pentagon papers, it is plain that the Kennedy

years brought more, much more of the same.

The "domino theory" was now expanded to embrace concern about the fate of Indonesia, loosely regarded as also in Southeast Asia. The fiasco in Cuba and tension over Berlin made it seem even more imperative to take a stand somewhere, if only for demonstration purposes.

Despite the Eisenhower warnings, Laos was deemed to be a poor place to make a stand. So it was partitioned among three rival factions, with the North Vietnamese gaining a convenient corridor for systematic infiltration into South Vietnam.

The deal had the effect of making the defense of South Vietnam vastly more difficult at the very moment when the American commitment to its defense was taking deeper root. The same paradoxical effect was achieved many times during the years of American involvement in Indochina.

The character of that involvement, it is now clear, also underwent a portentous though subtle change during the Kennedy years: American military and political activities came to be valued less for their intrinsic benefits than for the general encouragement they might give to the struggling South Vietnamese. They also came to be valued less for the damage they might inflict on the North Vietnamese than for the fear of still greater American involvement they were supposed to arouse.

Even though the Kennedy Administration knew the sad facts of instability, corruption and tyranny in South Vietnam, it consistently gave priority to military measures that would express its activism and bespeak its determination. Its vain but constant hope was that morale would improve in Saigon and that the threat of massive American intervention would somehow persuade Hanoi to relent.

Covert Operations Started

So for practical as well as domestic political reasons, private realism yielded even further to public expressions of optimism and confidence. Three weeks after the Bay of Pigs in April, 1961, Mr. Kennedy felt it necessary to order the start of new covert operations against the territory of North Vietnam and Communist regions in Laos.

Later in 1961, he heard so much debate about the growing need for American ground troops in Vietnam that the decisions to send several thousand military "advisers" seemed a relatively modest and cautious move.

But the pressure built for a more direct American management of the entire war, an impulse that found its ultimate expression in Washington's complicity in the overthrow of President Diem. Once again, more than the President realized and perhaps more than he wanted, the obligation of the United States had been simultaneously deepened and made more difficult to redeem.

Along with the Kennedy term and the Kennedy men, President Johnson thus inherited a broad Kennedy commitment to South Vietnam. And twice in Mr. Johnson's first four months in office, Secretary McNamara returned from Saigon with the news that things were going from bad to miserable. Stable government now seemed impossible to achieve and the countryside was fast falling into Vietcong control.

Mr. McNamara and many other officials began to press for action, including new covert attacks against North Vietnam and at least urgent planning for open bombing and border patrols. They acknowledged privately that the real problems were in the South, but they could not yet conceive of any effective form of intervention.

So they built on the old formula of the Kennedy years—action for action's sake, not because it would achieve anything tangible but because it might help morale in Saigon and cause Hanoi to recognize that it could never "win" the war without confronting American power.

Gamesmanship a Policy

As the Pentagon papers show, these "scenarios" for threat and escalation were written in the glib, cold but confident spirit of efficiency experts—the same experts whose careful plotting of moves and countermoves against the Soviet Union in the 1962 Cuban missile crisis had so gloriously vindicated the new political science of gamesmanship and probability theory.

Assistant Secretary of Defense John T. McNaughton, who eventually turned against the war with a pathetic confession of ignorance of the Vietnamese people, best typified this style of thought and planning at the upper levels of government.

In his memorandums, choices of more or less war were reduced to "options": "B—— fast full squeeze. Present policies plus a systematic program of military pressures against the North . . ."; "C—— progressive squeeze-and-talk. Present policies plus an orchestration of communications with Hanoi and a crescendo of additional military moves. . ."

Countries and peoples became "audiences": "The relevant audiences" of United States actions are the Communists (who must feel strong pressures), the South Vietnamese (whose morale must be buoyed), our allies (who must trust us as 'underwriters'), and the U. S. public (which must support our risk-taking with U. S. lives and prestige). . . . Because of the lack of 'rebuttal time' before election to justify particular actions which may be distorted to the U. S. public, we must act with special care—signaling to the D.R.V. that initiatives are being taken, to the GVN that we are behaving energetically despite the restraints of our political season, and to the U. S. public that we are behaving with good purpose and restraint."

Definition of Objectives

Many of these memorandums were only "contingency plans" that contemplated what else the United States might do in one or another eventuality. But there was nothing contingent in their definition of American purposes and objectives, in their analyses—in the crucial years of 1964–65—of the rapidly deteriorating situation in South Vietnam and in their revelation of the state of mind of the dozen or so top officials whose persistent clamor for action could be delayed but never ultimately denied by a President who shared their purpose.

And there was nothing "contingent" about the direct orders of the National Security Council and the Presidential messages that have turned up with the Pentagon papers. The lines of reasoning and decision from the action papers to the contingency papers are direct and unmistakable.

The Pentagon papers and The Times's

reports on them confirm the judgment of contemporary observers that President Johnson was reluctant and hesitant to take the final decision at every fateful turn of his plunge into large-scale war.

Mr. Johnson and other officials were often evasive or coy with the press by creating the impression that plans for bombing were only "recommendations" without "decision" or that "requests" for more troops from the field were not "on my desk at this moment" because they lay formally elsewhere.

But these are not the most important deceptions revealed in the Pentagon papers.

Deep Sense of Frustration

There is, above all, much evidence that the four administrations that progressively deepened the American involvement in the war felt a private commitment to resist Communist advance, and then a private readiness to wage war against North Vietnam and finally a private sense of frustration with the entire effort much sooner and to a much greater extent than they ever acknowledged to the Congress and the nation.

There is evidence in the papers that the Congress was rushed into passing a resolution to sanction the use of force in Vietnam in 1964, ostensibly to justify retaliation for an "unprovoked" attack on American vessels, even though the Administration really intended to use the resolution as the equivalent of a declaration of war and withheld information that would have shown the North Vietnamese to have had ample reason for "retaliating" against the U.S.

There is evidence that all the elaborately staged offers of negotiation and compro-

mise with the Communist adversary were privately acknowledged in the Administration as demands for his virtual "surrender."

And there is evidence, scattered over the years, that the oft-proclaimed goal of achieving "self-determination" for the South Vietnamese was in fact acceptable to the United States only as long as no South Vietnamese leader chose neutralism or any other form of nonalignment. As President Johnson put it in a cablegram to his ambassador in early 1964, "Your mission is precisely for the purpose of knocking down the idea of neutralization wherever it rears its ugly head."

The evidence for two very specific charges of deception that have been leveled against President Johnson since publication of the Pentagon papers is much less clear.

The Pentagon study itself did not make any charges, and neither did The Times in its reports on the findings of the study. But many readers concluded that Mr. Johnson had lied to the country in 1964, when he denounced his Republican opponent, Senator Barry Goldwater, for advocating full-scale air attacks against North Vietnam, and again in April, 1965, when he secretly authorized the use of American troops in an offensive combat role.

The Pentagon study describes a "general consensus" among the President's advisers, two months before the 1964 election, that air attacks against North Vietnam would probably have to be launched. It reports an expectation among them that these would begin early in the new year. As The Times report added, the papers also showed the President "moving and being moved toward war, but reluctant and hesitant to act until the end."

Search Through the Files

Mr. Johnson and those who defend his public statements at the time are undoubtedly right in their contention that the President made no formal decision to authorize more bombing until there were additional attacks on American bases in February, 1965.

But the President also knew that most of his major advisers regarded such a decision as "inevitable"—because they thought South Vietnam to be in danger of imminent collapse, because the forces to conduct more air attacks were in place, because the target lists had long ago been prepared and even sustained bombing was destined to be merely a stopgap measure until more troops could be rushed to South Vietnam.

In a search through his own dispatches from Washington at the time, this reporter has come upon three interesting accounts that help to explain the confusion but tend to support the much more thoroughly researched judgment of the Pentagon papers.

On Oct. 9, 1964, The Times reported on a news conference question to Secretary Rusk about reports "here and in Saigon that the Administration was considering a 'major turn' in policy but deferring a decision until after Election Day, Nov. 3." Mr. Rusk refused to predict "future events" but said that domestic politics had no bearing on any such decisions.

On Feb. 13, 1965, after a new "retaliatory" raid on North Vietnam but before the start of sustained bombing, this reporter quoted two unidentified high officials as follows:

"There is no doubt that the President remains skeptical about a deeper involvement in Asia, but he is getting some very belligerent advice from very intimate quarters."

"History may determine that it was already too late, that the die is cast, but I am sure that the Government's strategy is not yet determined."

In other words, even high officials sensed that their President was still reserving final judgment and "decision," but they did not really know how much real choice remained.

After the Decision

Even after the decision had been made, however, there was no simple way to get a straight answer from the Johnson Administration in those days, as is evident in the opening lines of a dispatch on March 2, 1965:

"The Administration described today's air strikes against North Vietnam as part of a 'continuing' effort to resist aggression and made no effort, as in the past, to relate them to particular provocation. . . . The White House said only that there had been no change in policy. The State Department said nothing. . . ."

Some officials at the time, and Mr. Johnson on at least one occasion since then, suggested that such coyness after decision had been deemed necessary to avoid provoking intervention in the war by Soviet or Chinese Communist forces. They never explained, however, why either nation would make such a grave decision on the basis of announcements in Washington rather than on the facts of the bombing, which were well known to them.

A far more plausible explanation, one that sounds strange in matters of such weight but rings true to those who could observe Lyndon Johnson closely and sympathetically in those days, has been offered by Stewart Alsop in Newsweek: "President Johnson was trying to fool not the people but himself—and temporarily succeeding."

What really emerges from the Pentagon papers, Mr. Alsop wrote approvingly, "is a picture of a desperately troubled man resisting the awful pressures to plunge deeper into the Vietnam quagmire—resisting them as instinctively as an old horse resists being led to the knackers. The President bucks, whinnies and shies away, but always in the end the reins tighten— the pressures are too much for him."

And, he adds: "A precisely similar sequence of events—mounting pressure from his advisers, instinctive resistance by the President, final agonized agreement—preceded the President's decision to commit additional troops and to give the marines an offensive role. When he made these decisions, the President did not realize—because he did not want to realize—that he had crossed his Rubicon. He still hoped and prayed that a bit more air power, a few more troops on the ground, would bring the Communists to the conference table in a mood to 'reason together.' Hence there really had been, in his own mind, nothing 'very dramatic' about his decisions, no 'far-reaching strategy.' "

As the Pentagon papers further show, Mr. Johnson was to make two or three other big decisions about troop commitments and carve them up into smaller, more digestible numbers, as if this could hide the magnitude of the American involvement. He knew that he was not winning the war and he knew that he was playing only for some unforeseeable stroke of good fortune, and it may be that his sense of statesmanship led him to conclude that the nation would be preserved longer if he minimized the task.

Whatever the motives, the methods for handling the awkwardness of Vietnam had then become almost traditional. But it was Mr. Johnson's misfortune to be President, as Mr. Gelb, the coordinator of the study has written, when the "minimum necessary became the functional equivalent of gradual escalation" and the "minimal necessity became the maximum" that international and domestic constraints would allow.

The overriding evidence in the Pentagon papers, quite apart from the timing of decisions or the candor with which they were disclosed, is that the United States Government involved itself deeply and consciously in a war that its leaders felt they probably could not win but that they also felt they could not afford to lose.

Gradually, some of the leading advocates of the war lost their enthusiasm for it, but even in disillusionment they felt a higher duty of loyalty to the President and his policy than to the public that had become deeply divided and tormented by the war.

As early as 1966, Mr. McNaughton perceived an "enormous miscalculation" and an "escalating military stalemate." By 1967, Mr. McNamara and probably others were recommending a reduction of objectives and perhaps a face-saving exit through the formation of a coalition government in Saigon.

But Mr. Johnson thought more unhappy Americans were hawks than doves and he was also forced, amid fears of noisy resignations, to negotiate with his military leaders, who were demanding more, rather than less, commitment.

Decisive Shock at Tet

Not until the shock of the enemy's Tet offensive in 1968, and the need to mobilize reserves if he was to meet the military's request for 206,000 additional men for the combat zone, did Mr. Johnson set a final limit on the American commitment, cut back the bombing of North Vietnam and announce his plan to retire without seeking a second term.

No one knows to this day whether by these moves the President intended to hurry out of the war in some face-saving manner or merely to buy still more time from the American voters for a final effort at vindication.

As the Pentagon papers disclose, his Administration did not expect much from the bombing limitation or the new offer to negotiate with Hanoi.

"We are not giving up anything really serious in this time frame" of four weeks, the State Department informed its embassies, noting that poor weather would have curtailed the raids for that period in any case. It said that some of the air power would be switched to targets in Laos and South Vietnam and that in any case Hanoi was expected to reject the bid for talks and this would "free our hand after a short period."

Hanoi accepted the bid for talks, but has offered very little so far that interests Washington. Neither on the way in nor on the way out, it is now clear, was the American hand in Vietnam ever "free." ■

Source: Rexford G. Tugwell, *Off Course: From Truman to Nixon* (New York: Praeger Publishers, Inc., 1971), pp. 198–267.

The Failure Of American Foreign Policy

The suspicion has grown with the years that excluding the Russians from any part in victory or occupation was indeed the reason for using the bomb on Japan. The long confrontation, presently to be called the "cold war," had begun. The United States' decision-makers certainly wanted sole control of Japan in the interest of hegemony over the whole of the Pacific. This was accomplished; the years of occupation were passed with MacArthur directing a military government; and the Russians were wholly excluded.

There was other evidence. During the war, assistance to the Russians by lend-lease had been accomplished by heroic means. The Murmansk run, through the Arctic seas past the German installations in Norway, had sometimes cost the loss of half the ships in the convoys. It was as dangerous as any duty ever exacted of seamen. Their ships were at such risk that it was later beyond belief that men could have accepted it. They were blown up in dozens, and life in the icy water was limited to minutes; there were very few rescues from the lost freighters. The other route, established by incredible engineering feats, ran from the Persian Gulf overland to southern Russia.

Both routes came into full use late in the conflict, and the Russians had throughout their development been ungrateful and demanding. They had suffered mightily and had withstood the battering of the *Wehrmacht* with stolid bravery; but it had been an ordeal of such magnitude that it seemed to them comparatively more than their share of a common conflict. They wanted

more help. Stalin practically ended communication with the Allies when the channel crossing was not put into operation in 1943; and he considered the invasion of North Africa a mere diversion. He was only grudgingly pacified by the successful operation when it was undertaken in June, 1944. By that time the Russian armies had driven out the invaders.

There had been heated arguments in the Congress during the 'thirties about Pearl Harbor: should it be improved as a base? Had the United States any business in the Pacific? The argument extended to the Philippines. They had been given independence. Did the obligation inherited from the Spanish-American war include defense of the islands? If so, the nation's reach would extend all the thousands of miles across the sea to Asiatic shores. There the two powers would have meeting lines if the Pacific and its islands were an American responsibility.

It had been Roosevelt's policy to give the Filipinos their independence; and when the Japanese had occupied the islands early in the war, he saw it as a responsibility to drive out the occupiers and restore the former status. This, however, was no more than an incident in the war with Japan. It was a job for the navy. The army became involved in this as in other battles for expulsion of the Japanese; but this did not imply that the Roosevelt plans included occupation of the Asiatic mainland. While he was President the Chinese were allies to be assisted, and the American intention was to free them as the Filipinos had been freed. He could not have imagined China as an enemy.

A whole series of failures began, it must

be admitted, when Hurley, Roosevelt's envoy, failed to negotiate a coalition between Chiang Kai-shek and Mao Tse-tung. Afterward, Marshall, acting for Truman, failed as well. It would not have happened if a more careful assessment of the situation had been made and more attention had been given to China's internal struggle. By the end of Truman's regime, the communists had won that struggle and were denouncing Americans as enemies. Chiang Kai-shek's faction was reduced to a government in exile on Formosa (Taiwan), to be a liability far into the future.

It has not been argued here that Roosevelt always made the right decisions or that he never made mistakes. He certainly should have understood that Mao was something more than an agrarian reformer; and, of all those who might have been available, General Patrick Hurley was the worst choice for bringing factions together and assisting in the formation of a Chinese government more friendly to the United States. What is argued is that Roosevelt recognized his mistakes and set about to correct them. He was an experimenter, not much worried if things went wrong temporarily; something else could be tried until a tolerable situation had been achieved. The difficulty was that he left to Truman many situations in flux with no more than tentative solutions and that nothing was tentative to Truman. Once fixed he turned away and refused to reconsider.

Truman not only considered any decision final, but belligerently regarded this as a virtue. It was his executive method. The way he put it was that he slept well after it was done and woke up to some-

thing else. For Roosevelt, nothing was ever quite done. Public matters were too complicated. There were too many fermentations. Adjustments always had to be made. Only the end in view was important.

One of his important ends was friendship with China. He was indignant about the Japanese attempt at conquest and wanted to see a new and more stable regime there. It was one thing the war had been about; and he would not have rested until such a solution seemed to be in prospect. When the Hurley mission failed he looked around for something else; he might even have recognized Mao and supported him in forming a new government. This is speculation; but it would not have been surprising.

On both fronts, across the Atlantic as well as the Pacific, initiatives were eventually crushed by irresistible forces. American ideology gave rise to impracticality. The venture in Vietnam would be no more successful than that in Korea. American soldiers would in time come home, having built vast installations costing billions. These would be left either to a military dictatorship or to the communists, if they should dominate an evacuated South Vietnam. By 1970 self-determination was a bankrupt policy, after having been endlessly preached by a stony-faced Rusk until his credibility was weaker than that of the Presidents he had served. The policy was containment, or it was nothing; but the lines had been drawn in defiance of geography. Control of the seas could be made good; invasion of the land beyond was a military impossibility.

In Germany there were still occupation forces whose presence there was becom-

ing harder and harder to explain. NATO headquarters had been expelled from France and was now in Belgium. American troops were deployed to defend West Germany; their number was no more than a quarter of those the communists maintained within a few days' march; only by the use of nuclear weapons could they make a convincing show of ability to resist a determined onrush toward the West; but American statesmen had said repeatedly that they would not be the first to use nuclear weapons. By 1970 it was not at all clear whether this pledge included the tactical ones by now perfected. If it only referred to intercontinental missiles it was of no use on a possible battlefield in Europe; and the distinction between "tactical" and "strategic" was difficult to make.

If Stalin had been given in to about Poland in 1945 he might not have felt it necessary to advance as far as East Germany. At any rate the Poles, as well as the rest of Eastern Europe, had not been protected by the Truman policies. Poland was a dictatorship under Russian control; the other countries (with Yugoslavia somewhat of an exception) were harshly dominated in the communist manner; and it was at least arguable that this might not have happened if the Russians had not felt themselves threatened by encirclement, and especially the fear of a revivified Germany.

As for West Germany, a remarkable economic recovery, with American help, had given it a position of comparative superiority among Europeans, but this was behind the allied armies still being maintained theoretically to prevent renewed aggression, but actually for protection against Russian invasion. As 1970 opened,

Burk Uzzle, Magnum

Brandt, the Prime Minister, was beginning
discussions with Russia to modify the hostility between East and West. This, if at
all successful, would leave the Allies with
nothing whatever to show for twenty-five
years of costly occupation.

It might be argued, in fact, that NATO's
containment had been for the Russians a
favorable policy. It had given them reason
for building a vast new army and navy,
for holding Eastern Europe in fief, for establishing a communist regime in East
Germany, for penetrating the Mediterranean and making subjects of the Arabs,
for putting North Korea and North Vietnam
in their debt, and for holding on to, and
possibly expanding, their Asiatic empire
with inscrutable determination.

All this the United States had opposed,
but never with the force to sustain the
policy. Deployment thousands of miles
from both coasts was simply an impossible
logistical task; and what had been done
had been at the cost of ruinous neglect at
home and the accumulation of problems
it had begun to seem almost too late to
overcome, even with quick and complete
reversal. The results seemed to many
young people, who must furnish the manpower and pay to support it, a failure not
worth going on with. It could be seen how
Russia and the United States together
could have unified the world, at least to
the extent of stabilizing the situations that
broke out into small wars in many places;
but neither could do it alone. Especially,
if they used their resources to oppose each
other, this was all they could do. A common policy toward China might even have
prevented its retreat from the affairs of the
world outside.

The first President after Truman's policies were clearly exposed as bankrupt would have to abandon the whole undertaking and do the best he could to create a new strategy. It had taken only two years after Roosevelt's death, and with Truman's management, to turn two great victorious allied powers into aggressive enemies. Russia and China would, in future, far overbalance the United States in population—in 1970 about a billion to two hundred million. Neither would be so productive per person, but neither would be in danger of starvation. Each would have drawn the United States into futile containment activities with troops deployed abroad on both fronts and actually fighting in Asia. Neither Russia nor China had soldiers in combat.

Could the situation have been avoided? To conclude that it could have been, it has only to be assumed that the Soviet Union and China might have been induced to remain American allies for the purposes of peace as they had been for the purposes of war. This would have required consent to the extension of Russia's sphere of influence into Eastern Europe short of Germany but with the Germans under compulsion not to rearm. For China it would have required recognition that the time had come to rid the nation of the reactionary—and corrupt—regime of Chiang Kai-shek, and bring that vast country into the twentieth century. Neither of these policies was tolerable to those in charge of American foreign relations; and in disregard of all reason they undertook the impossible.

The two most praised initiatives in the years immediately following Roosevelt's death were the Truman Doctrine and the Marshall Plan. Both were part of the general containment policy—the one to shut Russia off from the Mediterranean and the other to set up opposition to supposed communist designs on Western Europe.

The exclusion from the seas to the south had two obvious motives. One was to protect the British lifeline to the east; the other was to ensure that oil from Arabia would continue to be an exclusive Western resource. In spite of the enormous expenditures for these purposes the whole area had by 1970 fallen into Russian hegemony. The British had been forced to liquidate their imperial interests beyond the Red Sea, and so had no further use for a lifeline, and the oil for Europe was at such risk that new sources were being sought with frantic intensity. Both were therefore mistaken efforts. If they had never been undertaken the result would not have been much different; it might even have been more favorable. The Russians had no need for Arabian oil, having plenty of their own, and they might well have agreed to a sharing arrangement; the Suez Canal might have been open, and shipping not diverted to the tedious route around South Africa.

After years of effort neither Russia nor China would be contained. It would not be fair to blame Truman alone for these vast misfortunes. Only their beginnings and their early phases, when allies were turned into enemies and enemies into allies, are chargeable to him. That, however, may be the most serious criticism that can be made of any American President except Buchanan, who allowed the Civil War to develop. Even then it has to be recalled how many collaborators and what almost universal support Truman had. Still, he was the President who kept on his desk that inscribed motto saying "the buck stops here." He cannot be exonerated; nor, to do him justice, would he want to be.

The policy once begun, wars with communists on the Asian mainland were inevitable. Confrontation with Russia having been undertaken, it proved difficult for Truman's successors to abandon it. Instead, the confrontation was enlarged, and this would go on until Johnson faced failure in 1968 and Nixon, because of Johnson's forced abdication, was obliged to find means for liquidation. Seldom had people paid a higher price in dissension at home and lost opportunity abroad for decisions made in pursuit of futile aims.

It is impossible to exonerate Dean Acheson from a large part of the responsibility for these results. He was Assistant Secretary of State from 1941 to 1945, when Roosevelt was busy with the war, and he had much to do with drafting a United Nations charter that Roosevelt did not approve but thought could be modified. He was then Undersecretary from 1945 to 1947 and was Secretary from 1949 to 1953. He was the proximate author of the Truman Doctrine and of the Marshall Plan. His assistants in the Department included Rusk and Rostow, who went on after he left until Johnson was through. His influence was pervasive all this time. He persisted into the Nixon age in defending his part in making policy during the Truman years. Throughout his service, and even later, he continued to identify Russian communism with imperialism and to claim that the measures of those years were no more than an essential defense of the "free" world.

A necessary part of that defense gradually became the insistence that all disturbances, especially revolutionary ones, were instances of communist aggression and that they must be met everywhere with military opposition. This was true in Germany, in Persia, in Greece, in Asia, and in the Near East. This came to be called the domino theory and was used effectively to justify intervention in Southeast Asia.

George Kennan, who was ambassador to Russia in 1946, was the author of the "X" article in *Foreign Affairs* that first outlined the containment doctrine. In dispatches to the Department he spoke of the "Kremlin's neurotic view of world affairs." The Russians meant, he said, to "infiltrate, divide and weaken the West." Kennan, however, offered various proposals for accord with the Russians. These, Acheson rejected as useless. Kennan afterward said in his *Memoirs* (Boston: Atlantic, Little, Brown, 1967) that they failed because no other way to deal with the Russians was found than military opposition. There should have been a political solution. He said, also, looking back, that there had been a faulty interpretation of the North Korean attack on the South as inspired by Russia; actually the Russians had tried to stop it. This was an example of failure

. . . to take advantage of the opportunities for useful political discussion, when, in later years, such opportunities began to open up, and exerted itself, in its military preoccupations, to seal and perpetuate the very divisions of Europe which it should have been concerned to remove. . . .

The author of containment lived to regret the rationale he provided for the

politicians who had their own reasons for exaggerating his warnings about Russian intentions.

. . .

In June of 1950 the North Koreans invaded South Korea in an attempt to overrun the country before a defense could be organized. Truman reacted at once and, with United Nations backing (the Russians having some time before boycotted the Security Council), entrusted the joint command to MacArthur. A combat team opposed itself to the full force of the invaders and delayed them until two divisions stationed in Japan could arrive and begin effective defense.

There was something curious about the immediate undertaking to defend South Korea. It followed almost at once on the expulsion from China of Chiang Kai-shek and was, therefore, on the border of a hostile nation. It was assumed that the attack was inspired by Russia, although this assumption later appeared to have been false. Truman treated it as a provocation and met it as such even though there had been no promise of defense and American forces had been diminished. It had been omitted by Acheson himself when he had defined the defense perimeter of the United States in a policy statement; in April, 1948, he had said unequivocally that the nation should not become so involved in the Korean situation that an action taken by any faction in Korea or by any other power could be considered a *casus belli*.

The Joint Chiefs had felt, as General J. Lawton Collins reported later on, in *War in Peacetime: The History and Lessons of Korea* (Houghton Mifflin, 1968), that, in the

context of a general war, Korea was indefensible and "of little strategic value to the United States." Acheson had confirmed this conclusion in his speech (in 1950) drawing the defense perimeter. The line, he had said, "runs along the Aleutians to Japan and then goes on to the Ryukyus . . . and from the Ryukyus to the Philippines." Both Korea and Formosa were outside this perimeter. The defense of Korea was, then, a reversal, undertaken as a riposte to what was supposed to be a Russian thrust outward. It was unjustified either by the supposition supporting it or by the defense of any American interest.

The military tragedy in Korea was attributable to MacArthur. When reinforcements had driven the North Koreans back across the eighteenth parallel, MacArthur was not willing to stop there. As a military man he saw that if the territory across the Yalu remained an enemy sanctuary, there would never be an end to the threat of invasion. Besides, it seemed to him an opportunity to eliminate the Chinese communists from the world scene. He would not accept the confinement of a limited war. He grossly miscalculated the Chinese reaction and found himself facing hordes of foot soldiers, whose numbers and carelessness of losses he could not defeat. In March of 1951 Truman relieved him of command, and he returned to an outpouring of support and sympathy, in defiance of Truman, that had no match in American history.

The Korean conflict was still going on, but was somewhat stabilized, when Truman announced his intention not to run again. The Democrats nominated Adlai Stevenson—although Truman preferred his cold war assistant, Averell Harriman. Stevenson made a brave try but was defeated in a hopeless contest with General Eisenhower, who, in the multifarious troubles besetting the nation, appeared as a father figure who would become the stabilizer everyone was longing for. He had made that unfortunate statement about soldiers sticking to soldiering; but he allowed himself to be persuaded that a crusade to save America must be undertaken—and that only he could undertake it. His winning promise was that he would end the now unpopular war in Korea—and, because he was a victorious general, he was believed.

. . .

It can be seen why there is less to say about Eisenhower than about Truman: during his time so little was really begun! There was, however, one important change. This was the conclusion that the long-reach nuclear weapons had revolutionized warfare, and, at the moment, were, as well, an American monopoly. Until the Russians also possessed the same capability this would serve for defense policy. It was, however, a tactical, not a strategic change. The acceptance of containment was complete; it was a crusade with Dulles, the Secretary of State; but, for the most part, it is fair enough to say of Eisenhower that he merely acquiesced. Such mistakes as he himself made in foreign policy were not really ones of commission. There were, however, limits to his approval of aggression, and beyond them he stubbornly refused to go. This may have been illogical, but in fact he simply would not undertake a preventive war that, strictly considered, the policy called for. From 1952 to 1960 he

had such public prestige that his decisions were not challenged in any important way; and he had no cause to be worried by noisy dissenters. He drifted; but not over the edge. The word "brinkmanship" was appropriately applied to Dulles; but Eisenhower always pulled his associates back from the brink.

There was, however, deep in what often seemed an indecisive Presidential mind, a conviction that the apocalyptic proposals he was presented with were too extreme for acceptance and too fearsome to entertain; so, although he allowed Secretary Dulles to run loose around the world and seem to make commitments of the most horrific kind, and although he recalled—in a curiously intimate and naïve review, published in 1969—that he had often sat, at the end of a day in the White House, relaxed, talking at length with his friend Dulles, the fact is that he mostly listened; and ultimately he never let Dulles go too far. He was again and again urged by his Secretary of State and by Admiral Radford to open an attack; force must be used, they said, to save the world from the communist conspiracy. Now, they told him, as Mac-Arthur had told Truman, was the time to destroy the growing menace.

General Gavin described one such round of urging and refusal—perhaps the most important one (in *Crisis Now*, 1968, pp. 48–49):

Again, as at the time of Dien Bien Phu, the Joint Chiefs divided. Admiral Radford (the chairman) was emphatically in favor of landing a force in the Hanoi-Haiphong area, even if it meant risking war with Red China. In this he was fully supported by

the Chief of Staff of the Air Force and the Chief of Naval Operations. In my opinion such an operation meant a great risk of war. Just southeast of Haiphong harbor is the island of Hainan which is part of Red China. The Navy was unwilling to risk their ships in the Haiphong area without first invading and capturing the island. Admiral Radford and the chiefs of the Navy and Air Force felt that, faced with our overwhelming power, the Red Chinese would not react to his violation of their sovereignty. General Ridgway and I had grave doubts about the validity of this reasoning.

. . . Again, fortunately, the President decided not to commit U.S. forces to Southeast Asia.

However, there was a compromise. We would not attack North Vietnam, but we would support a South Vietnamese government that we hoped would provide a stable, independent government.

Eisenhower was not alone in this final reluctance. There were others who did not share the Dulles zeal. They might—and did—fully accept the necessity for containment, believing that the communists intended world conquest, and, when Chiang Kai-shek had been expelled, that all communists, including the Chinese, were unified and under one discipline; but there remained some sense of practical possibilities, perhaps also unwillingness to risk so many lives and so many billions. Besides, the deep isolationist sentiment, so evident before 1941, was still alive. Foreign adventures were to many Americans suspect. So, in April, 1954, when Dulles asked leading members of the Congress to approve a resolution permitting the President to use air and naval forces in Indo-China, he was advised that he had better locate some allies before undertaking such a venture. Whether Eisenhower really wanted that permission is not of record.

When Dien Bien Phu had settled matters for the French colonialists, and there took place in Geneva the conference of great powers, the outcome displeased Dulles. In that meeting a settlement of the Korean dispute had proved quite impossible, and it had been left as confused as it had been since Eisenhower had undertaken to make a settlement and had achieved no more than a cease-fire; but about Indo-China there had resulted what were afterward called the Geneva Accords. These had provided for a cease-fire, but had ended (in August) in a declaration reiterating the temporary nature of the separation between North and South at the 17th parallel and had said that democratic freedoms should be achieved by election—a secret ballot.

Neither the United States nor Vietnam signed the declaration; but France, the Soviet Union, and the United Kingdom did. Afterward there was a grudging unilateral statement, however, saying that the United States would not disturb the agreements by force and endorsing the suggested free election.

. . .

Eisenhower . . . made a number of proposals for conciliation and even for coexistence; but he was hampered for a long time by the McCarthy harassment and by his own acceptance of the communist conspiracy theory. When his eight years ended he left to Kennedy, his successor, a situation not much different from the one he had himself inherited from Truman. The nation was no safer; it was in fact far less safe, since commitments had been made, through treaties, in Europe, Southeast Asia, and the Middle East to support militarily no less than forty-three nations if they should be attacked; or if communists should start a "liberation war." Already in Vietnam there was a fomenting revolution in the South, and what was invited was what would readily enough develop within a short time. The Vietminh had not yet been adopted by Ho Chi Minh, but they were giving the American protégé, President Diem, plenty of trouble.

. . .

Kennedy's Presidency began with too little support and lasted too short a time for any substantial achievements to have been made. In foreign affairs he accepted the policy of containment and diminished confidence by consenting to a bizarre attempt, ending in miserable failure, to overthrow the Cuban Government. He gained only a little of it back by a successful interposition when the Russians attempted to place missile installations on the island.

He saw Vietnam as only one part of a general commitment to protect democratic nations in the pattern of the Korean and the West German defenses. The United States might be called on at any time and in any place to oppose communist expansion. It could not be done by the massive retaliation called for in the Eisenhower-Dulles strategy, since the Russians were well able by now to retaliate. If the walls of liberty were not to be breached at some spot chosen by the enemy for a test, it would be necessary to re-create "conventional" forces while continuing to maintain a lead in nuclear armament. He, with Secretary McNamara, therefore set out to create a police force for the free world, reconstituting the army, neglected since 1945, adding to it units trained for guerrilla fighting, and making it mobile with newly designed planes able to land troops anywhere at short notice. This system of armaments, including, as well as the navy, fleets of constantly airborne bombers, was enormously expensive; but it did keep a temporary lead over the Russians. Inevitably, however, they felt forced to compete; and what resulted in a very short time was spheres of interest, reluctantly recognized, and with provocative borders where confrontations were all too likely to take place.

This was an ideal situation for smaller nations plotting to use the superpowers in their own interests—in Africa, in the Middle East, in Europe, and in Southeast Asia. In Vietnam and in Egypt immediate advantage was taken of this weakness to lure both superpowers into courses they would not otherwise have followed. North and South Vietnam were supported, and both Israel and Egypt were massively armed. Neither superpower seemed able to negotiate or to do other than increase its commitments.

In Vietnam Kennedy enlarged Eisenhower's "limited involvement." He notified President Diem in December, 1961, that he had given orders to increase American aid for defense. A year later he wrote to Diem that he was "deeply disturbed" by the assault of the Liberation Front. "Our indignation has mounted," he said, "as the deliberate savagery of the communist program of assassination, kidnapping and wanton violence has become clear." When he was shot to death in Dallas this increased aid was in progress.

He had agreed to send 10,000 soldiers to support Vietnam's forces in addition to the considerable number of "advisers" already there. They were not supposed to do more than assist in logistical and counterguerrilla operations, but actually they were often in combat, and lives were lost. One effect of this was abandonment of any pressure for implementing the Geneva agreements by elections. This was because it was quite clear that the Diem regime, growing more and more dictatorial, was losing ground. The countryside was rapidly becoming a general battlefield. Neighbor was betraying neighbor, and attacks in the night were regularly expected. It was one of those most terrible of conflicts—civil war, with constant resort to torture, killings, and forced service.

Hardly anyone asked any more why it was necessary to send armed forces to Vietnam. It was accepted that they were sent to assist in establishing a barrier state against communist expansion into the rest of Southeast Asia, and the expectation, by 1963, was that whatever force was necessary would be used, although, of course, that would not be much. Dulles was gone, but the domino theory remained. Kennedy, on the advice of General Maxwell Taylor, Secretary Rusk, Allen Dulles, and others of his Security Council, set in motion the operations necessary to the cause. The enlargement of conventional forces was immense and rapid.

. . .

A reporter, who sometimes went with Johnson on his travels, said of him that he rode Air Force One like a stallion. The phrase sticks in the mind. He did ride the airways proudly, as though he were galloping over the plains. To his mind and manner the nation was his range. Presently, however, the watching people had had enough of it. Only if his immense undertakings had been successful and universally wanted could his style have been forgiven. For a while it seemed that they might be; but the disappointments came quickly. They accumulated; he refused to acknowledge their causes; nevertheless he began to squirm, equivocate, and try to make the record look better than it was. It was, as Eric Goldman, his historian in residence for a time, said, in the book he wrote afterward, "a tragedy." It ended an era of majorities for the Democratic Party; and left his successor to reassess, to reorganize, to retreat, and to liquidate.

It was Vietnam that was unendurable. There had been no considerable revulsion from that intervention during the other Presidencies since 1945. Until Johnson's accession it had been an acceptable program of assistance supported by a general belief in containment and in self-determination for nations threatened with subjection. There was a mission to defend the free world, but missions, costly ones, become tiresome; and moral reasons are soon found for their abandonment.

Kennedy, of course, had broken into war by sending the first few combat troops. How the escalation went after that can be seen by noting that 1964 was the year of decision—and also the year of Johnson's election for a term of his own. 1965 was the year when the Vietnamese were pushed aside and Americans took over the fighting, with Johnson commanding from the White House. The official figures of the Defense Department show how the expansion went; in successive year-end reports of troop strength in Vietnam, there were in 1964, 23,000; in 1965, 184,300; in 1966, 385,300; in 1967, 485,000; in 1968, 535,000. Casualties by 1968 were 30,000 killed and 192,000 wounded; and those figures quickly became obsolete; there were well over 40,000 dead by the year 1970.

The President gradually took to directing operations from his bed, his desk, or his plane; he gave orders; he shouted and swore at his assistants; he was furious at any check; he resented any questioning; and he allowed no latitude. The White House reporters found these idiosyncrasies interesting of course; and they were rather exaggerated than minimized. They were, however, regarded as unbecoming in a President, especially one whose domestic administration left much to be desired and whose direction of the military was being judged incompetent. He had believed those who told him that bombing would reduce the enemy to helplessness; he had failed to understand the resilience of pajama-clad guerrillas; and he had picked the wrong general to conduct operations in the field. Westmoreland, instead of acknowledging the requirements of jungle warfare, adopted a plan of "search and destroy." It assumed that there were enemy concentrations to be defeated by superior fire power. The fact was that the enemy faded into the jungles when massive armaments ploughed across the terrain. Military planners knew that the guerrillas could accept ten times the losses the Americans could have taken and still maintain the will to fight, but tactics in the field never seemed to admit this. Casualties made no difference to the enemy's characteristic resolution. Neither, as Johnson finally discovered, did reason or blandishment.

Johnson's skills as a professional politician proved to be of no use at all; and since tactics were mistaken, the situation was no nearer resolution in 1967 than it had been in 1965. He became desperate — there is no other word for it—and, as desperate men do, he demanded absolute obedience among his official family and expected concurrence from the public.

By 1968, opposition had become more vocal in the Congress, the press, and elsewhere, and although appropriations of increasing size were provided grudgingly, and although the further increases of troops requested by Westmoreland were pictured as making victory certain, Johnson's resolution collapsed under the weight of public disbelief and disapproval.

The governmental chaos in Vietnam had added to the confusion in people's minds about what Americans were doing there anyway. Their army seemed to be upholding a regime with more disposition to keep an elite in power than to defend their nation. Doubts grew; and it was gradually understood that the strongest nation in the world was, however improbably, unable to subdue one of the weakest.

This conviction, not acknowledged by Johnson and his associates, continued to spread. Growing numbers of citizens protested. Many of these, it is true, had discovered with suspicious suddenness that intervention was immoral. Lives wasted and resources diverted from domestic needs began to be a favorite theme, even

among those who had supported Kennedy's eloquent pleas for supporting "the free world" and had acquiesced in establishing a global police force. They now found Vietnam a special case. At any rate, they deserted Johnson. Finally, what he would not admit as commander in chief, he did admit as a politician. He had lost that majority he had so proudly counted on in 1964.

It was the defections that had forced Johnson and his associates—Rusk, McNamara, General Taylor, Bundy, Rostow, and the rest—to defend themselves in doubtful ways. Reports were doctored to make them more favorable; prospects were made more cheerful; the regime in Saigon, after elections, was pictured as democratic. Kept up awhile, these transparent fictions resulted in the famous "credibility gap." There were, after all, many experienced reporters both in Washington and Vietnam who told what they saw; and it was not what was being broadcast from the White House. The persistence of the enemy, the incapacity of the South Vietnamese, the waste of lives and material with no result —all were impossible to conceal. Even the "hawks" were discouraged, and the question began to be insistently asked: what would be gained if the North Vietnamese were kept out of the South and the Viet Cong were decimated. The Thieu government could hardly be said to be actually more democratic than that of the communists in the North. Then, too, questions concerning the national interest were at last being asked after years of concurrence in containment. What *were* Americans doing on the Asian mainland?

Johnson squirmed. He would not with-

draw, and he could not make progress. He came finally to humiliating attempts at negotiation. North Vietnamese representatives came to Paris but offered only vituperative propaganda. The bombing of the North was stopped, and reasonable offers for a ceasefire were made. Even admission of the Viet Cong to the Saigon government was suggested—if they could be elected. The communist representatives did not listen; they only talked. They said a hundred times that they would consider a peace only when all American forces were withdrawn. What was even more maddening, the North Vietnamese professed blandly not to have any forces of their own in the South. They insisted that it was a civil war and that the Americans were intervening. What to do with such an enemy ought to have been thought of before the intervention had begun. That could be seen now; but it was not this that sapped Johnson's morale; that resulted from the defection of his supporters. What had once been a crusade for liberty was now a cruel and immoral intervention.

As the elections of 1968 approached, the critics were so numerous and so bitter— demonstrations, often violent, had become frequent—that even if not defeated, Johnson would have been the center of the worst dissensions suffered by the nation since the Civil War. At the end of March, when he capitulated, he announced a decision not to increase the Vietnam involvement as Westmoreland advised him he must do if anything like victory were to be achieved.

It was the end for him. From one of the most popular and admired Presidents in the American line, he had become one

565

whose administration was a failure, and whose costly adventure as commander in chief had led the nation into humiliation. Even at the end he did not admit what by now was widely realized—that he had pictured to Americans a gradually worsening situation as one that was improving. A President had used his resources of communication for deliberate and prolonged misinforming. His reports had been more than merely optimistic. They had been misleading. A President could not survive that kind of relation with the public.

During this time, when Vietnam monopolized attention and polarized public opinion, other containment efforts were less active. Vietnam was the test of that policy. As Vietnam was withdrawn from, the domino theory would be tested. The United States would not again deploy its men and resources across the path of the Russians or Chinese if they did advance toward the south, and perhaps overrun all of former French Indo-China and even the Dutch East Indies. The nations involved would have to do the best they could for themselves. There would be aid, perhaps logistical support, but the incoming Nixon's half-hearted promise to carry out treaty engagements was an empty one. It contradicted any inference to be made from what was actually being done. Anyone could see that Dulles' Southeast Asia commitments would never be carried out. Americans were through with such involvements. The question was whether the nationalism of Thailand, say, or Malaysia, would withstand the pressures from China; and whether Pakistan, India, Iran, and Turkey would maintain their independence or would become other Hungarys or

Czechoslovakias. With the United States withdrawn from a quarter-century of consistent and increasing effort something like a vacuum was being created in all the border areas.

The withdrawal from South Vietnam was only one instance of a failing strategy; but with it went the holding efforts all around the communist borders. Of course the discovery, belatedly, that the communist bloc was not a monolith, contributed to this. This was another failure of American intelligence. Americans, blinded by the certainty of Dulles, Nixon, and others, only belatedly understood the inability of the communist ideology to overcome the far older and stronger bonds of nationalism. The Chinese and Russians had borders to dispute about. Americans had a continent of their own; there was no need to contain what had no possibility of expansion.

Still, there were defending forces in South Korea; there was NATO and 300,000 American troops with tactical nuclear arms in West Germany; there was the sixth fleet in Mediterranean waters and the seventh fleet in the Pacific. More important, there had been miraculous recovering among the former enemies, Japan and Germany, now next to the Americans and Russians in productive power. Both had profited from being disarmed; but disarmed, the Europeans faced hundreds of menacing Russian divisions; and the Japanese would be of no assistance in checking the Chinese drive to control Southeast Asia. The problem was not what the containers had conceived it to be. It was one of finding friends, or at least cooperators, not one of defeating aggressors by military means.

Containment, after the outpouring of resources, the deployment of weapons, and the encouragement of resistance among the border states, was ending in withdrawal. Americans were seeing how little different the situation was than it would have been without the quarter-century of effort, the loss of lives, the enormous diversion of resources. Those who asked now whether what had come about was more than could have been gained by an earnest pursuit of coexistence were at last being heard.

What needed to be contained was the missionary aggressiveness of ideologists and demagogues—not only in the communist enclaves but in capitalist ones as well; and the way to do this was for reasonable statesmen to build and operate a world order strong enough to resist challenge. This was the common interest of the great powers. Roosevelt had known this; now it was beginning to be seen by others as a necessity if genocide was to be escaped. ■

CONSTRUCTING A PUBLIC OPINION POLL

One of America's leading public opinion analysts, George Gallup, claimed as early as 1960 that polling had "come to be accepted as part of the democratic process" in large measure because it provided important information on what the common man thought about a wide range of issues confronting America in the modern age.

For over forty-five years public opinion polls have been systematically conducted and the processes of polling increasingly refined. In the course of this unit, you have been introduced to some of these refinements and have seen how they help us to understand more about various aspects of public opinion. There are still many problems in constructing and implementing a poll that adequately probes the intellectual, emotional, and moral dimensions of "public opinion."

Two obvious but most important aspects of polling concern what you ask and who you ask. For the type of question asked and the way it is phrased will determine the quality of the information obtained, while the sample of people selected for questioning will determine how truly representative of "the American public" the poll results are.

On the basis of what you have learned in this unit, construct a poll that will improve upon the type of polling you have studied in this chapter by probing more deeply into the intellectual, emotional, and moral aspects of opinion.

Some useful books and articles on question formation and sampling techniques are listed on this page. You will find others in your library.

Cantril, Hadley, *et al. Gauging Public Opinion.* Office of Public Opinion Research Center, Princeton University, 1947.

Gallup, George. *The Public Opinion Poll and How It Works.* New York: Simon and Schuster, 1940.

Gallup, George. *A Guide to Public Opinion Polls.* Princeton: Princeton University Press, 1948.

Public Opinion Quarterly. A journal of public opinion which contains articles on polling methods and problems along with recent polls. ■

ACKNOWLEDGMENTS

Charles Abrams, from *The City is The Frontier*. Reprinted by permission of Harper & Row, Publishers, Inc. Copyright © 1965 by Harper & Row, Publishers, Inc.

Jane Addams, from *Democracy and Social Ethics*. Reprinted by permission of The Harvard University Press. Copyright © 1964.

Edward Banfield, from *The Unheavenly City* in *The Conscience of the City*, ed. Martin Meyerson. Reprinted by permission of George Braziller Co. Copyright © 1970.

Roy P. Basler, ed., from *Collected Works of Abraham Lincoln*. Reprinted by permission of Rutgers University Press.

Merrill Beal, from *I Will Fight No More Forever*. Reprinted by permission of the University of Washington Press. Copyright © 1966.

Hadley Cantril, ed., from *Public Opinion, 1935–1946*. Reprinted by permission of Princeton University Press. Copyright 1951.

Kenneth Clark, from "Letter of Resignation from Board of Directors of Antioch College." Reprinted by permission of the A. Philip Randolph Institute.

John Collier, from *The Indians of the Americas*. Reprinted by permission of W. W. Norton & Co. Copyright 1947.

Vine DeLoria, from *Custer Died for Your Sins*. Reprinted by permission of The Macmillan Company. Copyright © 1969.

Max Frankel, "The Lessons of Vietnam." Reprinted by permission of the *New York Times*. Copyright © 1971.

Gallup Opinion Index and *Gallup Political Index*, portions reprinted by permission of Gallup International, Inc. Copyright © 1965 and 1967.

Herbert Gans, from *Commentary*. Reprinted by permission of *Commentary* magazine.

Milton M. Gordon, from *Assimilation in American Life: The Role of Race, Religion and National Origins*. Copyright © 1964 by Oxford University Press, Inc., and reprinted with their permission.

Victor Gruen, from *The Heart of Our Cities*. Reprinted by permission of Simon and Schuster, Inc. Copyright © 1964.

Oscar Handlin, from *The Newcomers*. Reprinted by permission of Harvard University Press. Copyright © 1959.

Samuel Hays, from "The Politics of Reform in Municipal Government in the Progressive Era." Reprinted by permission of the *Pacific Northwest Quarterly*. Copyright © 1964.

Jane Jacobs, from *The Death and Life of Great American Cities*. Reprinted by permission of Random House, Inc. Copyright © 1961.

Lyndon B. Johnson, from *The Vantage Point: Perspectives of the Presidency, 1963–1969*. Reprinted by permission of Holt, Rinehart and Winston. Copyright © 1971.

Winthrop D. Jordan, from *White Over Black*. Reprinted by permission of the University of North Carolina Press and the Institute of Early American History.

Alvin M. Josephy, Jr., from *The Patriot Chiefs: A Chronicle of American Indian Resistance*. Adapted by permission of The Viking Press, Inc. Copyright © 1958, 1961 by Alvin M. Josephy, Jr.

George F. Kennan, "The Sources of Soviet Conduct." Reprinted by permission of *Foreign Affairs*. Copyright 1947.

Martin Luther King, Jr., from *Speeches by the Leaders: The March on Washington for Jobs and Freedom*. Reprinted by permission of the National Association for the Advancement of Colored People. Copyright © 1963.

Harry H. L. Kitano, from *Japanese Americans: The Evolution of a Subculture*. Reprinted by permission of Prentice-Hall, Inc. Copyright © 1969.

Kevin Lahart, from "The Anger of the Ethnics: Was the Melting Pot a Myth; the American Dream Not Worth It?" Reprinted by permission of *Newsday*. Copyright © 1971.

Owen Lattimore, "Rebuilding Our Policy in Asia." Reprinted by permission of *Atlantic Monthly*. Copyright 1950.

Walter Lippmann, from *The Cold War*. Reprinted by permission of Harper & Row, Publishers, Inc. Copyright 1947.

Kay Longcope, from "The Identity Crisis of 'Harvard's Chicanos.'" Reprinted by permission of *The Boston Globe*. Copyright © 1971.

Roy Lubove, from *The Urban Community: Housing and Planning in the Progressive Era*. Reprinted by permission of Prentice-Hall, Inc. Copyright © 1967.

Malcolm X, from "Separation or Integration: A Debate." Reprinted by permission of *Dialogue* magazine. Copyright © 1962.

Alex Poinsett, from *Black Power, Gary Style*. Reprinted by permission of Johnson Publishing Co. Copyright © 1970.

INDEX

Polls, American public opinion Cold War
on American policy toward Russia, 495
on foreign aid, 492–493
on North Atlantic Security Pact, 496
on Russian character, 491
on Russian warlikeness, 491
on Russia's aims in, 491
on talks between Russia and United States, 494–495
on winner of, 497
on Korea and China, 516–518
on Vietnam War in 1965, 544–548
World War II
on German character, 469
on German warlikeness, 467
on Japanese character, 471
on Japanese warlikeness, 469
on post-war world organization, 472–473
on reasons for fighting, 471
treatment of Germany after, 466, 468
treatment of Japan after, 466, 467
Posters, American, during World War II, 469–471, 475–477
Potomac Institute, 427
Powell, John Wesley, 379
Powhatan, on Indian-White relations, 238–239
Prejudice. See specific group
Prendergast, Charles
Madison Square, New York, 324
The East River, 330
The Mall, Central Park, 328
Presidential power in American foreign policy, 448–449
Priest, Loring Benson, on Dawes Act, 240–244

Progressive Era and urban reform, 350–371
Prophet, the (Laulewasika), 221
Public opinion
in making of foreign policy, 448, 449
morality and, 410–413
types of, 448, 449
Puerto-Rican Americans, assimilation of, 308, 312–314

Quat, Phan Huy, 537

Racial discrimination. See specific group
Religion, and World War II, 450
Remington, Frederick
The Emigrants, 236
The Outlier, 232
The Sun Dance, 231
Removal Bill, 224
Reprisals after World War II, theory of, 459. See also Polls, American public opinion: World War II; World War II: reprisals
Reservations, Indian, 240–244. See also Indian Americans
Riis, Jacob, on pre-1900 New York slums, 342–345
"Rolling Thunder" operations, during Vietnam War, 529, 535
Roman Catholics. See Catholic Americans
Roosevelt, Franklin D.
on aims of World War II, 448–453
and American Indian policy, 245–247
and Chinese policy, 502
and Filipino–Japanese policy, 557
political character of, 558
Ropes, Ripley, 352

Rostow, Walt W., on guerrilla warfare, 523
Rusk, Dean, role in American policy in Vietnam, 534, 537, 555
Russell, Charles M.
Attack on the Wagon Train, 232–233
Salute to the Robe Trade, 237
The Buffalo Hunt, 230
Russia
aims after World War II, 479–482
American policy toward, during Cold War, 478–497
communist party in
and Chinese communists, 507, 508
after World War II, 479–482
entrance into World War II against Japan, 503
and India, 509
and Manchuria, 503, 504–505, 512, 514
relations with China, American policy toward, 510–511

St. Louis, government of, 334–338
Schools, decentralization of, 301–303, 418–419
SEATO, 519
Sectionalism in city government. See Cities: political bosses, era of; Cities: urban reform
Segregation and integration of minority groups. See specific group
Seminoles, 224–225
Senate Foreign Relations Committee, 448
Shawnees, 220–223
Shopping centers, regional, 388–391
Silent majority, 300

Sino-Soviet Treaty of 1945, 503
Sioux, 226–229
Sitting Bull, 228–229
Slavery
of Black Americans, 210, 256–260
of Indian Americans, 216
Sloan, John
Backyards, Greenwich Village, 323
Fifth Avenue Critics, 328–329
Pigeons, 326
Slums, urban. See also Cities: urban renewal
and Black Americans, 346–349, 408, 409
clearance of
failure of, 400–407
and minority groups, 406
under New Deal, 384–388
in Philadelphia, 346–349
in pre-1900 New York, 342–345
reasons for minority groups in, 387–388
Socialism
and capitalism, 479
Thomas, Norman, on, 452–453
Southeast Asia. See specific country
South Korea, pre-war situation of, 510. See also Korean War
Spanish Americans, percentage of, 297. See also specific nationality
Spilhaus, Athelstan, on the Experimental City, 429, 433–438
Stalin, Joseph
on communistic-capitalistic relations, 478
and Poland, 558
and recognition of Chinese government, 502–503
Steffens, Lincoln, on graft in government of St. Louis, 334–338

575

576